INSIDE THE KGB

INSIDE THE KGB

MY LIFE IN SOVIET ESPIONAGE

Vladimir Kuzichkin

TRANSLATED BY
Thomas B. Beattie

FOREWORD BY
Frederick Forsyth

Pantheon Books   New York

To My Mother and All My Friends

Library of Congress Cataloging-in-Publication Data
Kuzichkin, Vladimir, 1947–
Inside the KGB: my life in Soviet espionage / by Vladimir Kuzichkin.
p. cm.
Translation from the Russian.
Includes index.
ISBN 0-679-40146-6
1. Kuzichkin, Vladimir, 1947–. 2. Spies—Soviet Union—
Biography. 3. Defectors—Soviet Union—Biography. 4. Soviet
Union. Komitet gosudarstvennoĭ bezopasnosti. 5. Espionage—Soviet
Union—History—20th century. I. Title.
DK275.K89A3 1991
327.12'092—dc20
[B] 90-53439

Manufactured in the United States of America

First American Edition

CONTENTS

FOREWORD

Frederick Forsyth

It lasted for forty years. In truth it certainly started (on the Russian side) before the Berlin blockade of 1948 but we in the West hardly perceived it. And it may have continued for a while beyond 1988 but the writing was already on the Wall by then.

But for most people of my generation the forty years between those dates, almost all our lives, were dominated by one menacing presence – The Cold War.

During those extraordinary four decades world Communism did its utmost to triumph across the planet, and the nations and forces opposed to that triumph – simplistically called 'The West' – tried to thwart the expansionist ambition.

The struggle cost tens of thousands of lives and untold billions in treasure. Several times the degeneration into real war, and mutually assured destruction, was only narrowly averted. For all that time, behind the Cold War and yet intimately a part of it, was the Covert War. In this the secret intelligence agencies and counter-intelligence forces of each side sought to secure for their masters the dominating factor, the winning hand, the crucial edge. For Communism and the Soviet Union the primary organisation for this was the KGB and particularly its foreign-espionage arm, the First Chief Directorate.

At its best (qualitatively speaking) the KGB could be brilliant, ruthless, skilful and subtle; at its worst it could be crude, clumsy, naive and foolish. But then, so could we.

Perhaps it is a part of the human condition for opponents often to impute greater skill and efficiency to each other than they really merit. Certainly in the West the KGB became something of a legend, and not only in spy thriller novels. We tended to magnify their successes – Philby, Burgess, Maclean, Blake, Vassall – while over-looking the fact that over two hundred serving KGB men defected to us, utterly disillusioned by the cause they served. This one-sidedness was certainly because our failures usually hit the headlines of a free press, while we tended to mute all news of our triumphs.

One of the most fascinating of those KGB officers who 'came over' was Vladimir Kuzichkin. One thing of which we should not lose sight was that our defectors (to them) were often flawed, losers, cranks, no-hopers. But on the Soviet side the officers of the KGB, the GRU and the Foreign Ministry were the *crème de la crème*, treated in a manner so privileged that the ordinary Soviet citizen could not dream of such a lifestyle.

Vladimir was one such – tall, handsome, talented, highly educated, a brilliant linguist and heading for the top. And disillusioned; utterly and completely depressed by the nepotism, inefficiency, double standards, corruption and cheating that he saw all around him.

As he makes plain in this fascinating book he quickly reached a point, despite all his privileges, where he had penetrated the great lie of the so-called equality of the Communist system and could take no more of it. So, in Tehran where he had been posted, he 'walked'.

Not just a pen-pusher, he was a key staffer within the inner core of the First Chief Directorate, the Illegals Directorate, the cutting edge of covert espionage. That made him very valuable.

Now, years on, he has been able to write and publish his own story, in part the journey of a man who refused to sell his intelligence and his conscience for a finer apartment and smarter clothes, and in part an exposé of the flawed organisation and system that kept so many people in thraldom for so long east of the Iron Curtain.

To us in the West, who for years had to listen to the siren voices in our own society praising the men of Moscow and urging that we disarm ourselves before their might, this must be a fascinating book. For it is truly an insider's story, told by a man who for years walked the innermost corridors of our old adversary – the Soviet KGB.

London, July 1990

INSIDE THE KGB

INTRODUCTION

In 1984, the Central Committee of the British Communist Party sent Graham Atkinson, a journalist on the staff of its newspaper the *Morning Star*, to Bulgaria. He was to cover the press conference on Sergei Antonov, who had been accused by the Italian authorities of having taken part in the attempt on the life of Pope John Paul II. A Bulgarian calling himself Encho Mitov made contact in Sofia, and bluntly suggested that Atkinson should help him to find Vladimir Kuzichkin, a KGB major who had defected from Tehran to Britain. Kuzichkin was to be either 'abducted or thrown out'. If the operation succeeded, Atkinson would be paid $US100,000. Though he was obviously unenthusiastic, Mitov gave him the name of Radoslav Tsanchev, first secretary at the Bulgarian Embassy in London, as the leader of the operation. Atkinson was not to make direct contact with Tsanchev. To act as liaison, the Bulgarians gave him an Englishman, Len Dawson, a prominent figure in the British Communist Party, and a leading figure in the Anglo-Bulgarian Trade Union and Friendship Society. An alternative plan was also drawn up. Should Dawson be unavailable, Atkinson had to submit his report to Tsanchev by leaving it in a sealed envelope addressed to him in the offices of Balkan Airlines in London.

Atkinson returned home determined to play no part in these plans but unsure of what to do. Eventually, having heard about his story, Channel 4 suggested he should go through the motions of following Mitov's instructions. His experiences were filmed and the plot exposed in 'Working for the Comrades', part of Channel 4's 20/20 Vision series, broadcast in April 1986. In this way everybody learnt of the conspiracy.

*

It was not news that they were trying to find me. Every KGB officer who goes over to the West sentences himself to death in his absence. But while the KGB usually takes steps to find a defector, in general it uses only its own resources in the search, and these resources are not all that great. A photograph of the defector is sent to the local KGB residency, and the illegals operating in the country familiarise themselves with it. Specially trusted agents may be involved in the search. That, very likely, is all.

In this particular case, members of the British Communist Party were brought into the operation. This clearly indicates that the KGB was playing only a secondary role in this instance, and that the principal part belonged to the Central Committee of the Communist Party of the Soviet Union. Every intelligence officer in the KGB knows that the Central Committee of the Soviet Communist Party categorically forbids the KGB to approach members of other communist parties, still less to use them on their own initiative in operations of this kind. It is only the Central Committee of the Soviet Communist Party that could have instructed the British Communist Party to send Atkinson to Bulgaria, and it is only with the blessing of the Soviet Central Committee that the Bulgarians could have begun this operation.

These actions of the Central Committee are worth stressing here because they point to where the real power lies. A great deal has been written in the West about the KGB, much of it the product of the authors' unaided imaginations. The KGB is presented as a huge and faceless monster that terrorizes not only the entire Soviet Union, including the humble Politbureau, but many other countries in the world. Western society is mesmerized, against all logic, by the supposed omnipotence of the KGB inside its borders.

But can this creature be real? Is it a fact that the KGB is the power behind everything that happens in the Soviet Union, and that it reaches the same almighty hand abroad? Who benefits from the hype that surrounds the KGB throughout the world, and what does it conceal?

The truth about the KGB is known only to the officers who belong to it. The difference between the real and the imaginary organization may be hard both for Russians and for Westerners to credit, but the truth makes a sobering sense that the inventions cannot provide. In order to understand it, the reader needs to know something about the institutional corruption of the Soviet Union, and I can best describe the nature of the KGB and of my country's crumbling State machinery by relating my own career as a kind of case study.

The main content of this book is devoted to events and activities of the KGB that took place in Iran between 1977 and 1982, and of which the author was both an observer and a participant. Events in Iran were broadly interwoven with what was taking place at this time in the Soviet Union, Afghanistan and the Middle East, and this forms part of the background I describe.

I say as little as possible about my family, nor do I mention the names of my relatives or friends. They have remained in the Soviet Union, and are still under the control of the authorities.

PART ONE

In Preparation

CHAPTER 1

I was born in Moscow in 1947, into a large Russian family. My grandmother had eleven children. Two were killed in the Second World War. The others survived. My relatives followed a whole variety of professions. There were research assistants, and officials who worked in trade, both home and foreign. Some were military, and others white-collar and manual workers. All levels of Soviet society were represented in this one family, and naturally there was an extraordinary variety of opinions held within it. The missing category was professional Party officials. They got little respect from us, even though most of the adults in our family were Communist Party members. It always adopted a disrespectful, derisive attitude towards the Soviet regime. I remember that even when Stalin was alive, there were jokes about his appearance and the way he spoke.

Shortly after I was born, most members of my family went to live in a large country house outside Moscow. This house was sold in 1954, and we moved back to Moscow, to the Leningrad quarter. Using their savings and the money they had made on the sale of the house, my grandmother, mother and two brothers then bought a flat in a co-operative block. Or rather, they bought two rooms of a three-roomed flat, the third room being occupied by a woman neighbour. It may seem that this was very little for so many people, but at that time it was a luxury. Our seven-story block was the only building in large grounds, and it was completely surrounded by wooden shanties, in which the living conditions would be hard to describe as human. These living conditions in fact were just the same as those in labour camps, except that there were no escort guards, and people were not hounded to work. They went there under their own steam.

The adults living in the shanties and those in our block had nothing to do with each other. But their children were constantly coming into contact on the street. Sometimes we played together, but most of the time we had fights. The grounds of our block were entirely surrounded by a high metal fence 'to protect us from the hooligans', and this intensified the hatred felt towards us all. The local residents liked neither our block nor its inhabitants. They called it 'the Jewish fortress', and that was not far from the truth. About four-fifths of the residents were Jewish, working mainly in light industry and trade. Quite often there were battles fought between us and the shanty children, and naturally the hard cases from the shanties always won. The intelligent boys from the Jewish families never had a hope. I often chanced to be part of their crowd. Although I was a Russian, for our enemies I was just another resident of that hated block. In Khrushchev's time, a house-building programme began, and other high-rise blocks began to appear around ours. The shanties were pulled down and their occupants moved to other parts of the city. We, the children of our block, thus became the oldest inhabitants.

We children were old enough to grasp that 'secret disappearances' occurred from time to time among the residents of the block, and families became agitated. Papa Schpielberg has disappeared. Mama Schpielberg is in tears, and his children go around looking sorrowful. Papa Selsky disappears. His children go around looking sad, and Mama Selsky cries. Both 'disappeared' for eight years for business fraud. Then one of the residents hanged himself just before he could be arrested, thereby avoiding a trial, confiscation of his property and shame for his family. Now here is Auntie Lilya running round the neighbours trying to persuade them to hide crystal vases and other valuables, before her flat is searched in the wake of her husband's arrest. The neighbours take the crystal vases only, and when their owner goes back to recover them, they brazenly deny having ever received them. She makes a scene, naturally, but she can't make any official complaint against them. It is the law of the jungle. She just has to put up with it. Then Margulis, the highly respected professor of mathematics, is hounded from Moscow University for taking bribes in return for facilitating acceptance by the university.

Next, our own door-bell rings, and some grim-looking people come in, armed with a search warrant from the Protection of Socialist

Property Organization. It seems that someone has denounced my uncle to them for 'keeping gold ingots' in the flat. Of course they find no ingots. One of the searchers unofficially reveals the name of the informant. It turns out to be one of the neighbours, a 'friend of the family'.

In such conditions, there was naturally much talk among the children in the street about what was going on. This was the harsh reality that undermined our childhood faith in a radiant present and future. It became obvious from such talk that it was only excessively greedy or just stupid people who fell into the hands of the law. Any crooked character who wanted a quiet life had to have someone behind him inside the Party machine. A smart operator had real money, while a Party official had real power. The former paid the latter, who gave protection in return. Such friendly contacts became especially widespread in the early Sixties. The symbiosis between the Party and the wholesale criminal activities nowadays described as the Soviet mafia flourished particularly during the Brezhnev years.

All this was taking place before the very eyes of us children, and nothing escaped us. Very often I met Party officials who were visiting the families of my friends in the block. They were always seated around the dinner table, tipsy and glutted, telling vulgar jokes and inane stories, and trying to appear as persons of great significance. The grown-ups paid no attention to us, in the mistaken belief that all that was happening was going over our heads.

I once saw one of these people, pig-faced and rolling drunk, in the flat of one of my friends. He attempted to start playing with us, but he was so repellent that we quickly made ourselves scarce.

'Who was that man at your table who looked like a pig?' I asked my friend. 'A relation, or something?'

'He's no relation of ours!' my chum replied indignantly. 'He's from the Moscow municipal committee of the Party. He helps my father in his business. He's an indispensable man. That's why we've got to put up with him.' My friend was obviously repeating what he heard his parents say. 'Every time he comes to us, he stuffs his guts, drinks himself silly, and behaves like a lout to us all. My mother says that the place ought to be disinfected after he leaves!'

In this way, the abstract image I formed from my earliest childhood of a Party official was no different from that of a fat drunkard, a swindler and a thug. I held this opinion even more strongly with the passage of time. As I had known the obverse side of what the Party was doing, I was always very sceptical about ideological propaganda and about pioneer and Komsomol voluntary activities. When I was still at school, I could see very clearly that the more vile and two-faced a person was, the more active he was in the Komsomol and the higher he went up the Komsomol ladder, paying not the slightest attention to the contempt of his fellow members. All this revolted me, and led to my refusing to join the Komsomol at school, in spite of being put under pressure to do so.

When I left school, I was quite apathetic about my future and a career. This caused me to miss the chance to go to college, and instead I was called up into the Soviet Army. At that time the period of army service was three years. I ended up serving with the Soviet forces in Germany.

My unit was deployed in a garrison located not far from the town of Hagenow, which lay virtually on the western frontier of the GDR. I was serving in the secret guided missiles division, which no one, apart from us in the garrison, suspected existed. To all outsiders, the name of my unit was the evacuation company. The armament of the division contained three launchers for tactical nuclear missiles. In the event of war, the division's task was to annihilate Hamburg with six tactical nuclear missiles. Hamburg was thirty kilometres from us in a straight line. We went out fairly often into the frontier area, where we did training exercises in launching our missiles. I was a radio operator, and one of my jobs was to maintain communications between the batteries and the command post.

The idea of annihilating Hamburg was not particularly attractive to us, the soldiers of the division. We knew the city from West German television broadcasts, which we watched in the barracks, in spite of this being strictly forbidden by the command. There were always specialists in the division who could re-tune our television set on to the FRG television frequencies.

Since our unit was a secret one, we were forbidden to go beyond the confines of the garrison. During the three years I spent in the GDR, I was away from the unit three or four times in all, and then only as one of a group. In order to alleviate our existence, the commander of our division arranged for us to use the library in the Officers' Club. This gave us access to classical literature again, and proved that we had plenty of readers among us. Because of the special nature of the service performed by our unit, the command recruited only soldiers who had at least a secondary education. There were even some in our division who had had an institute education. Most of the soldiers in our unit were Muscovites or from Leningrad, and this was something that created quite a relaxed atmosphere. There was nothing like *dedovshchina* (the persecution of young soldiers by veterans) to be found among us. A glance at the neighbouring infantry regiment however was enough to make us realize how lucky we were. The law of the underworld reigned there, with young soldiers being beaten up and humiliated.

Judged as part of the Soviet system, army life differed little from civilian life. The same ideological waffle, which no one heeded and which you had to keep brushing away like a persistent fly. The same petty rackets, embezzlement, fraud and humbug. In order to have some fun during the obligatory political studies which were supervised by our deputy political officer, who held the rank of major, we pretended that we could not understand his explanations of Marxist-Leninist theory. He would turn purple, stamp his feet, scream in his high-pitched voice and use a ripe selection of epithets to describe us. But we did not give up, and went on pretending that we were thick as planks.

Every six months in the Soviet Army inspections take place, to check the combat readiness of the personnel. In our case, all these inspections were a complete farce. The inspecting officers were made dead drunk by our divisional commander and they then signed all the necessary papers. Our part in these inspections was a pure formality. On paper at least, the divisions always came through these inspections with a grading of excellent.

Three years is a long time, and I had plenty of time to think about the future and observe what was taking place around me. The Army was a microcosm of Soviet society with all its defects. Everything that happened in ordinary Soviet life was packed into this three-year period. Everybody began as a young soldier on an equal footing; what happened would be determined by the new recruit's convictions, talents or adaptability, exactly as in civilian life. Honest young men of principle, the seekers after truth, were never promoted during their service. They would not give up their principles to please their superiors. But those who were ready to crawl to the commanders made quick advances in the service and became commanders themselves. The particularly smart ones made their way by having themselves released from military duties to act as full-time Komsomol officials, after which their purely military service virtually ceased. All that remained for them to do was to drivel on about ideology. The honest ones simply despised those who tried to gain favour. They could do nothing else. The real authority and support of the command lay with the crawlers. This was further confirmation of the axiom with which I was already fully conversant – that the more ignoble and unprincipled a man is, the easier it is for him to make a career in Soviet society.

So I was faced with the time-honoured question, what is to be done? Should I refuse to make any compromises with the system, no matter what these might be, and so condemn myself to every possible difficulty, or join those who were holding up the system and in this way assure myself a career and an agreeable existence?

After thinking long and hard about it, I decided to follow the latter course, salving my conscience with the thought that I did not intend to betray my beliefs about the Soviet system, but only to conceal them until I had made a career. Then I would see what to do next. In the words of the old Russian proverb, you are lucky to find even one tuft of good wool on a mangy sheep. Having come to this conclusion, I decided that in order to achieve my aims, I needed first of all to obtain some higher education. It seemed to me that the most suitable place to get it would be the Institute of Law at Moscow University. With such a qualification, it was possible to work in any field, and particularly politics.

Unexpectedly I received a letter from an old girl-friend. Amongst other things she reminded me that my service in the Army was coming to an end and that I would have to think about the future. She mentioned my interest in foreign languages and asked if I would be interested in entering the Institute of Asian and African Countries in Moscow. She mentioned that the entry conditions were now

considerably lower and that the chances of acceptance for a man
with a military background were very good – the authorities gave
preference to former conscripts from workers' and peasants' families, whom they considered to be more ideologically reliable. At the
same time I sensed a hint that she herself intended to enrol at the
Institute and that she had connections there.

This letter got me thinking more seriously about my future. For
the Institute of Asian and African Countries was one of two higher
educational establishments in Moscow reserved for the elite. The
other was the Moscow Institute of International Relations, which
was intended for future members of the Foreign Ministry. The
doors into such institutes were practically closed to mere mortals.
Even to be accepted to sit the entrance exams you needed to have
a recommendation from a regional committee of the Party, if you
were a Party member, or from the regional Komsomol committee
if you belonged to the Komsomol. And such recommendations were
given only after a thorough examination at the office of the regional
party committee. To graduate from such an institute meant one thing
– the fast lane in Soviet society, the probability of future work abroad.
And by Soviet standards and by the law of the forbidden fruit, work
abroad was the apex of the dreams of many.

My first idea about entering the Moscow University Law Institute
was put to one side. Now a well defined plan of my future career
was taking shape before my eyes, and I decided to reinforce my
university chances with the weightiest argument of all – membership
of the Communist Party of the Soviet Union. First I approached the
deputy commander of our division in charge of the political unit, who
treated me in a fatherly way. He suggested how I should write the
application, and promised to give me a recommendation. But two
recommendations are needed to get into the Party, and for the second
I turned to the commander of our unit himself, Lieutenant-Colonel
Polyvyanny.

This was an act of sheer impudence on my part. I despised
Polyvyanny as a total scoundrel, and he was all too well aware of
my attitude. He knew that I had spoken critically about him, and
he held no burning affection for me. Quite the contrary: he took
every opportunity to do me harm. Yet here was I asking him to
give me a recommendation, not for any old purpose, but for the

Party itself! It was a fearful shock for our commander!

My calculation was simple. By giving me the recommendation, the commander would be acknowledging his trust in me, his harassment would come to an end, and I would serve out my final year in peace. There I sat, looking Polyvyanny straight in the eye, while he remained deep in thought. He was an intelligent man and understood my stratagem very well. He realized that he had been placed in a difficult position. He had no official reasons for refusing. In terms of battle readiness, I was an excellent soldier, and on record as such. He did not like me because I saw through him and I often spoke openly about his intrigues with other soldiers, but you don't bring your feelings into your work. What if I upped and complained one day to the highest quarters? Polyvyanny did not like rows. All this went through our minds as we looked one another in the eye, neither betraying what the other was thinking with even the slightest change of expression. At last Polyvyanny gave a sly smile and said that he would give me his recommendation. By doing so he was recognizing that this round had been won by me.

Entry into the CPSU became my first obligation to myself, and from that time onwards everything I did was subordinated to a precisely worked out plan. After returning to Moscow at the end of my service in the Army I had no great difficulty in gaining entry into the Institute of Asian and African Countries. Since I was a Party member, I was guaranteed the trust of both the teaching and administrative staffs. There was nothing to bar my progress.

CHAPTER 2

At the end of November 1973 I was preparing to leave for Iran to do pre-diploma practical work. The Institute of Asian and African Countries (ISAA) is located at No. 18 Marx Prospekt, in the old university building, which faces the Kremlin across Manezhnaya Square and forms an essential part of the architectural unity of the centre of Moscow.

My main subjects in the Institute of Asian and African Countries were the history of Iran and the Persian Language. But in addition to this, the students in the Faculty of History study a mass of other subjects, such as the history of the Soviet Union, and world history, which ranges from prehistoric society, Egypt, Greece and Rome, to the Middle Ages, modern times and the most recent history. We had separate lectures on the history of the East. We also had to study dialectical materialism, classical philosophy, Marxist-Leninist philosophy, and political economy. A fully trained orientalist needs to know more than one Eastern language. He must be able to read Western sources, and for this he must speak one of the Western languages. The students in the Institute study English or French, depending upon the colonial past of the countries of their interest. In my case, I learnt English. It is also a requirement to speak a second oriental language, in order to become a specialist in a whole region, and not simply in one Eastern country. I learnt Arabic. Not surprisingly, the training in the Institute lasts five years, or six years with practical work abroad. I enjoyed those years. The academic training in our Institute was the best in the country.

Almost every oriental language was taught, from the best-known, like Chinese, Japanese, Arabic and Hindi, to languages like Zulu

and Hausa, which only specialists encountered. It was considered
unrewarding to study such languages, since they were not spoken
officially in any country. Our graduates who spoke these languages
mainly worked with English, since there was no demand for specialists, for example, in Zulu. In fairness it must be said that groups to
study such languages were enrolled in the Institute once every five
years, but even so, they were still enrolled. Why this waste of time and
money, it may be asked, if there is no demand for such specialists?
But there was a demand. The specialists may not have been needed in
the academic field, but that left the political field. The International
Department of the Central Committee of the Soviet Communist
Party, which was the patron of our Institute, took a long-term view
of the future and was building up specialists. And as it turned out,
they had their reasons. From the mid-1970s onwards, pro-Soviet
regimes in African countries gradually began to establish themselves
in Angola, Mozambique and Ethiopia.

But the main target of the International Department still remained
the Republic of South Africa, not because the Soviet leaders wished
to crown the victorious progress of socialism through the continent
with the 'liberation' of Southern Africa, not because of apartheid,
and not even because of the strategic position of the RSA, but for
purely economic reasons. The RSA is the Soviet Union's main competitor on the international gold, platinum and diamond markets. If a
pro-Soviet government came to power in the RSA, or if its economy
collapsed, the Soviet Union would virtually gain the monopoly of
these markets in precious metals and diamonds, and could dictate
its prices and its conditions to the West.

Military training was another obligatory subject for all university
students. Young people who entered university were not called up
during their studies. Instead, they did military studies in the Military
Faculty, which was also located in the old university building, at 20
Marx Prospekt. Studies lasted four years in this Faculty, and on
completing them the student was given the rank of lieutenant in the
reserve. Students from the Institute, including the girls, were trained
for special jobs like military interpreting and military propaganda. (In
wartime propagandists broadcast to the enemy across the front line,
distribute leaflets and so on.) The Ministry of Defence has the right
to call up a student for one year's military service as an officer, should

he not have done any military service before going to university. If the student fails in military studies, he is sent down from the university and automatically goes into the Army as a private. Nothing would stop this happening, for the Army is very influential.

It was the practice for Institute students to be sent abroad, normally for one year, in order to gather material for diploma studies and to perfect the languages they were studying. But not everyone was sent abroad, of course. The chief criteria of selection were good progress in studies and naturally political reliability and moral stability. This last quality was easily maintained in our Institute, since the glowing prospect of work abroad kept the students' temperament in check. Discipline in the Institute was therefore the best in the University.

In other faculties, drunken parties, fights, orgies and drug-taking took place from time to time, and underground groups of various kinds were discovered. But nothing of this kind ever occurred in the Institute. This was also helped by the fact that approximately 70 per cent of the students came from families of the 'nomenklatura', the governing Party establishment, connected in one way or another with work abroad. Their parents held responsible posts in the Party Central Committee, the KGB, the Ministry of Foreign Affairs, the Ministry of Foreign Trade, TASS, the Novosti News Agency, and so on. A nomenklatura sense of caution had been instilled in these students from childhood. If you were going to drink and run riot, then you must do it on the quiet so that nobody saw. The remaining 30 per cent of the students, who made it to the Institute by their brains alone and without support, knew that this was their only opportunity to get on in the world and preferred to play safe.

Each department of the Institute had a lecturer who was responsible for the practical work of the students. He did not have much to do, since almost all the students whom it was proposed to send abroad had their own pre-arranged channels. It was like this in my case. The lecturer in charge of my practical work said that it had been decided to send me to Iran and asked whether I had any prospects of my own there. I confirmed that I had. The proposal that I go to Iran did not take me by surprise. I was considered politically reliable and morally sound. I had made good progress in studies. For three years I had been senior student of my course and a member of the Party bureau in our Institute. What was more, since I was a Muscovite, I lived at home and not in the university hostel. This meant that my personal life was not under the surveillance of informers.

So with these assets, I began to seek my own channel at the beginning of my fourth year, and quickly found it. Following the advice of one of our students on the senior course, who had already succeeded in going to Iran, I approached Tyazhpromeksport, a foreign trade association that built metallurgical plants and other works in developing countries. It came under the State Committee for Foreign Economic Relations (GKES). Thousands of specialists were working on their account in Tehran, and of course they needed interpreters. It turned out that they gave preference to students, for one simple reason. A student was paid only 70 per cent of the salary of a fully qualified interpreter. In this way they saved foreign currency. It also suited the students, for 70 per cent of an interpreter's salary abroad was much better than absolutely nothing at home. So both sides were satisfied.

As soon as the Institute suggested that I go to Iran, I obtained a letter from the dean's office and took it to Tyazhpromeksport, and the wheels of procedure began to turn. I had to fill up a clutch of questionnaires for persons travelling abroad, to write my life history on several forms, obtain references from the Party Committees of the Institute, and the University, and go through countless interviews.

The final stage of this merry-go-round is an interview in the old Party Central Committee building on Staraya Square. And God help you if you are late. The Central Committee building was guarded by people wearing militia uniform, but as I was to find out later, they were not militiamen at all, but officers of the Ninth Chief Directorate of the KGB, which is responsible for the physical security of our leaders.

I opened the massive entrance door and found myself in a lobby. I opened another door and entered a hall which was blocked by a barrier, at which stood a KGB sergeant. He checked my paper and passport and ordered me to wait. A few minutes later I heard my name being called. Another officer led me to a lift and told me which floor to go to. I was quite nervous. After all, this was my first meeting with superior State authority. On emerging from the lift, I saw a long corridor in front of me. A parquet floor, covered with a runner carpet, oak-panelled walls, soft light from the ceiling, and silence. Nobody in the corridor, the Land of Nod. I knocked on the door I had been sent to and went in. My nervousness grew.

It was not a large room. It had one window, a desk made of light wood with a chair in front of it, a portrait of Brezhnev and a map of the world on the wall. Sitting at the desk was a small grey-haired man, of commonplace appearance and with a hostile face.

'How do you do,' I said.

'Sit down.'

He indicated the chair without returning my greeting. I was immediately struck not so much by his failure to greet me as by his use of the familiar second person singular 'thou' form of address. I did not realize than that this was the usual boorish way in which Party officials addressed their inferiors.

'Right, you're going to Iran as an interpreter.'

He glanced at the file lying in front of him.

'Yes,' I answered. 'I'm going on pre-diploma practical work.'

'You can forget all about that.' His eyes grew even more bad-tempered. 'Diploma indeed! You're going there to work, as a representative of our State. You are the cause of all our troubles abroad, you interpreters. You'll mix with foreigners there under no control at all ... then come the scandals ... You mind your behaviour, for you'll see that we'll find out everything.'

I certainly had no doubt about that. Whatever else we might lack, we had no shortage of informers.

I was happy to leave the Central Committee building. It was a cold sunny day, and the disgust aroused by my conversation with the representative of superior authority gradually began to give way to a realization of a new reality. If I went to Iran before the New Year, then I should miss the winter exams! And what student does not dream of skipping the exam?

Shortly afterwards I was rung up by the GKES and told that the Central Committee's decision on my posting to Iran had been received and that it was planned to send me off somewhere at the beginning of December. What good news! I ran around the Institute, straightening out my affairs and sympathizing with my fellow students who were faced with the winter exams.

Then I was summoned unexpectedly to the dean's office, and told that someone wanted to have a talk with me. With whom and about what they did not say.

'But I don't have the time,' I said. 'I have to go and get my tickets and I still have to pack.'

'It doesn't matter, it won't take long.'

A group of students from my course was standing outside one of the rooms of the dean's offices. I asked them what was up. No one had the slightest idea. When I asked them to let me jump the queue, because I was in a great hurry to collect my plane tickets, nobody objected. Everyone was understanding towards someone who was going abroad. At that moment the door opened and one of our students emerged. His eyes were downcast, and he was red as a beetroot.

'What are they talking about in there, Kostya?' I asked.

'You'll find out yourself,' he replied flatly, and hurried down the stairs. I learnt afterwards that Kostya had given 'No' for an answer.

I went in. Sitting at a desk on the left of the door was a young man aged about thirty and of pleasant appearance, wearing a well cut grey suit. His expression was serious but friendly. We greeted each other and he invited me to sit down.

'I'm from the Committee of State Security,' he said, and flashed a red card-holder containing his identification document. I saw his photograph inside and was able to read his name and patronymic – Nikolai Vasilevich Sakalin.

'We know about you,' he continued, looking austerely at me, 'and you fit our requirements. We propose that you should join intelligence after you have finished university. Take a few days to think it over and then give your answer. Here's my telephone number' – he handed me a piece of paper. 'I must ask you not to mention our conversation to anyone, apart from your nearest relatives. You may discuss our proposition with them. We know that you are going to Iran and that you don't have much time, but please try to find a couple of hours to fill up our questionnaires, if of course you decide to accept our proposition.' He smiled.

I picked up the forms, and took my leave.

It must be said that the conversation with Nikolai Vasilevich made an agreeable impression. Outwardly, everything had been very proper. There had been no loutish familiarity, no patronizing tone, no piercing stare to show me my place, no intimidation, nor any threat that 'in the event of unauthorized disclosure ... our arm is long,' and the like. I was very flattered by this proposal that I should go into intelligence work. The fact is that Soviet society does not equate the KGB with the Soviet intelligence service. The uninitiated connect the KGB with all the terrible things which have happened and still happen in our society – the Cheka terror which followed the revolution, the horrors of 1937–49, the torture chambers in the Lubyanka prison, where thousands of people suffered. Today it is seen as devoting itself to the supervision of dissidents and of all other forms of protest, total surveillance, secret murders and telephone tapping.

Intelligence, on the other hand, is honourable, difficult, romantic work which is done for the good of our Motherland. Only the most able and patently honest people are accepted for it. Intelligence work is praised and glorified, in Soviet books and films that enjoy enormous popularity. The honour of becoming a member of this elite of intellectuals does not fall to everyone.

That is what people think. I also thought so after my conversation with the KGB officer.

Turning the matter over in my mind in this way, I decided to accept the proposal that I become an intelligence officer. I filled up all the necessary questionnaires, and telephoned Nikolai Vasilevich. We met on Kuznetsky Most, where at No. 27 the KGB Cadres Department was located. He suggested that I should pass a medical board before leaving, but I had only a few days left before my departure, and he did not insist. Before we parted, he said:

'In Iran you'll be an interpreter in constant contact with foreigners. The counter-intelligence branch of the local KGB residency are bound to try to recruit you. Our instructions to you are not to enter into contact with them. You must politely decline their proposals to collaborate, and they are not to know of our relationship. We don't want you involved in their grubby business. If our people need to make contact, they'll give you greetings from Nikolai Vasilevich.'

What the counter-intelligence branch of the residency was, what its grubby business was, and who 'our people' were, I had not the slightest idea. One thing I did understand was that I was dealing with a very serious organization, and that it had already begun to worry about my security. This convinced me once again that the choice I had made was the right one.

I flew out of Sheremetevo International Airport for Tehran on 6 December 1973. Because of the weather, I just made the plane, which is why I was the last to pass through customs and passport control. The customs official asked me a very strange question.

'What amounts of foodstuffs are you taking with you?'

'What foodstuffs?' I asked, not quite understanding.

He waved me through without an examination.

The flight took three and a half hours. It was near midnight when we approached Tehran, and the city lay below in a bright sea of twinkling multi-coloured lights that inter-played as in illuminations. It was hard to believe that the lighting was always like this. But in fact it was.

After another recurrence of the Arab–Israeli war in October 1973, the Arab countries had declared an embargo on the sale of oil to Western countries. Iran did not support this embargo, and was almost the only country in the region to go on selling oil. An incredible price was placed on the oil, and enormous revenues of up to 25 billion dollars annually flowed into the Iranian treasury. Iran's role in the world grew significantly. Western capital investment flooded into the economy. That is why Tehran shimmered with light, showing the whole world that there was no energy crisis in Iran, and attracting more and more capital into the country.

The door of the aircraft opened. As soon as I set foot on the gangway stairs, my nostrils were assailed by the smell of waste petroleum gases. The air was so saturated that it was difficult to breathe. There is no shortage of oil in Iran; but neither is there a shortage of that air pollution which comes as its by-product. The four million inhabitants of Tehran had one million private cars which emitted tons of poison into the atmosphere. Even the houses were heated by oil, which was also one of the main reasons for the smog that lay over the city. None of this however could cast a shadow over the mood of enthusiasm with which I was ready to greet the country whose history and language I had been studying for nearly four years now.

A smart young officer of the immigration service put an entry stamp into my passport, which he hardly glanced at, and I moved on to the customs hall. We were met there by a GKES interpreter, and once I had collected my luggage we moved off towards the exit. To my surprise, no one checked our bags – indeed there were no customs officers to be seen anywhere. Everything happened so quickly that I was already on the bus along with the other Soviet specialists before I realized what had happened. Then we set off towards the centre of the city.

The first thing I saw was the monument, floodlit by many searchlights, which had been raised to mark the 2500th anniversary of Iran, celebrated in 1971. It was called the 'Shahyad' ('Remembrances of the Shahs'), and was built by the Czechs on the orders of the Iranians. Iranian nationalism was enjoying an extraordinary upsurge, reinforced by the country's 2500 years of statehood. A strong state led by the Achaemenian dynasty arose in Iran at the beginning of the fourth century BC. Its territory stretched from Egypt to India. From that day to this, Iran has never lost her statehood. It existed alongside that of Egypt, Greece and Rome. Early in the seventh century AD, it was subjugated by Muslim Arab tribes, who imposed the Islamic religion. But the Arabs were still at an early stage of development, and Iranian culture absorbed them completely. The Arabs simply placed their rulers on the throne, while the entire State machine, operated by the Iranians, continued to work as before. The same thing happened with the Tartar tribes in the thirteenth century. At the beginning of the twentieth century, during the period of colonial possessions, Iran never became a colony but remained under the strong influence of only two countries, Russia and Britain. Even Stalin had to clear out of Iran in 1947, although everybody knew that he did not like doing so.

Iranian culture embraced philosophy, astronomy, mathematics and poetry. Iran gave the world such great poet philosophers as Firdawsi, Sa'adi, Hafiz and Khayyam. Many people identify the

Iranians with Arabs, but this is a fundamental error. The language of Iran is Farsi, which belongs to the Indo-European group of languages, while Arabic is a Semitic language.

We stopped at the Naderi Hotel, on the street of that name, and alighted from the bus. Although it was by then after midnight, the streets were still bubbling with life and there were even some shops still open, not to mention the restaurants. But I was not equal to any of this. Dropping with fatigue from my journey, I collapsed into bed.

Next morning the first thing to be done was to present myself to the GKES staff administration officer and collect my travelling expenses. After breakfast, I went down to the foyer and asked the head waiter in Farsi how I could get to the GKES. He smiled, and gave me the directions in beautiful Russian.

'Are you a Soviet?' I asked him in surprise.

'No,' he answered. 'I'm an Iranian, and an Armenian. My parents, like many Armenians here, are emigrants from Russia. It is traditional that we preserve our Russian language and teach it to our children in Armenian schools. We don't want to lose our links with the great Russian culture. By the way, there are many real Russians in Tehran, White Russians as we call them.'

I knew about the White Russians from history. They were the remnants of the White Army which was defeated in the Civil War. They escaped to Iran, and a number of them settled there. But we had been told nothing at university about Armenians from Russia. I was to learn later what had happened from conversations with local Armenians. Before the Revolution, the regions of northern Iran were under Russian influence, and the populace had no problem in moving from one country to the other. Many Iranian subjects of Armenian nationality thus preferred to live and work in Russia. They dwelt mainly in the Caucasus and in the regions of the southern Volga. The Tsarist government did not prevent them doing so. Stalin began to introduce the internal passport system in the 1930s, and in order to help him do so he carried out a census of the population. It was at this point that the foreigners living in the Soviet Union came to light. They were given the choice of either adopting Soviet citizenship or of leaving the country.

This placed the Armenians in a dilemma. To assume Soviet citizenship would mean their becoming slaves of the system. By that time, this had already become obvious. The alternative was to leave the Soviet Union. But that country had already become their Motherland. Third and fourth generations were already living on Russian soil. Some decided to accept Soviet citizenship, while others thought the matter over. But while they were pondering, Stalin took a new and, as always, radical decision. An order was issued that all those who had not adopted Soviet nationality should be arrested and forcibly deported. They were allowed to take only personal effects with them. All the rest of their possessions fell to Stalin. Thus all Armenians, Assyrians and Jews who were Iranian subjects were taken to Iran in ships and put ashore in Bandar Pahlavi (now Bandar Khomeini) on the Caspian Sea. The Soviet authorities had no further interest in their fate. Even after all that, the Armenians harboured no grievance against the Russians, as they knew full well that the Russian people was suffering at the hands of Soviet authority perhaps more than any other. The Armenians are a wise people.

It was 9 o'clock in the morning. Naderi Street was crammed with cars whose exhaust fumes gave the air a bluish tinge. The policeman at the crossroads had his mouth and nose covered with a damp handkerchief. I passed along Naderi, Stalin, Churchill and Hafez streets, and arrived at the entrance to GKES territory.

The territory of the Soviet mission, on which the GKES building is situated, is surrounded by a high red brick wall. What goes on behind it cannot be seen by passers-by. At the entrance were strong latticed metal gates for vehicles. These were automatically controlled by the duty guard from the guardroom premises. To the left of these gates was another small latticed gate for visitors on foot. I pressed the bell button. The guard's face appeared in the mirror, the lock buzzed and the door opened. I found myself facing a wide window, behind which sat the guard. He asked me who I was and where I was going. Fortunately for me, the Uzbek interpreter who had met us the previous evening came into the guardroom office. He recognized me, explained who I was and offered to take me to the administration staff officer.

I conversed with the interpreter and explained that I was being sent to a mine in the town of Bafq.

'Ah, into the wilderness,' he said. 'That place is much better than Tehran for practising the language. It's much quieter there.'

'What's wrong with Tehran?' I asked.

'This of course is the capital, with shops, cinemas and so on. Life is more cheerful than at the mine, but the work here is terrible. Most of my work is taken up with meeting and seeing off our specialist technicians. I'm permanently rushing back and forth between the station and the airport. I'm told to buy tickets, to see off some, to meet others, to be responsible for buses, luggage, it's a dog's life. And the specialists treat you like an errand boy. Sometimes I wonder whether it was worth while finishing Tashkent University simply in order to wait upon excavator drivers.'

'Why don't they give you real interpreting work, like negotiations?' I asked him. 'Surely your Farsi is very good?'

'Because English is the language of all negotiations and documents. This was okayed by some idiot when the economic agreement with Iran was signed. How is your English, by the way? They need an interpreter in Tehran right now.'

Such a turn of events had never entered my plans. I had come here to do a diploma and to polish my Farsi, not my English.

The interpreter led me along the corridor and pointed to a door with the inscription 'Deputy Head of Economic Section (Personnel)'. I knocked and entered. A black-haired middle-aged man sat at a desk. He was a typical Caucasian, an Armenian named Saringulyan. He was polite, and asked about my journey, the hotel and a little about university. Then he suddenly broke into English.

'And how is your English? We need an interpreter just now, and if you have a good standard in the language, we'll keep you in Tehran.'

I had to extricate myself from this, and after a long pause I mumbled something in English in reply.

'I see,' he said, disappointed. 'Ah, Moscow University, your standards are falling! You'll fly out to Bafq in two days' time. You'll find a complicated situation there. The Soviet colony is small and a long way from Tehran. You, as an interpreter, are obliged to let us know about all breaches of discipline. Be careful of the Persians. They have more than enough counter-intelligence there.'

I left Saringulyan and went to the finance office, where I was given both my travelling expenses and first month's pay in rials, the official currency unit in Iran, which everyone reckons in tumans. There are ten rials to a tuman, the word which the entire population uses. About 2,000 tumans (about 300 dollars) were put into my hand. Never before had I had so much money!

My next step was to register with the Party and the trade union organization. Here a brief explanation is needed. Before he leaves for abroad, every Soviet person must remove his name from the Party register, surrender his Party card to the Central Committee of the Soviet Communist Party, and be given a de-registration ticket in exchange. The same thing happens with his trade union card. He hands it in to the Central Committee of the Trade Unions and is likewise given a de-registration ticket in return. In Soviet colonies abroad, the Party organization is given the name of trade union; while the trade union organization is called the local committee organization. The Komsomol is called the physical culture organization. All this is done as camouflage, 'so that the enemy should not guess'! This measure has the purpose of concealing the communist activity of the Central Committee. Officially there is no Party organization in an embassy, which means that there can be no Party activity there either.

All Russians laugh at this. But it is not quite as silly as it seems. If for example an embassy were to be occupied by the host government, it would not find one word there about Party activity – about the trade unions' activities, yes, but nothing about the Party's.

Thus, when he arrives abroad, each Soviet citizen must hand over his de-registration cards. One card goes to the representative of the Party Central Committee, the other to the representative of the Central Committee of the Trade Unions, and in this way he becomes registered. The most important things he must now do are to pay his subscriptions regularly in foreign currency, and to attend meetings. There will be more on this subject in later chapters.

Once all formalities had been completed, I went out beyond the walls of the Soviet compound. I had two free days and I decided to see Tehran, about which I knew so much from books. Disregarding the warning that we should go to town only in groups, I set off to roam on my own. It was then, for the first time since my arrival, that I was able to turn my attention to the Farsi language. There were many people on the streets, all speaking in that splendid Tehran dialect. One did not have to eavesdrop to hear conversation. Iranians converse loudly, uninhibited by those round about them. To my surprise, I understood almost everything. Any language student knows that the main difficulty during his first days in the country of the language he is studying is to understand the local dialect. As it turned out, this was no problem for me. When I heard the lilting Iranian speech, I inwardly thanked my teachers for the excellent training in Farsi they had given me.

There are many shops on Naderi Street, occupying the ground floors of all the buildings on both sides of the street. Shops, shops, shops! They had everything – clothing of all kinds, footwear, plates and dishes from all over the world, lamps, and so much gold that it was hard to believe that it was real. How can you choose something here, I thought, when the same thing of even better quality is on sale somewhere else? In Moscow it was simpler. When you saw something good, it had to be grabbed without even thinking about it, otherwise the next minute it would be gone. But here your head spun. What is more, there were no queues, no jostling crowds in the shops. People simply came in quietly and looked around. I decided to buy myself a denim suit, and nothing more for the time being. No need to go mad. I came across some shops on Istanbul Street, their shelves piled from floor to ceiling with jeans. Every make was there. After looking at a dozen or so pairs of trousers and trying them on, I made no choice. Instead I became annoyed and returned towards evening to the hotel, cursing both the abundance of the capitalist market and Karl Marx and his free trade theories. It was only next day, when I was recovering from abundance shock and acquired a pair of Wrangler jeans, that I calmed down. I had had enough of shops, so I decided to spend the rest of the day seeing the sights of Tehran. I was due to set off for Bafq next day.

Bafq is a small town in the south-eastern part of the Iranian plateau, in the rock-salt wilderness of Dasht-e-Lut. The town had one mosque, rural cottages, built of rammed clay or gravel, and poverty. The small population was mostly engaged in cattle rearing and retail trade. The town would have remained in obscurity but for one factor that enabled Iran to develop its own metallurgical capability.

The Iranian authorities had been trying to set up a national metallurgical industry ever since the late nineteenth century. The most far-sighted people understood that, without its own heavy industry, Iran would always be economically dependent upon the developed countries, and they tried to rectify this situation. Mirza Tagi Khan Amir Kabir, who was then Prime Minister, imported the first blast furnace at the end of the century, but the project failed through lack of resources. In the 1930s, an agreement with Krupps to build a metallurgical plant was stopped by the outbreak of the Second World War. After the war, Iran negotiated with the Americans, the Swedes and the French, but all of them said with one voice that there was not enough iron ore in Iran, and that it would have to be obtained from abroad if a metallurgical plant were to operate there. For Iran, this meant continued dependence.

Then in the beginning of the 1960s, the Soviet Union appeared on the scene. After carrying out a geological survey, Soviet experts came to the conclusion that ore did exist in Iran, and in sufficient quantities to justify building a metallurgical plant. The Iranian government was wary of the Soviet Union's political influence, but its desire to establish an independent economy was stronger. So in 1963 an agreement on economic cooperation was signed between Iran and the Soviet Union. It also provided for the construction of a metallurgical combine in Isfahan. Cooperation between the two countries was to be purely economic and in no way political. The Shah remained an extreme anti-communist.

But purely economic aid had to be paid for in hard cash, and the Iranian treasury was dry. Oil was not bringing in sufficient revenue, as world oil prices were fairly low at the time. That left carpets and dried fruit as payment. And what else did it agree to accept? In the south of Iran there was natural gas which was being burnt off at that time as there was no use for it. The Iranians offered it to the Soviet Union to pay for the plant. But to do this meant building a gas pipeline. The Russians agreed to lay it, running it from the south along the western frontier of Iran on to the territory of Soviet Armenia. It must be said that some far-sighted Soviet experts considered the Shah an unreliable partner. They wanted the pipeline to be turned to the south-west and the gas sold to Turkey. If some conflict were to break out and the Iranians cut the supply, then it would be the Turks, and not us, who would suffer the consequences.

Everything moved in this direction until the start of the 1970s, when N. V. Podgorny, who was then Soviet President, met the Shah. He concluded that 'one can do business with that man', and the Turkish version of the gas pipeline project was cancelled. This, as it became clear later, was a great mistake. When the 1973 energy crisis began, oil and gas prices soared incredibly, and the Iranians wanted to raise the price of the gas being delivered to the Soviet Union. As the metallurgical plant was being paid for in gas, its cost would have been greatly reduced. What was more, world oil prices rose for reasons that were purely political and had nothing (or almost nothing) to do with either Iran or the Soviet Union. After agonizing negotiations, both sides came to an agreement that the price of gas would be increased slightly, but that it would remain well below the world price until the enterprise had been paid for in full. In order to offset its losses, the Soviet side slightly increased the price of spare parts for the plant, giving as its reason the increase in world metal prices.

The situation stayed that way until the revolution in Iran. The new Iranian authorities decided to bring 'order' to their economy, and having been convinced by Western propaganda that the Soviet Union was in urgent need of Iranian gas, presented the Soviet Union with an ultimatum – 'Either buy our gas at world prices, or we shall cut off supplies.' The Soviet side had no desire to start a quarrel. They simply refused to use Iranian gas any more, thereby demonstrating to the Iranians and everybody else just how much the Soviet Union needed it.

The metallurgical plant needed ore, and a deposit was opened up 14 kilometres from Bafq. It lay in a quite unique hill. The iron ore content in the stratum was more than 60 per cent and it was sent straight to the Isfahan plant without any enrichment. It was called the Chogart mine, taking its name from a nearby settlement. It was at this mine that I became interpreter to Mikhail Andreevich Volynets, the chief of the operational team that was directly involved in extracting the ore and sending it to the plant. Besides the operational team at the mine, there was also a team of geologists who were continuing to prospect for new deposits, and a team of hydro-geologists who were finding water for the local population.

The Soviet specialists lived side by side with the Iranian engineers in a settlement which had been specially built for them at Aryamehr, two kilometres from Bafq. The settlement stood on the plateau, surrounded by the Zagros Mountains. The temperature reached 50°C in summer, while the humidity was zero. The air was so clear and transparent that it created optical illusions. The hills, some tens of kilometres away, seemed so close that one could make out lesser details. The entire complex was surrounded by a barbed wire fence and was guarded by police. The Iranians said that the barbed wire was to keep out leopards and wild camels, but I imagine that it was a safeguard against contacts with the Russians. Workers were not allowed into the Aryamehr settlement. The Russians' movements were easy to control, since the complex had only one entrance.

Living conditions were comfortable. Each family had a small detached house with two, three or four rooms, air-conditioning, a bathroom, a washing machine and a refrigerator, in fact every necessity, including crockery. Under the agreement the Iranians paid for all this. All the Soviet specialists needed to spend money on was food and clothing.

Most Soviets there were specialists in iron ore extraction from Krivoi Rog in the Ukraine. Krivoi Rog is in the back of beyond, and getting away from there to go abroad is the chance of a lifetime. They take advantage of this chance. The main objective of every Soviet technician is to save enough money to buy a Volga car. This is not because they are mad about cars, but simply because it is not possible for the average inhabitant of the Soviet Union to buy a Volga. Assuming that the average wage is, say, 200 roubles a month, and a Volga costs 15,000, then one may calculate how many years it will take to save up sufficient money. Earnings are higher abroad, and the price of a Volga can be saved in two years. It is even more profitable to buy the car for 15,000 roubles in the Soviet Union and then sell it for 50,000 or more on the black market. 50,000 roubles is an enormous amount of money to the ordinary Soviet person, and with it he can consider himself secure for the rest of his days.

That is the theory, but first comes the money. So the technicians save, trying to spend as little as possible every month. If that expenditure is only on food, they can make savings here by bringing provisions from home. So they would cram their huge trunks, to the point of immovability, with all kinds of tinned fish and meat, boiled ham, dried sausage, flour (they did not even buy bread locally but baked it at home) and so on and on. When I saw all this, I understood the question about provisions which the customs officer at Sheremetevo had asked me. Some people exhausted themselves physically by trying to eke out these imported provisions until their next leave, to the point of fainting from hunger in front of the Iranians!

Superficially, it might be said that if provincial cattle are sent abroad, they will behave like cattle. But it is not quite as simple as that. These were in the main good people, and they could never be blamed for almost losing their human cast of mind in the effort to wrest this opportunity from life. The guilty parties were those who had deprived them of a normal life in the Soviet Union, who robbed them both at home and abroad – and I do mean robbed. This became clear to me when I was gathering material for my diploma and I found out how much the Iranians were paying the Soviet Union under the Treaty for the various types of specialists. My hair stood on end when I learnt that they were paying 5,000 dollars per month for each Soviet engineer. And from these, his own earnings, the engineer was given only 300 dollars! The rest went into the pockets of Soviet authorities. Pay even half of this money to these engineers and they would not become cattle.

There is another method, besides the financial one, of morally degrading the Soviet specialist. It is called *extension*. Officially, the specialist is sent abroad for one year only. When the year is up, his tour of duty is extended for another year, and so on each subsequent year. The extension of the specialist's posting is a matter for the Central Committee of the Soviet Communist Party in Moscow. In fact, however, it depends on his immediate superior at work. If he does not write him good reports, or fails to recommend an extension, then it will not be granted. No extension, no savings. The Party leadership uses the system as a method of exerting moral pressure. Extension is the cause of intrigues, scandalmongering, denunciations, coercion of others to make denunciations, seduction of the wives of others, and so on.

My tour of duty progressed normally, if you except the impressions described above. My boss was a good man, an intelligent well-read fellow with a sense of humour. Our relationship was a friendly one, and we often shared each other's company. I devoted great energy to writing my diploma on the subject of 'The History of the Metallurgical Industry in Iran', and sometimes I had to go to Tehran to gather information. My boss was understanding about this and quite often he arranged for me to make 'duty trips' to Tehran.

My diploma thesis was ready in draft by the end of the tenth month of my stay in Iran. I had succeeded in gathering good material from original sources, as the archives of the Iranian National Metallurgical Corporation proved to be. It was around this time that my boss said that he was writing his report on my extension and suggested that I should sign my application. I replied that I did not need an extension. I had gone to Iran for one year, and on completing it I intended to return to the university. I had told him this before, but it turned out that the boss had not taken my words seriously. Most students who came for a year's practical work remained in Iran for two or three years, thereby postponing finishing at university. They did this of course for purely financial considerations. The University adopted an indulgent attitude and did not put pressure on them.

'Well, I'll tell you what,' my boss said. 'I'm going to send my report on you to Tehran with or without your agreement, and you can work it out with them yourself.'

On my next trip to Tehran, I was sent for by the GKES deputy economic adviser on cadres. I expected to see the Armenian whom I already knew, but sitting in his place was another man of about fifty, with dark greying hair. He was short and aloof, and when he spoke he looked away from you. This was Anatolii Vasilevich Iunin, the new deputy adviser.

'I have received the report on your extension from Bafq,' he began, 'but you have forgotten to sign your agreement to it. You'd better take care, otherwise we might not extend your tour of duty.'

'I didn't forget,' I answered. 'I just don't want my tour extended.'

'What do you mean, you don't want?' He leaned back in his

chair in surprise, and for the first time looked straight at me.

'I came here for one year. That year is coming to an end, and I want to go back to the university.'

'Are you trying to be funny? You are given the honour of being offered another year *abroad*, and what do you do?'

'Thanks for the honour, but no thanks,' I said.

He stared at me in disbelief.

'The fact is we need an interpreter at this mine and you must take into account this imperative for production. I'm going to forward the documents to Moscow and I don't want to hear any more objections.'

'You are perfectly entitled to do so,' I said, 'only I too shall inform Moscow that you are coercing me.'

'Who do you think you're trying to frighten, you young upstart!' he hissed. 'I'll ruin your personal record for the rest of your life, and as for . . . '

'That's fine that you're giving me a warning, Comrade Iunin,' I said, rising to my feet. 'Now at least I know which way to look for trouble.'

He had begun to say something more, but I had already left the room. I had to act quickly before the old toadstool could create real problems for me. He would waste no time in sending a personal report to Moscow which would make even prisons refuse to have me for a jail sentence. And how could I have got out of that? For what is written by the pen, particularly on official paper, can never be cut out even with an axe. We believe paper rather than people.

On leaving Iunin, I went straight to the hotel, and quickly wrote a letter to the dean of my Institute. I described what had happened, and asked him to help me return to Moscow. My plan was simple. A KGB officer worked in the Institute. His cover was that of assistant to the director. The dean, knowing that the KGB wanted to take me on, would certainly show my letter to the assistant. He in his turn would get in touch with Nikolai Vasilevich, and he would do what was necessary. It was my good fortune that a student friend of mine from the Institute who had been in Iran for three years was flying back to Moscow that very day. I gave him the letter for the dean, and my friend said that he would deliver it next day.

I spent three days in Tehran on this occasion. I went to the cinema and spent hours browsing through bookshops. At that time Aleksandr Solzhenitsyn's book *The Gulag Archipelago* was on sale everywhere. Some shops even listed it among their latest titles. But I did not go near the book. An informer had only to see me with it in my hands for everything to come tumbling down. Solzhenitsyn was no longer popular with our leaders, even though there had been a time when Khrushchev called him a second Tolstoi, and almost awarded him the Lenin Prize for Literature. Before coming to Iran, I had read two of Solzhenitsyn's books in Moscow, *Cancer Ward* and *The First Circle*. They made a deep impression on me. But I could not discuss them with my friends, since the persistent view had begun to circulate in Moscow that 'The subject of Stalin's crimes belongs to the distant past. It might be interesting to our fathers, but not to us. Of course, mistakes and abuses of power did happen, but now everything has been put right, and there's no point in going over it all. Of course Solzhenitsyn is a talented writer, but he's gone off the rails on the subject of Stalin. He is always taking us back into the past when we should be looking to the future.' I had not realized at the time that all these sentiments held by people my own age owed their origins to the dissemination of rumours, which is the most insidious form of Party propaganda.

I looked at *The Gulag Archipelago*, and recalled the words of my friend from the internal service of the KGB, in whose house I had read Solzhenitsyn's books. 'If *The Gulag Archipelago* is found in your home,' he said, 'you'll get ten years in jail,' and he knew what he was talking about.

The day when I was going back to my mine in Bafq, I saw Aleksandr Titovich Golubev, another member of the cadre staff, standing outside the GKES building. He smiled and came over to me. An interpreter whom I knew had once told me that Golubev was a special member of staff. As he spoke, he put his hand to his brow, as though looking far into the distance and shielding his eyes from the sun. This meant that Golubev was an officer of the KGB.

'What's this, you've been rude to the deputy adviser, have you?' he said merrily. 'Never mind. You have to treat them like that, otherwise we'd have them all over us.' I didn't understand whom he meant by 'we', so I decided to play safe and say nothing.

'Who did you say sent you to Iran?' Golubev asked with a subtle smile. 'The Institute of Asian and African Countries,' I replied, 'for pre-diploma practical work.'

'All right, all right,' he said. 'Moscow is Moscow. We've been told not to keep you here. You'll get back to Moscow on time. And don't be upset with Iunin. He's a good chap on the whole. So it's the Institute, you say' – he gave me a sly grin. 'Well, all success to you,' and he shook my hand.

The conversation with Golubev was evidence that my letter had worked. I had no doubt about that. But the speed of Moscow's reaction was what surprised me. It had taken only two days.

My tour of duty came to an end. In spite of the gloomy impressions I have just described, I spent an excellent year in Iran. I had succeeded in seeing the country, not as a tourist, but from within. I had been to Yazd, Kerman, Isfahan, Shiraz and Persepolis. I had succeeded in getting to know and like the Iranians as they are in their everyday lives, and not as they are represented to tourists.

My departure date was fixed for 5 December. That night an incredible amount of snow fell on Tehran. In the morning all the streets were covered with it, there were traffic jams, and the snow went on falling. The bus came to collect us at the hotel and we set off for the airport. On the way, the interpreter who was accompanying us decided to go back home. He had left some papers behind. The specialists began to complain, as always, that we would be late. We really had no time to spare. In all, we lost about twenty minutes on that trip. When we were about 500 yards from the international airport terminal, we hit a traffic jam. You could see from the bus that something was happening at the airport building. The traffic had come to a halt, and I decided to go and see what was going on. When I got fairly close to the building I saw people running. They were covered in blood, and shouting. Police were bustling about, and I asked one policeman what had happened.

'I don't know,' he answered, agitated. 'About five minutes ago there was a crash and the ceiling collapsed. People are in a panic. They say it was a bomb.' He looked at me and added, 'Look, you'd better get out of here. SAVAK will turn up now and start arresting everyone in sight – and you're a foreigner.'

The airport was closed that day, and naturally our journey was cancelled. According to the news that evening, the roof of the central concourse of Mehrabad International Airport had collapsed under the weight of fallen snow. Most people on the concourse had been buried under the debris. Many victims, rescue work . . . It chilled our blood to realize that, but for being twenty minutes late through the 'fault' of the interpreter, we too would be lying under that pile of rubble. We went to the hotel bar and drank to our second birth.

Flights were resumed next day. The bus delivered us straight to the plane, but went quite close to the ruined building with its one and a half metres of rubble piled up in the main hall. It emerged later that most of the people there had died. My departure turned out to be an unhappy one.

CHAPTER 3

The day after I returned from Iran, I rang Nikolai Vasilevich Sakalin in the Cadres Department of the KGB. We agreed to meet as usual at No. 27 Kuznetsky Most. The first thing I did was to thank him for helping over my return from Iran. Then I made him the usual small present – a Ronson lighter. This was unhesitatingly accepted, and so the ice of our official relationship began to melt. Nikolai told me confidentially that my letter to him from Tehran had raised a real storm, since the Centre regarded me as a contingency replacement. Had my return been delayed, it would have disrupted plans already made for several years ahead. In my absence, he continued, the KGB had checked out both me and my family 'going back seven generations'. Nothing negative had been discovered. So there was no time to waste, and we should now proceed to the medical board, starting from the next day.

The KGB medical board is located in Kiselny Lane, not far from the Lubyanka. It is housed in an old grey building, typical of the centre of Moscow. The entrance is from a courtyard, so that passers-by on Dzerzhinsky Street cannot see who comes and goes. I was quite seriously worried about attending this board, since I did not know what was in store for me there, and I had heard many stories from those in the know about the special tricks it played. It was said for example that you might be sent down an empty corridor. Suddenly the light would go out, leaving you in total darkness. The floor would then open up, and you would fall through it and land on something soft. The lights would then be switched on, and the doctors would take your blood-pressure. Or else your chair would be removed from under you, as a pistol was fired close to your ear.

Then your blood-pressure would again be taken. There were other stories in the same vein.

In fact nothing of this kind happens – nor, as it turned out later, did it ever happen. The medical examination is a very ordinary one. The candidate is seen by ear, nose, and throat specialists, a surgeon, an oculist, a neuro-pathologist, and others. At the second stage there were tests to check concentration and aural and visual memory. There were no espionage tricks, and everything was quite straightforward. The concluding stage was a chat with a psychologist. It should be noted that the KGB almost never uses lie-detectors. It takes the view that the psychologist's live contact with the candidate is a much more reliable procedure.

My psychologist was a young fellow of about my age, which in no way surprised me. The Psychology Faculty in Moscow State University was in fact opened only at the end of the Sixties. Before this, psychology was not a subject of study in the Soviet Union, as it was considered to be a frivolous expression of bourgeois society. The first graduation of psychologists from Moscow University took place in 1973. That is why most of them were young people without any special practical experience. A high percentage of the first graduation were taken into the KGB. Where else were they to go? The national economy hardly needed psychologists. It was a profession that no one had heard of at the time. In the KGB however there was a wide field of work with candidates, colleagues, dissidents and others. The pay was much higher than in any other organization. In the event, my young psychologist did not put me through any special examination. He looked through the papers on my case, talked to me about the university and said that I was in good condition, giving his verdict as though to a fellow student.

It has to be noted that, in spite of its apparent simplicity, the KGB medical board is very important, especially its purely medical part. The slightest divergence from established health standards, and the candidate is disqualified. For example, his vision must be 100 per cent, including colour perception. People who wear spectacles are not accepted. The candidate is likewise unsuitable if he has had broken bones, or operations, or has suffered serious illness. The position of a candidate for KGB intelligence work is further complicated by the fact that his wife must also be passed by the medical board. The demands on her health are the same as for the candidate himself. If the candidate is healthy, but his wife is not, then he is not accepted. The KGB doctors are so powerful that no one can influence their decisions. But, as is widely said, laws exist to get round this. If a situation arises in which the KGB wishes to accept a candidate but the doctors do not pass him, then personal contacts, presents and the like come into play. In the Soviet Union these are much stronger than laws.

The decision of the KGB medical board on the candidate's fitness may also be used to resolve delicate situations. For example, if as a result of the vetting it is established that the candidate or his wife are unsuitable because of data revealed on the questionnaire (such as political views, or personal morality), then the candidate will not be told about it directly, but will learn that he or his wife has been failed on health grounds. I know of one student from my Institute who 'failed' this way because his wife's mother was a Jew. In another case the vetting established that a candidate's wife was secretly working as a prostitute. He too 'failed on grounds of health'.

In the Institute of Asian and African Countries, everything was following its normal course. My class had already completed the first half of its fifth year and was going off to do pre-diploma practical work. I had to begin my studies from the second term of the fourth year, the point I had reached when I left for Iran. I had lost a whole year. These were the rules, and there was nothing to be done about it. After I had reported back to the dean's office, I met Professor Mikhail Sergeevich Ivanov, the head of the Faculty of Iranian History, who was to be my director of studies. He asked whether my diploma work was ready. I replied that my research was finished in draft, but for the re-typing. Mikhail Sergeevich asked me to show him the rough draft, and a few days later he sent for me and said that he had read it and was satisfied with its contents.

'You will doubtless be interested to know that I didn't make a single correction to your work, and that very rarely happens,' he said. 'I think that you have an academic future before you, and I intend to recommend you for post-graduate study. And since your diploma work is finished, I don't see the point in your losing a whole year. I shall put it to the dean's office that they allow you to take the remaining examinations externally. That is, of course, if you have no objection,' he added.

Naturally I did not object. Then the ordeal began! In the six months that remained of the fifth year I had to sit three sets of examinations, one with my class and two unscheduled. That meant that I had to catch lecturers and arrange with them when I could take the examinations. Never in my life had I had to sweat so much as I did during these six months. I had to take a group of subjects, political economy, Marxist-Leninist philosophy, history of the West, history of the East, history of Iran, history of Iranian literature, the Farsi, English and Arab languages, military translation, and other things I can no longer remember. Overall, it was a nightmare time, but it went by. The examinations were taken and my diploma thesis defended, with top marks.

Professor Ivanov now told me that he had recommended me for post-graduate study. Matters were beginning to take a serious turn. I called Nikolai, and he advised me not to argue with my professor and to await assignment. 'The dean already knows where you're going after graduation, so Ivanov won't get in our way,' he added.

Another unforeseen development intervened during these six months. The Military Faculty in the university began to put pressure on me. My lecturer in military translation in Farsi suggested that I join the Army when I left. I got on well with him, and I told him straight that after three years' conscription I had no special love for the Army, in fact quite the contrary. But Major Panchekhin continued to press.

'We'll send you straight to Afghanistan. You won't even have to wear uniform,' he said, hinting that he was offering me service in the GRU. I declined, but he went on insisting and even handed me questionnaires to complete. I asked Nikolai to protect me from these GRU approaches.

'You know,' said Nikolai, 'there's no need to spoil your relationship with them. Fill up their questionnaires for the time being, and then we'll think of something afterwards. Don't say anything to him about your contacts with us, in case they end up making life difficult for you.'

I filled up the GRU forms and gave them to Panchekhin. But when they eventually learnt that the KGB had recruited me they still caused difficulties. It is a rule of the Military Faculty of the university that, before he graduates, every student must pass through training in the military camps near the town of Kovrov. Students who have previously served in the Army may be exempted, and I had already completed three years' service, but they wouldn't hear of my being excused. Instead of going on holiday when I finished at university, I had to spend two months in a military camp. That was the GRU's revenge for my having played cat and mouse with them. No matter how he tried, Nikolai could do nothing.

'So where is the famous long arm of the KGB?' it occurred to me to wonder.

But this happened a little later. Meanwhile assignment was approaching, the ceremony at which the graduate is told to where he is being sent to work. In essence, assignment is a pure formality at my Institute, since every graduate knows a year, or even more, in advance where he is going to work. As I mentioned before, most of the students at the Institute were children of the nomenklatura, or ruling Party establishment, who had used their official position, influence and contacts to find places for their children in advance.

Before assignment, I was summoned by the dean. She told me that the words 'Ministry of Defence' would be pencilled against my name on the assignment paper. I was not to be surprised, since this was the cover for my being assigned to the KGB.

The assignment ceremony takes place in the dean's office in the Institute. Excited graduates crowded the corridor, and were summoned one by one. My turn was approaching when somebody tugged my sleeve. I looked round and saw Professor Ivanov.

'Where are you being assigned to?' he asked.

'To the Ministry of Defence,' I replied after some hesitation.

'What do you mean, to the Ministry of Defence?' he shouted. 'There's already a place waiting for you in post-graduate studies. I told the dean to assign you to post-graduate studies!' And he hurried off down the corridor. I was sorry for the old man. We were not to meet again. But I still wonder what my fate would have been had I stayed with post-graduate studies.

Then it was my turn. Almost all the professors and lecturers of the Institute were sitting in the dean's office. I was glad to see, sitting smiling there, these people to whom I had been close these past five years. The chairman of the assignment commission was Professor Yuryev.

'This graduate especially needs no introduction,' he announced. 'We all know him well. Senior student of his year, a member of the Institute's Party bureau, and a good student. He has been in Iran on pre-diploma practical work. He has been recommended for post-graduate studies by the Faculty of Iranian History, but he has preferred to choose another path. Vladimir Andreevich Kuzichkin is assigned to the Ministry of Defence,' Professor Yuryev concluded with a touch of sadness in his voice.

On the document, the inscription 'Ministry of Defence' had been pencilled against my name. I signed and left the office. This chapter of my life history had ended.

It was the end of May. Nikolai rang and said that they wanted to talk to me. He did not say who 'they' were. We met in the usual place, walked up the Kuznetsky Most into Furkasov Lane and entered the building that housed the KGB Permits Bureau. I handed my passport through a small window to a KGB orderly in uniform. Once he had carefully compared my features with the photograph in the passport, he issued me with a one-time pass for visiting the KGB's main building, popularly known as the Lubyanka. The one-time pass is a small piece of paper, printed thus:

PASS

Surname
Forename
Patronymic
Date and Time of Issue
Entrance No.
Time of Exit
Signature of Recipient
Signature and Stamp of the Permits Bureau.

Nikolai was silent.

'Who wants to see me?' I asked.

Nikolai did not answer, but meaningfully raised his eyes skywards. This meant that it was some highly placed person who had sent for me. We crossed Furkasov Lane and went to entrance No. 5 of the main KGB building at No. 2 Dzerzhinsky Street. Facing us was a huge, fairly heavy door, about four metres high, and behind it a small glassed-in vestibule, and yet another door. Behind this one lay the quite extensive internal entrance hall. Some shallow steps led to the barrier that protected the entrance, with a narrow passage on either side, each one guarded by a KGB orderly in military uniform, who were both checking the passes. There was quite a bustle of people leaving and entering the building.

The guard looked me over carefully, unhurriedly scanned my passport photograph, checked the details on the pass against those given in the passport, once again looked me in the eye, and when he had finished he let me pass the barrier. Nikolai showed his KGB identity card and followed behind me. The process of closely examining credentials was repeated even in his case. Immediately behind the barrier was a wide ceremonial staircase that led to the entresol. To the left of the barrier was a corridor, which Nikolai and I walked down. The parquet floor was covered by brown linoleum; the walls painted light beige halfway up from the floor, and white from there to ceiling; heavy oak-stained office doors; plain white light globes hanging from the ceiling. People moving up and down the corridor. Grim faces, downcast looks, inaudible conversation, everybody hurrying somewhere. A bleak, oppressive atmosphere. Or did it just seem so to me? There were after all so many horrors in the history of our country connected with this building. At that moment I could not shake off one thought – 'Not long ago, down these corridors prisoners were led. Along here walked that monster Lavrenty Beria. What am I doing here?'

We reached the lift. It had an iron door with a small grated opening in the middle, just like the door of a prison cell, and when it clanged behind us I felt that I was not a future member of this organization, but its prisoner. It was a small lift; it held six of us, all frowning. Even Nikolai's usually cheerful face assumed this standard sullen look. As we ascended a tall, dark-haired, middle-aged man in a good quality dark brown suit stared at me. I had already gathered that this was not characteristic behaviour, and I lowered my eyes.

We emerged at the sixth floor. The iron lift door clattered behind us and again my flesh began to creep. The sixth floor corridor in no way differed from the one I had seen downstairs. We were halfway along the corridor when the dark-haired man came up from behind us and knocked on one of the oak-stained doors. The door opened, and he and I went inside, but Nikolai did not come in with us. The office was small with a high ceiling, one window and plain white curtains. Three people sat there, one at a desk with his back to the window, the other two at a table covered with a green cloth. They stood up when we appeared. The dark-haired man introduced me, and we exchanged handshakes, but they did not give their names. They invited me to sit down, then looked at me in silence while I looked back at them. Two of them were just like Caucasians. One was grey-haired, the other had black curly hair, both were aged around fifty. The man at the desk, whose office it was, was in the region of sixty. He had a noble face and intelligent eyes. His face seemed familiar, but I could not place him. The silence seemed to last an age, although probably only a few seconds passed.

'We understand that you've just returned from Iran. How did the country appeal to you?' asked the man whose office it was. I replied that I liked both the land and the people and we began to talk about the Shah and Iranian politics and economics. The Caucasians said nothing, but nodded now and then. Suddenly the curly-haired man said in perfect Farsi, 'You won't object if we talk in Farsi?' How could I object, I wondered. We spoke about my work in Iran, and I was struck by how purely this man spoke the Tehran dialect. The thought flashed that he might be an Iranian. When he brought the conversation to an end, the 'Iranian' looked at the occupant of the office and nodded approvingly.

'It was very good to meet you.' The office occupant stood up from behind his desk, signalling that the conversation was over. 'I hope to meet you again soon in this building.'

Where had I seen him, I kept wondering.

I came out of the office accompanied by the tall dark-haired man, and this time we walked down the wide staircase.

'Who was that man who spoke Farsi so well?' I asked.

'He's just an ordinary interpreter,' he answered curtly.

I understood that my question had been out of place.

Downstairs at the barrier the dark-haired man signed my one-time pass. The guard again unhurriedly checked my passport and took back the pass. Nikolai was already waiting for me at the other side of the barrier. He exchanged a significant look with the dark-haired man and we left the building. Once on the street, I could almost physically feel that bleak, cold, oppressive atmosphere of the Lubyanka lifting from my shoulders. I took a deep breath.

'Well, are you impressed?' Nikolai asked.

'Very impressed.'

'So tell me, what did Korznikov talk to you about?'

'Korznikov!' In a flash, the face of the occupant of the office suddenly acquired a name in my mind. I recalled that while I was looking through John Barron's book *KGB* in a Tehran bookshop, my attention had been drawn by a fine intelligent face in one of the photographs. The caption read 'Nikolai Alekseevich Korznikov, deputy head of the Directorate of Illegal Intelligence of the KGB.'

So that is where I'm going to work, I thought, and my heart beat faster. At that point I knew about illegal intelligence work only from books and films that told of heroic illegals who worked at Hitler's side during the war, and close to other Western leaders after it had ended. I had heard about Colonel Abel, who had been arrested by the Americans but who had not revealed his network consisting of hundreds of agents, and about our illegal Gunther Guillaume, who was able to position himself as a very close friend of Willy Brandt, then Chancellor of the German Federal Republic. Now I was going to work *there* with *these people*! There was every reason for becoming excited.

Shortly after my visit to the main KGB building, Nikolai summoned me to the Credentials Board. This is the final stage, where the candidate is told that he has been accepted into the KGB. The members are senior KGB officers, colonels and generals from various intelligence directorates. The Board is chaired as a rule by the head of the KGB Cadres Directorate. At that time the post was held by General Orlov. The candidate's cadre officer reports briefly to the Board about him. The candidate is then invited into the office. The Board generally meets in the premises of the KGB Cadres Department at No. 27 Kuznetsky Most.

Nikolai and I waited at the door for the summons. There were about another ten people in the corridor besides ourselves. When our turn came, Nikolai went into the office. I had to wait seven or eight minutes, and then I too was invited inside. It was a fairly large office, with some twenty elderly men in civilian clothes sitting on both sides of a long table that stretched almost the whole length of the room. Nikolai introduced me briefly. A man stood up from the head of the table. He was short, round-faced, snub-nosed and wide-eyed, and had rather a vacant smile. His sparse greasy hair was slicked back. I could never have imagined him as a KGB general, but rather as a promoter of popular shows or a low-level Party official, which in any case is much the same thing. But this was General Orlov. Smiling all the time, he asked me whether I was prepared to carry out any task for the Party. I naturally answered affirmatively. They put to me some questions on Iran, on the Institute, and on other matters.

'And how is your living accommodation? You won't be asking us for a flat immediately, will you?' Orlov asked suddenly, and gave a loud laugh, which was completely out of place. I said that I was all right for accommodation and that I did not need a flat.

'That's good,' said Orlov and laughed again. 'So, I congratulate you. You have been accepted as a student into the Red Banner Institute of the First Chief Directorate of the KGB.'

My meeting that day with this General-cum-Party worker filled me with a sense of aversion, rather than of satisfaction. I recalled how some people present had lowered their heads during his monologue in order to conceal their embarrassment at his idiotic words and behaviour, and I wondered whether I should have to meet many such characters in the KGB. It turned out subsequently that I should encounter a fair number. The higher one went, the more Orlovs one met, transferred into top KGB posts from full-time Party work.

'Cadres decide everything' was a popular Stalinist slogan in Soviet Party circles in the 1930s. Although it sounded simple, this expression embraced much, and could be interpreted in two ways. According to one version, everything, in all spheres of national life, was decided by carefully selected and highly qualified cadres, or specialists. According to the second version, everything was decided by the Bureaucracy, that is by cadre departments and their officials. In other words, these cadre departments kept practically all spheres of national life under their control. Appointments, pay increases, promotions and wages were all in their hands. Even the KGB did not escape this rule. Its Cadres Directorate has always had former Party functionaries occupying its leading posts. In this way the Party keeps all areas of life under its control, including its watchdog the KGB.

On 31 August 1975 I was ordered to report at 7 a.m. at the Dynamo Stadium swimming pool. Nikolai explained that this was the meeting place for students on their way to the Red Banner Institute of the First Directorate, or as it was called for short, 'School 101'. The meeting place itself quite surprised me. I had in fact spent all my childhood in this quarter. I began to swim in the Dynamo swimming pool when I was seven. I then took up boxing in the Dynamo Stadium, and used to go with my friends to the Dynamo cinema. But I had never heard that the KGB had the slightest connection with this sports club. I knew of course that the supporters called the players in the Dynamo football team 'rubbish and police informers', in the same way as they refer to any members of the Moscow militia, but I never imagined any KGB involvement. It was however widely known that the Dynamo sports association belonged to the Ministry of Internal Affairs, the MVD. Wide sections of Soviet society were likewise unaware that officials of the KGB were also making use of the services of the Dynamo club, and not just for the purposes of sport.

So it was seven o'clock in the morning when I emerged from the Dynamo metro station. Behind the railings surrounding the swimming pool I could see several buses, and quite a large group of some fifty people. The 31st of August was a Sunday. The streets were quite empty at such an early hour, so our gathering did not attract any attention. Even if some chance passer-by were to see a group of people and buses inside the pool area, they would simply think they were sportsmen going off somewhere. Everything had been thought of.

A man stood by the entrance recording the arrivals. I gave him my name. Looking around, I saw a fellow student from my Institute. I went up to him and we began a murmured conversation. It turned out that the group arriving at 7 a.m. had not been the first. The first group had been dispatched somewhere by bus at 6 a.m. Our conversation was soon interrupted by the order (it was more like a polite request) to take our places on the buses. We then departed. Since I knew that part of Moscow very well, it was easy to follow our progress. The buses drove along the Leningrad Prospekt in the direction of the ring road, passing the Aeroport and Sokol underground stations to emerge on to the Volokolamsk Chaussee. We passed through Tushino, crossed the ring road and then immediately turned right on to the Pyatnitsky Chaussee, which we followed in a north-westerly direction. Total silence reigned in the bus. No one spoke. We all sat with very serious expressions, although, and I am convinced of this, everyone wanted to know where they were taking us.

On reaching roughly kilometre 15, beyond the village of Yurlovo, the buses turned right and drove past a road-sign marked 'Entry Forbidden'. The road led us into the midst of a fairly dense forest. About three kilometres further on, we stopped at some high gates, beyond which nothing could be seen. The gates opened to let us through, and we alighted from the buses. Facing us was a four-storey building, built of light yellow brick. To the right of it was a second similar building, linked to the first by an overhead walkway at second floor level. There was a parking place for cars, several tennis courts, and flowers round about – in fact it was just like a typical holiday establishment in the Moscow area. We were taken past the glass doors of the main entrance into the spacious vestibule, and then along a corridor, before coming to a halt in front of a door. The person accompanying us explained that Volosov, the head of the school, would have a talk with each one of us separately. Each would be called by his name and patronymic; meanwhile we had to wait our turn in silence. He had no need to warn us to keep quiet, since the atmosphere of the unknown had deprived most of us of any desire to banter.

I was soon summoned into the office, where two individuals were seated at a table. They stood up when I appeared, and we shook hands.

'Colonel Volosov, the head of the school,' the tall stoutish man with pleasant features introduced himself, 'and this is Colonel Sterlikov, my deputy.' We sat down.

'I should like to acquaint you with some of the rules of our school,' Colonel Volosov continued. 'You will certainly have noticed that only your name and patronymic were used when you were called into the office. This was intentional. In order to foster the sense of secrecy in our students, and also out of security considerations, we shall change your surnames for the duration of your training. If you have no objection, we suggest that you assume the surname of Korsakov for one year. You can keep your first name and patronymic. A second point – the duration of the training in our school is one year. You will live the whole week in the school. You are only allowed to leave the school grounds from Saturday afternoon until 7 o'clock on Monday morning. You will share a room with another student, and I hope you will make friends with each other. However, the less he knows about you, the better. Is that all understood?' he asked with a friendly smile.

'Exactly, Comrade Colonel,' I replied smartly, in military fashion.

'Ah, and there's another thing. Although we have military ranks here, and the discipline in the school is military, we do not encourage military ways of dealing with one another. We are preparing you here for work abroad and therefore you must behave like ordinary civilians. If you are not used to the military way of behaving, it is not worth while to learn it; and if you are used to it, you'll have to get out of the habit. All right, go and settle in now.'

The person in charge of reception led me along the corridor, giving short explanations as he went. He showed me the dining room. Lunch was at 12.30. There was a lift and a staircase to the right of the entrance to the dining room, and he told me to go up to the third floor and move in to room no. 310. On emerging from the lift, I saw a long corridor with doors on both sides. The walls and doors were painted light grey. I knocked at door no. 310 and went in.

The student whom Volosov had mentioned was already in the room. He was a tall well-built young man, with black thinning hair, black eyebrows, and deep-set eyes with a restless expression. His entire appearance suggested a southerner, but not a Caucasian. We introduced ourselves. He was called Vladimir. They had given him the Russian surname of Paladin, although he did not look like a Russian. He had arrived with the first group and had already installed himself, having taken the bed by the window and the better half of the wardrobe. The room was furnished simply – two beds, a desk, a wardrobe and a wash-basin with a shaving mirror. A radio plugged into the local relay network hung on the wall. We were warned that the relay had to be permanently plugged into the network. I was to find out later what lay behind this requirement. The relay system could be used not just for transmission, but also for picking up everything that was said in the room. The students' conversations were monitored.

We conversed and began cautiously to draw out information from each other. It was obvious that Volosov's injunction was not working. We knew almost everything about each other after a few minutes. Vladimir was the same age as I. He had served three years in the Army in Germany, and had been a Komsomol Unit organizer when he was demobilized. (I certainly did not care for this feature, as it meant yet another Komsomol official.) He had completed studies at the Institute of International Relations, studying English and Arabic in the Faculty of Economics, with a period of practical work in Iraq. He was married and had a one-year-old daughter. His Komsomol work and daughter apart, his life history coincided exactly with mine. We were on an equal footing.

At eleven o'clock in the morning we were all assembled in the common lecture hall on the second floor. Volosov, Sterlikov, and about another six unknown people sat at a table on the platform.

'Before we get down to our routine work, we will have to take a test,' Volosov said.

A test! What sort of test? Most of us were expecting something unusual and dangerous to happen at any time. This was after all the intelligence school of the KGB. Each of us was given a sheet of paper and told to write his surname on the top right-hand corner. Someone came to the microphone and explained the purpose of the test. He would read out groups of figures which we had to write down as accurately as possible. In order to complicate our task, radio interference would be introduced as he read.

'Is that all?' we thought with relief. It was just like in the Army, an exercise in receiving a radio transmission with interference.

The test was over in a few minutes and we handed in our papers. I may say that we never found out the results of this test, and no one ever mentioned it again. If it did have a point to it, then I cannot see what it was.

We were told that there were 120 people on the course, divided up into four sections of thirty people in each. A leader was allotted to each section. They turned out to be the elderly men who had been sitting on the platform. The person appointed leader of my third section was Colonel Pavel Kuzmich Revizorov, about seventy years old, with thinning grey hair, a wide nose and a maliciously suspicious glimmer in his eye. A section senior student was appointed from among the students of each section. These section senior students had already served in directorates of the KGB, or of the KGBs in the republics, before coming to School 101. They then told us about the daily programme – reveille at 6.45 a.m., physical exercises 7.00–7.30, ablutions 7.30–8.00, breakfast 8.00–8.45; beginning of studies 9.00, lunch break 12.30–14.00; private study in the special library 20.00–22.00; end of the day 23.00. A typical Army regime, with no free time.

It was 12.30, and the time had come to get to know the mess. It was in a large room on the first floor, with a capacity for 120 people. Self-service. The menu was quite varied – tomato salad, cucumber salad, borshch, potato soup with meat, fish soup, soup with pickled cucumbers, solyanka (sharp-tasting vegetable soup with fish or meat), schnitzel, chops, meat cutlets stuffed with rice, meat pancakes, pancakes with cottage cheese, fowl, and so on; stewed fruit, sweet dishes and dairy produce. There was a bar in the mess, but only with non-alcoholic drinks. Not just wine, but even beer was banned in School 101. Provisions came from the nearest collective farm and were absolutely fresh. Local women from the nearest villages did the cooking. They did not use large cauldrons, but ordinary pots, which gave the food a taste of real home cooking.

We were given a tour of the school after lunch, and shown the classrooms, the rooms for the study of foreign languages, and the sports complex. Beside the sports premises stood a separate building, joined to the main building by an overhead bridge. There were three gyms and a swimming pool there, and outside it were four tennis courts.

Next day, on Monday, 1 September, our academic studies began. The first lecture was devoted to the structure of the Committee of State Security of the Council of Ministers of the Soviet Union. (At that time it was still 'of the Council of Ministers'. The separation took place later, in 1978, when Andropov had gained enough influence to be able to remove the KGB from the Council's control.) We were not shown any diagrams portraying the structure of the KGB. The content of the lecture was sketchy and quite brief.

The central KGB apparatus consists of nine Chief Directorates and Directorates.

The First Chief Directorate (PGU) deals with external intelligence. It has four Directorates: Directorate 'S' (illegal intelligence), Directorate 'T' (scientific and technical intelligence), Directorate 'K' (external counter-intelligence), and Directorate 'RT' (intelligence work carried out among foreigners on Soviet territory); two Services: Service 'I' (which processes intelligence received), and Service 'A' (active measures, or more simply, disinformation); and twelve geographical departments which work mainly on gathering political intelligence on the regions they cover. These departments are numbered in accordance with the importance of the areas they cover. They are:

First Department	United States and Canada.
Second Department	Latin America.
Third Department	Britain, Australia, New Zealand, Scandinavia.
Fourth Department	The Federal Republic and Austria.
Fifth Department	France, Italy, Spain, Netherlands, Belgium, Luxembourg and Ireland.

Sixth Department	China, Vietnam, Korea, Campuchea.
Seventh Department	Japan, Indonesia, Philippines, Thailand, Singapore.
Eighth Department	Iran, Afghanistan, Turkey, West Berlin.
Ninth Department	Francophone African countries.
Tenth Department	Anglophone African countries.
Seventeenth Department	India, Pakistan, Bangladesh, Sri Lanka.
Eighteenth Department	Arab countries of the Near East.

There are several specialized departments:

Eleventh Department	liaison with 'friends' (services of the socialist countries).*
Twelfth Department	developed into the RT Directorate.
Thirteenth Department	does not exist (superstition perhaps?).
Fourteenth Department	technical security of intelligence operations.
Fifteenth Department	has now grown into Service 'I', PGU archives.
Sixteenth Department	interception and deciphering of foreign communications.

In the PGU there is also a Cadres Department and a Party committee.

The Second Chief Directorate of the KGB is the equivalent of the British MI5. It carries out internal counter-intelligence, that is it tries to prevent foreign special services operating on Soviet territory.

The Third Chief Directorate of the KGB is the Army security and counter-intelligence service. It is the policy of the Central Committee of the Soviet Communist Party that the Army is forbidden to have its own counter-intelligence. This is how the Party exercises control over the Army.

The Fifth Chief Directorate of the KGB* is the ideological directorate, set up at the end of the Sixties to combat growing political opposition as the Party leaders recognized that the dissident movement was growing.

*In view of the recent upheavals in Eastern Europe, the Eleventh Department must be busy re-organizing these relationships.

*Under Gorbachev, the Fifth Chief Directorate has been re-styled under the title of Directorate for the Protection of the Constitution.

The Seventh Chief Directorate of the KGB carries out surveillance. It does not undertake independent operations, but collaborates with all other directorates.

The Eighth Directorate handles codes and cipher clerks' work.

The Ninth Chief Directorate provides personal security for Party leaders and government members, the protection of the most 'important' State targets, such as the Central Committee of the Party, the Kremlin, and the KGB. It is the most privileged directorate.

The Sixteenth KGB Directorate provides technical penetrations of foreign representations on Soviet territory (installation of listening and surveillance devices in embassies, digging tunnels, and so on).

There are no Fourth, Sixth or Tenth–Fifteenth Directorates. The KGB also runs the Chief Directorate of Frontier Troops, which has no number.

These comments on the functions of the various directorates are my own. They were not, of course, mentioned in the lecture.

The KGBs in the republics had the same structure, the only difference being that instead of directorates they had departments, and instead of departments they had sections.

From the beginning, days of intensive and interesting study flowed by. On general subjects, like the structure of intelligence in the main capitalist countries, lectures were given to the entire course. Intelligence subjects in detail were studied in the 30-strong sections. Unlike the lectures on the structures of the KGB, those on the structures of services of special interest like the CIA and the British Secret Service were accompanied by charts and diagrams showing a mass of detail and naming American and British intelligence officers. We were told that the main attention had to be concentrated on the Americans, first because the United States was the Main Enemy, and second because all the other services of special interest, including the British, were under their complete control. All this information was given us in such a way as to create the impression from the outset that the Western secret services were awash with Soviet agents, and that 'the activities of most intelligence services are an open book to us'. This whole approach was intended to rub in the fact that most of us knew nothing about intelligence. However the sceptical smirks on the faces of those students who had already spent some time working in PGU departments before coming to School 101 were not lost on me.

We studied the theory of intelligence, its problems, and targets for infiltration. We learnt that the structure of each country was divided up by the KGB into targets to be penetrated. For example, the political structure of a capitalist country is divided up in this way: the government, the ruling party, various ministries, the opposition party, other political parties, universities, economic targets, military and military-industrial targets. 'The basic task of intelligence is to obtain secret information by different means.' These are 'the penetration by technical means and by agents of targets of interest to us'. Put bluntly, this is to say that the KGB is constantly trying to plant eavesdropping devices in organizations of interest to it and to recruit agents in these organizations. 'We must select people as agents who have direct or indirect access to secret information. We do not need ballast. The time is past when we went after quantity in agent numbers to the detriment of their quality. The main product of intelligence is information. An agent who does not have the capability of acquiring information is no use to us.'

Now there's an effective approach to the problem, we thought! But again I saw the suppressed scepticism on the faces of some students.

In order to recruit somebody who is working in a target of interest to the KGB, and who has access to secret information, the intelligence officer must find a motive, or in the language of the professionals, a basis for recruitment. In the KGB's theory of intelligence, there are three such bases – ideological, where the person is prepared to work for the Soviet Union because he believes in communism; moral-psychological, a very broad category which can include anything at all, from mental illness, moral disintegration, non-recognition of talent and a search for adventure, to straightforward malice towards a boss who is blocking promotion at work; and financial, where the basic motive for collaboration is only money and nothing else.

Only the financial motive is found in its pure form. Generally speaking, the others overlap. The lecturer told us frankly during our studies that only the second and third motives now work. Recruitments on an ideological basis are extremely rare, and even if they do take place, they are treated with a high degree of suspicion. All this was told to us 'unofficially'. The reasons why the ideological basis has become unpopular were never discussed – there was no need. Everybody knew that Soviet internal and foreign policies had become so discredited in the eyes of the West, and indeed of the whole world, that the 'popularity' and authority of 'communism' were sustained in countries with pro-Soviet regimes only by force of arms and by the support of the Soviet Union, which after all is one and the same thing.

Anywhere in the world, whenever a pro-Soviet clique comes to power, the economy of the country collapses, living standards fall catastrophically, all human rights and liberty are suppressed, and a small knot of 'people's representatives' begins to terrorize the populace. It gives rise to civil wars, refugee camps and much else besides. All these facts are widely known everywhere. That being so, how can there be an ideological basis for collaborating with the Soviet Union? What is more, it is not only in the West that the ideological basis has become outdated. Belief in communist ideology has vanished from the minds of the Soviet people, which also means from the minds of Soviet intelligence officers, under the pressure of harsh, everyday reality.

Ever since the 1917 revolution the people have been promised a 'joyous future', constantly postponed. First it was foreign intervention and the civil war. Then it was the reconstruction of ruin in the Twenties, the search for 'enemies of the people' in the Thirties, the war with Hitler, the reconstruction of the economy after the war . . . The more we desired it, the further the glad horizon kept receding. But there was nobody to blame. There were objective reasons. Then suddenly in 1956, Khrushchev smashed the immaculate image of the ruling Soviet bosses. He laid responsibility for all the country's troubles on Stalin and his entourage, thereby trying to show that the bulk of the Party machine had had nothing to do with what happened. But it is very difficult to deceive the people. Everybody remembered the slogans 'When we say Stalin, we mean the Party. When we say Party, we mean Stalin.'

Herein perhaps lay Khrushchev's greatest service – he broke the faith of the people in the infallibility of the Communist Party and its leaders. But having broken it, as though to make a mockery of it, he then created a personal cult which was almost equal to Stalin's. It was here that the mass 'de-ideologization' of the Soviet population began. The people, who had begun to believe that changes were then possible, suddenly realized that nothing was happening. Everything was returning to square one. Dissatisfaction began to grow not so much against personalities as against the Party as a whole. Then in 1964 Khrushchev fell. The Stalinist element had not forgiven him for disrupting the 'authority' of the Party.

The new Brezhnev period began. Continuous slogans, fanfares, hot air, expansion throughout the world, economic and military assistance to Cuba, Vietnam, Angola, Ethiopia ... Meanwhile the economy continued to crumble and dissatisfaction among the people to increase. 'We don't have a home policy,' it was said among the masses. 'There is only a foreign policy.' This dissatisfaction expressed itself in an explosion of political anecdotes. Before, political jokes had been directed only at particular individuals. Now, the whole system was subjected to criticism. In a very typical story of that period, a patient went into a hospital. 'I want to see an ears and eyes specialist,' he said to the nurse.

'Perhaps you want the ear, nose, and throat doctor?' she asked.

'No,' he answered. 'It's an ears and eyes doctor I need.'

The nurse thought that he might be slightly mad, and without telling him, sent him to a psychiatrist.

'Doctor,' said the patient. 'Something has gone wrong with my eyes and ears. Wherever I go, I hear one thing, but then see something entirely different.'

'My dear fellow,' the psychiatrist replied. 'Unfortunately I can't do anything for you. We have no cure for socialism.'

Many might ask why it was that people in the Soviet Union did not stand up to their enslavers. Was the apparatus of repression, the militia and the KGB, really so strong? Yes, the apparatus was, and is, strong, but that was not the principal form of control. Everything, according to Marx – the basis of everything – is economics. Here the population was controlled by economic means. Every person in the Soviet Union was entirely dependent economically on the State, for his work, his pay, his accommodation and his holidays. All the means of existence were under Party control. If anyone expressed any dissatisfaction, then these means were removed. No one in that position could expect help from anywhere.

Yet the economic situation of the Soviet people is not so bad that they might be driven to stand up to the authorities under the slogan 'There's nothing to lose!' The people live neither in luxury nor poverty, and the authorities maintain this state of affairs for a purpose. When the question arises, do we protest and lose everything, or do we curse and forget and go on living a quiet life, it is the latter course that prevails. Everyone has families, relatives, and those near and dear who can suffer as well. Sayings begin to circulate like 'The weakest goes to the wall', and 'One man in the field is not a soldier.' As the poetry of Vladimir Vysotsky puts it: 'There are too few crazy hot-heads, that's why we lack mass leaders.' Only those who are so drunk that their tongues run freely shout anti-Soviet slogans on the street.

Very well, so there is no longer any ideological basis left. But it is not essential. We can get by without it. The siege mentality of the authorities was expressed in a KGB instruction which ran something like this: 'We can no longer influence what people think and say. Our main job now is to prevent practical anti-Soviet activity and the spread of arms among the population.'

But let us go back to the Red Banner Institute, and training for recruitment. After the basis has been selected, comes the stage of cultivating the target candidate. Cultivation is a complex and lengthy process during which the intelligence officer gradually and imperceptibly accustoms his candidate for recruitment to the idea of handing over secret information to the Soviet side. The intelligence officer's main job at this stage is to establish friendly relations with his target without evincing any interest whatever in his work. Before every meeting, a detailed scenario for the conversation is drawn up, with every detail aimed at achieving a definite purpose. It might go something like this:

1.   Congratulate on daughter's birthday and offer small gift.
2.   Talk about his health and family.
3.   Discuss latest political event, and find out target's attitude to his government's policy, stimulate his dissatisfaction and stress the Soviet Union's positive role on this issue.
4.   Discuss article published in press about target's organization (for instance about 'Irangate' political scandal) and see if target

is prepared to say more than is in the article. (We already know what information he is able to give.)

5. Establish with care whether target has reported his contacts with the Soviet representation to his superiors. If not, then imperceptibly reinforce in him the idea that it is not worth reporting them. Suitable moment to talk to him guardedly about security of contacts. If he reacts badly, turn everything into a joke. If reaction is positive, go a little further and suggest, for example, that there should be no more telephone calls and that meetings should be fixed henceforth in advance. If one of us cannot make the meeting, there is no need to ring to notify. The meeting will take place a week later, at the same time and place.

The intelligence officer thus accustoms his target to secrecy. The average cultivation will last roughly about a year. During this time, the target passes secrets both orally and in writing to the intelligence officer 'out of friendship', and does not decline to accept money. The acceptance of money is a great step forward in the cultivation. There exist many pretexts for handing over money. For example the intelligence officer tells his target that he has published an article in the confidential journal of his organization in Moscow, based on material which the target had given him. The intelligence officer has been given an honorarium and he considers it his duty to hand over half of it to his target as co-author. This usually works without a hitch. The purpose of giving money is to accustom the target to an extra income and to the comfort this brings. But it must not be thought that the KGB pays out enormous sums of money. The average remuneration does not exceed 500 convertible roubles, roughly equivalent to 500 US dollars. Vast sums of money however can be paid out in exceptional cases, when for example secret technology is being bought. Even so, sums spent in excess of $US10,000 must be approved by the chairman of the KGB himself. The money must not corrupt the target, nor must it attract the attention of those round about him. The intelligence officer is therefore always discussing with the target in order to work out a cover story to explain his extra income.

Then the moment arrives when the cultivation begins to qualify as one of 'near-agent relationship'. The target is giving us secret information and is accepting money, the meetings are being held secretly, and no suspicious features have been noticed. At this stage, the Centre may authorize a recruitment pitch to be made. (From the outset, cultivation takes place under the full control of the Centre, but more of this later.) Usually the target understands everything completely by the time the recruitment pitch is made. It only then remains to dot the i's and cross the t's. The pitch will take roughly the following form:

'You are giving us ['me' is discarded] great help. Your information is unfailingly highly valued in Moscow. I have been entrusted to thank you on behalf of the leadership and to express the hope that our fruitful collaboration will continue successfully. You are a very important person, and your safety is of prime importance to us. You must never do anything that might affect your safety.'

The words intelligence, espionage, agent and KGB are never used. On the whole, the less the target knows about the intelligence officer and his organization, the better. The target's response to the recruitment pitch is usually positive. But if moving the relationship on to a formal footing frightens him and he refuses to collaborate further, then no pressure is exerted. The intelligence officer tries quietly to convince the target to continue with his collaboration, but he will do no more than that.

The Western reader will find this hard to believe, since his concept of the KGB is totally unrealistic, but methods like blackmail, pressure and coercion to collaborate in intelligence work are no longer used by the KGB. These times have passed. We were told in the School that at the end of the Sixties the Americans and other Western countries introduced a new policy towards their citizens who were in contact with Soviet representatives. It was announced officially that if an individual came to one of their security services and reported having received a proposal to collaborate, or indeed that he was already collaborating with the Soviets, nothing would happen to him. This policy proved very effective, and many Soviet agents in the West were re-recruited by Western security services. In such a situation blackmail and coercion lost their point. It is also true that collaboration which is based upon fear and not friendship usually ends up badly.

Even after he has formally agreed to collaborate, a target of cultivation does not automatically become an agent. The intelligence officer must secretly check him by using technical resources. This is a very serious and difficult thing to do, and everything must be worked out down to the last detail. There are many ways of checking, but initiative for thinking up new methods is always encouraged. The check is aimed at discovering whether the target is collaborating honestly, or whether he has been planted by an enemy security service.

It must be noted that the process of checking up on the target is a continuous one, beginning from the time of the initial contacts. If he has already come into our sights, he is checked against traces held on him by the Centre. Everything he says about himself is also verified. The case officer constantly analyses the target's behaviour and notes any suspicious features. The reliability of his information is also tested. The target may be given the task of supplying information which we already have. We may ask him to give us information slightly outside his area of access. If he then gives us this information, he will be closely questioned as to how he was able to obtain it. All this is done very politely, on the pretext of concern about his security. If it is possible to do so, the target may be put under external surveillance, in order to find out where he goes after meeting his case officer.

The main operation to check up on him is always undertaken when the target is not expecting it. At a routine meeting, the case officer suddenly turns to the target, and makes the following sort of request. 'I have to go somewhere urgently. If you don't mind, we'll have to put our meeting back by two hours. My problem is that I've been in such a rush today that I haven't even had time to leave my briefcase in the embassy. I can't unfortunately take my briefcase where I'm going. Would you mind if I leave it with you and collect it again in two hours?' The target might then become curious and ask, 'Why can't you take your briefcase with you?' Here the main bait is cast – 'Officially I mustn't tell you this, but I shall tell you as a friend that there are secret documents in this briefcase, and there could be a disaster if I lose them! It's very important. I'll leave the briefcase with you because I trust you completely. You are my friend. Only for God's sake don't let the briefcase out of your hands' (in the most dramatic way possible!).

There are of course no secret documents in the briefcase, but there is a radio transmitter or a tape recorder. The briefcase itself has been treated with special chemicals that take fingerprints and make their recovery possible. Every verification cover story is designed in such a way that, should the target be working for us under control, and therefore be a 'plant', he will inevitably try to inform his security service that his case officer has left his briefcase containing secret documents with him for two hours. Two hours are sufficient for any security service 'to see the secret documents'. In order to convey this news, the target will probably use the telephone, and if he takes the briefcase with him we shall hear the entire conversation. Should he leave the briefcase unattended, this is also suspicious. The question then arises, what was he doing during this time? Well, if the security service officer running the case is fool enough to decide to look at the 'secrets', then at most we lose a briefcase, but on the other hand we have uncovered a 'plant'. He is simply dropped.

When the test has run its course, the briefcase is recovered from the target and subjected to a careful analysis. If no suspicious factors have been discovered then the verification of the target under cultivation is confirmed and he is included in the agent network of KGB intelligence. But the checking of the agent does not end here. It is in fact only beginning. According to the rules, every agent must be vetted at least once a year, or before each important operation in which he takes part.

All this information was news to most of us. It gripped and excited us. We could never become bored. We were studying a clutch of technical subjects all at the same time, such as photography, secret writing, the selection and preparation of dead letter-boxes, the use of special equipment for close contact with agents, and so on. Everything went smoothly for me. There were no problems. I very much enjoyed my studies.

After several months of study, caution disappeared, tongues loosened, and I began to find out who was on the course. The head of our thirty-strong section, Colonel Revizorov, was a former chief of the first department of Directorate 'S' (illegal intelligence) of the PGU who had left intelligence work on account of his age and transferred to teaching. He had specialized in his time in the United States and Canada, and had worked in both countries. We respected and rather feared him. There was something frightening about him. One student did not conceal his contempt for Revizorov and openly called him an old swine to the students. We never learnt why he hated him so, but his background made it likely that he knew something.

There were graduates on the course from Moscow University and the Institute of International Relations, specialists with a technical education, diplomats, journalists, interpreters who had already been abroad, officers from other directorates of the KGB and the KGBs in the republics, and Komsomol officials. One student in my section, a senior lieutenant from Kiev, showed everyone a photograph taken of himself with Kim Philby. It had been taken during a visit by Philby to Kiev. The photograph bore the dedicatory inscription 'To my friend Vladimir from Philby'. He was very proud of that photograph.

We had to solve many logical problems in group study. They would give us a real but depersonalized situation to work out, and we had to find our own solution to it, deciding on the basic motivation of the target and the method of approach and cultivation. Revizorov got us used to thinking creatively. He used to say, 'If the solution you come up with seems quite fantastic to you, you must not think that it is unacceptable. If your plan has a logical foundation, then you have not wasted your time. You must not be diffident. We shall discuss your plan together and we shall find the best solution.'

And it must be said that the plans which at first glance were the most unreal proved to be the most acceptable. They were usually put forward by former academic students who had not yet done any practical intelligence work, and whose logic had not been restricted by stereotyped solutions. Students who had done a stint in the KGB often found it difficult to break away from the habits of thought and logic which were practised in the internal organs of the KGB. These were entirely unacceptable for intelligence. Revizorov used to roar with laughter at the irritation of these 'experienced' students when their solutions to problems were not accepted.

The school had a special library, and we were obliged to read material from there during our private study in the evenings. The books were issued against a signature, and were recorded in a special log-book that was regularly checked by the section leader. He was thus able to monitor how much was being read, and by whom. When we realized this, we each began to take out, for instance, nine books for one evening, so that our log-book records took on a substantial appearance. But even so, those who had been academic students read far more than the KGB cadre officers. They would draw out ten books each for one evening, but they would not even open them, making out that they knew it all already.

'All that is theory,' they said. 'Everything is different in practice.'

All the books in the special library either dealt directly with intelligence work or had a bearing on it. The cases described in them were depersonalized, but they were real, and it was very interesting to read them. One of the most popular books in the special library was Dale Carnegie's *How to Win Friends and Influence People*. It had been translated into Russian in the KGB and bore the stamp 'For Service Use'. I did not know at the time that this book had been written for businessmen and not for spies, and was openly on sale in the West.

Great attention was paid to language training. All the students in School 101 already spoke one, two, three or more languages. The weakest was picked out during assessment and he was told to master the subject. Language groups were small, consisting of five to seven people. My group worked on English. Our teacher was Elena Akhmerova, the daughter of Akhmerov, a famous illegal who spent his entire career in the United States. He married an American woman when he was there and Elena was the fruit of the marriage. Naturally she spoke English like a native. The studies were very interesting. We had to listen to the radio each evening and tape evening news bulletins from the BBC. We then transcribed them into our exercise books from the tape and discussed them in class the following morning. The benefit of this way of working was beyond dispute. First, we improved our political vocabulary. Second, it accustomed us to perceive how the West treated political news and events both in the world and in the Soviet Union. Third, as we discussed the news, we were able to practise holding political debates.

Watching foreign films was the most interesting part of our language training. The most popular were the films in the James Bond series. We saw *From Russia with Love*, *Dr No* and *Casino Royale*. We were also shown contemporary French, Italian and even Chinese films, naturally according to our language groups. Our group was lucky. Elena Akhmerova loved the cinema, and it was never difficult to induce her to give a showing of any good film.

Where did all these films come from, it may be asked. Did

the Soviet government really spend vast sums of money to buy
them? Not at all. Under some agreement, in the village of Belye
Stolby near Moscow there is a repository of the copies of all (or
almost all) films produced anywhere in the world. It is from here
that these films are farmed out for film shows for our leaders, and
at the same time for the students in the intelligence school of the
KGB.

It was from the James Bond films that we first learnt how the
West saw Soviet intelligence officers. Bull necks, stupid faces, and
solving all their problems with their fists and not their brains. That
neither upset nor angered us. We were simply amused by it. 'The
more primitive you imagine us to be,' we thought, 'the worse for
you.'

By the way, about the fists. Due attention was paid in the
school to physical training, but it was not a main subject. Karate
was introduced in the KGB in 1975 as a basic and obligatory
physical subject. In school it was only taught us during morning
exercises. If someone was particularly attracted to it, he could train
during the hour allotted to sport. As to arms, I saw a Makarov pistol
only once during the entire year I was there, and I only fired three
cartridges from it. That was the sum total of arms training in the
KGB intelligence school. Some students said quite openly that they
could not understand this, but we were all told that an intelligence
officer who relied upon his fists and weapons in his work was not
an intelligence officer. The intelligence officer's main weapon is his
brain. Some other directorates do receive combat training, of course.
Direct action officers attend a special training school in Balashikhar,
near Moscow.

As a historian, I was particularly drawn to the history of the
KGB. We were told to read a book which had been issued in the
school under the title *From VCheka to KGB*. It was a small volume
of about 100 pages, written in quite a sketchy and boring way, a
continuous enumeration of data and titles. 'The All-Russian Extraordinary Commission [VChK, or Cheka for short] was set up on
20 December 1917, which even today is a pay-day in the KGB.
It was the armed vanguard of the PARTY, in the struggle against
counter-revolution, sabotage and speculation.' One idea ran through
the whole narrative like a red thread. 'This organization, from the

VChK to the KGB, is none other than the armed vanguard of the PARTY, the sword that destroys and punishes the enemies of the Revolution and the people.' The period of the Stalin cult was given only brief mention – 'During the personality cult, the organization was used illegally by certain individuals [a hint at Stalin] in order to attain personal aims. This state of affairs was corrected after the Twentieth Party Congress and the guilty were given the punishment they deserved [a hint at Beria]. We serve the PARTY and are ITS armed vanguard. This organization must never be placed above the PARTY.'

I had occasion to discuss the relations between the Party and the KGB in a private conversation with one of our students who was already an officer and had spent a few years working in one of the internal directorates of the KGB. It was then I found out for the first time that the Party stands not just above the KGB, but above the very law of the land. If for example the KGB or the militia are carrying out an investigation and it turns out that a professional Party official, or a member of his family, is involved in the affair, then standing orders lay down that the investigation ceases instantly and the case is handed over to the Central Committee of the Soviet Communist Party. As a rule, Party officials are never arraigned in a court of law. As an example, he quoted me a case where it had been established that a Western intelligence officer's mistress was the daughter of a highly placed Party official. (Names are not mentioned in such cases.) The case had to be stopped immediately and handed over to the Central Committee, from whence the instruction was quickly issued to leave that 'diplomat' in peace.

That was my first direct personal experience of learning how things really were at the top of the Soviet heap. It was by no means the last.

The surnames in *From VCheka to KGB* were extremely interesting. Everybody knows that Feliks Dzerzhinsky, a Pole by nationality, was appointed chairman of the Cheka. But not many people know who worked closely with him in this organization. It turned out that all the leading Cheka posts were occupied by foreigners and by non-Russian Soviet citizens, including Czechs, Austrians, Poles, Hungarians, Jews, Latvians, Finns and others. There were hardly any Russian surnames. We looked at each other in bewilderment.

The lecturers explained to us that many internationalist communists came to Russia at the time to help with the birth of the Bolshevik revolution. Assertions made in the West that it was a communist mafia that came to power in Russia have always been described in the Soviet Union as malicious hostile propaganda. Yet here before us was an official KGB book, with the words 'For Service Use' stamped upon it, which confirmed precisely this fact.

Historical facts which I had known before began to appear in a different light. For example, some weeks after the October coup d'état in Russia, representatives of the armed workers' guard of Petrograd who were protecting Lenin's government were suddenly replaced by a regiment of Latvian riflemen. It might appear at first glance that the workers were replaced by professional soldiers. But everything was not quite so simple. The workers' guards consisted mainly of Russian workers, and when they learnt that they had to protect the government, many members of whom spoke Russian with foreign accents, rumours went round town to the effect that Lenin had been replaced and God knows who was now in power. It was at that point that they were replaced by Latvian riflemen, who began to guard the entire State apparatus. Slogans appeared such as 'Soviets Yes, Communists No', where the communists were identified with aliens and foreigners. It became clear who had been brought to Russia along with Lenin in his sealed diplomatic railway carriage.

The Revolution in Russia is called Russian in the West. This is perfectly correct, if we are talking about the February Revolution of 1917, when the autocracy was overthrown. But the October coup d'état, and those who came to power as a result of it, are an entirely different matter. If anyone doubts these facts, I suggest they get hold of the collected edition of Lenin's works published in the Thirties and look at the surnames of the delegates who attended the Party congresses. Everything will then become clear. It would also be helpful to look up the names of the Old Bolsheviks in the *Great Soviet Encyclopedia*: many of them are Russian pseudonyms. Alternatively they might visit the cemetery in Moscow where the Old Bolsheviks are buried: they will have the utmost difficulty in finding a single Russian name.

From 1917 onwards, not one of the Soviet leaders was Russian.

The first real Russian by nationality is Mikhail Gorbachev.

In the spring of 1918 the Foreign Department was set up inside the VChK. The first head to be appointed was one of these same 'internationalists' whose name I can no longer recall, but it was something like Ackerman. According to the evidence of the same book, 'its staff included internationalist communists who had had experience in clandestine activities in European countries and in America.' The main task of the Foreign Department at that time was 'to organize and support the "Hands Off Soviet Russia" worldwide workers' movement'. Officials of the Foreign Department were smuggled into various countries where they made contact with the local communist parties and gave them Moscow's instructions. It was considered at that time that communists throughout the world had to follow Marxist ideology, according to which 'Communism does not recognize either frontiers or nationalities.' Thus communist parties throughout the world recognized the Bolshevik government in Russia as their own government. Russia became the bastion of international communism, whose main task at that point was to organize 'permanent world revolution'. But money was needed to organize world revolution. So at a time when Russia's economy lay in ruins and the people were starving, the Bolshevik government squandered enormous resources all over the world in order to support communist parties. Of course they did not use the international banking system. Members of the Foreign Department of the VChK acted as couriers. Nothing has ever changed in this state of affairs even to the present day, but we shall speak of this later.

'An intelligence officer cannot achieve success unless he is able to detect the surveillance which counter-intelligence has placed upon him.' The School attached great importance to this thesis. Right from the outset we were taught the theory of external surveillance and ways of detecting it. At first we were given general lectures on how surveillance was organized in the main capitalist countries, such as the United States and Britain. We were shown their methods of shadowing on charts, such as for example, shadowing a target along parallel streets or shadowing by overtaking, where one of the surveillance cars drives ahead of the target being shadowed, while the other keeps its distance to the rear.

We then began the theoretical study in each of our sections of the methods used to detect surveillance. Our lecturers were officers of the Seventh Chief Directorate of the KGB, which dealt only with external surveillance. They explained to us in detail which methods could be and had to be used, and which had to be avoided. The first basic rule was never to show the surveillants under any circumstances that you have found them out. The second was that surveillance officers in any country had to be respected, and never to forget that we were in their country and breaking their laws, which they were there to protect. We were told however that there were many examples of our officers adopting an arrogant attitude towards surveillance by trying to show the surveillance team by their whole behaviour that they had been detected. The first thing this type of behaviour does is to reveal that our man belongs to intelligence, and this can have negative consequences. His car, for instance, might be damaged, or he might be beaten up by 'hooligans'. Such examples exist all over the world, and as a rule any of our officers involved in them have had very low professional standards when it came to detecting surveillance, which required the most serious attention.

Above all, 'The good intelligence officer must know the city where he is located as well as a local inhabitant, or even better.' Before every operation a proven route must be selected, which must have a logical cover story. If the officer is going to move around the town, he must have an explanation for doing so. He may perhaps spend some time 'looking for a rare book'. The route must have certain places specially selected as traps, where surveillance can be spotted both naturally and with complete certainty. The officer for instance may go to a bus stop on an empty street, look back as he awaits the bus, and calmly appraise all those who had been walking behind him. When he boards the bus, he must try to stand near the rear window and see who is picked up by the surveillance car. All suspicious persons and cars must be memorized. One may also look naturally at a crossroads in the direction of oncoming traffic and pick out those who are following.

It is strictly forbidden to sit down and tie a shoe-lace while looking over one's shoulder, or glance round at an attractive woman, or jump out of an underground train as the doors are closing. In one of our lessons we were shown a film taken by the KGB external surveillance when they were shadowing an American intelligence officer in Moscow. This fellow got up to everything. He tied his shoe-lace, covered his face with a newspaper, jumped out of the train as the doors were closing. The film was shown to us as an example of what not to do. I have no doubt that it would win no medals for its subject from the CIA.

After theoretical studies, we got down to practical work. Having studied how to select verified routes, we began to work on real external surveillance. It is organized in this way. The Seventh Chief Directorate of the KGB has a school of external surveillance. It gives training to new recruits, and refresher courses to officers from all over the Soviet Union who have had some previous experience. These external surveillants practised their techniques on students at the KGB's School 101. There was a double advantage in this. External surveillance trained intelligence, and intelligence trained external surveillance.

On the day for working on external surveillance, the student goes to the pick-up point. This is usually the entrance to one of Moscow's underground stations. He has to identify himself by holding for example a newspaper or magazine. He does not know whether he will be followed that day or not. His task is to find this out. When he gets back to the school, the student writes a report, describing in detail his observations and any suspected surveillance officers. The surveillance team writes a similar report. Then an exchange takes place in which we compare our impressions. This is a very good form of training, since each side can see its mistakes and try not to repeat them subsequently. I recall that, after the first time I had embarked upon the verified route, I described ten surveillants and four cars. They all turned out to be mistakes. For a time I became the butt of my colleagues' jokes. This was what made me take external surveillance very seriously, and I became one of the two students in our section who ended the course with an 'excellent' grade for external surveillance work.

There was one great deficiency in our external surveillance training. Our studies in the detection of surveillance by using cars were only theoretical. The fact is that the private car is a luxury in the Soviet Union, so it is not surprising that our students did not have one car between them, nor did they even have driving licences. Most students took driving lessons at the school and obtained their driving licences only at the end of the course. It follows that when Soviet diplomats go on their first posting, they turn out to be very bad drivers.

The year of study at School 101 flew by almost imperceptibly. July 1976 arrived. We had to take examinations. They were in two parts, practical and theoretical.

The practical examinations were held at 'Villa', the code name for that extension of the training complex of School 101 which was located in a part of Moscow not far from the River Station stop on the Moscow Metro where Festival Street begins, just opposite a small Russian Orthodox Church. The complex is surrounded by a brick wall. A notice on the gates reads 'Technological Laboratory'. Beyond the gates is an extensive three-storey building built of sand-coloured brick. This complex is mainly used for holding USO courses (finishing courses for intelligence officers who have already had practical experience abroad, and who have been earmarked for promotion by the leadership), and for the practical work of the students from School 101.

We had to spend ten days at Villa. The set-up created there was exactly as in a residency abroad. The section head was the resident. Throughout the whole time, we lived continuously in the complex, as in an embassy. While we were there, we had to carry out a whole range of operations applying everything we had been taught in the year-long course and working with 'agents' whose roles were played by private teachers (retired officers from KGB intelligence). Each student was given two 'agents' and a total of nine operations to be mounted with them. These included secret rendezvous, the first contact with the use of a password; personal meeting; brush contact; two dead letter-box operations; exchange of intelligence by technical means; and a final personal meeting. ('Brush contact' involves the quick transfer of a document or verbal message while two people are passing each other, usually in some quiet place, so as to avoid being spotted by surveillance. 'Technical means' are special communications devices.) We had to spend three hours before each operation on the previously chosen verified route, trying to identify and throw off surveillance. It must be said here that we were told from the outset that these operations carried out under surveillance, and the shedding of surveillance, were for training purposes only. In real life this was not done abroad. There, as soon as an intelligence officer saw or suspected surveillance, he had to break off the operation and return to the embassy.

Before we left for a meeting, the 'resident' talked to us. There was a discussion on the cover story and of how the meeting was to be conducted. Some of us were categorically forbidden to offer our 'agents' alcoholic drinks during the meeting, since there were some heavy drinkers among the private teachers, who had only to be given one drink, and they would be unable to stop for a week.

Of course we all made mistakes in handling our 'agents'. Before my first secret meeting I had been unable to shake off surveillance. In accordance with the rules, they kept me under surveillance for three hours and then called it off. Because of this, I was late for my agent meeting, and had to fall back on the alternative arrangement which was half an hour later. The 'agent' was interested in the reason for my delay. I told him straight out that I had been under tight surveillance. My 'agent' became so angry that he wanted to break off the meeting, but seeing my complete naïvety, he took pity and explained that we must never talk about such things to our agents. That could frighten them off and lead to the loss of a source. There was another occasion when the 'agent', playing the role of minister counsellor at the Swiss Embassy, told me that his ambassador had gone off on holiday leaving him in charge of the embassy. I of course let this go over my head. It turned out that it had been a trap. I should have asked him to tell us about the embassy codes. But how could I have known about these codes? They had never been mentioned during our studies.

There were persistent rumours while we were in Villa that it was intended to have us picked up by the militia, the Soviet police. This meant that we could be arrested during an operation and subjected to interrogation under coercion, or to put it bluntly, be beaten up to see how we withstood it. But this also turned out to be rumour. An arrest was arranged for only one of our students, about whose courage Revizorov had some doubts. No one laid a finger on him. The militia held him for a short time and then released him.

These exhausting ten days finally ended and we returned to the main school premises. We all had a single dream, which was to sleep off all these operations, the write-ups of meetings, the surveillance reports, the use of technical resources . . . One thing we did learn very well during these ten days. That was that in our future work at least 50 per cent of our time would be absorbed in paper-pushing.

Immediately after our return, we had to take examinations in special subjects and in foreign languages. I passed them all. Then finally to the last assembly, where we were congratulated on successfully passing through the Red Banner Institute of the KGB, and wished success in our future work. Each one of us was told separately in which department or Directorate of the PGU we would continue our service. I was duly allotted to Directorate 'S'. This was followed by a banquet, with wine, served in the mess. We realized that the lecturers would be looking out for any excessive consumption of alcohol, but in spite of that and as always happens, many celebrated with every justification, including the lecturers. The following morning of 26 July 1976 we left School 101 for good, with hangovers!

CHAPTER 4

At nine o'clock in the morning on 1 September 1976, I arrived at the KGB Permits Bureau in Furkasov Lane which I had visited before. Again I was given a one-time pass. Slightly more confident than I had been on the first occasion, I now passed through entrance No. 5 as an official of the organization.

It is worthwhile to mention that the main KGB building has six entrances. The first is the ceremonial entrance on Dzerzhinsky Square. It is used only by the chairman of the KGB, his closest deputies, and high-ranking guests who come to visit the chairman in his den. The second entrance is on Dzerzhinsky Street. It is not in use, and its door remains firmly closed. The third and fourth entrances are mainly used by officials who work in the internal KGB directorates. The fifth and sixth entrances are used by intelligence officers and officers of the Chief Directorate of Frontier Troops. The first entrance apart, no official differentiation is made between any of them. Pedestrians are not forbidden to walk on the pavement directly adjoining the walls of the KGB building, but any passer-by with a trained eye might note two or three young fellows of athletic build strolling along the side of the wall trying to blend with the crowd. They belong to the external guard which is provided by the Ninth Chief Directorate.

The same tall dark man who had accompanied me on my last visit to the building was awaiting me on the other side of the barrier at entrance No. 5. This time he introduced himself. He was Colonel Valentin Ivanovich Erofeev, head of the Cadres Department of 'S' Directorate of the PGU. We went down a corridor on the left, then up in the lift with the prison cell door to the seventh floor. Room No.

701 of the Cadres Department was at the other end of the corridor. Two fairly young officials worked with Erofeev in this room. This time Valentin Ivanovich looked very friendly. He asked me how my family was, and about my holidays. He was clearly in no hurry to go anywhere. Nor, it seemed, was I. I still had not been given anywhere to work. So I told him of an incident which had happened to me during my holidays.

While I was at School 101, I had become friendly with Valery Maisuradze, one of the students there. He was the son of General Maisuradze, the deputy chairman of the KGB in Georgia. Being a kind-hearted and sociable fellow, Valery suggested that, when we were through with School 101, I should spend my holidays at Pitsunda, an international resort which was normally absolutely impossible to visit. But Valery promised that his father would fix everything. And that was what happened. General Maisuradze met us at Sochi airport. We had lunch at his guesthouse by the shore. The General had been an officer in KGB intelligence in the past. He was on first-name terms with highly placed officers in the PGU and he asked a lot of questions about School 101. He made an agreeable impression as an intelligent man. After the meal the General took us into Pitsunda in his chauffeur-driven Chaika. When the Chaika drew up outside the KGB building in Pitsunda, the chief of the KGB municipal department there thrust his head through the open door of the car.

'I wish you health, Comrade General!' he said with his head in the car, and stooping while holding his arms stiffly to attention at his sides.

'Is everything all right with you here?' the General asked.

The chief of the municipal department replied that it was.

'Fix up our comrade from Moscow with all the comforts,' the General ordered.

'Sir!' the chief bellowed.

He explained that the best thing would be for me to stay, not in the international resort zone itself but in a private flat, and have a pass to the beach in the international zone. We could eat in the canteen used by the local employees at the resort, where prices were about 70 per cent lower than for the general public. He wrote me out a pass, on the back of which he wrote 'KGB' in large letters. The weather was excellent, the accommodation terrific, and everything was proceeding normally. Then one day something happened. We had almost finished our meal in the resort mess, when a young Georgian came in. He was one of the resort workers. He went up to the hatch to collect his meal, only to be told that he was too late, and all the meals had already been served. The young Georgian exploded.

'What do you mean, there's nothing left? Is this your first day working here?' he shouted at the woman. 'Remember who has eaten here, and who hasn't! I'm a resort worker, this is my canteen, and there isn't enough for me! You feed anybody who drops in here!' He looked around the hall, and his eyes came to rest on me. 'Who's he? He isn't a resort worker! Why is he eating here?' he shouted, pointing at me.

'Quiet!' the woman in charge of the mess tried to calm him. 'He's from the KGB.'

'To hell with the KGB! Who do they think they are? What's the KGB doing eating my meal?' said the unmollified Georgian, on whom apparently the letters KGB had an exasperating rather than a frightening effect.

When he had heard my story Valentin Ivanovich looked at me somewhat sadly.

'And you, what did you think, that the word KGB would produce some magical result?' he asked. 'Don't worry. Once you've done a bit of work, then you'll find out what's what.'

After that introduction, Erofeev explained that, apart from my family, no one must ever know where I really worked. He said that the Ministry of Foreign Affairs of the Soviet Union would be my cover department, and it was then that the prospect opened of my going abroad as a diplomat. I was issued with a reference for my house management committee* that stated 'Official of the Foreign Ministry of the USSR'. As far as all my neighbours were concerned I was now a diplomat. Erofeev also said that, in the military registration and enlistment office, my name would be entered on the special list of KGB officials who fell outside the jurisdiction of the Army.

---

*Every block of flats in the Soviet Union has a house management committee, elected by the residents. It is responsible for liaison with the local authorities, including the police.

These formalities over, Erofeev said that I would be working in the Seventh Department of 'S' Directorate, and took me to room 714. There were two people there, Valentin Mikhailovich Piskunov, who was section head, and Rostislav Kozlov, an official. Piskunov was a small withered man with thin grey hair and a deeply wrinkled face. He appeared to be in his fifties, but unsuitably for his years, he was flashily dressed, with rather fussy manners. He had begun to explain to me how his section worked, when suddenly he turned to Kozlov, asked him some questions, and started talking about how tired he had felt on Sunday. Complete chaos, but I gathered that that section was responsible for work in Iran, Afghanistan and Turkey. No one explained to me what I had to do, so I simply sat and surveyed the room.

It was small, with one window, and four desks against the walls. Over one of them hung a small map of the Near East. The window looked out on to the 'well shaft', as the internal courtyard was called in KGB jargon, and from it were visible the great iron gates for cars driving in from Furkasov Lane. In Stalin's time hundreds of those arrested must have been driven through these very gates. I wondered where exactly the notorious internal prison was located.

Piskunov bustled about. He left the room, then came back, spoke to Kozlov about somebody called 'Konrad', and hurried out again. Rostislav Kozlov looked about fifty, and seemed to be a very agreeable individual with gentle manners, but with a sharp expression in his eyes. There was something of the priest in him. How astonished I was to learn later that he had worked in the Near East under Russian Orthodox Church cover, and had been secular secretary to its representative there. He had even been decorated with several ecclesiastical orders for his conscientious service. Under pressure from the State, the Orthodox Church has been compelled to allot lay posts in its missions abroad to 'S' Directorate officers, who run illegal agents in countries such as Israel for example, which have no diplomatic relations with the Soviet Union. On the other hand, the Church would never agree to the KGB using the pastoral calling of a priest for their purposes.

The lunch-break began at 12 noon. We went to the canteen, and Piskunov gave me a guided tour as we walked down the broad stairway.

'S' Directorate occupies the sixth and seventh floors in this wing of the building. The Chief Directorate of Frontier Troops is on the fifth floor. The chairman of the KGB sits on the fourth floor. You mustn't go there except on business. The Ninth Chief Directorate, responsible for personal protection, is on the third floor. On the second floor is the Third Chief Directorate, which handles Army counter-espionage. The administrative services occupy the first floor.

The canteen is in the lobby of the fifth entrance, to its right. You first select the meal from a menu, then pay for it in cash in return for a receipt at the cash-desk under the ceremonial staircase. The canteen is self-service. The queue moves fairly quickly along the service counter, until you surrender the receipt to the lady assistant and take the selected dishes on to a tray. Both the quality of the food and the cooking in the canteen are excellent.

Suddenly in the queue, someone grasped my elbow.

'Volodya, where have you been? Why haven't you come to work?' I looked round and saw behind me the Caucasian who had spoken Farsi with me in Korznikov's office during my first visit to the KGB building. 'We've got a desk all ready for you, and here you are wandering about,' he went on.

'I'm not wandering about,' I answered. 'The Cadres Department sent me to room 714 this morning.'

My colleague's eyes widened. 'All right,' he said, 'we'll sort it out after lunch.'

I went back to room 714 when we had finished and sat in idleness watching Piskunov fussing about again. Suddenly the door opened and my Caucasian came in.

'Volodya, would you mind waiting outside in the corridor? I have to talk with Valentin Mikhailovich.'

About five minutes later, he came out. 'Have you left any personal stuff there?' he asked. 'If not, then come with me.' As we went along, he introduced himself.

'Ismail Murtazaevich Aliev, head of the Eastern Section of the Second Department of "S" Directorate. I'm a colonel. You'd been earmarked for the Second Department right from the start, but Piskunov grabbed you illegally. I've said a few kind words to him. That man has no conscience.'

I did not know the details of this episode, but I somehow

felt at once that Aliev was speaking the truth about Piskunov.

We went down the staircase to the sixth floor and along to room 601. This room was larger than 714. There were six two-door steel safes lining the wall on each side of the room, leaving only a narrow space to squeeze through. Five desks were spaced along the walls. The one window, whose aperture was protected by netting on the outside, looked out on to Dzerzhinsky Square. I later learnt the story behind the netting. In the heat of summer, the rooms become intolerably stuffy. They do not have air-conditioning – the only air-conditioner in the building is installed in the KGB chairman's office. In hot weather, therefore, everybody opens their windows, and should anyone then open an office door it can cause a very strong draught. It happened on one occasion a few years ago that such a draught blew through a third floor office and swept some secret documents off the top of a desk and out through the open window. The official who had been working on them did not lose his head. He drew his pistol, jumped on to the window-sill and began to shout at the passers-by not to pick up the papers. After this incident all window openings were covered with netting.

There were another three people in room 601 besides Ismail Aliev and myself. I recognized one of them at once. He was Sergei Praottsev, who had completed his course, which included Japanese, at the Institute of Asian and African Countries a year before I finished there. The second was Vyacheslav Musikhin, a graduate of the Institute of International Relations, who had also done Japanese. The third was Vladimir Nalitov, who had learnt Arabic.

The atmosphere in room 601 was exactly the opposite to that in Piskunov's. There was no fuss, and everyone got on with his work. The head of the section had a friendly relationship with his staff. They all called him by his first name, Ismail, but without familiarity. Aliev was always ready to give help to anyone who asked for it. He gave me the impression of a highly intelligent Eastern philosopher, who devoted great thought to any problem, no matter how small. He had in his time completed the course of studies in the Persian Department of Baku University, and he had an excellent knowledge of Iran and its language. Naturally he was helped in this by being Talishi by nationality. The language of this small nation which lives on the frontier with Iran belongs to the Farsi group of languages. He had had three postings to Iran in the course of his career, but had to be withdrawn during his last tour because SAVAK, the Iranian secret police, was planning to frame him. They feared Ismail because of his quiet and self-confident ability to make himself indistinguishable from an Iranian. Although past fifty, he was noted for his robust health. The atmosphere of genial good humour in that section was very much to my liking.

My work in 'S' Directorate began with a study of its structure. We had in fact been told almost nothing about illegal intelligence at School 101. The one lecture we did receive on this subject dealt mainly with historical aspects. Right from the beginning of Soviet power, illegal intelligence was the main, and perhaps only, form of intelligence that the Bolsheviks practised. All diplomatic relations were broken off, and embassies closed. It was in these conditions that the International Department of the Cheka was set up, consisting, as I have said, of communist internationalists who were experienced in clandestine work abroad. It relied very heavily on the support of foreign communist parties which were members of the Comintern. This state of affairs continued until the end of the Second World War. After the cold war period had begun, more attention was devoted to acquiring secret intelligence through the 'legal' KGB rezidenturas who work under cover of Soviet embassies. Illegal intelligence began to move into the background. By the time I arrived in 'S' Directorate, it had the following structure.

It was headed by a chief of directorate, with general's rank. He had four deputies. The post of first deputy carried the rank of general, while that of the other three carried colonel's rank.

'S' Directorate had ten departments.

The First Department – illegals of the Centre. It worked with highly experienced illegals who were used to carrying out particularly important tasks.

The Second Department – documentation. It dealt with the selection, acquisition and processing of documents, cover documentation, and cover stories for illegals. It is the largest department, and its structure is a microcosm of the 'S' Directorate. It is divided into several geographical and specialized sections. The Eastern section embraces all countries in North Africa, the Near and Middle East, and the Indian sub-continent. The German section had a separate existence. When Germany was partitioned into two distinct states when the war ended, and the GDR was set up, Soviet illegal intelligence was presented with unbounded opportunities to avail itself of German cover documentation, the use of which for many years was basic to the work of 'S' Directorate. That is why it has become traditional that the KGB representation in East Berlin is always headed by senior 'S' Directorate officers.

The European section includes all Western European countries except the Federal Republic.

The Anglophone section – United States, Canada, and the British Commonwealth, including the United Kingdom.

The Latin American section – all Latin American countries.

The Chinese section – until 1978, it worked exclusively on China, but after the complete failure of this enterprise, Japan and the countries of South-East Asia were transferred to it.

The Infiltration section studies information on frontier procedures, and the systems used at check points in every country in the world.

The Information section receives a constant flow of information on all aspects of documentation procedures used in all countries. Codes of law governing the documentation of the local populations in almost every country in the world are kept here, as well as specimens of personal and other documents. There is no question on documentation to which an answer cannot be found in the archives of this section.

The Technical section is where the professional forgers work. They can counterfeit any document in such a way that it cannot be detected even by the most thorough chemical expert examination. When I was there, four people in all worked in this section. They could do anything at all. They had at their disposal not only office equipment from all over the world, but also a section in the Moscow mint where Soviet banknotes are printed. Paradoxically, however, KGB illegal intelligence very rarely used false documents. In the main it used only real documentation.

The Third Department of 'S' Directorate deals with the selection and training of illegals (see p. 82). The officials of this department are constantly studying students attending institutions of higher education which teach languages and other subjects in order to select candidates for the role of an illegal. For instance, at the Institute which I attended, we knew that Tsarkov, the dean's assistant, belonged to the KGB, and we believed that his main occupation was to keep tabs on the students. It then turned out that he was an officer in the Third Department of 'S' Directorate. After I had started working in the KGB, I ran across him in my own Directorate. The Third Department maintains close contact with the KGBs in the republics. There are sections there in their First Departments which select and study candidates to become illegals. They pay particular attention to ethnic minorities which have settled in the Soviet Union from neighbouring countries. In practical terms this means the whole of Asia and Europe.

The Fourth Department is a geographical one, covering the United States, Canada and Latin American countries. The main task of the officers in these geographical departments is to safeguard the operating conditions of illegals in the countries where they happen to be. Put simply, they maintain clandestine contact with the illegals.

The Fifth Department	Western European countries.
The Sixth Department	China, Japan, and the countries of South-East Asia.
The Seventh Department	Arabic-speaking North African countries, countries in the Near and Middle East, and the Indian sub-continent.
The Eighth Department	Execution of direct actions. Previously this was a specialized separate department and came under the direct control of the chairman of the KGB. It was then called Department 'V' and carried out direct actions, that is it physically eliminated those who had got on the wrong side of the authorities. It must be said however that the expression 'wet job', long popular with Western scribblers and attributed to the KGB, is not part of the KGB vocabulary. Murder is called 'direct action'. 'Wet job' is underworld jargon.

This department also had the responsibility for planning and preparing acts of sabotage and diversion abroad in the event of war, including for example the assassination of members of an enemy government and of its military high command, the destruction of power stations and the contamination of the water supply.

This department held a privileged position. The pay of its officers was 20 per cent higher than in the PGU. The direct action activities of 'V' Department ceased in 1972. There were three reasons for this. One was that the policy of détente had already begun between the United States and the Soviet Union; the second was that the Soviet leaders realized that the numbers of their political opponents were growing both in the West and in the Soviet Union and that it would now be simply impossible to exterminate them; while the third was that Oleg Lyalin, an officer of this department, had defected in Britain in 1971, and had then revealed many secrets. At that point, the active operations of this department were stopped, its officers recalled from countries all over the world, and the department itself changed from the independent 'V' Department into the Eighth Department of 'S' Directorate. The agents who had belonged to 'V' Department were then put under the control of the geographical departments in 'S' Directorate. All the Eighth Department did was to make contingency operational plans for war, and to train KGB officers and illegals in sabotage. The pay of these officers was reduced to the level of pay in 'S' Directorate. The importance and activity of this department increased when the war began in Afghanistan, but more will be written about this in subsequent chapters.

| The Ninth Department | Security. Its officials are responsible for the security of the conduct of operations involving illegals. They follow the progress of cases independently, and they may intervene if they see that the operation might lead to the downfall of the illegal. This department is not very popular, since it is always intervening to block risky operations. On the other hand, the existence of a second opinion helps maintain the standards of an illegal's security. |

The Tenth Department   Intelligence activity on Soviet territory. It tries to recruit foreign students studying in the Soviet Union, businessmen and other categories of foreigner, in order to use them in support of illegal intelligence.

There are more special categories in 'S' Directorate – illegals, agent illegals, and spetsagents, or special agents.

The *illegal* is a Soviet citizen, a KGB officer holding military rank, who has undergone special training and who has been documented as a citizen of a foreign country. Candidate illegals are selected by officials of the Third Department of 'S' Directorate from among young people throughout the Soviet Union. The selection criteria are suitable appearance and acceptable linguistic talent, all-round intellectual development, and membership of the requisite ethnic group.

It must not be thought that illegals are turned out in their hundreds. Dozens of candidates are selected, but only single individuals succeed in becoming illegals.

This is how it works. For example, there is a student in an institute of higher education which teaches languages. He reveals an excellent linguistic talent. He is well developed intellectually, has a strong personality, and his appearance is such that he could pass as a citizen of a certain country in Western Europe. He is morally sound. All this attracts the attention of the Third Department, and they begin secretly to check him out. Should the results of this vetting prove favourable, he will be offered work in the KGB. If he accepts, then he may be told that he is being considered as a candidate for the role of an illegal. If he accepts this as well, his special training will begin after he has finished his studies at his institute. Should the student not accept the proposition, a written undertaking of non-disclosure must be obtained from him and he is then left in peace. There are no repercussions.

The special training lasts on an average from four to six years. Most attention is given to language training. For four years, the candidate works in his main language to make it his 'mother' tongue. He is also given a second 'working' language. Illegals normally operate in countries where their 'working' language is spoken, and not their 'mother tongue' language. In this way the likelihood of discovery and downfall is reduced. For example, an illegal who is documented as an Englishman may work in France, using his 'working' French language while steering clear of English people who speak his 'mother' tongue and who might therefore detect even the slightest inaccuracies in his speech. If however the illegal belongs to an ethnic group and speaks the foreign language like a native, then most attention will be given to training him in his working language, and he may be sent to work in the land of his forefathers. The languages are taught in individual lessons given by former illegals. Area study also comes into it here. Stories about whole settlements that supposedly exist, where the entire atmosphere of a foreign country has been comprehensively re-created in order to train illegals, are nothing more than the figments of their authors' overworked imaginations.

At the outset of his training, the candidate's first name is changed, he is issued with new documents, and a cover life history is worked out for use while he is under training in Moscow. He begins to accustom himself to living as another person from the very first day. He is put up in an operational flat which is usually in a Moscow block and has 'no connection whatever' with the KGB. Neither candidates nor illegals themselves ever visit the KGB building, nor are they ever told anything about the structure of the KGB or about how its apparatus works. What a man does not know he cannot talk about in the event of arrest.

The special training includes receiving and decoding radio messages from the Centre, preparation of secret writing communications, the selection of dead letter-boxes, writing reports, cultivating and making recruitments.

Those in charge of the candidate place him under a microscope immediately. His flat is equipped with listening and surveillance devices, he is placed under external surveillance, and he must report his contacts, no matter who they are. His behaviour is analysed thoroughly, and he is subjected to continual check-ups. The candidates are unaware of course that most of the people they run across in the course of their daily lives in this period have been planted on them by the Third Department. Every officer of 'S' Directorate has a duty to help the Third Department in its training of illegals. A situation is engineered in which either an 'S' Directorate official gets to know the candidate 'by chance', or else the candidate is given the task of striking up an acquaintanceship with a given individual. I had to take part once in such a game. The candidate was told that I was a Foreign Ministry official who was suspected of disseminating anti-Soviet literature. He had to 'get to know me by chance' during my lunch-break in a café not far from the Foreign Ministry. It went like this. We established a friendly relationship, as a result of which he reported to his boss that, in his view, the 'suspicions' against me were unfounded. After each meeting, I wrote a report, along with my comments, on the candidate's performance. An officer from the Third Department and I then analysed the candidate's reports on the meetings and planned what we would do next.

With the passage of time, the tests devised for the candidate become more complicated. A woman may be planted on him to see how he reacts to the opposite sex. He may be sent to another town with the task of finding a job at a secret plant with a defence-related output. Before his training is over, he may be sent to those parts of the Soviet Union frequented by foreign tourists, under the guise of a foreigner and with a foreigner's documentation. On all these occasions he is of course surrounded by members of the local KGBs, who arrange various tests for him.

For instance, one candidate was sent to Baku as a Canadian tourist. Naturally the local friends appeared immediately. One day he was given a task involving his getting back to his hotel by 11 p.m. in order to receive a radio message. These 'friends' from the local KGB were told to create a situation in which it would be impossible for the candidate to get back to his hotel. They did this by arranging a magnificent meal, and then drove off to continue the feast in a villa outside town. The candidate tried to excuse himself from making the trip, but he was told that 'according to Eastern traditions, hospitality cannot be refused, in fact it would be a deadly insult to do so'. When evening was falling, the candidate began to ask his 'friends' to drive him back to the hotel. But they pretended to be quite drunk, and did not want to know. At that point, the candidate broke. He began to talk Russian, saying that he was a member of the KGB, and that he had to get back to town at once. Naturally, this candidate was removed from his training.

When the training of an illegal is approaching completion, a search begins to find him cover documentation, on which his cover life history will be built. As already mentioned, illegals use only real documents. In order to come by them, the officers of the Documentation Department of 'S' Directorate must go through the population registration records of the country in question and recruit an agent there, who will obtain the cover documentation for our illegal and then hand over real documents to us. (In theory, a different agent has to be recruited every time, for reasons of security.) There are many kinds of cover documentation. It all depends on the system of population registration in the country concerned. A 'dead' or a 'living' double might be used. A 'dead double' is cover documentation where our agent secretly neglects to register a death, and then hands us the dead person's documents which are then used by the illegal. A 'living' double is a method in which we specially recruit a foreigner whom we then take secretly to the Soviet Union, with his permission of course, for a prolonged stay. We then use his documents for our illegal. Alternatively the person we have recruited may go on living in his own country, but in this case we must be sure that he does not intend to go abroad, and we must keep him under control. Or a child who has never existed may be registered to parents who are already dead.

After the cover documentation has been found, the illegal's cover story has to be devised. Every point in it must be authentic and foolproof against any possible examination by enemy security services. All this involves an enormous amount of work for 'S' Directorate officers, both in the countries mentioned in the cover story, and in the Centre. The illegal must know every detail of his story, the names of people, addresses, descriptions of towns, streets, and houses where he 'lived' previously. In every case, this can take months and even years of hard work by 'S' Directorate officers.

Now at last everything is ready to bring out the illegal. In the present world climate illegals are usually launched through 'legal' channels. Using as a rule false travel documents, the illegal leaves the Soviet Union for a third country. An official of 'S' Directorate from the local residency arranges to meet him there and hands him the basic documents which have already been prepared to match his cover life story. The illegal then leaves for the country of his appointment. Other ways of exfiltrating an illegal can include official emigration, moving him across a land or sea frontier from a neighbouring country, or even having him 'escape from the Soviet Union'.

Now the euphoria of training the illegal, documenting and exfiltrating him, is over. All those who have taken part are suitably rewarded. A period of routine work with the illegal then sets in. And it becomes clear at this point that when it comes to producing secret intelligence, present-day illegals are quite useless. They cannot penetrate those secret enemy targets where serious personal vetting is practised. Places where they lived, and which are quoted in their cover life stories, will no longer exist. They will have been pulled down as a result of area redevelopment or destroyed by some natural disaster. People whom they 'knew' have either died or moved away to somewhere unknown, and relatives will have all died. The most important thing the present-day illegal can do is to run an important source of intelligence who either lives in a country that does not have diplomatic relations with the Soviet Union, or who works in an area to which the 'legal' rezidentura has no access. Even so, there are many obstacles in the way of conducting operations of this kind. For example, an illegal who is running an agent, let's say, in South Africa cannot take documentary intelligence the agent has given him out of the country, even on microfilm. A chance customs examination for drugs, for instance, can lead to both an illegal and an agent being unmasked.

Not all important agents in countries where there is a 'legal' residency belong to 'S' Directorate. The PGU departments are not bursting to hand over their best agents to 'S' Directorate, even though this may be the most secure procedure, since in that event they would lose all the dividends from all the work they have put in with these agents. This is the usual inter-departmental hostility. What is more, a dire warning hangs over the heads of the KGB. The Politburo ordains: 'Your activities must not have any negative influence on the conduct of the Soviet Union's peaceful foreign policy.' This means that if a KGB operation abroad should misfire and a political scandal ensue, intelligence officers can expect no mercy from the Politburo. It is one thing for a failure to occur in the 'legal' residency, when a Soviet diplomat may simply be expelled from the country. It is quite another when an illegal fails. Many countries do intelligence work under the cover of their diplomatic representation, and this is an internationally recognized fact. But when the intelligence of one country uses the documentation of another, it can seriously affect the relations between these two countries. The downfall of an illegal therefore usually brings very damaging consequences for those responsible. At best, a culprit may be thrown out of the KGB without a pension. At worst, criminal proceedings may be instituted against him. Who then would risk the security of illegals in these circumstances? And the Ninth Department keeps a strict watch to see that the least risk possible is taken. Because of that, illegals spend most of their time building their cover life stories, devising reliable cover, and organizing their personal business affairs and their travel to other parts of the world. These illegals therefore produce no real intelligence.

An *illegal agent* can either be a Soviet citizen or a foreigner. He is not a KGB officer, he does not hold military rank, and has been brought into intelligence in order to do a one-time operation. The illegal agent is documented as a citizen of a foreign country and undergoes special training. His training is exactly the same as that given to an illegal, and everything said above about illegals applies also to illegal agents. The difference is that the illegal agent goes back to his civilian work, while the illegal remains an official of the KGB. Although there is a rule that he may be used only once, an illegal agent can be used on more than one occasion.

A special agent, or *spetsagent*, is a foreigner who has been recruited by the KGB intelligence, who has undergone special training in the Soviet Union, and who works in the country where he operates using his own documents and biographical data. He is not a KGB officer, nor does he hold military rank.

Spetsagents are either taken from among already existing and particularly trusted agents, or else they are recruited specially for this purpose by 'S' Directorate officers either abroad or in the Soviet Union. Young university students, many of whom have left-wing views and Soviet sympathies, are usually suitable for this role. 'S' Directorate takes great care over their cultivation and recruitment, since if skilfully handled this group can use their own legitimate identity to penetrate whatever target may be required, including the secret services of the enemy. Their cultivation is usually conducted very slowly, and care is taken to reinforce their Soviet sympathies. When someone is recruited, he is sent secretly to Moscow. His training lasts about a year. Particular attention is paid to teaching him intelligence subjects. After his training is over the spetsagent may either be sent back to his own country, or to the country of the main enemy, the United States. A suitable cover story is created to explain his absence, and nobody will ever find out that he has been in the Soviet Union. Work with spetsagents abroad is conducted in the same way as it is for illegals.

There is also a category of support agents, recruited by officers in the field in order to provide genuine documents, cover, radio flats, etc.

In 1976, the head of 'S' Directorate was General Kirpichenko. He was a 'Varangian'. In the language of 'S' Directorate, this means that the person concerned neither originated nor was trained in that Directorate, and that he had come into it from elsewhere. Kirpichenko had had a quite interesting career. He came from the Eighteenth Department of the PGU, which specialized in Arab countries. He had been KGB resident in Egypt when relations with Sadat were beginning to show signs of cracking. The KGB rezidentura learnt through its sources that Sadat was planning to expel all Soviet advisers from Egypt. The sources were reliable. One of them was actually Sami Sharaf, the head of the Egyptian Security Service. The rezidentura sent this intelligence to the Centre, but to its astonishment, no reaction followed. On the contrary the Centre began to ask questions about the status of the intelligence.

What had happened in fact was that Vladimir Mikhailovich Vinogradov, the Soviet Ambassador to Egypt, had at the same time sent back information to the Soviet Party Central Committee which said exactly the opposite, convincing Moscow that Sadat would continue to remain a 'true friend' of the Soviet Union. Alarming intelligence continued to arrive in the residency from its agents, and Kirpichenko continued to send it to the Centre, but the Ambassador stuck to his line and the Politburo believed him, since he was a member of the Party Central Committee. Nevertheless, Kirpichenko's intelligence put Moscow on the alert and the Ambassador was asked to confirm his reports. In July 1972, the Ambassador was still insisting that everything was normal. In fact, on the 18th, the day Sadat announced the expulsion of the Soviet advisers, Ambassador Vinogradov had a meeting with him and was given personal assurances of cordial sentiments. Next day the Russians were thrown out of Egypt.

Kosygin, who was then Chairman of the Council of Ministers of which the KGB was part at that time, ordered that 'that intelligence resident should be made a general and given a top post in the Centre'. That is how Kirpichenko became head of 'S' Directorate. What did they do with the Ambassador? Nothing. He returned to Moscow and was given the post of deputy minister of foreign affairs. We do not punish members of the Central Committee.

I used a temporary pass for about a month while working in 'S' Directorate. It takes a long time to prepare a permanent identification card for a member of the KGB. First, a photograph has to be taken in a special KGB studio, which is at one end of Komsomolsky Prospekt. He must be photographed in military uniform, and as intelligence officers do not have a uniform, they have to use one which is specially kept for them in the photographic studio. He uses only the upper part of the uniform, with shirt, tie and military jacket.

Intelligence officers not only do not wear uniforms, they do not possess them either. To make up for this, they are paid a grant equivalent to the cost of fitting themselves out with military uniforms. When I was there it was more than 700 roubles, a quite considerable sum by Soviet standards. There are special 'wear and tear' dates applied to separate articles of military uniform, and when these periods are up, fixed grants are paid, for instance for the wearing out of shoes or trousers.

When the photographs are ready they are sent to the Cadres Department, and about a month later the identification card is ready. A KGB officer's identification card is a small red rectangular booklet with the crest of the Soviet Union embossed in gold in the centre of the cover. Under the crest, written in gold, there is an inscription, 'Committee of State Security of the Council of Ministers of the USSR'. The official's photograph showing him in military uniform is inside the card, on the left, against a grey background.

To the right of the photograph, in beautiful lettering in black Indian ink, appear his name, patronymic and surname, each on a separate line. His personal military number appears in the lower left-hand corner. His military rank and function are shown on the right side. Identification cards with a grey background inside are issued to junior officers up to and including the rank of captain. In the cards of senior officers from major upwards, the background colour inside is pale red. The inside of the identification card, including the photograph, is covered with a thin film of lacquer as protection against forgery. When the card is being examined at the entrance to the KGB building, the guard turns it to the light and checks whether the lacquer covering has been broken.

My own identification card had the details: rank, lieutenant; grade, junior executive.

The grades within the KGB are more important than military ranks. This is their order:

> junior executive – cannot rank higher than first lieutenant;
> executive – captain;
> senior executive – major;
> assistant head of department – lieutenant-colonel;
> senior assistant head of department – colonel;
> head of section – colonel;
> deputy head of department – colonel;
> head of department in 'S' Directorate – colonel; in PGU – general;
> head of directorate in 'S' Directorate – general; in PGU – lieutenant-general;
> deputy chairman of the KGB – colonel-general;
> chairman of the KGB – full general.

Appointments depend upon the success attained at work. When ranks are awarded, a time factor counts. The period separating second and first lieutenant appointments is two years; between first lieutenant, captain and major it is three years; between major, lieutenant-colonel and colonel, four years. The generals' ranks depend only on the posts, and the time factor does not then apply. So that the rank can be bestowed in its due time, the post must have precedence over the rank. For instance, a major may be appointed to the post of head of section, which carries the rank of colonel. But he will be given colonel's rank only when the due time has elapsed. Such a situation arose because a decree was issued early in the 1970s abolishing the granting of military ranks out of turn, and establishing that they should be conferred strictly according to seniority. But this does not particularly affect the lives of the executive staff, who get a considerable increase in pay when they are promoted in their function. Promotion in rank brings only a rise of 10 roubles to salary.

KGB officials are well paid by Soviet standards. Whereas the average monthly pay in the Soviet Union is 150 roubles, or less, a junior executive officer in the KGB is paid 250 roubles a month. In addition to this he is paid 10 roubles for his military rank, 10 per cent for knowledge of a Western language, and 20 per cent for knowledge of an oriental one. Something like 60 roubles is added to his pay on promotion. Thus the pay of a colonel, who is senior assistant to a head of department, is 600 roubles.

Yes, the pay is high. Here however I must disappoint the reader who is expecting a story about KGB privileges. Apart from their high pay, KGB officers do not have any privileges. They have no special shops exclusive to them, where they may buy at low prices high-quality foodstuffs, or fashionable clothes made in the West. They are unable to jump the queue to buy a car. Privileges exist only for KGB officers who hold the rank of general and above. They join the nomenklatura, the Party ruling class, and enjoy the same blessings as the workers on the Central Committee of the Soviet Communist Party. They are selected with special care. The granting of a general's rank or general's post is confirmed *by the Politburo itself*. Many writers claim that all KGB officers belong to the nomenklatura. This is quite wrong.

Even a KGB colonel, when he receives his high salary, must choose either to take his place in the queue for food products like an honest Soviet citizen, or to find his own personal channels in order to obtain products in short supply, thereby directly involving himself in corruption. He will either pay black market prices or, for example, offer things such as foreign produce, to which the supplier has no access. Everyone, without exception, is involved in this process. At first, such a state of affairs is repellent. How can it be that I, a KGB officer, guardian of legality, am involved in corruption? But you gradually get used to it. Such is Soviet reality.

The mother of one of my fellow officers was the manager of a large grocery store on the outskirts of Moscow. This was our channel to 'privileges'. I was given access to this gravy train because I was the only person in the section to own a car, which I bought when I returned from Iran. I was used therefore as a means of transport once or twice a month. Each person in the office compiled a list of the provisions he wished to buy and, accompanied by someone else, I would set off to the store. It was quite a large self-service shop, with nothing much on display on the counters – no good meat, sausage or frankfurters, let alone goods like crab and caviare. But in the basement of the shop, the picture was entirely different. Whatever you might wish could be found there in abundance. Naturally we paid State prices, but in addition, there was a special surcharge: a good attitude towards the son of the manager. I once asked the lady, after we had established a good relationship, why she kept the foodstuffs in the basement and did not sell them to the general public.

'If I had my way,' she answered, 'I would sell the lot right now. But I'm forbidden to do so by the local regional committee of the Party. Most of these provisions leave here as orders for regional committee officials and their families.'

The day came when in the Cadres Department I was given my identification card as an officer of the KGB. It was in red leather, with the coat of arms on the cover. No doubt every KGB officer experiences the same emotion when he receives his card. It gives the feeling of having been handed a symbol of authority – that you have only to produce it and, like magic, your every wish will be fulfilled. This feeling that the young officer experiences comes from the rumours about the all-powerful KGB that circulate throughout the country.

My personnel officer then threw a bucket of cold water over me. *The identification card must not be shown to anyone.* Above all to members of the militia. This was not at all because an intelligence officer must keep his connection with the KGB secret. It was for an entirely different reason. There was real hostility, from the top downwards, between the militia and the KGB. Andropov, the KGB chairman, and Shchelokov, the interior minister, hated each other.

The KGB, which had its agents inside the militia, had previously been able to control it. But then Shchelokov came along. He was a friend of Brezhnev's, and induced the Secretary General to make the militia independent of the KGB. This idea was to Brezhnev's liking, since the measure would weaken the KGB's influence, and make the militia a competitor on an equal footing with the KGB.

All this allowed Brezhnev to pursue his policy of divide and rule. By setting the two organizations against each other, the Party directed the rancour of one against the other, while it remained safe from both. If one of these organizations were to move against the Party, it would always be possible to oppose it with the other. In spite of the hostility, Brezhnev, Andropov and Shchelokov all lived in the same block at No. 26 Kutuzov Prospekt, and the block was guarded by both KGB and MVD personnel.

The hostility descended to the lower levels. In accordance with a secret instruction from above, the militia would hound KGB officers for no particular reason. If for example a KGB official had a car accident or did something that drew the attention of the militia, such as getting involved in a drunken brawl, members of the militia were not to be counted upon to have any sympathy for their 'colleague' from the KGB. Outwardly of course everything was above-board. There was no compulsion of any kind. But the official complaint from the MVD to the KGB would as a rule exaggerate the facts so much that the victim would come very badly out of it. Soviet society believes paper and not people. 'What has been written down cannot be cut out, not even with an axe.' In a situation like this, the KGB would come off the loser.

The KGB in fact has no executive powers in Soviet society. It does not even have the right to make an arrest. An arrest can be made only with the approval of the public prosecutor's office, and only by MVD organs. That is why officers of the KGB's internal directorates who work on Soviet citizens always use credentials provided by the Criminal Investigation Department – naturally with the agreement of the MVD. This graphically illustrates that, in such a situation, the KGB can do nothing against the MVD. 'Don't get caught' was Andropov's very strict instruction to his officials, and if someone did get caught there was no mercy from the leadership. He usually ended up by being either expelled from the KGB or transferred somewhere deep into the provinces.

Such an alignment of forces between the KGB and the MVD caused a fearful outbreak of corruption in the ranks of the MVD from top to bottom. There was no doubt whom Brezhnev was supporting. His daughter's husband, who had formerly been his MVD bodyguard, was made a deputy minister in the MVD, and not in the KGB. Brezhnev could fix up his son-in-law wherever he wanted. But Brezhnev had other personal plans. Having freed the MVD of KGB control and having placed his friends and relations in the highest posts, Brezhnev converted this organization into his own personal guard. (The MVD incidentally has far more troops than the KGB.) The pay of MVD officials was raised to the level of pay in the KGB.

The facts about the scale on which Brezhnev's family was involved in corruption are now widely known throughout the world, so there is no need to rehearse them here. But it is still worth saying something about what happened inside the MVD. The highest MVD posts were held by Shchelokov and the reliable Churbanov. Posts lower down were not given on merit, but were sold for money. There was even a price list showing how much each post cost. (Unfortunately I do not know these figures.) It followed that every scoundrel who held a high position in the MVD surrounded himself with people of his ilk. The same thing went on lower down.

The Criminal Investigation Department, whose job was the investigation of crimes, was turned into a business. It worked like this. If you stole three roubles, you would go to jail. But if you stole 300,000 roubles, your case would be dropped, but half of the money would go to the officials in the Criminal Investigation Department.

The OBKhSS, or Department for Combating the Theft of Socialist Property, became a full accomplice in these embezzlements. One of its responsibilities was to exercise control over the observation of financial disciplines in trade and other branches of the economy. Its officials had to make surprise visits, for example to a trading enterprise, and carry out a financial audit. But it was quite different in practice. Before making a raid, OBKhSS officials would ring their friends in the trading body and warn them about the planned operation. It goes without saying that this information did not come cheap. In most cases, teams who arrived, for example to carry out an audit at a restaurant, never did so. They would be given a sumptuous banquet, with women if necessary, and big pay-offs in ready cash. The OBKhSS was so rotten that rumours began to circulate that its functions were to be handed over to the KGB, but they were only rumours. What minister would wish to lose such a source of income?

How, incidentally, does this tainted money reach the top? Quite simply. Let us take the OBKhSS. One of its officials makes a raid on a restaurant and is given a bribe there of 1,000 roubles. He keeps 60 per cent for himself, and gives the remaining 40 per cent to his boss. The boss, who has been receiving similar percentages from all his other officials, keeps 60 per cent of what he has had from them for himself and passes the remaining 40 per cent on to his superiors. The process is repeated right up to the summit of the organization. The Brezhnevs of course had no need of money in notes. They took their share in gold, precious stones and expensive gifts.

Everyone in the Soviet Union knows about the affairs of the GAI, or State Automobile Inspectorate. The GAI has a high profile. At its head is the special GAI, or SPETSGAI, which was formed to make sure that members of the Politburo and government could drive around without being held up by traffic. They always led motorcades in Mercedes and BMW cars specially bought for them by Shchelokov in West Germany with hard currency. It was the only organization in Moscow that officially used cars of this kind. In the KGB, only Andropov had a government ZIL. The others had to be content with the usual black Volgas.

The changes in the MVD's position naturally affected the GAI. There was a time when the traffic policemen on the streets of Moscow used to wear the uniforms of sergeants and sergeant majors. At the beginning of the Seventies however they all became officers. The streets in the centre of Moscow came under the control of first and second lieutenants, captains and even majors. Street traffic policing was tightened in Draconian fashion, not in order to improve the movement of street traffic but to collect more fines, which are an unofficial source of income for a GAI officer. It was such a profitable business that anyone who wanted a job in the GAI first had to pay a bribe of 5,000 roubles. This, when the average wage of the ordinary Soviet person was 150 roubles a month!

In Moscow there was a GAI official on almost every intersection, and their main job was to collect as much money as they could in fines that they had to share out at the end of the day with their bosses. Their speciality was setting traps. GAI patrol cars would conceal themselves behind bushes while the speed limit signs were intentionally hidden by tree branches. Every driver who was stopped knew what to expect. It was traditional for drivers to keep money, usually three roubles, in their driving licences. When one of them had to produce his licence for the GAI official, the three roubles disappeared. If the driver had been drinking (under Soviet law it is forbidden to drive a car having taken any alcohol at all), then the size of the take shot up to something between 50 and 100 roubles. It goes without saying that the GAI officials never gave receipts.

With the country-wide increase in the number of private cars, the issue of licences to new drivers became a lucrative business. A driving licence could be bought almost openly in the GAI for 150 roubles. A neighbour of mine obtained one for his wife in this way. He went to see the head of the GAI regional office, explained what he wanted, placed an envelope with the money in front of him. (Note that my neighbour was seeing this GAI fellow for the first time.) Straight away, his wife was given papers to sign, with examination questions and their answers already filled in. She received her official driving licence two days later.

As a driver, I kept on having dealings with the GAI. If you are stopped only once a week in Moscow, you can consider yourself very fortunate. A driver is stopped on an average every second day. On occasions I decided to test the validity of the warning given by our Cadres Department, and presented my KGB identification card. In most cases, the reaction was hostile, and I was fined, but they did issue me with a receipt. On two cases I asked why the GAI was behaving in this way towards their KGB 'colleagues'. I was given the straight answer that they had orders from above to come down on anyone from the KGB. On another occasion I was trying to retrieve my broken down car. The GAI lieutenant quoted the law, and I had to hurry up. I explained to him that I was KGB, but that only complicated matters. I then decided to follow the route taken by the ordinary Russian, and offered the lieutenant 25 roubles. He took the money, but knowing that I was KGB, he asked at the same time whether I would lodge a complaint against him.

All this corruption was taking place under the nose of the KGB, but they could do nothing about it. They did not have any warrant to do so. KGB officials called their organization an invalid with no arms, who sees everything, but can do nothing. But the paradox was that only the Party Central Committee and the KGB itself realized that this was the position. Even in the MVD, the truth was known to only a few of the highest-ranking personages. Rumours continued to circulate throughout the country about the unbelievable omnipotence and influence of the KGB, and many Soviet citizens, unhappy about the spread of corruption, openly asked where the KGB's eyes were. In most cases, KGB officers kept their mouths shut and said nothing about the true position, for two reasons. First, it was embarrassing to admit that this 'all-powerful' organization had in fact been turned into a paper tiger by the Party. Second, nobody would believe it, so improbable would it sound. I once tried to explain the real position of the KGB to some friends. They simply brushed me aside, saying that I was making it all up.

This blind belief among the people in the power and ubiquity of the KGB was skilfully exploited by Party officials, who deflected the general dissatisfaction away from the Party and directed it against the KGB.

What, on the whole, was the KGB doing at this time? Intelligence abroad, counter-espionage against foreigners in the Soviet Union, protecting the State frontiers, intercepting foreign radio communications, protecting top Party leaders, and working on dissidents and currency speculators. The KGB was totally uninvolved in the fight against corruption. Nor did it have any access to that fight. The Party had no desire to combat its own enrichment.

Of course, the KGB was not free of corruption, but it was not on the terrifying scale it had reached in the MVD. Andropov severely punished any involvement in corruption. In 1972, for instance, some KGB officials working on currency speculators were arrested for having taken bribes. Their punishment was severe. Most of them were shot.

I am not in any way maintaining that KGB officers are a

breed apart. They are just ordinary Soviet people like everyone else. But their strict discipline, and the fact that they have no direct involvement with the sources of corruption, have checked its spread among them. Corruption in the KGB took the form of modest gifts to immediate superiors after returning from a foreign posting, or arranging dinners either in restaurants or at home. Yet even these 'innocent' things were strictly forbidden, and it did not stop there. Inviting colleagues to celebrate birthdays or promotions in office or in rank was also strictly forbidden in the KGB. Of course it did go on, but very much on the quiet and at great risk. If anyone was caught in a drunken state by the militia after such an event, it was not only he who suffered, but also the person who had organized it and all who had attended it. The culprit could be dismissed from the KGB without a pension, and the careers of the others could be considered frozen for many years. The reason for this was that same hostility between Andropov and Shchelokov. The interior minister gave instructions that every case of a KGB officer being arrested by the militia should be reported to him personally. He would then go running to Brezhnev, who in his turn would haul Andropov over the coals.

Why did Party officials have such hatred for the KGB? The answer is simple: because of the events of 1937, when Stalin's repression began. Not because the NKVD liquidated the Party's Lenin Guard on Stalin's orders, but because the present leaders had played a direct part in it. It will be very obvious from a glance at the official biographies of people like Brezhnev, Kosygin, Podgorny and others, that they began their professional Party activities in 1937–38. That means that they took the places of those people who were tortured and liquidated. In order to be noticed at that time, promotion was essential. And there was only one way to be promoted, and that was by unconditionally supporting the repressions and taking part in them. I do not have participation in executions in mind, but active participation in 'exposing enemies of the people' and in writing denunciations for the NKVD.

The NKVD underwent considerable changes in the Thirties.

It too had purges carried out in the ranks of the old guard. Stalin gathered new people to replace them. These were the children of the 'enemies' who had been liquidated after the revolution, the children of dispossessed kulaks and deported peasants, all of whom were embittered towards the Soviet authorities and who were thirsting for revenge. That explains the unimaginable terror of the repressions of the 1930s. The newly fledged officials of the NKVD had no pity for the Party members of the Lenin Guard. They were liquidating the people who had liquidated their families.

After Stalin's death, Khrushchev accused him of every crime, but tried not to sully the Party. In 1964, however, the Stalinists threw out Khrushchev and began to 'restore the leader's image'. But the milk had already been spilt, and it had become necessary to find a scapegoat for Stalin's crimes. They found one in the KGB. With Brezhnev's coming to power in 1964, the unofficial persecution of the KGB began. It must be said that by that time there was hardly anybody left in the KGB who had taken part in the repressions. Immediately after Khrushchev's revelations, most of those who had blood on their hands were removed from the KGB machine and transferred to other work. The father of one of my acquaintances was a colonel in State security. In 1956 he was sent from Moscow to the Far East, where he became the head of one of the oilfields in the Kurile Islands. But his spacious flat in the KGB block on Smolensk Square was kept for him.

A grim-faced, taciturn man called Andrei Dimitrievich lived in my block of flats. He wore military uniform without insignia and said that he worked in 'the organs'. Once I heard him say in a conversation about masculine physical qualities, 'I could break a collar-bone with one chop with the edge of my hand.' I was a boy of about eight at that time, and what struck me was not that he could break the collar-bone with one blow, but that he was talking about it in the present day. How can it be, I kept thinking, that now, when the war is over, he goes on breaking collar-bones? One night in 1956, Andrei Dimitrievich suddenly disappeared from our block. I only found out later that he had been one of the executioners of the KGB.

These were the sort of people the Brezhnevs had willingly collaborated with. That is why they hated the KGB, where their real face was known.

*

Brezhnev's personality cult seemed to have reached its apogee in 1976. He had already become the personal leader of the country. He hung three stars of the Order of Hero of the Soviet Union on his chest, bestowed the rank of marshal upon himself, made himself Chairman of the Defence Council and collected an incredible number of international decorations. The history of the Second World War was rehashed to please him. The only military operation in which he took part was a naval assault landing at Malaya Zemlya in the Crimea. Now this operation began to be offered up as almost the most decisive one in the victory over Germany. The first edition of Marshal Zhukov's memoirs, in which he described the Malaya Zemlya assault landing as 'a stupid operation which led to the pointless loss of thousands of lives', was withdrawn from circulation and replaced by a second edition in which the piece about Malaya Zemlya was missing.

This caused vague dissatisfaction in the country. But there was a place where the dissatisfaction was openly expressed – the KGB. Does it appear unlikely, the KGB and open dissatisfaction? But that is how it was. During my first weeks in 'S' Directorate I could not believe my ears, and thought that they were testing me with all these 'anti-Soviet' conversations. But no one was thinking about testing me. It was simply that what under Gorbachev is now called perestroika and glasnost had begun in the KGB in the mid-1970s. In 1988, the announcer on Moscow Radio could be heard saying that 'a positive result of perestroika is that we can now discuss any problem and criticize anyone we wish without having to be on our guard. Yet ten years ago we were not just afraid to speak, but to think!' But we were not afraid in the KGB, not because we were at the summit of power (as has been mentioned already, power was almost non-existent), but because we knew far more about all that dirt at the top than anyone else.

There is a Russian proverb which says, 'A fish begins to rot from the head.' It was impossible to imagine anything more rotten than our head, Brezhnev. He could not pronounce his words properly, and it was said that he had cancer of the jaw-bone. This was an invention. The truth was otherwise. Brezhnev was a ladies' man. When he reached the very summit of power, his physical capabilities began to let him down with increasing frequency. His personal doctors were given the order, 'Cure me.' When ordinary treatment did not help, he demanded more radical methods. The doctors warned that hormone treatment could fundamentally undermine his health, but it turned out that Brezhnev cared nothing for that. The main thing was that he could still perform. The hormone treatment gave him several strokes, and it also affected his ability to speak. I learnt these details from doctors of the Fourth Chief Directorate of the Ministry of Health, or as it is better known, the Kremlin hospital, where there is every kind of medicine from all parts of the world, obtained for the benefit of the Soviet elite.

I met one of my school friends in the KGB. He was from the Ninth Chief Directorate and a member of Brezhnev's personal bodyguard. I learnt many details from him about the life of our leader. He had women all over the Soviet Union. No matter where he went, there was always a selection of women lined up in case he wanted them. Perhaps he would keep turning his attention to a woman in the crowd who had come to meet him. She would later be approached by a bodyguard who would invite her very politely to visit the 'highly placed guest'. If she agreed, she and her family would be showered with favours after the encounter. (A fine fellow, Brezhnev.) If the woman refused, which very rarely occurred, nothing would happen to her. She would only be asked to put her signature on a document of non-disclosure. We knew that many well-known Moscow actresses had intimate relations with the Secretary General, after which their careers took off.

The bestowal of a series of Hero of the Soviet Union awards on Brezhnev and those closest to him had a serious practical point to it. A gold star and the Order of Lenin are handed over along with these decorations. They are made of purest gold. A gold star weighs around 25 grams, the Order of Lenin 40 grams. Brezhnev was a Hero of Socialist Labour (25 grams) and a Hero of the Soviet Union four times over. In contrast to marshals' stars and orders decorated with diamonds, which must be returned to the State on the death of the holder, the families are allowed to keep the gold heroes' stars and Orders of Lenin. Thus, on Brezhnev's death, his family inherited 285 grams of gold from these five decorations alone. In addition to this he received many decorations from other countries throughout his career, and these were not made of aluminium either. Quite a lot of gold in nett weight. In addition a considerable sum of money was paid along with every decoration. This is only one of the official ways of accumulating capital, but it was well known that Brezhnev's family was up to its eyes in corruption.

It must not be thought that it was only Brezhnev who did these things. Everyone in his entourage was like him. No honest man could survive there. Here is an example. A marshal's privileges are extended to his children even after his death, and they continue to enjoy them until they themselves die. Marshal Grechko, the former Minister of Defence, adopted his own grandchildren, despite the fact that their parents were still alive, so that they could go on enjoying the privileges of a marshal. Real life in the Soviet Union has countless instances like this.

All these and many other things caused deep dissatisfaction in the ranks of the KGB. We could see that the Party had kept the KGB out of the combat against corruption and placed itself above the law, granting immunity to its members, solely in order to make use of this corruption for its own ends. So whom were we working for and whom were we defending? Crooks! Some young officers began to gain the impression that Stalin's repressions in the 1930s against the Party's 'Lenin Guard' had been justified. Supposing this 'Lenin Guard' had been caught stealing just like the bosses today? It was appalling just to think about it. Where were we going? It seemed that, in the words of the anecdote, 'We were overtaking capitalism as it rushed headlong towards the precipice.'

In this situation, the KGB relapsed into apathy. Weaker characters began to reach for the bottle. Others preferred not to think. They sat out the day at work, and that was fine. Yet others tried to find an explanation for what they were doing, saying that we were not working for these riffraff, but for Russia and her future. But somehow these fine phrases did not quite sound as they used to, nor did they set the mind at rest.

It was particularly hard for those who were working on dissidents. I am not talking about those 'dissidents' whose main objective is to emigrate from the Soviet Union. These did not indulge in anti-Soviet activities. I have in mind the dissidents who were in conflict with the regime and had no intention of going anywhere. Not that there was anywhere to go to. The Jews have Israel, but where can a Russian go? I had to talk on occasion with officers from the Fifth (ideological) Chief Directorate of the KGB. They had been instructed by the Party Central Committee to suppress precisely this type of dissident. If the activities of such a person could be dealt with under the criminal law, then he went to prison. But if what he had done did not fall under the criminal code, he was sent to a psychiatric hospital.

'This man comes in and sits down in front of me and spells out frankly the reasons why he is a dissident, quoting real honest facts from the life we live here. And I know that everything is true, and what's more I know it better than he does and I agree with him. He is in no way a criminal, but an ordinary honest man, whose patience has run out. But I have had orders from above to conclude my report with a recommendation that this dissident should be sent to a psychiatric hospital. How can I possibly live with myself after this?' said my collocutor, pouring himself a full glass of vodka.

Such instances happened fairly often in the KGB. A jingle was circulating in Moscow at the time, which fairly accurately reflected the KGB's position. (The MUR is the Moscow Criminal Detection Department; the OBKhSS is the Organization for the Protection of Socialist Property, and the GAI is the State Automobile Inspectorate, to which the traffic police belong.)

> The MUR step out in front,
> They're always drunk and always frown.
> Next come the OBKhSS,
> They've cash and girls all over town.
> The GAI are next to make their way,
> They always drink, but others pay.
> The KGB come last, their hands are clean.
> They even stop the rest from cashing in.

The reader will peruse this account and consider it unlikely. There may be others who will say, 'This Kuzichkin must have been sent to the West by Andropov to whitewash the KGB.' But I did warn in the preface that the truth can seem much more improbable than fiction.

CHAPTER 5

I went on working in the Second Department of 'S' Directorate. After I had completed my training and had 'mastered' all the subtleties of illegal intelligence, I was earmarked to go to Iran, the country of my future intelligence career. An officer of our section called Sasha Yashchenko was working out his time there. He was in his fourth year in Iran, and had asked to be replaced when his four years were up. I had never met him personally, but I had already learnt a great deal about him. He was constantly mentioned at meetings as an officer who knew what he was doing. In private conversations my colleagues always spoke of him with cordial respect. He seemed to be a friend of one and all. Ismail, the head of our section, spoke of him with great affection. He always read out his personal letters, written in a good style and with a sense of humour. All this made me despondent when I was appointed to replace him. To take over from one of the best officers and maintain his standards is no easy thing to do.

The day came when Ismail handed over all Iranian matters to me. Two cases lay on my desk. It appeared to me at that point 'S' Directorate had *only two* agents in Iran. I could not believe my eyes, but it was a fact, and facts do not go away.

One of these agents was not an Iranian, but an Afghan diplomat. His pseudonym was 'Ram', and he was the head of the consular department of the Afghan Embassy in Tehran. Yashchenko had recruited him in 1974. 'Ram' was used to obtain authentic Afghan documents for our illegals, 'Akbar' and 'Stella'. It was in this that Yashchenko's success lay.

Yashchenko had inherited his second agent, 'Timur', from his predecessor. 'Timur' had no intelligence capability. He had been recruited because his brother worked in an Iranian target of interest to us, and it was planned to reach the brother through 'Timur'. But this did not happen, so 'Timur' simply became ballast. He produced absolutely nothing. Reports consisted of a constant debate on his situation and health. The 'Timur' file was full of receipts for money we had given him. It was a complete waste of time and resources. Before I left for Iran, and at my insistence and with Ismail's full support, the 'Timur' case was closed and contacts with him broken off.

Apart from these, we had a couple more illegals in Iran, 'Konrad' and 'Evi'. They were documented as Europeans, 'Konrad' as a Luxemburger of German nationality, and 'Evi' as a citizen of the FRG. In fact he was a Latvian, and she a GDR German. They were exfiltrated from the Soviet Union through Finland, where they exchanged their travel documents for 'real' ones, and continued on to Denmark, where they were officially married. (This marriage was regarded as operational by Moscow. After their tour of duty had ended, they would no longer be considered man and wife, if they so wished.) They then went round Europe to complete their cover life stories before they proceeded to Pakistan, the country to which they had been appointed. Why Pakistan? Because Pakistan is a close friend of the United States, the main enemy. But they did not succeed in settling in Pakistan, so after visiting India and Afghanistan, they finally settled in Iran. 'Konrad' managed to find work in Pasavant Werke, a West German company. The Centre had no objection. It might be possible to place them somewhere.

Yashchenko was the only representative of 'S' Directorate in Iran, and almost all his time was taken up working with illegals.

I was very surprised by the small number of agents in Iran, and began to compare this with the position in other countries. It soon turned out that the state of affairs in other countries was not much better, and on occasions, worse. For example, the Chinese section did not have a single agent, not just in China itself, but in any other country anywhere else in the world. It was the same in Pakistan, Turkey and Japan. Since coming to the West, I have heard it claimed that the KGB residency in Tokyo had 200 agents. That is just non-science fiction of the purest kind. I remember when Valery

Vdovin was being prepared in our room for his posting to Japan. In his own words, what we had in Japan was a round zero. He combed the archives for agents who had been put on ice, and who might be resurrected. It was clear from conversations with friends from other departments that they were no better placed.

It was at this point that I recalled the sceptical grins on the faces of some of the students during lectures on recruitment at School 101.

The nearer the time of my posting approached, the more I understood the real (as opposed to the textbook-version) philosophy and credo of KGB intelligence officers. Like everything else in the Soviet Union, they were very different from what was written on paper.

The fundamental rule is to survive, and to endure until the end of the posting without being expelled from the country. If an intelligence officer is expelled then his career abroad may be considered at an end. He cannot go to the Main Enemy, NATO countries or their allies, as he would not be given a visa. There remain countries friendly to the Soviet Union, but who would want to work in one of them – say in black Africa? The Centre is understanding towards expulsions, since as a rule it is active intelligence officers who are expelled. Another rule flows from this: don't be specially active.

In order not to be expelled, the following unwritten rules must be observed:

1 Don't touch Americans, British, Germans, or French in their own countries or in countries where their influence is strong.
2 Try to touch local nationals of the country where you are as little as possible, but concentrate your attention on representatives of third countries. Generally speaking, local security services do not pay much attention to contacts between Russians and third countries' nationals.
3 Respect the local security services, and under no circumstances try to recruit their officials, even if they offer their services. In most cases this turns out to involve enemy frame-up operations. Any such operation mounted by these security services usually ends with an expulsion.

4   Do not accept anything that falls into your lap, no matter how tempting it might appear. The more tempting, the more dangerous it is. It is better to lose a good source than to run into a frame-up.

5   Never intentionally become involved with terrorists, like Palestinians, Lebanese and others. That can be dangerous to life and limb.

6   Concentrate your attention on nationals of third countries who are in the easily recruitable category, like Indians, Pakistanis, Arabs, Latin Americans and South-East Asians. After all, any recruitment can be counted as a success, especially in the present-day situation, when KGB agents throughout the world can be counted on the fingers of two hands.

This philosophy was the direct practical expression of that previously mentioned inner apathy. In the West, the Soviet Union's structure and economy are rightly considered to be stagnant, ineffectual and inflexible. So why should the KGB be described in quite opposite terms, although this organization is part of the same Soviet system? How can the KGB be effective, when the whole country is in the grip of stagnation, loss of ideology, and absence of enthusiasm? It is absurd to imagine that, in the whole of this rusted machine, there is a component which has remained free from corrosion and is still working perfectly.

The KGB working day begins at 9 o'clock in the morning. Late arrival is discouraged, although nobody makes any particular record of it. 'S' Directorate late-comers usually take the lift to the fifth floor, pass through the Chief Directorate of Frontier Troops and then go up the staircase at the end of the corridor to the sixth and seventh floor. This stratagem reduces the likelihood of being noticed by the bosses after nine o'clock.

The day begins with an exchange of news taken from our newspapers and from the 'hostile voices', as Russian language broadcasts from Western radio stations are unofficially called in Moscow, and with an exchange of new anecdotes. In the late 1970s, political stories directed against the Party leaders were highly popular. For example, what does the word 'syskemastisk' mean? Answer, it's Brezhnev trying to pronounce the word 'systematic'. According to a secret decree of the Communist Party of the KGB and of the Interior Ministry, people who spread such stories were to suffer criminal prosecution. A prison sentence could well have resulted from the following four-line rhyming stanza, which commented on the exchange of Vladimir Bukovsky, the Soviet dissident, for Luis Corvalan, the leader of the Communist Party of Chile.

> They changed a hooligan
> For Luis Corvalan.
> Who can they swap
> For the man at the top?

The vindictiveness of Party leaders towards such joke-telling was reflected in the story about some Western correspondents asking Brezhnev whether he had any hobbies. 'Of course,' says Brezhnev. 'I collect anecdotes against myself.' 'Have you collected many?' the correspondents ask. 'Yes,' says Brezhnev. 'Two prison camps full.'

After the papers, the news, the anecdotes and a break for a smoke, work gradually begins. The safes are opened, the papers taken out and laid on the desks. Another new story: more distraction. As soon as you do begin to write, somebody from another directorate or department looks in, 'just for a chat'. Everything stops again. At 11 o'clock, everyone is chased out into the corridor for physical training. KGB officers must not put on weight. The exercises go on for fifteen minutes, which leaves only forty-five minutes before the lunch break. What can you do in forty-five minutes? Especially when everybody tries to slip away early, so as to leave some spare time after eating. Some people hurry off to the shops, others play chess, while still others simply smoke and gossip. This state of affairs is typical for the ordinary members of the Directorate. The hard work begins with the section heads. They have to be constantly at the end of a telephone, in case the chiefs should ring. The section head keeps in touch with all the higher levels, and they pester him with all sorts of trivialities.

'Life is a struggle. Before lunch with hunger, after lunch with sleep.' As happens everywhere, after lunch officers feel drowsy, and are no longer up to working. But work goes on, however slowly. Letters to the residencies are written in time to catch the diplomatic bags, and answers to telegrams are given quite quickly. On the whole, the tempo of work in 'S' Directorate is considerably faster than in the First Chief Directorate.

The working day ends at 6 o'clock in the evening. You may leave early with the permission of the section head, but if you want to stay behind to work after six o'clock, the permission of a Directorate deputy head must be obtained.

The officers of 'S' Directorate operate a duty system. Fifteen minutes before the working day ends, the duty officer goes to the reception room of the chief of Directorate and begins to receive the room-keys, which are deposited in small sealed wooden boxes. Each box is sealed with the section head's personal seal. Each officer has his own personal bronze seal. It is circular, about two centimetres in diameter, with an embossed number on its face. These personal seals are used by officers to seal their own safes.

After all the keys have been collected and recorded in a special book, the duty officer goes along the corridors checking the seals on every door. Should he find the seal of any room broken, he can summon the official responsible for the room back to the office from his home, and find out the reason why. The duty officer then mans the telephones. Calls out of office hours are rare, but sometimes a call may come in on a telephone which, instead of a dialling disc, has the coat of arms of the Soviet Union fitted to it. This is the link to the government. The duty officer must take the message and pass it immediately to his chief of Directorate, whose whereabouts are always known.

At ten o'clock in the evening the duty officer hands over to the professional guard and sets off home. He must be back in the Directorate at 7 o'clock next morning to open all the doors, having first checked their seals, open the small hinged casement windows in the rooms in order to ventilate the offices, again close the doors, wait for the working day to begin, and finally hand over his duty to the secretary of the chief of the Directorate.

Deputy heads of Directorates and heads of departments usually come to work about an hour and a half early so as to be able to read their letters and telegrams from all parts of the world without interruption. They do not manage this during the working day, since all their time is programmed down to the last minute for holding meetings and seeing other Directorate officials.

After working in the main KGB building for a time, you gradually come to realize that the organization of internal security is not all that strict. As I have mentioned, there is a round-the-clock guard on the entrances inside the main doors of the building. An armed guard admits the officials, having checked their passes. There is only one permanent guard inside the building, and that is on the fourth floor, at the reception room of the KGB chairman. In addition to this, the corridors are patrolled. The guard passes along each corridor once an hour. A special box fixed to the wall at the end of each corridor contains a book in which the guard has to write his signature and the time when he makes his check. The main purpose of the patrol is fire prevention. Smoking in the building is permitted only in places in the corridors which have been specially set aside for this purpose. Smoking in offices is forbidden.

The KGB does not have concealed laser beams, nor guards with automatic weapons on every corner.

It is forbidden to carry bags and briefcases into the KGB building. They have to be handed in to the guard room opposite the building. Should it be necessary to take a briefcase into the building, then a special insert slip, issued by the secretary of the chief of Directorate, is required to be put inside the officer's pass. The guards do not subject KGB officials to any sudden stop-and-search procedures.

Sometimes curious things can happen involving the guards.

An old peasant woman was once found in a corridor in the main KGB building, looking for the department that sold children's toys. She thought that she was in the Children's World department store, which is next door to the KGB. The guard, thinking that she was a cleaner, had let her in without asking any questions.

On another occasion, a man who had nothing whatever to do with the KGB was found dead drunk and asleep on one of the wide window sills in a corridor. No one knows to this day how he got into the building. None of the guards admitted to having seen the man, nor could the man himself remember when or how he had got in in the first place.

My efforts to see the prison inside the Lubyanka were finally crowned with success. An officer with whom I had become friendly promised to show me the internal prison. He took me to the internal courtyard known as the 'well-shaft', and we crossed it, passed along a narrow corridor under the building, and passed through a doorway into a dining room.

'Are you kidding me?' I asked my friend.

'Not at all,' he answered. 'Allow me to introduce you to the Café Prisoner.' That is now the slang name for the premises of the old KGB internal prison where prisoners were held while under interrogation, which was closed in 1956 and converted into a dining hall. There is now no internal prison in the KGB. Archives occupy the cellars. Several metro tunnels terminate in the building at that level, and these link the KGB with the Kremlin, the Central Committee building, and the general network of the Moscow Underground.

Before he leaves on a lengthy foreign posting, every officer goes through one more period of special personal briefing which lasts six months. All intelligence officers pass through this briefing period, irrespective of whether they are going on their first posting abroad, or as a resident. The departing official draws up a Briefing Plan which is approved by those in authority. In accordance with this plan, the officer has to make a thorough study of all the matters that will arise in the country of destination, and contact other 'S' Directorate departments to establish whether they have any interests there.

I had to have discussions with the heads of most departments, including Krasovsky, the head of the Eighth Department of 'S' Directorate. Among the usual office objects on his desk, there was a cigarette lighter mounted on the casing of a fragmentation hand grenade. This was quite significant, given the function of his department.

'I shall be leaving shortly for Iran on a long posting,' I said. 'Have you any interests there, and can I be of help to you in anything?'

'No, we have no interests there. Neither there nor anywhere

else!' Krasovsky grumbled. 'We move paper from place to place, but that's all the work we do.'

As already mentioned, the Eighth Department ceased carrying out direct actions in 1972. This had clearly irked Krasovsky.

An official who is to be posted abroad must also go through preparatory periods in the relevant geographical section of the First Chief Directorate, in the Directorate of Foreign Counter-Intelligence, and in the Information Service of the First Chief Directorate.

The First Chief Directorate building is located outside Moscow, immediately beyond the ring road near Yasenevo. That is why it is known in KGB jargon as 'the Village'. The building was built by the Finns and was originally intended to house the International Department of the Central Committee of the Soviet Communist Party, but for some reason they took against it, and the Central Committee decided to hand it over to the KGB. It is made of glass, concrete and aluminium and designed in the form of a three-pointed star. Inside there are huge windows stretching almost from floor to ceiling, light parquet flooring, wide corridors, and doors and furniture made of light coloured wood. All this makes quite an agreeable impression.

The entire compound of the First Chief Directorate is surrounded by a high fence. The only way in is through the main entrance. The inscription 'Bureau of Information' appears on the wall, which is a fairly exact reflection of the work of this organization, since information is the basic product of intelligence.

The special pass needed to gain entry is a rectangular card made of plastic, with a photograph inside it showing the official in civilian clothing and bearing his personal military number. That is all. Should this pass be lost, then no one, apart from people in the know, will realize to whom it belongs. First Chief Directorate officials also have a KGB card, but they do not present it on entry and scarcely ever use it. Each 'S' Directorate officer has a pass to admit him to the First Chief Directorate, and he may go there at any time. But not every First Chief Directorate officer may go into the main building of the KGB. In order to do this, his card must bear a small special stamp giving him the right to visit the Lubyanka. This stamp is only given to senior officers. Junior officers must obtain a one-time pass.

The First Chief Directorate building is surrounded by woods and constant fresh air, not at all as in the centre of Moscow. It contains splendid sports facilities, a swimming pool, and various gymnasia. On the orders of the Chairman, every officer must practise sports for one hour's working time thrice weekly. They have a free choice. They may do karate, swim, run, or simply go walking in the woods gathering mushrooms.

There is only one snag throughout this organization, and that is how to get there. Not everyone has his own private car, and so 'those without horses' have to use special buses. There are pick-up points for First Chief Directorate officials all over Moscow, usually near the main Underground stations, with buses leaving at fixed times. If anyone misses the bus, he has a problem. He has to take a taxi, but taxis may not approach the building of the First Chief Directorate. The road to it is blocked by an 'Entry Forbidden' sign, at which the latecomer must get out of his taxi and then walk for about two kilometres.

It was precisely because of the inconvenience over transport that 'S' Directorate remained in the centre of Moscow. All the places needed for its work, such as safe flats for training illegals, and for language courses, are in the centre of the city. They lie within easy reach of the main KGB building, while it would take several hours from 'the Village'.

In 1976, the head of the First Chief Directorate was General Vladimir Kryuchkov. As happens in many other cases in the Soviet system, General Kryuchkov, the head of the KGB intelligence service, was not a professional intelligence officer, but simply a Party bureaucrat. He was an Andropov man. He had worked with Andropov first in the Komsomol, then in the Party. Andropov was appointed KGB Chairman in 1967. He made Kryuchkov one of his deputies. Kryuchkov was appointed head of the First Chief Directorate some time in 1974. From an intelligence point of view, he was a mere figurehead, and all the professional work was done by his deputies. It was said that he particularly did not aspire to a James Bond role, and relied upon advice. His main asset was his closeness to Andropov: he could resolve the First Chief Directorate's problems over the heads of the bureaucracy. Discipline in the Directorate was not specially severe in Kryuchkov's time, although he banned the sale of beer in the canteens, following the occasion when he summoned one of his senior officers of the Directorate and found him drunk. Many officials considered him a snob, because for example he did not use the standard service black car to which his position entitled him, but drove around in a white Mercedes 230, the only one of its kind in Moscow at the time, complete with chauffeur and television set.

My briefing in the First Chief Directorate began in the Eighth Department which dealt with work in Iran, Afghanistan, Turkey and West Berlin. Its work embraced West Berlin because there were many Turks, Afghans and Iranians living there, and it was much easier to work with them there than in their own countries.

General Polonik was head of the Eighth Department. He had specialized in the United States and Canada throughout his career, and during his last posting abroad had been the resident in the United States. When he returned from there to the KGB headquarters, all the posts that carried the rank of general in his First Department had already been taken. He could not be demoted, as this is not done, so he was appointed head of the Eighth Department. Polonik did not have the foggiest understanding of the Middle East or the ways of working there, nor did he make any special effort to learn about them, so all the work fell on to the shoulders of his deputy, Kostromin, who was an orientalist by education and who had spent his entire career in the area.

The head of the Iranian desk was Colonel Anatoli Mikhailovich Lezhnin, approaching fifty, balding, and with a dull-witted expression. I had seen him twice before. The first time was in the Tehran bookshop in 1974, when my interpreter friend pointed him out to me, saying meaningfully that he was the 'special consul', thereby hinting that he belonged to the KGB. On the second occasion he was a member of the commission during the final examinations at School 101. He did not remember me, nor would there have been any point in my reminding him.

Lezhnin led me into the section, after telling me that the acquisition of political information must be part of the duties of every intelligence officer, no matter what his specialization. They had warned me in 'S' Directorate that such things would be said to me during my briefing in the First Chief Directorate. I should not argue with them by pointing out that I had my own responsibilities. Listen and agree, I was told, and make a good impression, and so I did. Only once did I have a clash. When my briefing on the political problems of Iran was almost over, Lezhnin asked me what I thought about the position of the monarch. I answered that I had formed the impression while I was in Iran that the heir to the Iranian throne would never become Shah, and that this impression had now strengthened. This simply caused Lezhnin to explode, and his eyes flashed in anger.

'So, you have understood nothing! I am not going to sign off your briefing form. The strongest economy in the Middle East, the strongest army, the all-powerful SAVAK secret police, and the full support of the Americans, yet after all this you say that the regime is not stable? Complete political illiteracy,' he concluded.

It was manifestly useless to argue with him. Apology had to be made for the 'political illiteracy' which had so upset Lezhnin. Looking ahead for a moment, let me say that later on, when I was on leave and Iran was on the brink of revolution, I jokingly reminded Lezhnin of our conversation. He looked me straight in the eye and said that he could not remember any such conversation.

My briefing in the Eighth Department of the First Chief Directorate gave me a complete overview of the situation in Iran as seen by our political intelligence. I read through tomes of political information according to subject. The Shah's court had the code-name 'Casket', SAVAK had 'Barracks', and so on. The sheer volume of the material caused the impression that political intelligence in Iran had a multitude of agents; the true state of affairs became clear only later when I was working in the Residency in Tehran.

After finishing my briefing in the Eighth Department, I went over to be briefed by the Iranian line in the Directorate of Foreign Counter-Intelligence of the First Chief Directorate. It must be noted that there is a distinction between officers belonging to foreign counter-intelligence ('CI') and those in political intelligence ('PI'). Most PI officers are given special country training in customs and institutions, and they speak the language of the country or area of their posting. As a general rule, they spend their entire career in the areas in which they are specialized. For example, the career of an official in the Eighth Department will be mainly in Iran, Afghanistan and Turkey. Most PI officials are graduates of universities or advanced language institutes.

In most cases CI officials come to the First Chief Directorate either from the internal directorates or the provincial KGBs, already having had experience of counter-intelligence work in the internal organs. As a rule they speak only one Western language, and they will be moved anywhere in the world in the course of their careers. The main CI task is to penetrate the special services of the enemy. In Iran this meant SAVAK, military counter-intelligence, the police, CIA stations abroad, and stations of other capitalist countries. In the CI Directorate I acquainted myself in detail with a mass of information on SAVAK and the other Iranian special services. Again the impression was created that CI had agents in almost every department of SAVAK. For instance, information on SAVAK's surveillance work was so detailed that it seemed that it was not they who were following us, but we them.

The next stage of the briefing was with Service No. 1, at the Information Service of the First Chief Directorate. This service processes political intelligence from all over the world and prepares it to be forwarded to the International Department of the Party's Central Committee and to other departments. The KGB does not gather intelligence for its own consumption. The intelligence it receives must be acted upon, otherwise it is useless.

In spite of all the apparent advantages, the impression made upon me by the atmosphere of the First Chief Directorate was not a positive one. This was not only the result of mixing with the officials in the Eighth Department. I met up with most of my fellow course members from School 101, who were now working in almost every department of the Directorate. Most of them noticed the same thing. The atmosphere reeked of careerism, arrogance, self-importance and hypocrisy. The agents of residencies abroad could be counted on the fingers of one hand. The information was fabricated. It was not intelligence, but sheer journalism.

At the same time a belief prevailed that the agent situation in 'S' Directorate was considerably better than in the First Chief Directorate. It was considered that 'S' Directorate was more workmanlike and friendly. When people have much work to do, they have no time for squabbling. But on the subject of the agent situation, my friends were mistaken. Nevertheless, in our conversations on the subject I preferred to keep silent, thereby sustaining the reputation of my office.

As my predecessor in Tehran held a diplomatic post, I would be assuming the same position, which was that of attaché in the consular department of the embassy. It was necessary for this purpose to do an attachment with the 'cover establishment', in this case the Consular Directorate of the Soviet Ministry of Foreign Affairs.

The Soviet Foreign Ministry is located in Smolensk Square, in one of Moscow's high-rise buildings, those monstrous monuments to Stalinist classicism put up in the Fifties to show that 'we are not inferior to the Americans and we too have skycrapers.' The Moscow State University was put into one building, the Ministry of Foreign Affairs and the Ministry of Foreign Trade into another, while the rest were given over to housing for the nomenklatura, Party officials, scientists, artists and rogues of all kinds who had connections to the highest levels of the Party. So here, when the greater part of the Moscow population was mouldering in barracks and ramshackle wooden houses without the most elementary facilities, our superior personages were occupying incredibly spacious flats, finished in marble, redwood and oak. At the same time they were holding forth about the equality in our country and the poverty in the West.

The Consular Directorate of the Foreign Ministry is situated in a separate house away from the high-rise building. My attachment there presented no problems, since two-thirds of the people working there were 'under-cover'. An 'under-cover' officer is someone from the KGB or GRU who works permanently 'under the cover' of the Foreign Ministry, TASS, the Novosti News Agency, the Committee on Science and Technology, and various newspapers. Only *Pravda*, the newspaper of the Party Central Committee, is not used as a cover organization by the intelligence services. This has been forbidden by the Central Committee.

There is quite a considerable difference between the under-cover officers of the KGB and the GRU. The KGB in the main sends officers whom it does not need to work under cover. Let us say that an officer has returned from a tour abroad without having achieved any results, and without having revealed any special aptitudes. All the ordinary posts at his level in his department are already occupied. None of the other departments wants to take him. It is here that the cover organization comes to the rescue. Those First Chief Directorate officers who leave to work 'under cover' do not do any work for the KGB. They only go to Party meetings once a month and come to the Directorate for the difference in pay, which is higher in the KGB than in other organizations. In 'S' Directorate the under-cover officers are not released from doing intelligence work. They work half and half, and are useless in both capacities.

In the GRU it is another matter. The GRU sends its best officers 'under cover', apparently considering that this practice best protects their objectives. Actually this is a complete illusion, since in all these organizations everybody knows who is who.

There were two under-cover officers in my section who were working in the Consulate Directorate of the Foreign Ministry. They were Colonel Viktor Ganykin and Lieutenant-Colonel Nikolai Snetkov. Personally, they were excellent fellows, with a sense of humour, kind and helpful. But when it came to work . . . Some time earlier, their careers had ground to a halt, and they had ceased to be concerned about them, following the typical philosophy of Soviet civil servants – the pay's the same, but the responsibility is less. And we'll still be colonels. It was these two who were entrusted with introducing me to my future job.

According to standing orders, a KGB official who is to go abroad as a diplomat must spend no less than three months in the Foreign Ministry. This rule is largely observed, but it was decided in my case that a two-week attachment would be quite sufficient. Ganykin and Snetkov took me into the Foreign Ministry Consular Directorate, introduced me to Aganin, the head of the Middle East Department, and said that they would take charge of my briefing. Aganin did not object.

As they conducted me along the corridors of the Directorate, my colleagues would indicate people we came across and say, 'He's one of us, that one's GRU, he's ours . . .'

'And are there any straight Foreign Ministry people here?' I asked.

'Yes, there are of course,' was the answer. 'But they just sit in their offices and write papers. Someone has to write all that drivel. The 'straight' Foreign Ministry people have all the top jobs. The Foreign Ministry doesn't give them either to us or the GRU.'

I sat in a room for two days with some 'straight' officials, reading instructions on consular matters. I then spent three days in the visa section, where I was shown how to draw up Soviet visas. While this was going on, my diplomatic passport was got ready – a dark green booklet with a photograph and a stamped coat of arms, and showing my name and professional description. My passport had been signed by an officer from my department in the KGB, who had worked in an under-cover capacity in the Passport Department of the Foreign Ministry's Consular Directorate. At the end of the week, on the Friday, my attachment came to an end.

Finally, my briefing was over. I returned to 'S' Directorate and drew up the Work Plan for the period of my posting. Since we had closed the 'Timur' agent case, only one agent was handed over to me to run. This was 'Ram', the Afghan consul in Tehran. Otherwise, a start would have to be made from scratch. The main targets of interest to my Department in Iran were the population records office and the foreign passport department. Work had to continue on the Consular Corps in Tehran, on clarifying all changes which were made in the documentation needed in Iran, and on monitoring changes in the procedures followed in all of the country's frontier check-points. With illegals in mind, the position of any foreigners in Iran had also to be monitored.

The tasks I had to do for the Seventh Geographical Department of 'S' Directorate were not very extensive, since the number of operational officers working on the N line (that was the name for illegal intelligence in residencies abroad) had been increased in Tehran, and an official of the Seventh Department had been sent there. He was Sergei Pavlovich Kharlashkin, aged about sixty, a colonel, of slight build, with greying hair and a frightened expression in his eyes. He gave the impression of a man who was weighed down by life. Kharlashkin had spent his entire previous career in counter-intelligence. He had done one tour of duty abroad, in the Netherlands, and had learnt only the language of that country. He could not even speak English, to say nothing of Farsi. His chief duty was to do work aimed at maintaining communications with illegals. He had arrived recently in the Seventh Department as a protégé of Petr Shein, the head of that department.

Kharlashkin had been assigned to work under cover in the Soviet hospital in Tehran as deputy director for administration. Everybody knew that his bosses had sent him there so that he could keep them supplied with scarce and expensive Western medicines. Everybody knew too that all the work would be laid on my shoulders. Kharlashkin could not be relied upon, and this was hinted to me, both directly and indirectly, by highly placed superiors.

Before leaving, I had to go back to the Party Central Committee for a discussion. It turned out that even officials of the KGB are allowed to go abroad only with the permission of the Central Committee. This rule is extended to illegals as well. It was Aleksandr Vasilevich Polyakov who spoke with me in the Central Committee on this occasion. Before going to the Central Committee he had been a diplomat and had specialized in Iran. I was to meet up with Aleksandr Vasilevich in the future.

'Your departure for Tehran is planned for the eleventh of June,' said Ismail Aliev, the head of my section. 'What you must do now is to get tickets for the Moscow–Tehran train.'

'What do you mean "I must get"?' I asked in astonishment. 'Does the KGB intelligence service really not have a supply of tickets for its departing officers?'

'Yes it has, but only for the senior heads,' Ismail replied quite irritably. 'I too have to make my own personal arrangements when I go on an official trip. Now you find a way.'

I was astonished by this turn of events, which was against all logic. Did it mean that, if I personally did not obtain tickets for myself, my departure on an official mission would be held up? It was hard to believe, but true.

Here a brief explanation about tickets is called for. At that time, there were nearly 8,000 Soviet experts working in Iran on the building of various economic constructions. The movement between the two countries was both continuous and quite intensive. So the organizations concerned booked train and airline tickets roughly a year in advance. That was why there were never any tickets freely available on sale. A paradox had come about. For metal workers and excavator operators, there were always tickets. But for intelligence officers and diplomats, there were none. Such a situation delighted the booking clerks, since they could extract bribes from people like me. As I was going on a posting under diplomatic cover, the application for my ticket had been issued to me by the Foreign Ministry. (Air line and rail tickets for trips abroad are not sold freely in the Soviet Union. The traveller must have an official ticket application issued by the organization that is sending him.) I took my Foreign Ministry application form to the international counters, which are located in the Metropole Hotel not far from the KGB. There I was told that the train was booked solid for six months ahead. I tried to explain to the girl at the counter that I was from the Foreign Ministry and that I was going on an official mission.

'I don't care even if you're from the KGB,' the young thing shrugged, evidently used to situations of this kind. 'There are no tickets, and that's all there is to it.'

I reported to Ismail that there were no tickets for the appointed day, and that there would be quite a long wait to get one.

'Find a way,' he said again. 'You're an intelligence officer.'

'I don't have any contacts like that,' I answered, losing patience. 'I didn't become an intelligence officer to waste my skills on scraping acquaintance in ticket offices and giving bribes. No tickets means no tickets.'

In fact, until that time the course of my life had never involved me in corruption. Being a straightforward and honest man, I did not take to all this swindling – it was one of my reasons for agreeing to work in the KGB. Now however it turned out that the KGB was not only not immune from corruption, but even depended upon it in its official dealings. I could not swallow this.

The situation was saved by Kolya Snetkov, who had connections everywhere. He arranged a rail ticket for the appointed day, and told me that in order to do this, he had had to buy a box of chocolates for a girl acquaintance in the ticket office. This was a hint that I was in his debt.

Shortly before my departure, I was sent for by Gumenyuk, deputy head of the Cadres Directorate of the KGB. Nobody would tell me why, and that worried me a little, but my fears proved groundless. Gumenyuk had a son working as a cipher clerk in the KGB residency in Tehran, and wanted me to take him a box of foodstuffs. Gumenyuk turned out to be jolly and affable. He said that he only wanted to obtain my consent, as he would deliver the box direct to the train.

The day before my departure, and in spite of the official ban, I arranged a farewell party in the Berlin restaurant for the officers in my department. Everything passed off smoothly, there were plenty of jokes and final farewells. Everyone realized that it would be hard for me to make a start in the shadow of my predecessor's successes. When the evening ended, it was decided that Volodya Nalitov would help me to load my things and would come to the station to see me off.

At home on 11 June, there was bustle and farewell parties as friends and relatives came to say goodbye. The train was to leave the Kursk Station at 9 o'clock in the evening, and we decided to go there early, so as to avoid any unexpected delays. There were quite a lot of things, four trunks and several whisky cartons used for packing. Once at the station, we quietly unloaded on the platform indicated and began our wait for the train. There was still an hour and a half until departure time. To my surprise, Ismail and his wife appeared. He said that they had decided to come and say 'au revoir' once again, and perhaps to help with something. Soon Gumenyuk and his wife turned up. They had brought a parcel for their son. Platform 4 was gradually filling up with people who were going to Iran, most of them Soviet experts bringing enormous plywood trunks. While we were waiting, several people approached me to ask if I would take parcels for their children who were working in the embassy. I took them.

Everything was going normally, but the train had still not arrived at the platform. Then, with only fifteen minutes left before departure time, it was suddenly announced over the loudspeaker that our train would be leaving from platform 8, instead of platform 4. Panic broke out. Everybody grabbed their things and ran. To reach platform 8, you had to go down a flight of stairs and then along a tunnel. I realized at this point how very lucky it was that I was being seen off by several people. All of us, women included, grabbed the first thing that came to hand and scrambled for the other platform. The deputy head of the KGB Cadres Directorate got the heaviest trunk, but he stuck it like a hero. Perspiring, we reached platform 8, where another surprise was awaiting us. The two international carriages bound for Tehran were at the front of the train, beyond the end of the platform, which was too short. That meant that we had to load up from ground level, which was about a metre and a half below the door. Five minutes remained before the train left. A fearful situation resulted. There was only one door open at one end of the carriage, with a bottleneck at the entrance because the way was blocked by the enormous trunks of the visiting experts and technicians. The train conductors were nowhere to be seen. People were squeezing into the carriage through the windows, and trying to drag their trunks behind them. It all appeared unreal, and reminiscent of some film on the Russian Civil War, which showed the last ship leaving the Crimea with the remains of the smashed White Army aboard.

Nalitov and I succeeded in fighting our way on to the carriage, and dragged a couple of trunks into the compartment. Volodya stayed to stack the things while I rushed for the rest. Suddenly the train started to move. Shouts and women's screams rang out. The crowd went mad. Somebody pulled the emergency lever, and the train stopped, then started, and was halted again by a second pull at the lever. There was no way of getting back into the carriage. The narrow entrance was occupied by a hulk of a man who was allowing only his own trunks on board. As to the others, women included, he was simply booting them away. I too got a kick in the chest, and I fell off the footboard on to the track. I was all set to go over to the attack when the hulk, with his hands clasped in front of him in the pose of a champion diver, came flying through the carriage doorway and thudded to the ground. In the doorway stood Nalitov, who had propelled the lout off the train with a kick on his backside.

'This man is the consul from our embassy in Tehran!' he shouted at the crowd, pointing at me. 'And if you don't put a stop to this shambles right now, not one of you will get across the frontier!'

I had of course no powers to do anything of the kind, but at that instant it worked, hot heads cooled, and we managed to complete the boarding in comparative calm. I had a separate compartment, very small and crammed solid with my stuff immediately after departure, and once again I had to rearrange everything. After that, I collapsed on the bed and fell asleep.

PART TWO

Comrade Saidov

CHAPTER 6

The journey from Moscow to Tehran takes four days. The train headed south-eastwards towards the Caucasus, and there was nothing to do but to lie back and recover the energy burnt up in the effort to board the train. But rest was a relative thing. It was a very hot summer in 1977, and the further south we moved, the hotter the weather became. The international carriages had air-conditioning, but as usual it was out of order. The atmosphere became incredibly stuffy.

The restaurant car was in the middle of the train. It was so dirty, and the food so unwholesome, that after trying it once, I preferred to live on what I had brought from home. What is more, service in the Soviet Union is hardly obtrusive – 'Take it or leave it!' The Azerbaijani stewards cheat the passengers in the most incredible way.

Finally we reached Dzhul'fa, the frontier station where the train crosses the Soviet–Iranian border. The Dzhul'fa customs people appeared, black-haired, dark-eyed Azerbaijanis wearing the dark-grey uniforms of the customs service. One of them passed through the carriage and spread out several huge sacks on the floor.

The first thing that the most senior of the customs officers asked was whether there were any passengers in the carriage with diplomatic passports. It turned out that I was the only one. Under Soviet customs regulations, even the personal luggage of a diplomat is exempt from examination. The customs man gave me the key to my compartment and said that I could go and sit out the proceedings in the station restaurant. This I did, as I had no desire to watch the customs experts in action.

About an hour after the inspection began, I decided to go back to my compartment for cigarettes, and I then saw what was going on. The customs men were confiscating food supplies from the experts – tinned meat and fish of different kinds, dried sausage, caviare, vodka and cognac. They filled their enormous sacks with all these things and emerged another hour later, dragging sacks now full of booty on their backs. Soon the international carriages set off for the frontier.

I conversed with the Soviet specialists as we travelled, and they described what had happened during the customs search. Along with what I had already been told about the Dzhul'fa customs in Tehran, the following picture emerged.

Soviet customs regulations lay down the quotas of foodstuffs and alcoholic drinks which may be exported from the country. It is thus permitted to export one litre of vodka or cognac, and fixed quantities of tinned meat and fish, sausage, and so forth. Soviet experts know these rules, but deliberately break them. As I explained earlier, they take provisions with them so as to avoid spending money, because the Soviet government pays them a beggarly salary abroad. The customs seize the excess provisions, but not all of them. They allow their victims to take a little more than the quota away with them, and in return for such kindness the victims do not ask for receipts for the confiscated provisions. The customs officials then simply split up the take among themselves.

The tastes of the customs officials have become increasingly more refined with the years. They will not for instance touch tinned pork. The Dzhul'fa customs were particularly punctilious before important holidays, when they stocked up with goods for entertaining their guests. All these facts were known in Tehran, Moscow and Baku, and the head of the customs branch there was changed on a couple of occasions, but the situation persisted. It was natural that the specialists tried to outwit these jackals. In particular they excelled in taking vodka which had been soldered into tinned food containers, or poured into rubber hot water bottles, or maybe made up to look like preserves, with brine replaced by vodka in a jar of pickled cucumbers.

It is worth noting that, during all these years when experts had been passing through Dzhul'fa, not one of them was ever taken off the train and then prosecuted for carrying contraband. The customs did not want to lose this source of income. Likewise, no expert ever submitted an official complaint against the customs. One hand washes another.

We approached the frontier where control was exercised by Soviet frontier guards, young conscripts doing their military service. They worked unhurriedly and in silence. Some checked passports, while others examined the carriage to see if they could find anyone hiding there who wanted to leave the country illegally. The examination over, we were let through into the neutral zone, where the train ran along between rows of barbed wire which went on for kilometres. In the Soviet vocabulary, this is exactly what is meant by a 'locked frontier'.

The train came to a halt on Iranian territory. Soldiers of the Iranian gendarmerie, who guard the Iranian border, boarded the train and took away our passports. The train then proceeded a little further to the Iranian Dzhul'fa station, where Iranian customs representatives now began their inspection. One of them came into my compartment and told me to open my trunks. I explained that I was a diplomat and that my luggage was not liable to customs examination. The customs official asked for my passport; but it was still being held by the frontier guards. The official grinned slyly, and then asked me, this time more insistently, to open my trunks. I flatly refused. He went off somewhere, came back with a soldier, and repeated his order, this time in a more commanding tone.

Things were taking a bad turn. Of course there was nothing prohibited in my luggage, but the principle of diplomatic immunity was important. I told the customs official that he could open my trunk himself, but if he did so it would no longer be a customs inspection, but a search. The Iranian understood this, yet he continued to insist, and threatened not to allow me across the frontier. I stopped arguing and sat down, saying nothing. At that moment another Iranian appeared. He called the customs official out of the compartment, and a minute later returned my diplomatic passport to me. The second Iranian told me that the incident had been a mistake, and apologized. My customs official left the carriage, unhappily muttering something to himself under his breath.

The customs inspection over, our carriage was hoisted into the air by a special crane then lowered on to a different set of wheels. In Iran, the gauge of the railway track is narrower than in the Soviet Union.

The train drew in to the platform. Although the customs inspection was over, the Iranians would not allow us out of the carriage. People, Soviet experts apparently, were walking up and down outside. One of them, a short fair-haired man wearing grey trousers that were too short for him, had a particularly self-assured bearing. Smiling broadly, he was talking with the Iranians and patting them on the shoulder. He obviously spoke Farsi. Then in spite of the ban imposed by the Iranians, he boarded the carriage and went into the compartment alongside mine, where, as it turned out, his wife and two children had been travelling. I was standing in the corridor when this same short man emerged from the neighbouring compartment and stopped beside me.

'Are you going to Tehran?' he asked me, with a sly smile. I answered that I was.

'And to which organization, may I ask?'

'You may,' I replied coldly. 'To the embassy.'

'Ah yes,' he went on. 'And may I ask whom you are replacing?' His smile had become even more cunning.

This character had begun to irritate me, and I had a strong desire to tell him where to go, but a sixth sense warned me that he might just be from the Residency.

'Yashchenko,' I answered after a brief pause.

'Ah, we've been expecting you for some time! Yura Perepelkin,' he introduced himself. 'We're from the same office. Come into my compartment right away. My wife has brought some cognac. We must celebrate your arrival!'

It was only eight o'clock in the morning, and I told Perepelkin that it was rather too early for drinks.

'This will be your first lesson on work abroad,' Yura stated meaningfully. 'An intelligence officer must know how to drink at any time, anywhere, and with anybody.'

I went into his compartment, but I did not take a drink. Perepelkin's wife naturally told him about my encounter with the customs official. Pointing at a group of Iranians standing on the platform, he asked which one it was who had tried to examine my luggage. I pointed out my opponent.

'Ah, Mr ... [I can no longer remember the surname.] He's no customs official. He's known to us as a member of the local SAVAK office. He's not a bad chap on the whole, when you get to know him, but he is quite open in his hatred of us.'

It then became clear who had organized the incident over the customs inspection.

It is a thirty-six-hour train journey from Dzhul'fa on the Iranian side to Tehran. Thus, having left Moscow on Saturday evening, we arrived in Tehran after midday on Wednesday. Sasha Yashchenko, whom I was to replace, met me at the station. He was a tall young man of thirty, with black hair and a friendly expression in his eyes. He had engaged two porters earlier, so there were no problems over unloading the luggage. I was immediately and agreeably struck by the way he spoke Farsi with the Iranians, fluently and without any accent. We loaded our things on to two light vans in the station square, and drove off.

The traffic in Tehran was just as chaotic as before. Iranians do not recognize any traffic rules, and it seemed that everyone wanted to shoot ahead. Yashchenko drove his white Peugeot 504 fast and skilfully as he manoeuvred through the chaos. Finally, the car drove up to the Soviet Embassy in Tehran, which I already knew, situated on Churchill Street right in the heart of the city. The white automatic grilled metal gates opened and we drove on to Soviet territory. Gate duty is performed round the clock by officers of the KGB frontier service in civilian clothes. The car turned right and drove along a shady avenue under the arches of tall trees towards the building that housed the embassy living quarters. This was a five-storey block, built to a Soviet design. All the doors of the flats opened on to balconied galleries on one side of the building. I was accommodated on the fourth floor, in an unprepossessing one-roomed flat with a very small kitchen, a lavatory and a bathroom. All the walls were coloured grey. The rickety old furniture had been brought from the Soviet Union about fifteen years before, and must have been ancient then. After stowing my things and taking a shower, I set off for the embassy's summer residence, situated at Zargande to the north of Tehran, some 14 kilometres from the city centre.

Tehran is built on the slope of a hill, and its northern quarter is some 400 metres higher than the city centre. That is why the climate is considerably cooler in summer in Zargande than in the centre. Most well-to-do Iranians prefer to live in the north of Tehran, leaving the south to the poor. Diplomats follow the same rule. The residences of most embassies are situated in the northern part of the capital.

The Soviet residence occupies a quite extensive area, which is surrounded by a high brick wall. Inside are single-storey detached bungalows with one, two and three rooms, and standing apart from them the ambassador's residence. These bungalows are shared out among the diplomats, the senior of whom are given the larger ones, the junior, the smaller.

Yashchenko had a one-roomed bungalow, since his rank was that of attaché. It had already begun to grow dark when we arrived in Zargande, and Sasha's wife had prepared a good supper. After it was over, Sasha asked for news of the Centre, and went on to say that his departure had been fixed for next Wednesday, in one week's time. He wanted to start handing over to me the following morning, and we agreed to meet at 8 a.m. in the embassy guard office. Sasha also explained that the flat in the embassy had only been given to me temporarily, and that after he had left I would live permanently in Zargande.

At night it was very stuffy in the flat in the embassy block. Having been baked by the sun all day, the walls gave out heat, and there was no coolness anywhere. The room had an air-conditioner built into the frame of a window which occupied the whole of one wall, but it rattled so loudly that it was like sleeping next to a tractor at work. The first night in Tehran did not bring the rest I had looked forward to after the journey.

I arrived at the embassy guard-room at 8 o'clock next morning but found nobody there. I waited a little, and then asked the embassy guard whether he had seen Yashchenko. He replied without a trace of embarrassment that Sasha had gone for a beer with a friend to a café across the road, and that he would soon be back. It was evident from the way he spoke that such things were the usual practice here and surprised nobody.

While I was waiting for Yashchenko and watching people coming and going, I recalled how those who had previously worked in this embassy had described the Soviet community in Tehran. The social atmosphere in the embassy has always been extremely bad. This is because both the Foreign Ministry and the KGB arrange their work on the geographical principle, which requires officials to specialize in their own particular regions. There are only two countries, Iran and Afghanistan, in the Farsi-speaking region, so most officials spend their entire careers from beginning to end in these countries. This brings about a situation in which everybody knows everybody else, and everyone knows everything about each other. The outcome is friction from gossip, intrigue and cliques. I had no idea while I was in Moscow how serious all this actually was in reality.

Yashchenko soon turned up, and we went into the embassy. The entrance door is kept constantly closed, and is guarded from inside by an orderly. Sasha pressed the button of the bell, the automatic lock buzzed, and we found ourselves in the lobby of the reception hall. A woman orderly sat at a table to the left of the door. She was the wife of Rassadin, the embassy security officer. She at once broke into a broad smile and welcomed me. On the wall inside the hall there were two plaques commemorating the meeting that took place in Tehran during the Second World War between the heads of the three Allied powers, Stalin, Churchill and Roosevelt. This meeting was held in the great reception hall of this same building.

We passed down a long airy corridor that linked the representative part of the embassy with the six-storey administration block. On the first floor were the living quarters of the minister counsellor in charge of the secret registry, and of two cipher clerks. The second floor contained the embassy internal security room used by the duty guard, two other rooms used by the representatives of the Party Central Committee, the embassy security officer's room and a room for secretaries and typists. The ambassador's reception room and office were on the third floor. The remaining rooms were occupied by Foreign Ministry people. The fourth floor held the KGB Residency, with the secret registry on the fifth floor. The Residency of the GRU was on the sixth floor.

We went up to the fourth floor and into the office of the KGB resident, Colonel Lev Petrovich Kostromin. He had arrived in Tehran about a month before I did, in order to take temporary charge of the

Residency. In the Centre he had held the post of deputy head of the Eighth Department of the First Chief Directorate, and I had had a lengthy talk with him there during my briefing. On this occasion, therefore, we simply exchanged pleasantries, and he told Sasha to introduce me himself to the ambassador, as he did not have the time. In fact, however, as I was to learn later, Kostromin did not like the ambassador and preferred to steer clear of him.

There were several people in the ambassador's waiting room. The ambassador's private secretary sat at the table. He was Maxim Peshkov, an attaché, and grandson of the famous writer Maxim Gorky. Everyone greeted us affably and winked knowingly at Sasha. I had the feeling that they all knew that I was a KGB officer. As it turned out later, I was right. Because of the geographic principle adopted by both the Foreign Ministry and the KGB, everybody in the Embassy knew who was who, and it would have been simply stupid of me, for example, to pretend to be a straight diplomat.

The ambassador in Iran at that time was Vladimir Mikhailovich Vinogradov, that same Vinogradov who had returned home in disgrace from Egypt after Sadat expelled the Soviet advisers in 1972. He had then spent four years as a deputy foreign minister without portfolio, and now here he was, appointed ambassador again. It is certain that he enjoyed strong backing inside the Party Central Committee. Vinogradov arrived in Iran in February 1977, and at the time I got there he was still learning the ropes, so he did not ask me many questions and made a fairly quiet impression. But those who knew him said that the impression was deceptive. Vinogradov always hated the KGB, especially after Egypt, when it was the resident, Kirpichenko, and not Vinogradov, who had proved to be right in his assessment of events. For the time being he was keeping his head down.

'So what's wrong in Vinogradov hating the KGB?' the reader may ask. Let me advise a little patience, and no drawing of hasty conclusions.

Yashchenko began his hand-over to me by explaining the structure of the embassy.

An embassy of the Soviet Union is headed by an ambassador, who is always a straight diplomat, in most cases a member of the Party Central Committee, and whose salary is the highest in a Soviet community abroad – no one can be paid more. The ambassador is the supreme representative of the Soviet government, and everything in the country of his appointment, including the KGB, is subordinated to him. The myth that the KGB is above the ambassador is no more than the product of over-active imaginations.

After the ambassador comes the minister counsellor. He is second to the ambassador in rank, but not in importance. The minister counsellor is almost always the representative of the Foreign Ministry, and one of his duties is to stand in for the ambassador when he is absent. In Tehran this post was held by Fedor Saulchenkov. Both the local authorities and the Americans thought that he was the KGB resident, and he is named as such in John Barron's book, *KGB: The Secret Work of Soviet Secret Agents* (1974). But in fact Saulchenkov had never been a KGB officer. He was just an ordinary diplomat.

The official structure of the embassy looks like this:

the political section;
the economic section;
the administration section;
the consular department;
the military attachés' office.

The Trade Delegation is separate, and mainly in developing countries there is the Delegation of the State Committee on Economic Relations.

As the Soviet system is centralized in everything, the structure of all Soviet embassies is the same, with small variations, all over the world. But the real structure of an embassy is radically different from the official one. It is like this:

straight diplomats from the Foreign Ministry;
representatives of the Party Central Committee;
representatives of the Central Committee of Trade Unions;
the KGB;
the GRU.

Like diplomats of all countries, straight Soviet diplomats are supposed to maintain contacts with various organizations in the country of their appointment, hold negotiations, start up personal relationships and obtain political information. In practice only part of this is done. Straight diplomats maintain contacts with foreigners only on an official level. Personal diplomatic contacts hardly exist. Even today, it is very rarely that a straight diplomat will be seen having a meeting with his contact in a restaurant. No one has ever officially banned such contacts. It is simply that the ambassador as a rule has the funds for representational expenditure under his control, and he does not encourage his officials to have contacts in restaurants. In most countries Soviet ambassadors live off these representational funds, so as not to spend their own salaries. Most of the work done by straight diplomats consists in 'extracting' information from the open press, translating it, and sending it back to the Foreign Ministry.

The representative of the Party Central Committee is equal in importance to the ambassador. He is usually an official belonging to the International Department of the Party Central Committee. He holds the post of counsellor in the embassy and his duties include maintaining links with the local communist party in those countries where it has a legal existence. Since the communist party was then outlawed in Iran, there was no such duty for an official of the International Department. As there were 8,000 Soviet experts then working in the country, this post was handed over to the Party Central Committee's Department for Cadres Abroad. Its tasks included the organization of Party ideological work among Soviet workers throughout Iran, and the collection, in foreign currency, of Party members' dues. Since all Soviet citizens abroad are Party members, these contributions amount each month to a respectable sum.

This representative must also oversee the moral condition in the Soviet colony. It is not the KGB that does this, be it noted, but the representative of the Party Central Committee. It is to him that all gossip and denunciations of moral conduct find their way. It is he who has a string of his own informants. In practice, his is the decision as to whether to extend the tour of duty of everybody working in a Soviet embassy, including those in the KGB.

At that time the representative of the Party Central Committee in Iran was Ibrahim Azhievich Amangaliev, a Kazakh by nationality. He had previously run the Komsomol in Kazakhstan – and, it was said, completely ruined it. For this he was transferred to Moscow 'as a punishment' and ended up a member of the Central Committee.

Although he does not hold a diplomatic post, the representative of the Central Committee of Trade Unions is an indispensable part of the system. His duties include organizing 'cultural recreation' for Soviet citizens living abroad, which involves arranging amateur concerts and shows of Soviet films – measures intended to divert the Soviet citizen from 'local capitalist entertainments'. But his main job once again resides in the collection of contributions in foreign currency from members of the Soviet community. As has been often observed, 'The Soviet regime never lets go of its own.'

The consular department, my cover work place, was housed in a separate two-storey building across the street from the embassy. When I arrived there were five people working there, one straight and four from the KGB. The consul was Boris Kabanov, who was a political intelligence officer. The vice consul, Anatoli Sazonov, was from counter-intelligence. Viktor Kazakov, a political intelligence officer, issued visas to Iranians visiting relatives in the Soviet Union. My job was to issue visas to Iranians and foreigners visiting the Soviet Union as diplomats, businessmen, tourists and those travelling in transit across Soviet territory. Our only straight colleague, Sulyadin Kasumov, did the formal paper work.

Yashchenko explained that I should take special care not to allow undesirable foreigners into the Soviet Union. That was why every visa applicant had to be checked against the 'black lists' or, in official language, 'lists of persons whose entry into the Soviet Union is forbidden'. Were such a person to slip through our control unnoticed, then whoever had let him through would be in big trouble. The 'black lists' were kept in my safe. They consisted of two bulky files, each of some 400 pages, that contained the names of all undesirable persons, beginning with out-and-out anti-Soviet enemies and political opponents and ending with small-time smugglers.

It is quite difficult to obtain a Soviet entry visa. Tourist visas are only issued to those already in possession of an itinerary obtained from Intourist, the Soviet tourist bureau. It is simply not possible for a foreigner to enter the country as a tourist without such preliminary arrangements. Transit visas are only issued to foreigners if they have a ticket showing a date of departure from the Soviet Union. There must not be more than four days between the dates of entry and departure. Diplomatic and service visas are issued only on prior agreement and instructions from Moscow.

All Soviet visas, with the exception of a diplomatic visa, which is stamped into the passport, are issued on special separate slips of watermarked paper. All entry and exit stamps are put on to this slip when the Soviet border is crossed. In this way nothing remains in a foreigner's passport to show that he has visited the Soviet Union. This is done in order to avoid pinpointing foreigners who have secretly visited the Soviet Union by travelling along the communication lines of the international communist movement. Such people are issued with service visas in which only the words 'by invitation' are written in the column marked 'Purpose of Visit'. For the initiated, this means that the foreigner is travelling along lines laid down by the Party Central Committee, and that he must be treated with particular respect, if you do not want to land in trouble. In the cases of persons arriving in the Soviet Union under Ministry of Defence arrangements for secret purchases of equipment or for military training, the word 'specialization' appears in the 'Purpose of Visit' column of their visa. Such visas are given, for example, to groups of Palestinians who undergo training in the Soviet Union.

Afghan travellers in transit were a particular problem at that time for the consular department. The Afghan traveller in transit was not just a category, it was a profession, a business. Young Afghans 'in search of a better life' arrived in Iran and travelled on by train, transiting the Soviet Union, Poland or Czechoslovakia, to Western Europe. In Iran they bought goods that were scarce in the USSR and then they sold these to the Soviets. In the Federal Republic they bought goods which were in short supply in the countries in the Soviet sphere of influence, and retraced the same route to Iran. Those with more money returned to Iran in another way. They would buy cars in the Federal Republic – a Mercedes or a BMW for instance – and drive them back through Austria, Yugoslavia, Bulgaria, Turkey and Iran all the way to the frontier with Afghanistan, where they sold them to Afghan dealers at prices three times higher than they had paid. Since Afghanistan has no car industry of its own, the authorities did not object to operations of this kind, and imposed no customs duty on their import. Having made a treble profit from the sale of the cars, the travellers returned to Western Europe, repeating the routine.

The travellers in transit preferred to travel across the Soviet Union for various reasons. First, Soviet rail fares are cheaper than anywhere else. Second, by selling their goods on the way to Moscow, they completely recouped the cost of their rail ticket, and were still left with a decent profit. Third, according to their own account most Afghans just liked to be in Moscow among ordinary Russians. Many of them had Russian girl-friends, and a few even had Russian wives. On the whole, the Afghans liked the Russians. These warm feelings were not destined to last long.

When I began working in the consular department, we were issuing about seventy visas a week to these travellers in transit, and the number kept growing, the business was so profitable. The customs were continually arresting Afghans for infringing customs regulations and for carrying contraband and drugs. These law-breakers were thrown out of the Soviet Union and their names entered on the black lists, but more and more young Afghans came forward to take the places of the fallen. Instructions were continually reaching us from Moscow to restrict the numbers of Afghan travellers in transit. But what could we do? We had no basis in international law for refusing them visas.

The consular department of our Tehran embassy was open to receive visitors from 8 till 11 in the morning. But in fact these were its entire working hours. There was an unwritten agreement between the Foreign Ministry, the KGB and the GRU that intelligence officers should work only three hours a day in their cover departments. Since four of the five officials working in my own were from the KGB, it meant simply that there was no one working in the consulate after 11 o'clock. Our only straight official either took papers to the Foreign Ministry, or else just disappeared for an early lunch-break.

After I had done three hours in the consular department, my main work began in the Residency of the KGB.

CHAPTER 7

The KGB Residency is situated on the fourth floor of the administrative building of the embassy. It occupies two-thirds of the area served by a corridor in which the first four offices are used by straight diplomats. Past these, the corridor is sealed off by a double folding wooden door, which is kept permanently closed. This is the entrance to the Residency. Entry could be gained only by pressing the right buttons on an automatic lock, placed to the left of the door. The lock was rectangular and made of metal, with four buttons in a row. To enter from outside, you had to press simultaneously, for example, the first, second and fourth buttons. The lock then emitted a buzzing sound, during which the door could be opened. The combinations of the locks were changed from time to time, and they were known only to KGB officers. The door could be opened from the inside simply by turning the knob on the lock.

The door leading into the resident's office was immediately on the right of the entrance. Yashchenko pointed out a tiny glass eyelet above the door, and explained that when it glowed red we had to keep out of the resident's office. It meant that he either had someone with him, or did not wish to be disturbed.

The premises of the Residency were not large. On the right, behind the resident's office, was the office of his deputy. On the left were the offices of the head of the counter-intelligence line, the head of scientific and technical intelligence, the typing pool, the information officer's room, and a common work room for the ordinary officers.

Since Yashchenko did not have a room to himself in the Residency, we went into the common work room. It was quite large, measuring approximately 5 x 10 metres. The entire furniture consisted of ten ordinary plastic tables and chairs placed round the walls. A huge double window occupied the whole wall opposite the door. Its outside pane was of ordinary glass, but inside, the frame had been fitted with a pane of opaque corrugated glass with metal netting on its inner surface. The outer and inside frames were half a metre apart, which created a reliable defence against hostile long-distance or laser microphones. The window had heavy double blinds. The rules laid down that the blinds on the Residency windows had to be drawn without fail as soon as darkness fell, so that no one could see from outside in which rooms the lights were constantly burning.

There was no one in the common room. On entering it, Sasha immediately pressed what looked like an ordinary light switch, but no light came on. Instead, a faint buzzing sound filled the room. Sasha explained that this was a sonic defence against eavesdropping by hostile services. It always had to be switched on before anything could be said. This protection was organized in the following way. Behind the walls, made from sound-proofing slabs, there was a wooden frame that went round the perimeter of the room. This frame had thin steel sheets nailed to it. Counting the metal netting in the window, it was therefore as though the room were inside a metal box. Electric vibrators were fixed to the steel sheets about one metre apart. When they were switched on, vibration was transmitted to the metal sheets, which created both an electromagnetic and a sonic field. Our technical experts maintained that this type of defence guaranteed almost one hundred per cent security. Even if a hostile transmitting device were placed in that room, its signal would not pass through the field of electromagnetic protection. Nevertheless we were under instructions to be especially careful in our conversations, particularly if they concerned Residency operations. Excessive care taken in intelligence work never does any harm.

Yashchenko began my briefing by explaining the structure of the Residency.

A KGB Residency abroad is headed by a resident, who is almost always a representative of the geographical department of political intelligence. The resident usually holds the rank of colonel or general, depending upon the importance of the country where he is serving.

He is the master of the Residency, with full powers over it. No communication is ever sent to the Centre except under his signature. All communications from the Centre are addressed without exception to the resident. He has discretion to send information to anyone he wishes in the KGB, from the head of his geographical department to the head of the First Chief Directorate and the Chairman of the KGB. The resident does not have the right to communicate with the Party Central Committee. As has been mentioned already, the resident in Tehran was Colonel Kostromin, a deputy head of the Eighth Department of the First Chief Directorate.

After the resident comes his deputy. As a rule, the deputy is also the head of the PI line, as political intelligence is always called in residencies. When the resident is out of the country, the deputy assumes his full authority. The rest of the time he is simply in charge of the PI line, which is responsible for obtaining political information and processing it for transmission to the Centre. Lieutenant-Colonel Gennadi Kazankin was head of the PI line in the Residency. He was only just past forty, and of pleasant appearance, but gave the impression of being a lightweight and not very serious person. He had five KGB officers working under him in the embassy.

External counter-intelligence was represented in the Residency by the CI line. Among its tasks were the penetration of hostile special services and safeguarding the security of Soviet citizens abroad. Lieutenant-Colonel Yuri Denisov was in charge.

The X line dealt with scientific and technical intelligence in the Residency. The only two people who worked on the X line in Tehran were Colonel Valentin Shkapkin, its chief, and Colonel Anatoli Zgerski, his only officer. Shkapkin worked under cover of our trade delegation, while Zgerski held the post of scientific first secretary in the embassy. They jokingly referred to themselves as the line of the 'black colonels' (the Soviet name for the Greek military regime of 1967–74). It turned out that all their line had to show for their work was indeed a joke. They never produced anything of practical value.

Illegal work in the Residency was called line N. We shall deal later in detail with what it did. The main task of N line was to safeguard the work of our illegals in the country. Yashchenko was the sole representative of the N line in the embassy. The other N line officer worked under cover of the Soviet hospital. Sergei Pavlovich

Kharlashkin arrived in Tehran three months before I did, and had already succeeded in gaining a reputation for himself. Sasha told me bluntly that I could not count on any help from Kharlashkin, since he tried to get out of doing anything by saying that he could speak neither English nor the local language.

The moment came for handing all the documentary material over to me, and it immediately became clear that no documents at all, to say nothing of secret documents, were kept in the Residency. All papers were held in the secret registry on the fifth floor of the embassy.

We emerged from the Residency, walked up one floor, and stopped in front of a wooden door exactly like the one in the Residency. There were two rectangular button-lights at eye level on either side of the door. Sasha pressed twice on the one on the right, and I heard two faint rings from somewhere inside.

It had been explained to me that cipher clerks and radio operators from every organization represented in the embassy worked in the secret registry. There were two cipher clerks and one radio operator from the Soviet Foreign Ministry, one of whom was in charge of the secret registry and held the diplomatic rank of attaché. There were two cipher clerks and one radio operator from the KGB; two cipher clerks and one radio operator from the GRU; one cipher clerk from the trade delegation and one from the State Committee for Foreign Economic Relations. The cipher clerks work only for their own organisations and use separate codes and cipher machines. The radio operators work to schedules, and transmit enciphered messages to the Centre by using the usual Morse radio station. The rings for entry are accordingly allocated thus – one ring for the straight people, two for the KGB, and three for the GRU.

After a time there was a metallic clanking sound and the door opened. It turned out that the wooden door was only a screen, behind which was a thick steel door. This was opened for us by Anatoli Gumenyuk, the son of the deputy head of the KGB Cadres Directorate, for whom I had brought the parcel from his father which I had already succeeded in delivering. We found ourselves in a corridor exactly similar to the one in the Residency. The KGB room was immediately to the right of the door, while to the left were two rooms with separate cubicles where straight diplomats could work.

These diplomats were forbidden to write any papers of a secret nature outside the secret registry. The corridor was blocked further along by a ceiling-to-floor curtain. With the exception of the people working in the secret registry, the ambassador, the two residents and the embassy security officer, everyone was categorically forbidden to pass beyond this curtain, behind which were the cipher clerks' rooms and the safes containing secret papers.

Inside the KGB room Gumenyuk introduced me to Ivan Polunin, the KGB radio operator, who was also responsible for the clerical work of the Residency. Gumenyuk asked me whether Polunin's facial features reminded me of any well-known person. I looked at him closely. The bald, high forehead, the high Asiatic cheekbones, the eyes screwed up in a smile. Lenin! And indeed Polunin's unofficial alias in the Residency was 'Lenin'. The first thing Polunin did was to issue me with a plastic working folder with a zip fastener, a working notebook with a hundred numbered sheets and a personal seal for securing my folder. The seal was metal and circular, about one centimetre in diameter. Its impression was imprinted in a special book. I had to sign my name against it, thus assuming the responsibility for the safe-keeping of the seal. I had to sign in another book for the folder and working notebook. I never signed in my own name, but always used Saidov, which was my operational KGB alias.

Each KGB and GRU intelligence officer has his own operational alias. Aliases are used in correspondence between the Centre and the Residency in order to encipher the identity of officers, in case for example an operational letter were to fall into hostile hands, or the special services were to decipher an encoded telegram. The rules lay down that intelligence officers should use their aliases when dealing with each other on Residency premises, but in practice this is hardly ever done. Everybody has an operational alias. In my time, these were:

Chairman of the KGB – Sviridov
Head of Intelligence – Aleshin
Head of Eighth Dept, First Chief Directorate – Ardov
Head of 'S' Directorate – Lebedev
All deputy heads of 'S' Directorate – Leonov

The personalities in these appointments might change, but the aliases always remained with the posts.

An intelligence officer's alias is always chosen by the Centre. There have been different rules at different times governing the selection of pseudonyms. In most cases, intelligence officers have Russian aliases, and when these are written down, inverted commas are never used. Foreign agents of the KGB are given foreign aliases, which are always written in inverted commas. In the mid-1970s the rules were changed. Officers began to adopt foreign aliases, while agents were given Russian aliases. About three years later the rule changed again. Officers were able to assume both foreign and Russian aliases. The same practice was extended to agents. Now the difference is that agents' aliases are always written in inverted commas, while the word 'comrade' always appears before an intelligence officer's pseudonym. For example, the telegram about my arrival in the Residency looked like this:

To Comrade Leonov

Comrade SAIDOV arrived safely in the Residency on 15 June. Comrade YASNOV has begun his hand-over to this operative. The process of handing over the agent 'Ram' to be run by Comrade Saidov is planned for 19 June. Comrade Yasnov's departure for the Soviet Union is planned for 21 June.

Svetlov (Resident's signature)

Once I had received my working folders, Sasha and I returned to the common work room in the Residency, where he began to hand over the documentary material. It consisted of one working notebook. Every officer has such a notebook, which is used for making brief notes on matters concerning agents and cultivations. The table of contents sets aside about ten pages for each item. The summarized content of incoming and outgoing letters and telegrams dealing with agents and cultivation matters is written down in the notebook. That done, the originals of the letters and telegrams are destroyed. (It is strictly forbidden to accumulate operationally unnecessary papers in the Residency. The secret registrar and cipher clerk are responsible for their destruction at the right time. Nor is it permitted to make any notes on separate unrecorded sheets of paper.) When work is completed, the notebook is put away into the folder, which is then secured with the officer's own personal seal. The folder is then handed in to the secret registry, where the cipher clerk checks the seal in the officer's presence. No one except the head of his line or the resident may open the folder without the officer's knowledge.

A huge map of Tehran, covered with transparent plastic, took up almost the entire wall of the common work room to the left of the door. Places to be avoided by officers of the Residency were indicated with various coloured markings. These places included SAVAK and its strong points throughout the entire city, military locations, police stations, various ministries and other places which were under guard. The map was divided into squares. On the day when he was to carry out an operation, an officer would cover with a sheet of white paper the square on the map relating to the area where he would be operating. He would then write on the sheet of paper the date and time when the square was covered. This was done in order to let the other officers in the Residency know that they should steer clear of that area at the time shown. Before going into town, every officer in the Residency had to look at the map and make sure that his personal plans would not cut across any operation in progress. Identical maps were in the resident's office and in the 'Impulse' operator's room.

Impulse is the Residency's radio interception post. Our technical expert's room, and the room of the Impulse operator, were right at the end of the corridor on the sixth floor of the embassy. In the Impulse room there was a multitude of enormous radio receivers and tape recorders, with whose help the Impulse operator intercepted and recorded the radio conversations of SAVAK's external surveillance teams, and, among others, of Iran's military counter-intelligence, and the criminal police. We knew the frequencies. We were thus able to monitor the environment in which the Residency officers were moving, the area around the Soviet embassy and the city as a whole.

'Mars' was also located in a separate room on the sixth floor. Mars was the post for intercepting encoded Iranian communications involving such targets as various ministries, the SAVAK headquarters and the American embassy. It was protected by special secrecy. Apart from Vitali Nekrasov, the operator, and the resident, no one was allowed to go into that room. The intercepted material was regularly sent back to the Centre to be decoded, but whether it ever was in fact deciphered we never found out. The Residency was never told.

The operator at the Impulse post was Viktor Kirichenko, an officer of the CI line. He was of middle height, round-faced and balding, with very malicious eyes. He was so supercilious that, even when seated, he somehow contrived to look down on anyone standing before him. He began his career as an ordinary intelligence officer, but this did not work out for him, apparently because of his character, so he was made operator of the Impulse post, and it became his main job. But to give him his due, he did this work well. His Farsi was quite adequate, and his ear good enough to understand quickly what the external surveillance teams were talking about. His speed of reaction to a developing operational situation was very important in our work, but his professionalism did not improve his human qualities. I was warned that Kirichenko was no great prize, but since it was impossible to avoid associating with him at work, it was better, in spite of everything, to keep on good terms with him.

Sasha told Kirichenko that the operation in which the agent 'Ram' would be handed over to me would take place in two days' time. He picked up a sheet of paper, quickly wrote down the operational plan, including the route which had been designed to detect any external surveillance, and handed it over. Kirichenko muttered something, but signed the plan without raising any objections. Sasha then left to have the plan signed by the head of the CI line. As soon as the door had closed behind him, Kirichenko spoke up in an appallingly arrogant voice.

'Don't think that you'll find it as easy as that to produce operational plans like the one Yashchenko has just written. I passed it because he is leaving. But you, my dear chap, I shall pressure until the pips squeak, and until you get to know the city like the back of your hand.'

I said nothing, but it was obvious that the man was not joking.

'We'll see,' Kirichenko continued to mutter, 'whether this Ram of yours will turn up at all for the meeting.'

'What a surly man,' I thought. But, as it turned out, Kirichenko was to be proved right on one thing.

On the day of the operation, we looked in to the Impulse post to find out what the external surveillance situation was. Kirichenko barked offhandedly that so far everything was clear. We drove out of the embassy at 10 a.m. The meeting with 'Ram' had been fixed for 12.30. Yashchenko began to drive around Tehran in his car in order to establish whether we were under external surveillance. It was obvious that he knew the city extremely well. We drove along small deserted streets for two hours, never emerging on to the main roads.

It was only after Sasha had convinced himself that we had no one tailing us that we proceeded to the area where the meeting was to be held. The rendezvous was on Zohre Street in the north of Tehran. 'Ram' turned up about five minutes late. He was a tall, black-haired, nice young Afghan with fervent, if not to say flashing eyes. I had seen his photograph in the Centre, but he made a more agreeable impression in the flesh. Sasha introduced me, and I noticed that 'Ram' had been taken aback by my presence. His real name was Khomayun Akram. He was first secretary in the Afghan embassy in Tehran, in charge of the consular section. He had already been used on one occasion to document a couple of our illegals as Afghan citizens, and now it was planned to profit from the opportunity afforded by 'Ram' to extend the validity of the passport of 'Beduin', one of our illegals working outside Iran.

Our meeting took place in Maxim's, one of the most expensive restaurants in Tehran. Sasha conducted the entire conversation. I sat and listened. Even if I had had to say something, I should not have been able to, since right from the start of the meeting I had been in a flap. The first meeting of one's life with a real agent in a hostile environment is no joke, the more so with an agent who knows the identities of our own illegals. There was something here to be in a flap about. Sasha asked 'Ram' about his family and work, and then, in what seemed to be a very cautious way, he explained to the agent that he was leaving for Moscow, and that from now onwards it would be I who would be meeting 'Ram'.

'Ram' was very surprised, and it was obvious that he was hearing about Yashchenko's departure for the first time. I didn't like this at all. According to the rules, Sasha should have gradually prepared the agent for the hand-over, in order to avoid any shock reaction. He had clearly not done this, and I would have to repair the situation. Sasha asked 'Ram' to help us by extending the validity of the passport, and the agent mumbled something in reply. We agreed that I would have the next meeting with 'Ram' in about six weeks' time, at the end of July.

We returned to the embassy, and it was only then that I realized how drained I had been by the emotional tension of the meeting.

The operation transferring 'Ram' to my control marked the completion of my hand-over from Yashchenko. No operations had been planned to hand over 'Konrad' and 'Evi', our illegals, since they had gone on leave. Kharlashkin, the second officer in N line, was acting as receiving point for signals from them. Everything was working out quite successfully, since the opportunity had arisen for me, although only in a small way, to study the city in an operational context.

After completing the hand-over, Sasha gave me a run-down on the moral and psychological atmosphere prevailing both in the embassy and the Residency at the time I arrived. This atmosphere was not good. An air of permanent holiday pervaded the Residency. Everybody drank, from the resident downwards. There were parties every day behind closed doors. Russians, including Residency officers, were always to be seen in cafés near the embassy. Since there had been a considerable turnover in Residency staff in the course of the preceding year, there were hardly any operational experts left. Gennadi Kazankin, the head of the PI line and deputy resident, and Yuri Denisov, the head of the CI line, did not have any special experience of practical work, and they were therefore unable to set high standards. Their incompetence had already led to two serious operational failures.

It was only later that I succeeded in tracing these Residency failures about which Yashchenko had spoken. The first had occurred in May 1977. A highly placed official of the Iranian Ministry of Education named Rabbani, who was a KGB agent, was arrested by SAVAK officers when he went out to meet Evgeni Venediktov, an officer in our Residency. Venediktov managed to avoid arrest because Kirichenko, who was manning the Impulse post, became suspicious at the very last moment of the activities of SAVAK external surveillance teams in the area where the meeting was being held and succeeded in giving the danger signal. As our officer had not been caught red-handed, the Iranians did not raise a scandal afterwards, nor did they demand that Venediktov be thrown out.

The agent Rabbani had been recruited by Soviet intelligence some time in the Forties, in the period when the Soviet Union had real clout in postwar Iran, and he had collaborated continuously with the KGB ever since. According to what I heard from those who had worked with him, his position in the Ministry of Education did not give him access to real secret information, but he used to pass on intelligence obtained in private conversations with his highly placed acquaintances and relatives, and this was sometimes quite interesting. Rabbani was run by the PI line in the Residency, and many officers of the Eighth Department of the First Chief Directorate remained in successful contact with him over the many years of his collaboration. One of the last to work with him was Gennadi Kazankin. Suddenly he handed this agent over to be run by Venediktov, the youngest officer on his line, who was almost arrested when he went out to have his very first meeting with Rabbani. Mutterings were then heard among the PI line officers, that there was something fishy here – there was a general feeling that Kazankin must have made some slip-up with Rabbani – but ... Let me say, moving ahead of events, that Venediktov was thrown out of Iran six months later. SAVAK had been trying to drop hints to the KGB resident prior to this that Venediktov's presence in Tehran was unwelcome. They drained the brake fluid from Venediktov's car, and it was only by a miracle that he escaped with his life from the ensuing accident.

The second case happened in June 1977, immediately before my arrival. Boris Checherin, an officer of the PI line working under TASS correspondent cover, was cultivating an Iranian, and this cultivation was about to come to a head. Then during the meeting, at which it had been planned to make the recruitment pitch, two unknown persons appeared at the villa outside town which belonged to the target of the cultivation. They introduced themselves to Checherin as members of SAVAK. No arrest followed, and everything passed off extremely politely. They simply proposed collaboration to our officer. Checherin naturally refused, and walked out. This meant that throughout the whole period of cultivation our officer had been working with an Iranian 'plant', and nobody had realized this, although the entire cultivation should have been thoroughly analysed both in the Residency and in the Centre. Boris Checherin was also expelled from Iran, but without any fuss in the press. This was still to come.

It is interesting that, as on previous occasions of this nature, the Iranians always summoned Fedor Saulchenkov, the minister counsellor in our embassy, to their Foreign Ministry, for they thought he was the KGB resident. The poor old fellow suffered fearfully over this, but there was nothing to be done about it. So it would seem that his name will go down in the annals of Soviet–Iranian relations as a KGB officer, although he has never been one.

The falling standards in the Residency were due to the replacement of many officers, including the heads in the Residency, at the beginning of 1977. The following left Tehran when their tours of duty ended: Leonid Bogdanov, the resident; Vlasov, the deputy resident and head of the PI line; Lev Kostromin, the head of the CI line; and two other officers named Dmitri Kuzmin and Vladimir Fisenko. They had all specialized in Iran and were experts in their subject.

The resident was not replaced. Gennadi Kazankin, the new head of the PI line, temporarily carried out the resident's duties. He had begun his career in 'S' Directorate as a candidate illegal, but never became one, because he failed a final psychological test right at the end of his training. But as he was already a KGB officer, he was moved to a geographical department in the First Chief Directorate, where he studied Farsi and began to specialize in Afghanistan. He spent about a year on a posting in Afghanistan, but illness compelled him to return to Moscow. In the Centre he completed finals courses, after which he was sent to Iran. It was while he was in charge that these two failures happened.

Yuri Denisov, head of the CI line, was no kind of expert on Iran, and spoke no Farsi. He came to K Directorate of the First Chief Directorate from internal counter-intelligence, was once on a posting to Burma, and after that came to Iran as head of the CI line. Above all other things, the head of the CI line must be responsible for the security of Residency operations. In order to perform this role, he should speak the local language and have a thorough knowledge of the agent running and operational environment in the city. Denisov had neither of these qualifications.

It was into this situation, and because of these failures, that Lev Petrovich Kostromin, by now deputy head of the Eighth Department of the First Chief Directorate, was temporarily sent to Iran in order to 'strengthen' the Residency.

On 21 June, I saw off Yashchenko for Moscow. When I got back to the embassy from the station, I felt that I had been left entirely on my own, to sink or swim.

Every morning at eight o'clock, I went to the consulate, where a crowd of Afghan applicants for visas were already waiting. There were always those among them who needed visas urgently. They agitated, they implored, they grabbed you by the arm. The reception of callers, 99 per cent of whom are the same Afghans who have been there before, goes on until 11 a.m. That over, you have to leave the office and again force a way through the crowd of screaming Afghans, answering all questions and entreaties in the same way: 'Tomorrow morning at eight o'clock.' The crowd accompanies you along the street right up to the embassy entrance, and salvation only comes when the grilled door slams shut behind you. The Afghans had absolutely no need for such impatient behaviour. We always issued visas on time, and turned down only those people named on the black lists. But all this went on day after day. It had apparently already become a tradition.

There was practically nothing for me to do in the Residency. KGB intelligence rules laid down that an officer arriving on his first tour of duty must be given six months to build up his cover for the benefit of the hostile special services and to study the city. But usually it did not work out like this, since a young officer is taking the place of his predecessor, and he must continue the work which was being done before he arrived. In addition, those in charge of the Residency tended to be sceptical about this six-month rule for preparation. What they needed was results.

I personally was lucky over this. Since I was the only N line officer in the embassy, there was no head of line breathing down my neck, and I had to be given my orders directly from the Centre. I had even agreed with them while at the Centre that they would not trouble me until I felt sure of myself in the agent running and operational environment in Tehran.

As it rapidly proved, there was little point in worrying about anybody's cover in relation to SAVAK, the secret police. They mounted continuous surveillance on us from observation posts placed all round the embassy. The main one was a house on the corner of Stalin and Churchill Streets, and they also ran a small kiosk for selling non-alcoholic drinks across the street and directly opposite the entrance to the embassy. The same SAVAK employees had the Soviet nationals under constant round-the-clock surveillance. This was their main job, and some had been working in the same places for twenty years. They were highly qualified experts on the Soviet community, and they had no great difficulty in determining the organization to which a newly arrived official at the embassy belonged. It took them about a month from his date of arrival to do this.

The SAVAK observers took photographs of the Russians from the drinks kiosk. They also had a radio transmitter there which they used in order to tip off the surveillance teams deployed around the embassy when the target of surveillance appeared. This kiosk was open every day from 7 a.m. until 11 p.m., on all holidays and rest days and in all weathers. At night, surveillance was carried out from concealed posts. We knew that they knew that we knew who they were, but this did not worry them, since they were in their own country. We had been accustomed to that kiosk for so long that it had become part of our existence. Sometimes its presence could even be helpful. For instance, during the protracted Iranian holidays, when all the shops were shut, you could buy drinks like Pepsi, Seven Up and Canada Dry there, and contribute to SAVAK's budget.

But in the matter of personal cover, the main enemy for intelligence officers of both the KGB and the GRU was certainly not SAVAK. Paradoxical as it may sound, the main enemy of intelligence was our own countrymen. The blame for this lies with the geographical work principle already referred to. People who end up in the geographical departments stay there in most cases until the end of their careers. They work together in Moscow and in embassies and they all know everything about each other. When some outsider appears, for example in the Iranian Department of the Foreign Ministry, no one has any doubt that he is from either the KGB or the GRU. Even before an intelligence officer arrives in a country, the embassy grapevine already knows who he is, whom he is replacing, whether he is KGB or GRU and what his military rank is. That would not matter if it stopped there. But alas, our dear straight diplomats and embassy officials rehash all the gossip in their flats in town, and town flats occupied by Soviets in any country are bugged by the local special services.

We knew all this in the Residency, so our basic credo was: 'SAVAK knows who we are. Our main task in this situation is to ensure the complete security of operations in order not to give them the opportunity to catch us out.' An intelligence officer's main security job is above all else to get to know his city well and its agent running and operational conditions. Having been left to my own devices in the Residency, that was exactly where I decided to begin.

Since, once my predecessor had gone, I should have to drive back and forward to Zargande, some 14 kilometres to the north of the embassy, I needed a private car. The one I inherited was my predecessor's white Peugeot 504.

The fleet of embassy cars, like everything else, is divided into three parts, one each for the Foreign Ministry, the KGB and the GRU. Each of these organizations has its own cars and a staff of drivers to service them. Legally, and in their documentation, the cars in a Soviet embassy are the personal property of its diplomats and are registered as such in the Foreign Ministry of the host country. In fact however the cars belong to the three organizations that pay for them. The names of the diplomats are used so that the cars may be bought free of tax, but this certainly does not mean that the diplomat in whose name the vehicle has been bought will use it. The decision as to who should use which car depends variously on either the ambassador, the KGB resident or the GRU resident.

The ambassador, the minister counsellor and the representative of the Party Central Committee are the only persons to have a personal driver. The other straight diplomats either have their own cars or use the services of Foreign Ministry drivers to make journeys on official business. Of the straight diplomats, the youngest (third secretaries and attachés) did not have cars for their personal use at all. The cars belonging to the straight diplomats consisted mainly of Soviet-manufactured cars like the Volga and the Lada. The ambassador had an establishment Chaika, but he almost never used it, preferring a red Mercedes.

The cars of the KGB and the GRU were basically different

from the straight cars: not one was Soviet-manufactured. There were three Mercedes cars in the KGB Residency, a silver 380 that belonged to the resident, two 230s, a BMW 520, four Peugeot 504s, two Toyotas and some others. The KGB uses cars of foreign make, not for show, but for purely operational reasons. During operations a car must not betray the fact that it belongs to the Soviet embassy and attract attention to itself. Another reason is that foreign cars are technically much more reliable.

The Western reader will no doubt think that the KGB drives around in Mercedes cars because it has unlimited financial resources, while the Foreign Ministry has to count its kopecks. That is not so. KGB rules lay down that every intelligence officer abroad must have a car for operational purposes. When he goes abroad, a certain sum of money is earmarked for him to buy a car of medium standard. The purchase of expensive cars like Mercedes, BMWs and Volvos is not sanctioned for two reasons. First, the intelligence officer's car must not stand out too ostentatiously from the general run of cars in the country of his appointment. Second, and this is more serious, the KGB is always under the most strict instructions to save foreign currency.

It was quite fortuitously that expensive cars began to appear in the Tehran Residency. The fact was that Iran had a very high customs duty, in the order of 200 per cent, on the importation of foreign cars. Diplomats naturally bought cars for themselves without paying tax. The rules of both the Foreign Ministry and the customs in Iran stipulated that, after he had used it for four years, a diplomat might sell his car on the domestic market at the going price. Because of the customs duty, the price of a four-year-old car was double the price of a tax-free new car. In this way diplomats made a great profit when they sold their old cars, so we were able to buy a higher grade of tax-free car with the money made on the deal. The Centre did not object to these operations. The most important thing for them was that we worked within the system of paying our way without subsidy and did not ask for the usual grants to buy new cars.

Each residency has a minimum of two operational drivers, who work under cover of ordinary embassy chauffeurs. In fact they are officers of the Seventh Chief Directorate of the KGB, which deals with the organization of external surveillance. This Directorate supplies its officers to the First Chief Directorate for work abroad as operational drivers. Their main job is to familiarize themselves with the town, and to provide professional means of checking whether hostile surveillance is present on the more crucial operations, in particular those involving illegals and the most valuable agents. Good residencies look after operational drivers, trying not to blow them to hostile special services by having them make too many trips from the embassy with Residency officers. Ideally they should be involved as much as possible in the work of the Foreign Ministry line, in order not to stand out from the crowd of other drivers.

But all that is theory. Our Residency had two operational drivers, Mikhail Titkin and Ivan Yegorovich Shabanov. Titkin was a master of his trade and had a nose for hostile surveillance. He was used on all the important operations. At the same time he was to all intents and purposes the resident's personal driver, which naturally gave it away that he belonged to the KGB. Operationally, Shabanov was quite useless. He never spotted surveillance, was unfamiliar with the town, and was used only as the personal driver of the deputy resident. Chauffeurs are traditionally looked upon in the Soviet Union as inveterate drunkards. This was a tradition with which our operational drivers did not break.

So, once I had the white Peugeot 504 in my personal possession, I set about studying the city. After three hours' work in the consulate, I would go to the embassy and up to the Impulse post on the sixth floor. In spite of his surly nature, Kirichenko, the Impulse operator, was an expert on Tehran, and it was far from a waste of time to pick his brains. Since I was living in the summer residence of the embassy, we agreed that I should go there by different routes every two or three days. It was thus possible to study the city for cover story purposes. Kirichenko, who knew in advance my time of departure and the route I would follow, checked my movements to see whether any surveillance appeared behind me.

It is normally quite difficult to lose oneself in Tehran. High mountains to the north of the capital are visible from anywhere in the city. If you do get lost, you simply move in their direction and this will lead you northwards. It was likewise necessary to learn the network of the main Tehran streets by heart. Kennedy Street, Amir Abad Street, Pahlavi Street and Shemiran Street all go from south to north. Shah Reza Street, Tahte Dzhamshid Street, Tahte Tavuz

Street and Kerim Khan Zand Street, among others, run from east to west. Anybody who is lost in the side-streets has only to take bearings from the hills to locate his position or emerge on to one of the main streets. It could not be more simple in theory. But in practice it means days and weeks of hard work.

Some time later, as he realized that I was genuinely interested in studying the city, Kirichenko gradually softened and began to give me advice which was operationally very useful. He showed me 'holes' all over Tehran. 'Holes' are places in the city through which it is possible to drive without emerging on to the main streets. Practical experience showed that checking for surveillance had to be done on quiet, deserted town streets which did not lead on to the main arterial roads. There you could feel more confident as to whether surveillance was present or not. When emerging into a busy street, it is especially difficult to note surveillance in the flow of traffic; even if you have been clean up until that point, you may pick up a mobile surveillance. But knowing these 'holes', it was possible to drive practically all the way through Tehran without touching the main roads.

Everything was going normally, but one thing worried me. I never saw any external surveillance on myself. I am sure that every intelligence officer who goes on a foreign posting for the first time knows that feeling that surveillance is always there. In these early days you think that you carry a tail wherever you go. You have the feeling that you are exposed and that everybody is looking at you, knowing you for an intelligence officer. It is this tension that makes you want constantly to be looking over your shoulder to see who is following you. But common sense wins in the end, and the surveillance paranoia passes, overwhelmed by everyday problems.

The paranoia passes – but not for everyone. I have come across cases where surveillance fever begins on day one and lasts until the final day of departure from the country. For most intelligence officers surveillance, although still a serious matter, becomes an ordinary everyday factor in their work. My fears in those first days incidentally proved to be quite unfounded. SAVAK did not impose serious surveillance upon Soviet diplomats until they had been in the place for nine months. During these nine months, they studied the new arrival and reached a conclusion as to whether he belonged to one of the Soviet intelligence services, or was a straight diplomat. As a rule they did not err and imposed surveillance on intelligence officers only, leaving the straight ones in peace.

I waited for my own time to come. SAVAK put me under external surveillance exactly nine months after my arrival, and from then onwards they became my fairly frequent travelling companions. I recall how I felt on the first occasion I saw in my rear mirror the blue BMW of SAVAK's surveillance following me at quite a distance. It was a feeling of unimaginable relief and joy. 'At last they've turned up! I've been wrong to blame myself for not observing surveillance before. They simply weren't there till now.' But that was for the future. Meanwhile I went on studying the city.

The working day in the embassy ended at 2.30 p.m., after which people were left to their own devices. It was natural that Party and trade union leaders in the Soviet community tried to involve people in 'mass cultural activities' in order to distract their attention from the universal bourgeois contagion served up in the shape of cinema, restaurants and magazines.

The Soviet club was on Stalin Street, right opposite the embassy. It was quite a large two-storey building with a cinema and music rooms. Soviet films were shown in the club four times a week. A concert of amateur performances was staged for every Soviet holiday. The club was not just for embassy officials. People working in other Soviet organizations in Tehran were allowed in as well. Iranians were not admitted.

The bookshop enjoyed enormous popularity and was opened before the beginning of every film or concert in the club, which is hardly surprising, seeing that in Russia literature has always occupied a special honoured place in society. But there was something else here. For years there had been a famine of books – that is, of good books – in the Soviet Union. The authorities blamed it on shortfalls in paper production, but this was not true. There had been quite enough paper to print rubbish like Brezhnev's articles, speeches and memoirs – which, may it be said in passing, were written for him by the Institute of Marxism–Leninism. But no one ever came forward to buy this kind of literature. After they had been placed in the shops, these books would be removed somewhere in order to make it appear as though they had all been snapped up by the populace. Yet books by such popular authors as Pushkin, Bulgakov, and contemporary authors such as Belov, Pikul, Rasputin and others were published in editions of a hundred thousand copies. One hundred thousand copies for a population of 270 million was less than a drop in the ocean. What is more, the greater part of these editions was sold in accordance with 'the lists', that is to members of the ruling Party establishment.

Another quota of these editions was sent abroad, where the books were sold for foreign currency to Soviet citizens working beyond the national borders. This is how the Soviet authorities manage to obtain an income in foreign currency by selling Soviet books to Soviet people. But even abroad it is not always possible to buy what you want. The fact is that 'lists' exist abroad as well. When new books arrived at our shop in Tehran, an order list was sent to the ambassador, the Party Central Committee representative, the head of the trade delegation, and to counsellors, who included the residents of both the KGB and the GRU. The other diplomats tried to make friends with the salesgirl in the shop, to get her to set good books aside for them. In this way yet another unofficial list was created. Ordinary mortals could obtain virtually nothing in short supply without the right connections.

Yet another place of note in the club was the canteen, situated in the internal courtyard and rented out to a local Armenian who ran it with his family. It was used mainly by those Soviets whose wives had gone off to the Soviet Union leaving no one behind to cook for them. But the main attraction of this institution was its bar, where Misho the Armenian sold alcoholic drinks and beer along with excellent highly seasoned hors d'oeuvres. There was never any shortage of customers here. They came before the cinema, after the cinema, instead of the cinema, mainly the young diplomats, embassy staff, and Soviet experts. They usually started here, and then, so as not to be seen to be drinking too much, they would graduate to one of the many cafés near the embassy and end up after midnight in somebody's flat. In the morning, it was work until 2.30 p.m. with a hangover, and then it began all over again.

The senior diplomats stayed away from the canteen, out of concern for their reputation, but this certainly did not mean that they did not drink. They quenched their thirsts indoors, in restricted private parties. But the outcome was no different. The embassy lived in something akin to an atmosphere of permanent holiday, each reveller appearing to think that since everything was transient, they had to seize the day. Such an atmosphere had an adverse effect on the moral climate of the community. In the embassy, as in other organizations as well, extramarital and inter-marital relationships were commonplace, and these caused gossip. Young Foreign Ministry secretaries who had arrived in Tehran as innocent girls would drift into this society and rapidly become the mistresses of diplomats, a process that usually ended in tears. All this was known both to the KGB and the Party heads in the embassy, but the KGB did not deal in these matters, and the Party heads simply closed their eyes to everything. They were following a Party Central Committee instruction according to which it was not worth while taking severe measures against seductions in the embassy, provided that everything took place discreetly and without causing scandal. But Soviets had better stick to Soviets, and thus reduce the likelihood of local involvements. Well, such a philosophy suited everybody, and the resulting sexual licence was quite widespread.

The embassy was protected by duty guards who were officers of the KGB frontier troops. These young lads performed round-the-clock duty in shifts. Every night after 11 o'clock, they turned loose their charges, a pack of enormous guard dogs which had been brought to Iran from frontier posts in the south of the Soviet Union. Kept locked up during the day, and out of contact with people, they were utterly wild, and could attack anybody on command. We all knew that we could only go into the embassy grounds after 11 p.m. if we had previously warned the guards, so that they could remove the dogs.

At night, one guard remained in the guard-room building, while another went round the perimeter of the embassy compound with the dogs. Sometimes the guards would stop when they reached the embassy living quarters in order to see what was going on. All the doors of the flats opened on to galleried balconies, and any furtive comings and goings could be clearly seen. The guards knew who was pairing with who, but the information stayed with them.

Besides, to whom could the information be of interest, when it was part of the fabric of Soviet reality? Vladimir Mikhailovich Vinogradov, our ambassador and a member of the Party Central Committee, took a doctor/masseuse along with him to every country he went to. This was Skvortsova, his mistress. She lived in a separate flat in the embassy block. The ambassador had his detached residence not far from there, and our guards often saw her going over to the ambassador's house at nights. To be fair, it must be said that the ambassador's elderly wife spent most of her time in Moscow.

The ambassador also had a personal valet and a cook. The cook was a niece of the ambassador's wife, and the valet was her husband. Officially such situations do not exist in the Soviet Foreign Ministry system, so masseuse, cook and valet were all registered as duty guards. This meant that our lads had to put in many extra hours on duty. Some of them resented this injustice and threatened to turn the dogs on the masseuse as she hurried through the night. The threat was a joke, but the reality was galling. A member of the Party Central Committee may follow his fancies with impunity. All this of course was known about in the KGB Residency, but nothing could be done about it. The most interesting thing was that people were outraged, not because the ambassador had a mistress, a cook and a valet, but because he had registered them as guards. He had thus violated the unwritten Soviet law of all-permissiveness, 'Live and let live.'

CHAPTER 8

The second N line officer worked under Soviet Red Cross Hospital cover, holding the post of Deputy Director for Administration and Supplies. Since he spoke no foreign languages, apart from Dutch, he was entrusted with supervising the signals sent us by our illegals in the form of marks left at pre-arranged places which he would visit three times a week, on his way from the hospital to the embassy. Since Sergei Pavlovich Kharlashkin had come to Tehran three months before I did, he had already grasped the set-up in the hospital. He was the first person to tell me about what went on there.

The Soviet Red Cross Hospital had been built in Tehran as a result of an economic cooperation agreement signed in the early 1960s between Iran and the Soviet Union. Under it, the Iranians received the usual package of Soviet economic assistance, consisting of metallurgical plant, mines, pits, and a hospital. In order that the hospital should be able to pay for itself, it was run like a commercial concern, accepting payment for treatment from the local populace. These charges however were purely nominal – no more than three dollars per visit to the doctor. Not surprisingly, our hospital was very popular with these locals, particularly with the poor people among them. Iranian doctors charged astronomical fees for medical services.

The Soviet doctors working in the hospital were competent people in the main, and provided the Iranians with qualified help. But they did not speak Farsi, so a female interpreter taken from among the local community worked with each doctor in his surgery. These were local Russian-speaking Armenians, Aysors, Azerbaijanis and second- and third-generation White Russians.

The hospital had medical, surgical, X-ray and physiotherapy

departments, but no highly specialized departments. That is why it was such a goldmine for our doctors. I had heard previously that our people were making huge sums of money there, but it was Kharlashkin who explained to me exactly how the system worked.

This is what happened. When he examines a patient, the Soviet doctor establishes what the patient needs, let us say a neuro-surgical type of operation. But the Soviet hospital does not have a neuro-surgical specialist, so our doctor gives the patient a chit to take to a local Iranian specialist who performs the operation. This operation naturally has to be paid for, and costs let us say four thousand dollars. The Iranian surgeon performs it and receives the money from the patient. However, since the surgeon played no part in making the diagnosis, but only in performing the operation, he hands over half of what he receives, or two thousand dollars, to the Soviet doctor who made the diagnosis. In the medical world it is considered that to establish a correct diagnosis is half the battle in the successful treatment of a patient. That is how the Soviet doctor came to receive 50 per cent of the cost of the operation. Diagnostics in the Soviet hospital were of a higher order than in Iran, but the Iranian specialists were not complaining. Their cooperation was profitable for both sides. Those Iranian doctors who maintained contact with the Soviet hospital had a continuous stream of clients, and their reputations enhanced, while the Soviet doctors received sums of money which, by Soviet standards, were enormous.

The reader may find this situation commonplace enough, especially if he is from the West. For what is so special about an Iranian doctor handing over 50 per cent to a Soviet colleague with whom he is collaborating? These are ordinary business relations. For the Iranian doctor, it is indeed ordinary business, but not for the Soviet doctor. The fact is that this money is not included in the profits of the hospital, nor does it pass through the hospital accounts. It is quite simply pocketed by our doctors. Here was a system well established by years of practice. Once he had obtained the money, the Soviet doctor would keep half of it for himself, and hand over the other half to the director of the hospital, who ran this entire enterprise.

When I arrived, the director of the hospital was Ashurko. He had instituted a very precise system for handling these profits.

Each doctor had to send at least one patient a month to an Iranian specialist. If he sent more, all the better. Should a Soviet doctor take offence against the arrangement, and refuse to have anything to do with this medical corruption, Ashurko would have a private talk with him, after which the rebel would either back down and fall into line or else he would be quietly sent back to Moscow as a result of a negative personal report.

'And where was the KGB?' the reader may ask.

In the KGB all these facts were known down to the last detail, but nothing could be done about them. The hospital was under the protection of the ambassador and of the representative of the Party Central Committee. What is more, most of the Soviet doctors were from the Fourth Chief Directorate of the Ministry of Health, or more simply from the 'Kremlin hospital', and had their own links to the highest reaches of the Party.

The Residency regularly sent the Centre reports on the situation in the Soviet hospital in Tehran. These facts were reported to the Party Central Committee, and there the matter rested. Sometimes the Central Committee would ask their representative or the ambassador to verify the facts in these KGB reports. The answer sent to Moscow was always the same – 'As a result of a check carried out at the hospital, the facts you refer to have not been confirmed.' How could they be confirmed, when the director of the hospital was the best friend of Amangaliev, the Party Central Committee representative, and of the ambassador, who both had their snouts dug into this golden feeding trough?

Amangaliev also fed in the hospital in the literal sense. His wife spent the greater part of her time in the Soviet Union, and when she was away he ate in the staff canteen, but did not pay. Amangaliev was frequently the guest of Ashurko, the hospital director. We knew what cemented this friendship. The hospital director had money, and the Party Central Committee representative had authority. A typical merging of corruption with Party position. In the Soviet Union, such instances were more the rule than the exception. That is why in Brezhnev's time corruption grew to unbelievable proportions.

We had first-hand knowledge of all this. One of the hospital doctors was a Residency officer. He was a genuine doctor who had been coopted into the KGB intelligence service to work for the PI line, gathering political information. It was considered that interesting people might turn up in the hospital. But most of his time was absorbed by working on patient reception, some twenty-five to thirty a day. He was a good specialist, with a conscientious attitude, and he knew everything that went on in the hospital, not because he sought the information but simply because it came to him.

In the hospital, as happened everywhere with us, it was common knowledge who was who. The straight doctors knew that Dr Volodya Kuzmin was KGB, that Kharlashkin, the deputy director for administration, was also KGB, and that the deputy director of the treatment unit was GRU. So the straight doctors used to come to our officers and the GRU officer and tell them that the director was compelling them to make money by sending patients to have operations they did not need. In their naïvety, they thought that the KGB would send the director straight back to Moscow under guard and all the way to prison. But nothing ever happened, so it began to dawn on the doctors that the KGB was not going to help them, and that it was better to do as the director required.

The director meanwhile was spreading himself more and more widely. The term of his posting was running out, and he was making the best of his final moments by changing local Iranian currency into dollars and converting some of his money into gold and diamonds. Feeling his position to be completely secure, he used to say openly that he would buy himself the post of deputy minister of health, and that the KGB would not be able to stop him. 'To hell with the KGB,' he often said when he was among his friends. 'They don't have the real power!'

Of course, he was quite right. He knew the true state of affairs from his Party friends. But most of the Soviet citizens who saw Ashurko in action in Tehran thought of course that the KGB would never do anything against him because he was their agent and he could do as he pleased. During Ashurko's last two months in Tehran, according to the official accounts, the hospital made no profit whatever. In fact, the profits that were made went to line the hospital director's pockets.

Everything that the director and his circle were doing outraged not only Soviet people, but also the Iranians working in the hospital.

They sent written complaints to the embassy and the consulate, and called personally to tell us what was going on. Nothing changed.

All the same, it is one thing to accumulate a fortune abroad, and quite another to bring the loot back to the Soviet Union. For all the doctors posted to Iran, the director included, held ordinary Soviet foreign passports. This meant that they did not have immunity, and were liable to a strict customs examination on both the Iranian and Soviet sides of the border. But our 'businessmen' were too smart to be thwarted by such a triviality. Each doctor tried to make friends with some embassy official who would be willing to carry a package or two for his friend from the hospital! Their exemption even from Soviet customs inspection enables Soviet diplomats to take back anything they want to the Soviet Union, both for themselves and for their non-diplomatic friends. Diplomats, including KGB officers with diplomatic passports, have no illusions as to what they are carrying. They may not know precisely what it is, but they are certainly sure that it is either taxable by the Soviet Customs, or actually illegal.

Nobody was an exception. I also had friends at the hospital, and I carried packages for them. It goes without saying that the diplomats did not do all this for purely altruistic motives. Health is a matter of fundamental concern for each and every one of us, if not in our young years, then certainly later in life. It was therefore far from a waste of time to have a doctor among one's friends, particularly when he came from the 'Kremlin hospital'. As always, it all worked out the Soviet way, on the basis of mutual advantage.

In itself, this corruption in no way worried the KGB. It had already become a normal and accustomed factor in Soviet reality. The KGB sounded the alarm because here State security matters were being affected: Iranians were working in the hospital, and most of them were informers for the Iranian secret police. In Iran, SAVAK worked in close collaboration with the CIA, the British Secret Service and the Israeli Mossad, for all of whom the Soviet Union was the main enemy. The Iranians were well informed about the Soviets' activities in the hospital. They knew this from the contacts which the female interpreters established with the local doctors. So if the Iranians knew all about the corruption, it follows that the Western intelligence services knew about it too.

From the professional viewpoint, we could only draw one conclusion. A recruitment pitch, based on compromising material, could be made to many doctors in the hospital, and particularly to the director. And these intelligence services certainly had more than enough of this kind of material on which to base a recruitment pitch. Both the ambassador and the representative of the Party Central Committee were numbered among the director's friends. So there you have, if you please, a penetration of the highest organ of authority in the Soviet Union. There was certainly something here to cause alarm.

All that material, and the conclusions drawn from it by the Residency, were sent to the Centre. This elicited flaccid enquiries as to whether the Residency had specific evidence that Western intelligence officers were active around the hospital. The Centre was well aware that without specific proof, there would be no wish even to discuss the matter in the Central Committee, the more so since some of its members were close to those mixed up in the affair. The Residency did not have specific evidence, and this put us even more on our guard. We did not believe, and indeed no professional intelligence officer in the world would believe, that the world's leading Western intelligence services were not taking advantage of such a favourable situation. It meant that recruitment pitches had been made, and that either they had been crowned with success, or else the Soviets to whom the pitch had been made had refused to collaborate, but had not reported it to the Residency for fear of being sent home before their time. We had had reports that some doctors had suddenly fallen into a state of depression and fear for no apparent reason, and this could stem from the causes just suggested, since almost all these people were involved in corruption. We had no facts of substance, but it would have been absurd to expect to see them on the surface. Secret services are called secret because they do their work discreetly and with thoroughness.

Meanwhile everything followed its course. The hospital director came to the end of his tour of duty and calmly returned to the Soviet Union. And yet, not quite so calmly. The KGB did at least manage to do what lay within its power without the sanction of the Central Committee, and when he crossed the Soviet border Ashurko was subjected to a thorough Customs examination. As was to be expected, no contraband was found in his luggage.

His entire fortune in gold, diamonds and dollars had already been conveyed to the Soviet Union by his friend Amangaliev, the Party Central Committee representative, who not only enjoyed diplomatic immunity but made use of the VIP channel every time he crossed the Soviet border. I do not know what became of Ashurko in the Soviet Union, but no doubt he bought himself a cushy job in Soviet medicine.

The new director of the hospital was Sirak, and he proved to be even worse than his predecessor. But more of that later.

The hospital was not the only charge of our Party Central Committee representative. He was also responsible for monitoring the moral and political climate prevailing in other Soviet organizations which were scattered throughout the whole of Iran. This was like leaving a goat to guard the cabbages. When the heads of these organizations came to Tehran, they went to report to Amangaliev, but never to the KGB. Sometimes they would simply drop in on Amangaliev's secretary and leave carefully packed little packages marked 'For Ibrahim Azhievich, PERSONAL', which meant that the secretary had to hand over these packages to her boss without opening them. We knew what they contained – money and other valuables. The heads of the different organizations thus indulged the local boss of bosses upon whom their well-being depended. Some complained to the security officer about this state of affairs, believing in their innocence that if the KGB was doing nothing about this bribery and corruption, it was merely because it did not know what was going on. They did not realize that the KGB simply could not raise a finger, even if it tried, against the Party Central Committee representative.

Lenya Lozbenko, born in the provincial Ukrainian town of Shakhty, was an English-language interpreter working with a group of hydrologists in Tehran. He had completed a course of studies at the International Relations Institute in Moscow, so his position in Tehran was a clear signal that this lad had no connections. To graduate from the IRI, and then work as an ordinary interpreter, especially with mere hydrologists, fell some way short of his qualifications. But Lenya Lozbenko was not downcast. Agreeable, always smiling, he was everybody's friend. He took an active part in amateur theatricals, and he sang patriotic songs at concerts with fire in his eyes. His best friends worked in the hospital. Sometimes he was seen in Amangaliev's company. A fine fellow from every point of view.

We then learnt that when he had gone back to the Soviet Union at the end of his tour of duty, Lenya Lozbenko had left a sum of money in local currency equivalent to $US12,000 with one of his friends, giving him strict instructions to find a way of converting this money into convertible 'golden' Soviet roubles.* This friend could not believe that Lenya could be mixed up in business of this kind. For how inspiringly he had sung patriotic songs with tears in his eyes ... But it was quite obvious that, on Lenya's pay, the money could not be clean. He earned in all something around $US200 a month, on which he still had to live. Lozbenko warned his friend that when he got back to Moscow he would be starting work in the Party Central Committee, and that if his friend attempted to denounce him, then Lenya would destroy him. But this friend proved to be an honest man, and after thinking it over at length, he reported what had happened.

By that time Lenya Lozbenko was already working in the Central Committee of the Soviet Communist Party, living in a beautiful flat in Moscow, and had a car and driver for his personal use. This meant that he was already above the law and could not be touched. An unofficial check established that Amangaliev had recommended Lenya Lozbenko for a job with the Central Committee.

Two Iranian Kazakhs from the province of Khorasan, in north-east Iran, once called on me in my office. They did not ask, but brazenly demanded, that I issue them with visas to enable them to visit relatives in Soviet Kazakhstan. Following the rules, I asked if they had an invitation from their relatives.

'We don't need any invitation,' blustered one of them. 'Now give us the visas, if you don't want to lose your job!'

I was so taken aback by their insolence that I could not even summon up the strength to become angry. I had never encountered

*Usable in Soviet beriozka shops, which sell foreign goods to Soviet citizens who have been able to acquire hard currency through travel abroad.

anything like it before. I patiently explained that they would have to write a letter asking their relatives to send them an official invitation.

'We already have a letter. Here it is,' they said, and produced a letter from their relatives in Kazakhstan. The letter stated that they should apply to the embassy, where their relative would help them get visas.

'Who is your relative in the embassy?' I asked.

'He is the top chief here, and you must always stand up in our presence, when you talk to your chief's relatives,' they said, starting up their theme-song again.

'Are you suggesting that your relative is the Soviet ambassador?' Things were beginning to take quite an interesting turn.

'Who's the ambassador?' the elder of the two asked indignantly. 'The ambassador here works for our nephew. He's the most important chief, I'm telling you!'

'Very well then, but has he got a name?' I was beginning to think that these two old men were not quite right in the head.

'Of course he has. It's Ibrahim Amangaliev.'

So that was it. It was no longer funny. I suggested to the old men that they should come back next day, and in spite of their protests they were led out of the consulate. Then I went straight to the embassy and reported the visit to the KGB resident, whose jaw almost dropped off. It is regarded as almost a criminal offence in the Soviet Union to have relatives abroad, and the subject figures in every questionnaire. This circumstance was of particular importance for persons working abroad, for such a relationship could be used for organizing provocations, recruitment pitches and who knows what else. Kostromin, the resident, ordered me to keep my mouth shut, and hastened off immediately to report what had happened to Amangaliev. They went from there to see the ambassador. After he had returned, the resident's face was wreathed in a satisfied smile.

'You should have seen our Party boss's face when he heard about his uncles at the door of the consulate,' he said. 'But here is the official story. There are no relatives. This is a provocation by SAVAK. Give them back their passports tomorrow and send them home. Don't issue visas. And keep your mouth shut, or it's your neck.'

I had no doubt about that. Next day I did as I was told. The old men were fearfully indignant and demanded a meeting with

Amangaliev. They were told that he did not want to see them, since they were no relatives of his. At this point an unimaginable storm broke out. The old men shouted that Amangaliev had disgraced their family, that he would be cursed by all his relations, and that they would murder him at the first opportunity. They were very temperamental people, those Kazakhs. They besieged the embassy gates for two days in an effort to catch their relation. But once they had let off all their steam, they returned home. Amangaliev was so stunned by what had happened that he did not leave his office nor raise his eyes from the floor for a whole week. He was scared stiff, for it was clear that the relations were real, and also that he had never reported them to anybody. The Residency had a feeling of satisfaction. At least something had managed to spoil this crook's life for him. All the same, there was nothing special to celebrate. The case was never officially followed up.

But this representative of the Party Central Committee did not have a monopoly of corruption in the Soviet community in Iran. Once Vladimir Mikhailovich Vinogradov, our ambassador, had settled in to his new surroundings, he got down to some feverish activity. While he was spending his first summer in the summer residence of the embassy in Zargande, he decided that it was not his intention to share the grounds with other ranks, so in the best traditions of the Central Committee of the Communist Party of the Soviet Union he took over roughly one third of the grounds for his own personal use and surrounded it with an iron fence. Only those who had obtained the ambassador's approval could go in, and everyone was warned to observe total silence near his domain – the ambassador did not like noise, especially children's voices. Indignation was openly expressed in the Soviet community. No previous ambassador had given himself such airs. But this was only the beginning.

Vladimir Mikhailovich soon decided that his private residence, a large villa, no longer suited him. In the ambassador's opinion, you see, this villa had been built in such a way that there was no decent view from the dining room. So he decided to build himself a new villa alongside the old one. At this point we got the picture. It is well known in the Soviet Union that if you want to rob the State blind, you begin with construction. Vladimir Mikhailovich knew these rules very well, for he had started his career in the Ministry of Foreign Trade, where he worked his way up to become head of the trade delegation in Paris. After that, a quite unusual transformation took place. He transferred to the Foreign Ministry, shortly afterwards became a member of the Central Committee of the Communist Party, and was then sent as ambassador first to Japan, then to Egypt.

In order to carry out his building plans, the ambassador needed a reliable man to work as domestic manager in charge of the staff accommodation in the embassy. The man he summoned from Moscow was Anatoli Kazakov, who had worked with him in the past, and knew his mind. Petrakov, the domestic manager who preceded him, was sent back to Moscow before the end of his tour of duty.

Domestic managers, with their direct access to assets of value, have traditionally had a reputation in Soviet society as accomplished thieves. Stealing from the State has become so commonplace in our life that it no longer surprises anyone. The enterprising thief is seen as being smart, while honest people are called idealistic fools. This is the normal process. The State, which has taken everything away from its people, including their initiative at work, cannot count on an honest attitude toward itself. There was a dismal saying current at the time to the effect that: 'Russia is a very rich country. Everyone from the top downwards has been plundering her ever since 1917, and yet there's always something left to steal.'

Kazakov quickly got down to business. He soon found an Iranian building company that undertook to build the new villa for the ambassador. Kazakov did not speak Farsi, and his English was rudimentary. Nevertheless, when negotiations with the builders touched on the financial accounts, he preferred to get by without an interpreter. I once drove Kazakov in my car to the building company office. It surprised me that he was alone without an interpreter, but he explained that the junior embassy officials were 'always busy and you can never get hold of them'. Without the slightest ulterior thought, I suggested that I might help him by interpreting. He flatly turned down my offer.

'But how can you negotiate with them over anything when you don't speak the language?' I asked in surprise.

'I do it in the language of business and figures,' Kazakov answered, with a brazen wink.

How can a personal profit be made in such circumstances? It is easily done. The embassy gives an order to the building contractor to build the house. The contractor prepares all the estimates and building costs. The embassy's representative, in this case our friend Kazakov, offers a sum which is higher than the original tender, provided that the contractor raises the building costs even higher in all the official documents and accounts. Suppose that it costs $100,000 to build the house. Kazakov pays the building company $120,000, and the cost of the house is shown as $200,000 in all the documents. Thus the company's profit grows by $20,000, while Kazakov creams off $80,000. Agreements like this one are made verbally, and no papers are ever signed. This system of robbery is used by Soviets the world over. Foreigners are surprised at first to find Soviets looking for kickbacks, but they soon get used to it. What does it matter to them, when they still make their profit, especially as Soviet fixers prefer to make deals of this nature with ailing companies for whom the contract may come almost as salvation?

So, how does the ambassador come into this?

The ambassador comes in because if he had wished to forestall the plundering of State resources he could easily have kept his domestic manager's activities under his control. What happened here was the exact opposite. The ambassador approved all expenditure personally. Kazakov was given a completely free hand.

As always happens in such cases, the building of the ambassador's house lagged behind schedule. But no one thought of fining the building company for breach of contract. Quite the contrary, unfinished work kept on coming to light, and the embassy had to pay more and more money to have it put right. Then appetites grew, and the ambassador decided to build himself a private swimming pool alongside his new villa. The large pool, for general use, which had been good enough for all of Vinogradov's predecessors, did not suit the new ambassador.

Did the KGB Residency know all about this? Of course it did. But for reasons already given, nobody wanted to have anything to do with this can of worms. It would have been simply useless. The documents showed everything in order.

One of our officers dealt with Armenian matters in the embassy consular department. Both Soviets and Iranians called him 'the Armenian consul'. One of his jobs was to issue visas to Iranian

Armenians visiting relatives in Soviet Armenia and arranging the repatriation of Iranian Armenians to the Motherland. There was a constant flow of repatriates from Iran to Armenia – at the end of the Seventies, about 2,000 migrants a month. The 'Armenian consul' had always traditionally been an officer in the Armenian KGB and represented the Repatriation Committee. But this is not the point.

Most Armenians who left Iran to take up permanent residence in Armenia were poor people whose lives in Iran had been fairly hard. They returned to Armenia out of purely patriotic sentiments. Everybody throughout the world knows how strong is the Armenians' love for their Motherland. Some of them were so poor that they could not afford to pay for their move. In order to help these poor Armenians to return home, wealthy Armenians, of whom incidentally there are quite a few in Iran, set up the Armenian Charitable Fund and placed it at the disposal of the 'Armenian consul', who then used it to pay for the resettlement of indigent Armenians. This Fund existed for many years, and had always been supported by donations from richer native Armenians, as well as from those who remained behind in Iran. It helped many poor Armenians to go to settle in Armenia. The Fund had no connection whatever with the finances of the embassy. It was simply that local Armenians had traditionally chosen the 'Armenian consul' as its chairman.

But then Ambassador Vinogradov got to hear of the Fund, which incidentally was no small amount – several hundred thousand dollars. 'What's this Armenian Fund?' he asked with studied surprise in his usual loutish manner. 'All finances in the embassy must go through the accounts. These Armenians have got themselves on to a really good thing here! These goings-on have got to stop!'

The ambassador then issued an order for all the money in the Armenian Fund to be transferred to the embassy accounts. Aleksan Ovsepyan, the 'Armenian consul', who had put so much effort into building up the Fund, was almost struck dumb when he learned of this order. He flatly refused to hand over the money to the embassy.

'It's nothing to do with me when that crook steals government money!' he shouted. 'He's got the authority to do it. But he won't get his paws on the local Armenians' money!'

So Vinogradov put pressure on Kazankin, the resident, who, not wishing to harm his relations with the ambassador, in his turn put pressure on the Armenian consul, his KGB colleague. Ovsepyan dug his heels in as best he could, and even threatened to tell everything to the local Armenians, but it did not come to that. They finally reached an agreement that the money in the Fund would be held in the embassy accounts, but that the 'Armenian consul' would have the right to audit the money, which would be used only for its intended purpose. All these were only promises. We soon began to receive reports that the ambassador already had his fingers in the Armenian Fund. Money from the Fund was used to purchase an expensive Xerox copying machine, and also to cover expenditure on the building of the ambassador's house.

The Soviet Union has a lower level of political structure called the Primary Party Organization. This organization exists in all undertakings and institutions throughout the country, and has all the ordinary, that is non-professional, members of the Party in its ranks. The embassy also had its primary Party organization. It was headed by the Party bureau, which was headed by the secretary of the Party organization. But the secretary and members of the Party bureau are not professional Party officials, and they do their Party work as a sideline. The Party bureau and its secretary are elected each year from among the officials of the embassy. Only Party members may be elected. This incidentally causes no problems, since in the Soviet Union only Party members are allowed abroad. The Party bureau comes under the Party Central Committee representative in the embassy, who is a professional Party official.

One must not confuse the position of the Party Central Committee representative in the embassy, who is usually on the same level as the ambassador, with that of the secretary of the embassy's primary Party organization. The latter has no real authority. The only advantage is that his holding the position will be mentioned in his end of tour personal report, and this may benefit his later career. The secretary of the primary organization is in fact an obedient pawn in the hands of the Central Committee representative and of the ambassador. His main job is to organize Party meetings – hardly a difficult task, since the procedure for holding meetings both in the embassy and throughout the country has been strictly laid down.

Many years ago the Party Central Committee worked out a system for holding meetings which is still unswervingly observed. The Party meeting is held at the end of each month, round about the 24th or 25th. The subject of the report to be made to the meeting is known beforehand, since the Party Central Committee selects the themes of the meetings a year in advance and circulates them to the Party organizers. Exceptions are made, again on the orders of the Central Committee, only when there is a need 'to discuss the latest report or initiative of the general secretary of the Central Committee'. The draft of the resolutions to be passed by the meeting is also known in advance. It recapitulates the points in the report.

The only thing that the secretary of the primary Party organization must do is to find speakers. This is quite a hard job. Usually none of the ordinary Party members wishes to speak at meetings, for you cannot speak the truth there – that was a habit Stalin knocked out of the heads of the populace for good and all – and most people have no desire simply to parrot the thesis of the report. The only people who are active at Party meetings are those who want to be noticed and make a career for themselves, but they are not plentiful. That is why the secretary has to run round the embassy, trying to line up speakers: there have to be no fewer than six at every meeting.

A good secretary always maintains a list of who spoke, and when. In this way it is easier for him to put pressure on people by telling them that their turn has now come. It is not just because they have to say something that people do not like to speak at Party meetings. Rather it is because they have to put what they will say in writing and then submit it to the secretary for approval. All this takes time. Attendance by members of the Party organization is compulsory. Missing a meeting without valid reason can involve the absentee in trouble at work. All this is done to let the Central Committee see the enthusiasm, or at least the obedience, of the ordinary communists. So, in order to guarantee the best attendance, the meetings are held during working hours. Non-attendance is therefore the equivalent of playing truant.

The meeting itself follows a completely automatic course, the secretary starting with the usual stereotyped phrases.

'There are fifty-two members on the roll of our Party organization. There are forty-seven present at this meeting. Are there any views about opening the meeting?'

'Begin!' someone says from the floor.

'A proposal has been made to open the meeting,' the secretary continues. 'Those in favour, please raise your hands. Carried unanimously,' he says, without even a glance at the floor. Hands are raised automatically. 'For the work of our meeting, it is necessary to elect a working presidium. What are the proposals on its numbers?'

'Five people,' says an organization member, who has already been primed by the secretary.

'And who has nominations on the membership of the presidium?'

'I move the election of . . .' and a person who has been put up in advance to do so reads out names from a piece of paper. The Party Central Committee representative and the secretary of the Party organization always decide beforehand who shall sit on the presidium.

Candidatures for the presidium are then put to the vote, usually 'by list', so as not to waste time. Next the procedures for running the meeting are voted upon. Hands are again raised automatically. Finally the presidium take their places and the reading of the report begins. It may be safely said that practically nobody listens to the report. People read newspapers and books placed on their laps, they doze, or whisper among themselves . . . Even if you want to take in the report, it is very difficult to do so, since it is written in such turgid, bureaucratic jargon that you begin to nod off after the first few sentences. The speaker may make mistakes, or he might say the same thing twice, but no one pays any attention.

After the report, the speeches begin. Here again nobody listens, unless the speaker, on his own initiative, strays from the main thrust of the meeting and begins to talk about matters of topical interest at work. At this point the audience might begin to wake up a little. But this is unusual. Generally the audience do not listen, but time the speaker by looking at their watches. The speeches over, the previously prepared draft resolutions to be passed by the meeting are heard, and then they are voted upon. I cannot recall even one occasion on which a debate took place on the draft resolutions of a meeting. Everything was unanimous.

With this the meeting ends. Another month of Party time has been served.

Ambassador Vinogradov was a member of the embassy's Party organization, and according to the rules he should have attended every meeting. But in reality this did not happen. He showed up two or three times a year, and only when he wanted to say something, although his regular attendance was precisely recorded on all the documents. The representative of the Party Central Committee did likewise. This gave rise to open dissatisfaction in the embassy, particularly among KGB and GRU officers, who were compelled to sit through these meetings. We knew that the ambassador 'couldn't stand that rubber-stamping nonsense', but others were not overjoyed about it either. It was simply that by everything he did, the ambassador felt compelled to prove that he was above the rest.

For the same reason, Vinogradov fixed himself up with private film shows in the embassy cinema. All new films that arrived from the Soviet Union were shown to him first, and only then to all the others. Once, after he and the Central Committee representative had seen the film *Pena* ('Foam') he decided to ban it from general viewing. This was the first film to touch on the subject of corruption at the top, where the ambassador belonged. But the film had been passed by the official Soviet censorship. A scandal flared up which began to spread beyond the confines of the embassy. Vinogradov was compelled reluctantly to back down.

I keep saying, 'We knew ... from information reaching us ... ' The reader may wonder where this information was coming from.

Information about what is going on in the Soviet community reaches the KGB Residency from agents among Soviet citizens, or more simply from informers. They are popularly known as 'knockers' – those who knock at the KGB officer's door in order to hand in a denunciation. In the KGB they are also referred to as 'the striped ones', because their personal files, which are kept in Moscow, are marked with a bright red stripe. For the sake of clarity we shall simply call them informers.

An anecdote used to go the rounds, and probably still does, in the internal departments of the KGB, to the effect that the entire population of the city of Odessa was divided into 'active agents, agents on ice, and candidates for recruitment'. I do not know about the population of Odessa, but such a description could be quite fairly applied to the Soviet State machine, which swarms with KGB informers. The informer system has existed throughout history and in every country, but it certainly never reached such proportions anywhere as it did in Stalin's time, when it was necessary to inform in order to survive in the State machine. So the informers generally survived. After Stalin died, the Party became the master, with full power, and forbade the KGB to recruit informers from among full-time Party workers and their families. Otherwise, everything remained as before, except that the compulsion to collaborate was outlawed. But only the heads of the Party and KGB knew that this was the case, and naturally the broad strata of society were not told about these changes. This belief was reinforced by the self-inflicted paranoia of the people, and by the fact that, particularly in the State apparatus, refusal to cooperate with the KGB could still entail considerable trouble. That is how things were at the end of the Seventies.

I recall an interesting conversation with a fairly highly placed official in the Foreign Ministry just before graduating from University. Unaware that I was going to work for the KGB, he gave me some friendly advice.

'When you go abroad, or perhaps even before, the KGB will be bound to approach you and suggest collaboration. Don't even think of refusing! They can ruin your whole life and career. Just agree, and your life will be much more peaceful. You don't need to be active. Just sit and wait until they ask you. You can then pretend that you don't know anything. But collaborating has its advantages. If you get into any trouble, they'll pull you out of it. And they can also help your career.'

This, as I was to find out later in the embassy, was the typical philosophy held by most Foreign Ministry officials. It can be said for certain that all such officials have at one time or another been KGB informers. The only exceptions are members of the Central Committee and their children. The recruitment of Foreign Ministry officials presents no great difficulty. Self-hypnotized by fear before the KGB, they do not refuse.

In 1978, out of twenty-three straight diplomats in the Soviet embassy in Tehran, twenty were KGB informers. The exceptions were Vinogradov the ambassador, who was a member of the Central Committee, Amangaliev, the Central Committee representative, and Fenopetov, a second secretary who was married to the daughter of a Central Committee member. All the straight technical officials in the embassy, the cipher clerks and the drivers were also informers. Of course, these people had not been recruited in the embassy but a considerable time before, many perhaps while they were still in college. Certainly nobody twisted their arms or forced them into it. They were pushed into collaborating by fear of the KGB, by the anticipation of an easy career, or simply by the enjoyment of a feeling of superiority over others, though this latter category was not quite so simple when almost all the informer's colleagues were themselves informers.

Informers who are used to obtain information on the Soviet community are run by officers of the CI line and by the embassy security officer. The KGB tries not to blow its own informers, so that among those who are straight, no one knows for sure who is a knocker and who is not. In a situation like this everybody suspects everyone else. Such a state of affairs is particularly helpful to the embassy security officer. If some incident arises, he can obtain an exact picture of what occurred from conversing with several informers, which enables him not only to discard inventions and guesswork but also to see whether a source is telling the truth about what has happened.

If an informer suddenly declines to collaborate, no special pressure is brought to bear. When Yarikov, a third secretary in our embassy, was acting as an informer, he did not get on with Denisov, the head of the CI line, who maintained contact with him. Yarikov refused to collaborate, and when Denisov tried to pressurize him, he threatened to report everything to the ambassador, and complain against the KGB. The head of the CI line was forced to climb down, since the ambassador hated the KGB and the Residency had no desire to clash with him over a minor matter. The CI line lost the agent, while Yarikov was simply left in peace, and this incident did not affect his career.

If the informer rises high up the promotional ladder, then it is entirely up to him whether he continues. Evgeni Ostrovenko had been an informer since his student days, but when he attained the rank of minister counsellor the resident decided to consult him about his future collaboration.

It is known that informants constantly worry about how the KGB regards them, whether it considers them indispensable helpers, as they are told at meetings by their officers, or . . . The truth is that the KGB's attitude to informers is in most cases negative, and it is even contemptuous towards the specially zealous. Where and when have informers ever been respected, and by whom? But if the tasks set by the Party were to be achieved, they could not be done without.

Even though most straight people maintain contact with the KGB, they cannot shake off their own paranoia about the organization. Not just in Tehran, but throughout the world, straight Soviet diplomats believe that the KGB's main task is to keep them under surveillance. They believe that the KGB taps their telephones, bugs their flats, and tails them in town, even using foreign agents to do so. In our embassy in Tehran, its straight members believed that Mars and Impulse, the two radio interception posts, did nothing but listen in to their telephones. If a straight diplomat bumped into a KGB officer in town, he would assume that he was under surveillance.

In fact nothing of the kind used to happen. The embassy had an automatic internal telephone communication system. Its central control box was in the embassy cellar, and it was serviced by a straight engineer. As far as I know, the Residency had never shown the slightest interest in this control box. One could not even consider the installation of microphones in Soviets' flats. It was simply forbidden. And why complicate matters by going to such lengths when straight informers tell everything about each other, and the KGB knows perfectly well who said what about whom, who bought and who sold, who is sleeping with whom, who has stolen what and hidden it where, what the ambassador is thinking, and what he is writing to Moscow in his secret dispatches.

But straight diplomats certainly do not have a monopoly in paranoia about the KGB. The embassy houses yet another organization which can outdo the straight diplomats in this. It is the Residency of the Chief Intelligence Directorate of the General Staff of the Soviet Army, GRU for short.

Of the Tehran embassy's fifty diplomats, twenty-three were straight, fifteen were KGB and twelve GRU. Do not assume that the GRU ranked as poor relations. There was a far larger number of officers attached to the trade delegation. The GRU deals with the collection of military intelligence of all categories, political, economic and technological.

A great deal has been written about the GRU in the West in recent years, both by Western researchers and by former GRU officers. Two themes run through all this information. The first is that the GRU is a super-secret, exceptionally successful intelligence service with an iron discipline and successfully staged operations in all parts of the world. Its steely-eyed, robotic officers are fanatically devoted to the cause of communism, every second one having SPETSNAZ training. The second theme, constantly harped upon, concerns the enmity that rages between the GRU and the KGB in the triangle of power whose three sides are the Party, the KGB and the GRU.

On the first point I can only say that, having worked for five years in one embassy along with many GRU officers, I never noticed any among them with Superman qualities. They were ordinary fellows with the shortcomings inherent in any Soviet man. Their Residency had everything – drunkenness, corruption, loose living, and more than enough operational failures. All in all, right in the Soviet vein.

Yes, enmity exists, but it is unilateral. The GRU hates the KGB. The KGB has no similar feeling towards its 'distant neighbours', as the GRU is code-named in KGB documents. The KGB adopts a condescending attitude to the GRU, and there is no more to it than that. It is roughly as an older man might relate to a young one of fiery temperament who still has much to learn. The theory current in the GRU about the triangle of power is quite naïve, because it presents KGB and GRU as 'two equal independent forces in relation to the Party'. According to this theory, it is the Party that stands at the summit of power, skilfully manoeuvring between the KGB and the GRU. The Party forbids the KGB to interfere in the affairs of the GRU, and vice versa. All KGB activity against the GRU is nothing but a violation of Party directives and confirms the 'brutal face of the

KGB'. Responsible officials in the Central Committee in Moscow allegedly tell GRU officers when they meet them that from the moment they join the GRU they pass outside KGB jurisdiction, that the KGB has no right to arrest or interrogate them, and that they must report all contacts with the KGB to their leaders, who in their turn will report these provocations to the Central Committee.

I have no doubt that something of this kind is said to GRU officers. But this is an excellent example of how the Party leadership dupes the hot-heads among our military intelligence officers, palming them off with hare-brained theories. In fact, something quite different goes on. The KGB, which is officially the 'sword and shield and armed detachment of the Party', is the obedient servant of its masters. Everything the KGB does is done solely on the instructions of the Party. That is why all the KGB chairmen are appointed from the ranks of the professional Party officials. Their own interests do not lie with the KGB. They only watch over the Party's interests.

The Party has decreed that the Army, including the GRU, must not have a security organization of its own. The Third Chief Directorate of the KGB is responsible for security in that area. According to the Central Committee's wish, the GRU is forbidden to recruit agents from among Soviet citizens. According to the Central Committee's instructions, the KGB recruits informers from among GRU officers, but not for reasons of some far-fetched rivalry.

KGB total obedience to the Party is borne out by many specific examples. At the end of the Fifties, Khrushchev, intending to improve relations with China, ordered the KGB to hand over all the agents it had in China to the Chinese authorities. This order was unquestioningly carried out. As a result of this 'act of friendship', the whole of the intelligence potential on China was lost, but this was not the point. In the mid-1970s, Brezhnev ordered the KGB to keep clear of the militia, and removed the Ministry of the Interior from all KGB secret service control. What happened as a result has already been discussed. But for some reason or other, the KGB was not given similar instructions regarding the GRU. Consequently the Central Committee benefits from the present position in which the Army, including the GRU, is under full control, while all the resulting anger and dissatisfaction is directed against the KGB. 'Long live the wise policy of the Central Committee of the Communist Party of the Soviet Union.'

In the Soviet embassy in Tehran, the GRU Residency was located on the sixth floor of the administration building. It occupied the whole floor, except for the two rooms that accommodated the KGB's Mars and Impulse radio interception posts. These posts had been placed there for reasons of pure practical convenience, in order to be nearer to the necessary aerials on the roof. The GRU officers were convinced however that both eavesdropping and surveillance were being mounted against them from these posts. They knew of course what the main purpose was of both Mars and Impulse. They had similar posts themselves. But that did not matter. Just like the straight people, they believed that the KGB was spying on them through 'holes in walls and was eavesdropping with microphones'. We found out that they sometimes conversed in their offices in cautious whispers, or even passed each other notes, so as not to be overheard.

They also staged searches for KGB listening devices. Vladimir Plakhti, the GRU resident, once went for our resident, accusing the KGB of tapping a telephone in his office. It so happened that one of his zealous young telephone engineers had checked his boss's telephone and discovered an unusual aperture, with a fine small grid stuck over it, in the microphone section of the instrument. The same thing was discovered in other GRU telephones. There was a scandal. Plakhti threatened to report this 'illegality' to Moscow. Our resident, who quite honestly did not understand what Plakhti was talking about, mollified him by promising to look into the matter. He called in our technical specialist and demanded an explanation. And this is what transpired. All the telephones of the embassy's internal system had recently been replaced. Security rules laid down that new telephone instruments had always to be supplied from the Soviet Union, and this was what had happened. All these instruments had the same sinister apertures. They were part of a new design.

When he learnt of this, our resident had a hearty laugh, invited the GRU resident into his office and showed him his own telephone, which had the same aperture. Plakhti was shown other telephones in the Residency as well. The GRU's blunder was obvious and it placed them in an embarrassing position. But the KGB Residency had no wish to make capital out of the incident. It had once again demonstrated the GRU's naivety. If they had stopped to think, it would have become quite clear that there would be no point in tapping the telephone of even their resident. As a professional and highly experienced intelligence officer, he would only use the telephone to summon this or the other officer to see him, and that was all. So what was there to listen to? But on this occasion the GRU resident had been guided, not by logic, but by blind hatred and a desire to catch the KGB red-handed.

The KGB however had no need to use either surveillance or eavesdropping devices. We knew everything that went on in the GRU Residency from informers in their ranks who were working for the KGB. There were not as many of them as there were among the straight diplomats, but there were quite enough. At one time our counter-intelligence even had access to their secret documents.

The KGB recruits agents in the GRU in various stages. Some are recruited by the Third Chief Directorate of the KGB (military counter-intelligence) even before they join the GRU, while they are still serving with the forces. Others are recruited in Moscow while they are working there in their cover establishments. A third category is recruited while serving in GRU residencies abroad. GRU officers may have various motives for collaborating with the KGB, but one more prevalent than all the others was the belief that the KGB could stop them travelling abroad by making them 'un-postable'. There was even a tale circulating among them that there existed a large black rubber stamp bearing the word 'un-postable' which was stamped on the cover of a GRU officer's personal record in the event of his coming into conflict with the KGB.

The representation of Aeroflot, the Soviet airline company, is in the gift of the GRU. Aeroflot's representation in Tehran was headed by a GRU officer named Nikolai Demidenko. His Ukrainian face with its wide cheek-bones and screwed up eyes always bore a malicious expression. He was already on his third tour of duty in Iran, and he felt quite sure of himself, but this assurance did not spring from any particular successes in his operational work. We knew that he was not active in the GRU Residency, and his post, in practical terms, was looked upon as a vacant slot. He drew his confidence from his financial position and from his sense of utter impunity, although there was plenty to punish him for.

Aeroflot worked with Iran Air, the Iranian airlines company. Two of their representatives sat in Aeroflot, where they were responsible for direct sales of tickets and payments from passengers. At that time there were many Europeans and Americans working in Iran who preferred to travel on leave by transiting the Soviet Union. There were two reasons for this. First, Aeroflot tickets were much cheaper than those of other airlines. Second, it afforded an opportunity to visit the Soviet Union, which for them was a mysterious country. Here was a situation which had potential for making money. It worked in this way. An Aeroflot aircraft ticket to make a flight in transit to Europe costs, let us say, $250. The same journey costs $750 travelling with a Western airline. Aeroflot used to sell these tickets to unsuspecting foreigners for $500, thus making a profit of $250 on the sale of every ticket. And these tickets were sold in their hundreds. Payments were in cash only. The profits were split between the two Iranians and Demidenko. Two other Soviet citizens worked in Aeroflot in addition to Demidenko, and this whole racket took place before their eyes. They tried to talk with Demidenko, but he simply threatened to get even if they revealed what was going on, and they kept silent.

Demidenko was involved in falsifying his representational expenses. I myself was once witness to this in Mehrabad Airport, where I often used to go on consular business. The aeroplane was late and Demidenko bought drinks for some of the passengers in the airport bar. When they gave him the bill, before he signed it Demidenko increased the sum shown by writing in his own hand the figure 3 in front of the total shown. The result was that, if $35 had in fact been spent, Demidenko's account, after amendment, was for $335. Again this is only an isolated incident directly observed by an uninvolved person, yet things like this were going on all the time. Straight people were afraid to make official complaints against Demidenko because they thought that he was KGB. It turned out that he himself had put this rumour about. But of course it was not so far from the truth. Demidenko had been an agent (informer) of the KGB throughout his GRU career.

The Residency finally obtained documentary material on Demidenko, proving his involvement in all these financial swindles, and sent it to the Centre. There was no reaction whatever. It cannot be ruled out that he had support in the Central Committee. On his income, he could afford it. After they saw that Demidenko continued unpunished in his job, the straight people refused to talk with us. The Iranians who were mixed up in the ticket racket were assuredly SAVAK agents, which meant that SAVAK knew everything about it. Nor was Demidenko an exceptional example in the GRU.

CHAPTER 9

Fortunately I did not have any Residency informers to run from among Soviet citizens, and nothing which has been catalogued above had any direct effect on my morale. We in the Residency always referred to working with informers as washing dirty linen, and no one would do it willingly. The CI line did the job. The N line had no need for informers, so I had a wonderful opportunity to do purely intelligence work.

Here I focused my attention on the consular corps in Tehran. First, it enabled me to fulfil one of the main requirements in my brief, namely to cultivate and recruit consular corps colleagues from the capitalist countries, with the aim of obtaining authentic documents for our illegals. Second, it gave me the chance to build up the cover, and the cover story, for my relationship with Ram, my only agent, who was consul in the Afghan embassy.

Work in the diplomatic and consular corps might appear to be among the easiest to perform. And so on the whole it is. But two quite considerable difficulties exist here for Soviets. The first is a total ignorance of etiquette and accepted social manners, for until quite recently such things were regarded in the Soviet Union as relics of capitalism. This makes our people abroad awkward and constrained, and sometimes gives them an inferiority complex, and as a result they prefer to avoid being diplomatically active. The second difficulty is the conversational barrier. I am not referring to ignorance of foreign languages. These our diplomats and intelligence officers speak quite well. But Soviet people are not used to expressing their thoughts directly and openly. That is the fault of the Soviet system, which has compelled the Soviet citizen to think one thing and say something completely different, and even then with circumspection.

When they converse on political subjects, Soviet diplomats follow the national convention and communicate with hints, innuendoes and winks. The same thing happens in conversations with foreigners. Before answering a foreign diplomat's straight question, let us say on the state of dissidents in the Soviet Union, this is what will run through the mind of a Soviet diplomat: 'I'm not going to tell you what I really think. Suppose you're KGB, and they've sent you to me specially? Or if not, what if you take it into your head to quote me to my ambassador? On the other hand I can't bring myself to repeat the rubbish in our rubber-stamp press. Therefore it's better to make a joke of it.' So the Soviet diplomat makes his joke, with a nudge and a wink.

It was slightly easier in this scheme of things for KGB intelligence officers. We at least knew that no one was putting us through any tests, and that a foreigner would not go running to report our conversation either to the KGB or the ambassador. In the field of manners and etiquette, it was every man for himself. These subjects were not taught in the intelligence school.

In the first two months, I had made around seventeen personal consular contacts, which were developing quite well. According to standing orders, every foreigner who comes into contact with a KGB intelligence officer has to be traced in the Centre's records. In practice it is only those foreigners who are of operational interest who are traced in this way. The Centre sends a minimum of basic data on them, and if any information is held in 'T' Directorate records, that will be sent to the Residency. Tracing takes quite a long time, since everything is done by hand in the Centre. There are no computers: reports are kept on microfiches. The speed of the tracing also depends on the efficiency of the officer who handles it. Generally speaking, the reply to a telegraphic trace takes about three or four weeks to reach the Residency, and that is still quite quick. As a result of the tracing, established foreign intelligence officers emerge from among the contacts. The N line does not entrust the identities of illegals to these people. The remainder are studied as targets for possible recruitment. Usually, if two or three candidates are left in the net when this fishing is over, then you may count yourself lucky.

The moment then arrived for my first solo meeting with the agent 'Ram'. By this time I had got to know the city well enough to be able to drive along the surveillance checking route on my own. Setting up the meeting was quite a complex process.

The plan for organizing the meeting is drawn up by the intelligence officer the day before the operation is to take place, and it looks like this:

Plan for Setting Up Meeting
with Agent Ram

1.	Date of Meeting	31 July 1977.
2.	Time of Meeting	12.30–14.30.
3.	Place of Meeting	Maxim's Restaurant, Zohre Street.
4.	Car	Peugeot 504.
5.	Driver	Comrade Saidov (if an operational driver is to be used, indicate his alias).
6.	Technical safeguards	The Impulse post: radio receiver in the car (the receiver has been adapted for listening in to external surveillance frequencies and for receiving the danger signal from the Residency) and a Sony pocket receiver (also equipped for receiving the danger signal when on foot).
7.	Danger signal	– – – ·· (Morse signal).
8.	Cover story for trip	Visiting bookshops.
9.	Route	Comrade Saidov will drive out of the embassy on his own at 9.30, taking the following route: (here follows a detailed description giving the names of the streets which the operational officer has to follow, and indications of times and places of stops and visits to shops).

10. Should hostile surveillance be spotted before the meeting takes place, the operational officer will act out his cover story and then return to the embassy.

11. Return to the embassy by 15.30. (Here all possible delays must be allowed for, since after this time the alarm will be raised in the Residency and steps taken to find the missing officer.)

12. Check-point. (The exact place and time are given at which the intelligence officer will appear there.) The check-point is fixed at a place not far from the area where the meeting is to take place. It is to be a physical version of the danger signal. In the event of the Impulse post discovering surveillance, the operator will send the tonal signal, and at

the same time send to the check-point a stand-by intelligence officer, who will park his car in a fixed place and at a fixed time. If for any reason the intelligence officer running the operation has not received the radio danger signal, he will clearly see the back-up version as he passes the check-point.

The intelligence officer then signs the plan for the meeting in his operational alias and shows it to the operator of the Impulse post. Agreeing the plan with the Impulse post operator, especially with our Kirichenko, was always a difficult stage to pass through. Knowing what was going on in town from his radio interceptions, he could insist on making changes. This usually earned him a mouthful of abuse from the operational officers, because they then had to change parts of the surveillance checking routes, and not everybody could do this easily. Intelligence officers in the Residency who knew the town well could be counted on the fingers of one hand. Kirichenko's demands boiled down to this: don't mount operations in the same place; don't use the same surveillance checking routes several times; and when selecting places for operations and surveillance checking routes, follow the elementary principles of security – that is, don't drive past places which are guarded, and don't have meetings in restaurants which are frequented by Soviet citizens. But what this demanded was a good operational knowledge of the city. Sometimes the route had to be changed simply because a SAVAK team carrying out surveillance on a target who had nothing to do with us would start work on the day of the operation in one of the sectors where it was to take place.

After sharpening up the details, the Impulse operator would then sign the operational plan and return it to the intelligence officer.

The next step is to meet the technical expert who must prepare all the necessary equipment in case it will have to be used. He has to tune the car's receiver to the external surveillance frequencies, and enable it to receive the danger signal; prepare the pocket radio interception receiver; and prepare the special tape machine for recording conversations. Generally speaking, the intelligence officer can festoon himself with these toys if he wants to. In practice, however, he dislikes using operational technical equipment, for reasons of security. If, for example, officer and agent are arrested during a meeting, operational equipment like a special tape recorder is direct evidence that espionage activity is taking place, and it is very hard to get clear. Or take the case in which by sheer chance the intelligence officer is picked up by the police as he goes to or returns from a meeting: here again operational technical equipment can be incriminating. Then, again, if he has to wear, for example, a concealed tape recorder for taping conversations, the officer has to run a network of wires inside his shirt, and make holes in the pockets of his trousers where he keeps the remote control. This is not particularly popular with intelligence officers. In practice, therefore, they prefer to use only a minimum of equipment.

The technical expert also puts his signature on the meeting plan.

The next person to sign the plan is the officer who will man the check-point. This was never a very easy matter in our Residency. It was up to the case officer to find someone to man the check-point, and as a rule, nobody wanted to spend time on someone else's operations. What was more, the check-point officer had to know the town well, so that he could quickly find the exact position of the check-point, and we did not shine at this.

Thereafter the plan is signed by the head of the line to which the officer running the operation belongs. Usually at this point they discuss not only the security plan, but also the planned conduct of the meeting. This includes all details of the contact, and the projected course of the conversation with the agent.

The head of the CI line, who is in effect responsible for the security of all Residency operations, is next to sign the plan. Here the Tehran Residency had a built-in handicap. Yuri Denisov, the head of the CI line, was no expert on Iran. He did not speak Farsi, and knew next to nothing of local traditions and conditions, and absolutely nothing about the city in the operational context. All this meant that to discuss an operational plan with him was for all practical purposes useless, and in fact worse than useless. He could make no practical or constructive observations about the route, so he concentrated on petty details or put forward quite unacceptable proposals. He was also a pathologically malicious and stubborn man, and discussions of the plan usually ended up in a slanging match. Finally, after wasting a vast amount of nervous energy, Denisov would sign the plan. It seemed to us that all these confrontations with people gave him a charge of energy. In fact he was simply afraid of accepting the responsibility for operations, and was unable to make any contribution to organizing their operational security.

The last stage of this 'progress through Purgatory' is the resident. It must be noted here that the resident does not usually approve all operations personally, but only those in which especially important agents and illegals are involved. In the other cases, approval may be finalized at the level of the head of the CI line. This was not possible in the Tehran Residency for the reasons described, so the resident had to sign the plans of virtually all operations.

When all the signatures have been collected, the intelligence officer hands over the operational plan to the operator of the Impulse post.

It takes at least half a working day to pass through all this bureaucratic machinery. But there is no way of circumventing it. All these signatures are needed so that, in the event of the operation going wrong, no one can say that he did not know, or that nobody warned him.

On the day of the operation, the operational officer must look in on the Impulse post and find out about any late changes in the agent-running and operational conditions in the city. Only after doing so does he leave for the meeting. The meeting may be postponed at the last minute if for instance the operator should discover surveillance activity in the area where the rendezvous is to be held, irrespective of its target. Nobody needs risks on those occasions. It is better to lose one piece of intelligence than its source.

Nothing like that happened when I had my first meeting with 'Ram', and I set off happily on the route. When I had assured myself that I had no tail following me, and after passing the check-point, I came to the quarter where the meeting would take place. I left my car quite some way from the meeting place for one simple reason. The number-plate revealed that the car belonged to the Soviet embassy.

When I came to the meeting place, all my nerves were on edge. It was a quiet street with private houses on each side, and I had to hang around as though rooted to the spot. It seemed to me that all the passers-by were giving me suspicious looks, knowing full well that I was awaiting a meeting with my secret agent.

The appointed time of the meeting passed, and my feeling of paranoia gave way to one of unease. 'Ram' had not appeared. If I complied with the rules, I should wait no more than ten minutes for the agent. However, because of that voice that will be familiar to any intelligence officer, which says, 'Just a little longer, for he'll turn up the minute I leave', I hung about there for forty minutes. 'Ram' did not come. My disappointment was indescribable. All that effort and excitement, and all in vain. But one had to get used to such things. Failure to turn up for meetings occurs fairly often in intelligence work.

'Ram' did not appear at the emergency meeting one week later, nor at the second emergency meeting either. I knew for certain from my Afghan transit travellers that he was alive and well, so I was compelled to make contact on the diplomatic level, by paying him a visit in the embassy. Only after that did our meetings become fairly regular.

The nervous strain of preparing for a meeting, the tension induced on driving along the surveillance checking route, and the stress engendered at a meeting make themselves felt. Fatigue sets in after returning to the embassy. They told us 'unofficially' during lectures at School 101 that in order to dispel the nervous tension that followed an operation it was essential to relax, and that vodka or whisky provided the only natural means of doing so. They did warn against making this method into a habit, but this is precisely what happened in our Residency. Drinks after every operation were traditional. After a meeting, everybody who had taken part in it – the case officer himself, the stand-by officer, the Impulse post operator, the operational driver, the heads of the lines and the resident – all went to the garage. In that section of the garage which belonged to the KGB, there was a back room without windows where the Residency's liquor store was kept.

Like all the other organizations represented in the embassy, the KGB Residency bought all its drinks from the list of the Danish firm Ostermann and Petersen. Officially, these drinks should have been used for operational needs, such as presents for agents and contacts. However they were used also to meet the needs of the operational staff. (Only the resident was allowed to hand out spirits, and it must be said in fairness that with the sole exception of those post-operational visits to the garage, it was practically impossible to obtain the resident's permission to buy spirits from the Residency reserves. All present got through one or two bottles of vodka, which were paid for by the officer who had run the operation. Then everybody went home. For some it was only an episode, for others it was everyday practice. Sometimes after the garage, people would set off for town and spend the rest of the evening sitting in a restaurant. Sometimes they would invite straight people to accompany them, naturally at the expense of the KGB.

Such behaviour on the part of officers of the KGB Residency was, and most likely still is, the reason why many people believe that KGB officers are paid more, and therefore can afford this sort of lifestyle. Unfortunately I have to disappoint the proponents of this theory. KGB officers abroad are paid in foreign currency according to their diplomatic rank, in exactly the same way as the straight diplomats. Since however most KGB officers hold the lowest diplomatic posts, a system of levelling up exists in KGB residencies. Under this system, an officer who, let us say, holds the rank of attaché, has his salary levelled up to that of a second secretary, and is paid the difference in money from the Residency accounts. This is a perfectly fair system, since normal promotion for KGB officers in diplomatic posts abroad scarcely exists. My predecessor spent four years in Tehran, and was still an attaché at the end of this period.

Sixty per cent of the earnings of all Soviet citizens working abroad is retained in Soviet currency, and the money paid into their personal accounts in Moscow. The KGB of course wins here, since the KGB officer's pay is double that of Foreign Ministry officials. This however in no way allows KGB officers to feel themselves the least bit more free in financial matters. A system of operational expenses exists in KGB residencies abroad. All expenses incurred on reconnoitring the city, the selection of routes, the setting up and holding of meetings with agents and targets for cultivation, and the payment of bonuses, come under operational expenditure. Bankers' cheques and credit cards were not popular in Iran, so ready cash was used to make all payments. That being so, at the beginning of every month intelligence officers would draw from Residency accounts what in their judgement was the amount they would need for their operational expenditure. They had to account for this money at the end of the month, by filling up a special form on which they had to itemize all money spent. Receipts and accounts might be attached, but were usually displaced by the formula 'receipt or account not taken for operational reasons'.

These expenses are approved by the resident, after which the Centre passes them without question. Given such circumstances, it is not at all difficult for an officer to inflate his real expenses, and this is common practice throughout the Residencies. No vast expenditure is covered in this way, however, and in comparison with what our Party bosses do, these are mere trivialities. But, for example, when we received and entertained visitors from the Centre, who naturally do not spend their own money, the whole cost fell on the shoulders of the officers whom they were visiting. After these inspecting visitors had gone, the costs were shared between the officers and then charged up to operations.

At the end of 1977, operations were being mounted quite frequently by the Residency, such as meetings with agents and targets of cultivation, and operations on behalf of the Centre. Centre operations included posting letters, which had been prepared in Moscow, to Iranian leaders. These letters were of course unofficial. They were written in Farsi by the Active Measures Service − Service 'A' − of the First Chief Directorate, and then sent anonymously by the Residency to members of the Iranian government, to the Shah and to SAVAK. The content of the letters was unknown to us, but no doubt they must have contained something which would undermine the United States' position in Iran, destabilize the Shah's regime, undermine SAVAK's position, and so on.

In KGB language, these operations were referred to as 'letter posting' and our Residency attached great importance to them. At that time they were being undertaken frequently, and the letters were sent in batches. The resident roped in most of our officers for the job, and I too had to take part. These operations are set up just like any other, with a plan, a surveillance checking route and the observation of all security measures. Post-boxes are selected in advance in various parts of the city − one post-box, one letter. The officer posting a letter must wear gloves, so as not to leave his fingerprints on the envelope. The entire operation is carried out with such care that there is not one Soviet fingerprint either on the envelope or the letter.

At the beginning of September 1977, I was involved for three days in a PI line operation. My task included the manning of a temporary Impulse post which we had deployed to Zargande in case it should be needed there for operations to be mounted in the northern parts of Tehran. Something was slightly out of gear with the PI line, so they were using the fall-back variants. On the third day, I was on duty in Zargande along with Viktor Kazakov, a PI line officer. We were listening in to the frequencies used by SAVAK surveillance. Everything was proceeding boringly as usual. We had to sit through the three hours allocated to the operation, after which we were to be stood down by a coded signal from the embassy that the operation had been concluded.

In the evening, somewhere close to the time when the operation was due to begin, traffic suddenly started up on those SAVAK radio frequencies that we were monitoring. We snatched up our pencils and the tape machine began to record. We quickly realized that something unusual was happening. The SAVAK surveillance personnel were speaking in clear, and not in their usual veiled sentences. But the most interesting thing of all was that this conversation was completely personal. Two SAVAK officers were discussing the difficulties of their work, lack of money, and the fact that one of the American advisers, a man called Long, was constantly complaining about them to their chiefs, this was landing them in trouble. We could hardly believe our ears, and scarcely managed to record it all. The conversation continued for about thirty minutes, after which it ended as though it had never happened. Total silence returned. Nothing else went out over the air waves.

We were excited. Just think, we had succeeded in recording an expression of dissatisfaction in the ranks of SAVAK. But soon our excitement began to change to something else. An hour had passed by since the operation had ended, but we had not received any recall signal from the embassy. Another hour went by, and then another. By then it was 11 p.m. and we had already begun to make plans to take revenge on whoever forgot to ring Zargande and give us the signal to stand down. We could not ring the embassy ourselves, since that would have been a breach of security rules. Finally, at 11.30 p.m. we received the long-awaited signal and set off for the embassy.

We almost burst into the resident's office, ready to complain, but there was something wrong. In the office were Kazankin, the head of the PI line, who had been acting resident since Kostromin left, and Denisov, the head of the CI line. The room was so smoky that you could have cut the air with a knife. We asked what had happened. Denisov answered that it had been nothing in particular, and we might as well go home. But we were not satisfied with such an answer, and we had no intention of leaving. We wanted to know what had confined us all evening in a cramped stuffy room. And the answer came.

'There was an arrest during the operation,' Kazankin said in a flat voice. 'Boris Kabanov and the agent 'Man' were arrested by SAVAK. Rassadin [the security officer] has gone to the Foreign Ministry to pick up Kabanov and bring him back to the embassy. The Iranians can't detain him as he's a diplomat.'

This news was stunning. I knew nothing at all at that moment about the agent 'Man', but Boris Kabanov's arrest really flabbergasted me. Kabanov was a PI line officer, and his cover was head of the consular department in the embassy. Everybody's favourite, with a sense of humour, good-natured, quiet, always smiling, always ready to help, conscientious, industrious . . . and now he had been arrested. Instead of just anybody, they had picked the best one of all. But that is how it goes with intelligence work. The officer who works hardest and is most active is the one who gets caught. Or to paraphrase the well-known saying, 'He who does nothing never gets caught.'

Soon Kabanov and Rassadin, back from the Iranian Foreign Ministry, came into the office. Boris looked calm, but he was slightly pale. There was a bloodstain on the right side of his shirt front.

The following picture emerged from what Kabanov said and from what transpired later.

Contact with 'Man' was maintained through the Close Information Link system, which was used both to receive intelligence and to transmit signals. This line consisted of an ordinary medium-sized transistor radio tape recorder, which had been adapted by KGB experts both to receive and transmit information. A few days before, a signal had been received at our end of the line from 'Man', calling urgently for a meeting. Kabanov went to the rendezvous two days running, but there was nobody there. Nevertheless the signal calling for an urgent meeting kept on registering at our end of the line. I myself had heard Kabanov, before he went out on the final occasion, telling Kazankin that he smelt a rat. Kazankin only brushed these suspicions aside, saying that the signal had most probably been caused by a technical fault. He had no time for discussion, as he was hurrying off to a diplomatic reception in our embassy.

On that final occasion Kabanov, accompanied as usual by Titkin the operational driver, drove along the surveillance checking route and arrived at the scene of the operation. Their car was parked in the appointed place and Kabanov began to flick the switches of the Close Information Link system in a routine attempt to receive information from 'Man'. Suddenly a light vehicle cut in front of them, stopped with a screech of brakes, then reversed and hit the front bumper of Kabanov's car. At that same instant, a second vehicle ran into the rear of the Mercedes, while a third SAVAK car pulled in to block it from the left. On the right of our car there was an irrigation canal which firmly blocked the way. The blockade was complete.

SAVAK men jumped out of their vehicles and surrounded Kabanov's car, their pistols drawn. One of them ordered our officers out of the car. At this Kabanov lowered his window slightly and poked out his diplomatic card, thereby declaring his immunity. This did not satisfy the Iranians. With an expert kick, one of them smashed the back right-hand window of the car and opened the door. Against all the rules of diplomatic immunity, our officers were dragged from their car by rabid SAVAK officers. Kabanov was injured by the glass, now strewn all over the car. Following standing orders, our officers offered no resistance. They were bundled into the SAVAK vehicle and taken – without any questions being asked – to the Iranian Foreign Ministry building. Foreign Ministry officials rang the embassy, offered no explanations, but ordered us to come and collect our officers.

I was unable to sleep that night. It is one thing to read about such happenings in the newspapers, but quite another to experience them close at hand. But the most interesting part was yet to come.

Shortly afterwards, a representative of the Soviet embassy was summoned to the Iranian Foreign Ministry. This, as usual, was Fedor Saulchenkov, the minister counsellor whom the Iranians mistook for the KGB resident. Kabanov and Titkin were declared guilty of espionage and required to leave the country in forty-eight hours. They did so of course.

This was followed by an event that marked a new stage in Soviet–Iranian relations. The Iranian authorities, no doubt under pressure from the Americans, headlined the affair in the press. There had been incidents previously where KGB or GRU officers were arrested with their agents, but everything had always passed off quietly. The Iranians would expel our people and there was never any publicity. This time everything had changed. All the Iranian national newspapers came out with banner headlines like 'KGB Agent Network Uncovered in Iran' and 'KGB Inside Iranian Leadership'.

Immediately after this débâcle, all officers in the Residency were warned that there must be no leak of information about it. But it was clear next day that everyone knew what had happened. The straight people looked past us when they met us, while GRU officers wore gloating smiles. Leaks of this kind usually happen through officers' wives, who share it with their girl-friends, who in turn pass them on to their girl-friends, and so the news spreads like wildfire.

All that was known to Residency officers not connected with the case was that the PI line had lost its best agent. We learnt of his identity only from what was published in the press. Later, the tongues of the PI line officers began to wag as well.

'Man' was a brigadier-general in the Iranian Army named Mogarebi. He had been a KGB agent for thirty years, ever since his recruitment as a young officer in 1947. He was regarded as the Residency's best agent, and provided really secret intelligence which was of great importance to the Soviet Union. In recent years he had risen high, and had been responsible for Iranian Army arms purchasing from the Americans and other countries of the West. As American activity in Iran had always been a matter of the utmost importance to the Soviet authorities, General Mogarebi's intelligence was invaluable. Apart from his direct access to secret information, he had innumerable connections in various spheres of Iranian life, including the court of the Shah, the government and SAVAK. Now he proved irreplaceable, for the hard fact was that Mogarebi was the Residency's only agent who supplied serious intelligence. The others could not be compared to him, and even they were few in number.

With the loss of Mogarebi, an intelligence vacuum developed in the Residency. What was more, he had got to know practically all of the PI line officers who had worked with him at different times during his long period of collaboration.

As always happens in these cases, an order came from the Centre to stop all the intelligence activity of the Residency, and to produce a damage assessment. A period of enforced rest began for the operational officers. Not that I noticed anybody objecting to it. Failures of this kind always backfire on the morale of the operational staff.

Publicity about the Mogarebi case grew into an international sensation in newspapers and magazines all over the world. In particular, the weekly magazines *Time* and *Newsweek* made great play with the story. At first we took every new item published as yet another blow from the enemy, but we came gradually to assess all that information with a more critical eye. The outcome was that the American special services, who were doubtless behind all the uproar, did an excellent advertising job for the KGB intelligence service.

Everything published proclaimed the incredible efficacy of KGB intelligence, saying that the KGB did not waste time on small fry, but only had agents among generals, members of government and senior officers of Western intelligence services, and ran them, at a conservative estimate, for decades, paying vast sums for their collaboration. If something did go wrong, the KGB made every effort to rescue its agents ... and much more in the same vein. As an example, the names of the British intelligence officers Kim Philby and George Blake were advanced, as well as that of Colonel Abel, the Soviet illegal who refused to reveal the names of 'hundreds of his agents' after he had been arrested in the United States.

We could not have wished for anything better. If there was anybody in any country still in two minds about whether to collaborate with the KGB, then this sort of information would encourage a positive decision. A great deal of money, absolute security, rescue in the event of arrest – what was there to think about? What was more, this type of advertisement could be used when insisting on the rigorous observation of security rules with active agents.

In reality however, all this information in the Western press made a mountain out of a molehill. Agents like Philby and Mogarebi were isolated individuals. They belonged to the generation before and during the Second World War, when the Soviet Union was regarded by the West as an ally in the struggle with Nazism, and communism enjoyed a certain popularity. The retrieval of agents was a complete invention. When an agent is arrested, the KGB simply abandons him, and questions about his 'rescue' just do not arise. Legally, an agent, being a foreigner, has no connection with the Soviet Union, which therefore cannot demand that he be freed or extradited, although promises of this kind are made to agents while the KGB is working with them. Illegals who are citizens of the Soviet Union, are another matter. In their cases, every effort is made to bring them back to the Soviet Union.

We discussed all these subjects in private conversations in the Residency, together with the possible causes of the Mogarebi débâcle. Various alternatives, including treachery, were put forward, but the most sober minds came to the conclusion that General Mogarebi had simply been burnt out. In the last year or eighteen months, we had involved him in operations every other week, which was totally against the rules for running agents. But the Centre was demanding intelligence and Mogarebi was its only source. Intelligence was obtained from him on the Close Information Link Line, and Mogarebi categorically refused to work from anywhere except his home. This meant that our car, equipped with Soviet embassy diplomatic number plates, drove into the area where the agent lived every two weeks. Why look any further for the reasons? Nowadays I expect they blame it all on me.

About six months later, Mogarebi was tried and sentenced to be shot. The sentence was only carried out in December 1978, two months before the Iranian Revolution. The Residency's suggestion that it should help the dead man's family was turned down by the Centre as too risky.

In the aftermath of the Mogarebi case, a new uproar began in the Iranian and world press about the espionage activities of the KGB. On this occasion, publicity was given to the damage done by Rabbani, the official in the Ministry of Education who was arrested in May 1977. I have written earlier about this agent, and here I can only say that the media proceeded in the same spirit, choking with hysteria over the triumphs and effectiveness of the KGB. But we in the Residency had already grown accustomed to this.

CHAPTER 10

The redesigning of the Residency had been planned for some time, but apparently it was brought forward as a result of the recent failures. In the autumn of 1977, there arrived in Tehran a team of builders whose orders were to renovate the premises that housed the KGB Residency, to secure the offices of the ambassador and his deputy with operational protection, and finally to renovate the Residency of the GRU. As they rebuilt the premises, they were also to check them for hostile eavesdropping devices. Checks of this kind are carried out only on the official premises occupied by the embassy, the residencies and the consulate. The private flats in town occupied by the Soviet staff were not checked. According to the KGB's security rules, we were instructed to take it for granted that our unprotected living quarters could have been bugged by some hostile special service, and never to allow any conversation to take place on an official matter. It was particularly forbidden to look for listening devices, but if one were to be discovered, we had to keep quiet about it, except for reporting it at once to the resident, as the situation might be of use for feeding disinformation to the enemy.

Since the building team belonged to the KGB Technical Directorate, their work naturally began with our Residency. Under the new plans, the general work room in the Residency was to disappear. Each line was given one room for its chief, and a second room for its officers. All the rooms were equipped with new vibrating metal frames as protection against eavesdropping, and this meant considerably reducing the dimensions of the rooms. Thus, only the resident's remained comparatively large. The other rooms were very small, but for that reason it was possible to work quietly in them.

With the flames of civil war in the Lebanon burning higher and higher, at this time the illegal Residency for the region was transferred from Beirut to Tehran.* As a result, the number of N line officers was increased to three, and Vladimir Golovanov, the chief of N line, was sent to us on transfer from Beirut. This suited me very well, since I preferred to work under an experienced officer, rather than beaver away at everything on my own. Golovanov had previously been in Iran on a posting between 1968 and 1973. He spoke Farsi and was a serious officer, although many people in the Centre considered him rather dull.

The transfer to Tehran of the regional illegal Residency meant that we should have had to deal with a large number of illegals who would in future visit Tehran from various countries in the region. But this was destined not to happen, since the first signs of the coming disorders were already emerging in Tehran. Opposition posters and inscriptions reading 'Death to the Shah' began to appear with increasing frequency on the walls. At that time these inscriptions were immediately wiped off by the police and the walls repainted, but the inscriptions went on appearing.

The opposition which was actively fighting for the overthrow of the Shah's regime was mainly represented at that time by the Mujahidin and Fedayin underground organizations, both of which had made their appearance in the late Fifties under the influence of Islamic Marxism, which was popular in the Near East at the time, and with the support of countries like China, Syria and Libya. Their slogans were anti-imperialist, anti-American, and anti-Israeli, their main objectives to overthrow the Shah's regime and remove Iran from the influence of the United States. These aims coincided with the interests of Soviet foreign policy in the region, but the Soviet Union never had any direct contacts with either the Mujahidin or Fedayin organizations, and there were two very solid reasons for this.

First, the Soviet Union has never given direct support to political or other organizations if it saw that they had no prospects of coming to power. The Soviet authorities viewed the Shah's regime as being

---

*An illegal Residency is a group of illegals working together. An illegal Residency in Tehran might cover the whole of the Middle East, but maintain contact with the N line in the Tehran Residency.

so stable, and the support of the United States so strong, that they did not believe that the Mujahidin and Fedayin organizations could ever mount a serious threat with their terrorist acts. These groups were fairly small, and drew their support from student youth. What is more, both organizations had been so heavily infiltrated by SAVAK secret agents ever since their formation that the authorities knew all about their plans and activities both in Iran and abroad. This was illustrated by the subsequent arrest, and the trial in Tehran in 1973, of practically all the leaders of the two organizations, when they had only got as far as planning to begin active terrorism inside Iran.

Second, there was the dampening effect of the Shah's warning that, should he learn that representatives of any country were in touch with the Iranian opposition either in Iran or abroad, Iran would break off diplomatic relations with that country immediately. This warning was of course directed at the Soviet Union and its allies. The Shah was true to his word. As soon as he learnt that Fidel Castro, the head of the Cuban regime, was planning to meet Iraj Eskandari, the secretary general of the Tudeh People's Party of Iran (which is the Iranian Communist Party), in Moscow during the Twenty-Sixth Congress of the Soviet Communist Party in February 1976, the Cuban government was warned that Iran would sever diplomatic relations at once if the meeting was held. Castro was not popular with the Shah because of the presence of his troops in Angola and Ethiopia. This meeting did of course take place, and diplomatic relations between Iran and Cuba were instantly broken off.

Inside Iran itself, the Tudeh Party was practically non-existent. After it had been routed by the authorities at the end of the 1940s, those of its members who had fled from Iran set up their centres in Moscow and East Berlin. In Iran, Tudeh Party members, who were quite few in number, were to be found only in the prisons. There were then no Tudeh activities at all in Iran itself, and it presented no threat to the regime.

It was quite clear to the Soviet authorities that if the Shah could react so strongly to Castro's meeting with a tiny opposition party, and one which in any case was only represented abroad, it would not hesitate to break off diplomatic relations even with the Soviet Union, if it learnt of any contacts with the Mujahidin and

Fedayin. The strictest instruction from the Central Committee of the Soviet Communist Party was therefore issued to all Soviet missions abroad, that there should be no contacts of any kind with members of these organizations. This instruction was observed by everybody, including the KGB. All approaches made to us by members of the Mujahidin and Fedayin organizations – and these were especially numerous until the mid-1970s – were simply ignored.

That the Soviet leaders were not anxious to have a break in diplomatic relations with Iran was not of course due to any fondness for the Shah. Such a move would play right into the hands of the United States, whose influence in Iran the Soviet Union did not wish to see increased.

The south of the Soviet Union shares a 2,500-kilometre common frontier with Iran. Although the Shah was an out-and-out anti-Soviet, he preferred at that time to follow a policy of balance between the US and the USSR. He kept few troops on the Soviet-Iranian frontier, there were no American military advisers in the area, and Iran took economic aid from both of the rival powers. Although the Shah bought most of his armaments in the United States, even in this sphere he tried to keep a balance, and bought certain types of weapons from the Soviet Union as well. The Americans sold Iran up-to-date weaponry that the Iranians were to all intents and purposes unable to use without instructions. This practice was regarded in the Soviet Union as stockpiling arms in a strategically convenient region for possible use by the US army in the event of war with the Soviet Union. There was no doubt that a Soviet-Iranian split would greatly suit the United States, and this was a risk that the Soviet authorities were not prepared to run.

The proposition is advanced in the West that the Soviet Union in general, and the KGB in particular, support all kinds of terrorist groups all over the world. The facts are not as simple as this.

The Soviet Union has supported, and continues to support, what are known as national liberation movements which, according to the Soviet definition, 'are struggling to overthrow imperialist reaction in their own countries'. In common parlance, this translates into movements struggling to overthrow a pro-American government in order to replace it with a pro-Soviet one. Who counts as a national liberation movement, and who does not, is decided in Moscow, and the criterion is the chance of coming to power. If the Soviet leadership sees such a prospect and considers the movement pro-Soviet, then it will give political support and material help. A good example is Soviet policy towards the Kurds of Iraq. The Soviet Union had supported the national liberation struggle of the Kurds for many years. When the pro-Soviet Ba'ath Party came to power in Iraq in 1963, support to the Kurds was stopped. What was more, the Soviet authorities made no objections against anything the Ba'athists did to suppress the Kurdish movement.

The Soviet Union makes no direct contact with the small groups of European terrorists like for example the Red Brigades and Action Directe. At the same time however the Soviet leadership closes its eyes to the fact that members of these organizations undergo training in several pro-Soviet countries in the Near East and are given weapons by them. What role does the KGB play in all this? Practically none. The task of maintaining relations with national liberation movements is in the hands of the International Department of the Central Committee of the Soviet Communist Party. Meetings with the leaders of these movements take place in third countries. Whether they wish to use the KGB or the army for this purpose, the authority is theirs. So arms deliveries, including secret ones, are made by the army and the GRU. The training of fighting men from these movements is done by the army. Arabs were trained in special camps in the deserts of Central Asia, and learned underwater sabotage in naval camps near Odessa.

If the Central Committee bosses feel the need to call on KGB specialists to do this sort of work, it is easy for them to do so. To take an example, a large delegation from the Palestine Liberation Organization came to Moscow in 1976. They asked among other things to be given advice about turning out false documents, or more exactly about one particular aspect of this process, the portable production of watermarks on documents. The equipment may be carried in a small case or briefcase, and is for use in 'field conditions', for example in a hotel room or at an airport. The International Department of the Central Committee instructed the documentation department of the KGB's 'S' Directorate to receive the Palestinian specialists as cordially and politely as possible, but not to give them any practical help or reveal any secrets.

While the aims of high strategy and tactics may differ among the various intelligence services of the world, the main attention of all intelligence officers in their everyday work is concentrated on their confrontation with the local security services.

In the United States, Soviet intelligence officers are up against the FBI and the CIA. In the Soviet Union, American intelligence officers are up against the KGB. In Iran, we had SAVAK to contend with. 'Come on!' some readers may say. 'Surely SAVAK was just a minor organization?' I would argue against that view.

SAVAK or Sazman-i Amniyat va Ittila'at-i Kishvar, the Organization for Security and Intelligence in the Country, was set up by the Americans in 1956. This move came in the wake of the following historical events.

After the Second World War began, the influence of Nazi Germany increased in Iran. As a consequence of this, the Soviet Union and Britain, who were then allies, sent their troops into Iran on 25 August 1941 in order to forestall the Germans. The British troops entered Iran from the south, the Soviet troops from the north. Tehran thus found itself in the sphere of influence of the Soviet troops, and as a side-effect the forces of the Left in Iran began to grow active with the full support of the Soviet authorities. After the Second World War had ended, and following some unsuccessful attempts to set up a pro-Soviet regime in the north, the Soviet Union had to withdraw its troops from Iran in 1946. This process was helped along not just by pressure from the Allies, but especially by the fact that the United States already had a nuclear weapon and was prepared to use it. The Soviet Union did not have the atomic bomb till 1949. After the Soviet troops had withdrawn, the Iranian Communist Tudeh Party was crushed and its remnants exiled.

Mossadeq, the leader of the Iranian National Front, was opposed to Britain's economic influence. When he became Iranian prime minister in 1951, he immediately acted to nationalize the Iranian oil industry, previously under British control. At first the United States remained on the sidelines in the ensuing crisis. Fearing however that Mossadeq might adopt a pro-Soviet policy, they organized a military coup in 1953, and Mossadeq was overthrown. The hitherto weak authority of the Shah was thereby asserted, and all the country's left-wing and democratic movements routed. The Americans wanted to see the Shah as a strong dictator who would carry out a tough anti-Soviet policy. The National Iranian Oil Company I considered to be nationalized only on paper, American oil corporations seeming to take the leading role that had previously belonged to the British.

In order to become a personal ruler, the Shah needed reliable backing. The Iranian army of that time was not suited to such a role, since there was a strong left-wing influence in its ranks. Something new was needed, guaranteed pure from communist influence.

SAVAK was controlled and financed by the United States. Everything it did was aimed at buttressing the Shah's regime, and at suppressing any opposition, particularly on the left. In addition, SAVAK joined an international grouping of special services which was code-named Trident. The two other members were the CIA and Mossad, the Israeli intelligence service. Trident was of course aimed at the Soviet Union and its allies in the region. This was the 'community' with which the officers of the KGB Residency had to deal.

SAVAK consisted of eight directorates with different functions. The Eighth Department, which carried out counter-intelligence control of foreigners, was the one that dealt with us. The Soviet embassy was surrounded by a network of observation posts located in the multi-storey apartment blocks that stood around the embassy grounds. We were thoroughly convinced that these posts overlooked the entire grounds of our embassy. The main one was situated in the house opposite the main entrance of the embassy. It was from there that all movements of Soviet people were kept under round-the-clock surveillance, persons of interest were secretly photographed, and communications maintained with all the other observation points.

SAVAK mobile surveillance teams, each with four or five cars at its disposal, were stationed in streets adjacent to the embassy. There were never fewer than two men in each car. What usually happened was that one team would take the target under observation, and follow him as he moved about town. The SAVAK teams were quite professional at managing surveillance. They very rarely came close to the target and preferred to keep a respectable distance. In nine out of ten cases, the SAVAK cars that followed me kept a distance of 300 metres back, and sometimes even further. Thus if you looked at the cars right behind you, you would not see any surveillance. You would have to look as far back as you could in your rear mirror and memorize the cars you saw there.

No matter how well the surveillance is mounted, however, the intelligence officer target is at a certain advantage. He always knows what his next step will be, and he has some tricks up his sleeve to help him identify surveillance, while the surveillance officers can only guess what lies one moment ahead. Sometimes this leads to a flap. It is then that the surveillants can be discovered.

It may happen like this. The car of the intelligence officer under surveillance turns off a main road into a quarter with quiet deserted streets. He makes one turn, then another, then a third, and stops immediately round the corner. The surveillance car turns that same corner, sees the stationary car, stops instinctively, and in order not to be noticed, goes into reverse. The intelligence officer is instantaneously tipped off. This method is a very old one, and is known both to intelligence officers and to surveillants, but even so, the surprise and panic factor almost always works. There is a multitude of other examples. Moreover, intelligence officers' cars are usually equipped with special radio receivers which enable them to eavesdrop on the opposition. It can be very amusing to sit in a car and listen to what the surveillance officers are saying about you. But radio interception is only an auxiliary resource. If the intelligence officer does not see the surveillance behind him, then no amount of technical devices will help him.

SAVAK operations against us were not defensive. They did not sit and wait until they caught us on the hop, but acted in an aggressive, offensive way, with full support from the top. Their constant pressure was calculated to make our lives as intolerable as possible. Sometimes the surveillance was carried out in a style of overt psychological warfare. The target was openly followed both by car and on foot, breathing down his neck and treading on his heels. Surveillance of women and children was done in this way in order to intimidate them, and with the aim of paralysing the intelligence officer's morale by showing him that physical provocation was possible. I myself had SAVAK deliberately breathing down my neck at one time. The most important thing in such a situation is not to react and not to notice whatever they are doing. They will drop you after a time and set to work on someone else.

Soviet staff who lived in town flats in Tehran were subjected to special pressure. Here SAVAK was the undisputed master. All these flats were bugged, of course, but that was not blatant enough, and 'secret' visits were always being paid when the occupants were out. Again, psychological pressure was their main purpose.

After living for several months in the summer residence of the Soviet embassy in Zargande, I decided to move to a town flat, on the assumption that operationally it would be much more helpful. Everything went normally at first. I found myself an attractive furnished flat in the north of Tehran, the landlord agreed to rent it to me and we arranged to sign the contract the following day. Next day I was received not by the landlord but by an employee with a shifty eye who explained that there'd been a mistake, the flat had been promised earlier to someone else. Well, these things happen, I thought, and found myself another flat. But the same thing happened again. It also happened with the third, the fourth, the fifth ... I tried sixteen flats one after the other with the same result. After the landlords' provisional agreement, obviously they had complied with the rules and reported that a Soviet diplomat wanted to rent the flat, and clearly SAVAK then forbade it. In this way they led me nearer and nearer to the embassy. Finally they allowed me to rent a flat on Gazali Street, directly adjoining the embassy, where SAVAK could keep me under observation without spreading its resources.

Life now proceeded in accordance with long-established traditions. Fairly frequently I saw traces of hostile visits – pockets of jackets and trousers intentionally turned inside out, stubbed-out cigarette ends on the floor and in the bathroom wash-basin, books scattered about, and so on. Sometimes someone would scratch at the front door, as though trying to open it. Sometimes the telephone would ring in the night, with heavy breathing at the other end ... It was hard, but absolutely necessary, to become accustomed to this, since if the perpetrators were to see any weakness, they would just go on and on. Wives who had to stay alone in their flats while their husbands were absent were particularly vulnerable.

Nor did SAVAK leave our cover organizations unattended. The consular department of the embassy was a particular target. Some very odd customers kept turning up in order to put us on edge and obstruct our work. One particularly colourful figure was a mentally ill Iranian who at the time of my arrival in Tehran had been coming regularly to the consulate as though to work for a year and a half. It was difficult to know whether he was just putting on an act, or whether he was in fact violent, but it was a noisy monologue that he delivered in the waiting room:

'I have slaughtered lots of people! Probably five thousand! And it's not enough for me! Now I want to go and live in the Soviet Union, and if you don't give me a visa, I'll slaughter you lot too!'

At first, our security guards tried to get rid of him by calling the police, but our violent visitor continued to appear. It was clear who was behind all this, so a decision was taken to handle this fellow with care. The guards gave him tea and treated him to biscuits, and he would sit there quietly, only to explode now and then, come up to one of us, grab him by the arm and threaten to murder him. Although we tried not to react, on one occasion he set upon me when I was not in a particularly good mood, and I swung round so hard and held him against the wall that the fellow was thoroughly shaken. He still continued to turn up after this, but whenever I appeared he would fall silent and sit as quiet as a mouse. He was not so mad, it seemed, as to risk his health.

Fairly often SAVAK would send us provocateurs, offering all kinds of collaboration, and merchandise including the designs of the latest American tanks, aircraft, submarines and anything else you can think of. But I followed one principle, which was: 'Don't react to anything, no matter how tempting it sounds. It is better to lose a lead than to walk into a frame-up. Whatever I need I shall find myself.'

SAVAK's reputation over human rights was notorious all over the world. There was much talk about the incredible tortures suffered by the Shah's opponents, ranging from the medievally primitive, like caning the soles of the feet, to the most modern, like lowering the naked body on to a white-hot fine grid, electric shocks, chemical preparations that paralysed the will, and many others.

Just how reliable all this information was, we did not exactly know. We were unable either to confirm or refute these reports, because the fact is that the KGB intelligence service did not have even a single agent inside SAVAK throughout its existence from 1956 to 1979. All the reports we received were obtained either by radio intercepts or from indirect sources who knew something about the organization. The KGB never succeeded in achieving a direct agent penetration of SAVAK. Of course, it cannot be said that the counter-intelligence officers in the Residency actually tried to achieve this in practice. We had almost no direct access to members of SAVAK, and those few whom we did bump into hated us so openly that there could never be any question of establishing friendly relations. I do not know to what indoctrination these people had been subjected, but when they met us, they invariably wore expressions of fear and hatred, as if they expected an assault. What made them like this, I do not know.

In the wake of the previously mentioned failures in the KGB Residency and the publicity that followed them, both the PI and CI lines continued to keep their heads down. The ban on operational activity however did not extend to the N line, and we went on working as before. All the Centre did was to nag us about the need for special care, as if we ourselves would have failed to understand this. We made use of the contrast effect in our work. Both we and the enemy special services knew that following the KGB Residency failures, all activity had ceased for the time being. The GRU Residency also slowed down a little, fearing that it might stop a blow in a general brawl. It was only in the lives of the straight diplomats that nothing changed. They continued to work and move around town just as before, and we in N line did exactly the same, showing that what had happened had nothing to do with us, and thus misleading SAVAK.

I continued to work with the agent known as 'Ram' as I prepared the operation to extend the foreign passports of our illegal 'Beduin', who had been documented as an Afghan citizen. Everything seemed to be going to plan, when I learnt quite by chance from my Afghan transit travellers that the Afghan consul (who was 'Ram') was finishing his posting and would be returning to Kabul in two weeks' time. At our next meeting, which took place two days later,

I asked 'Ram' when his tour of duty was due to end. Without batting an eyelid, he replied that it would be in about three or four months, and proposed to extend the validity of our illegal's passport in about a month's time. This put me on my guard, and I reported everything to my superior at the Residency. We checked the information about 'Ram''s departure through other sources, and were able to establish that my agent was indeed planning to return home in two weeks' time.

It was quite obvious that 'Ram' wanted to get out without fulfilling his commitment. I contacted him again, but he stuck to his story, and since there was no point in waiting any longer, we decided to use surprise tactics. Next morning I intercepted the agent on his way to the embassy, and told him that the passport extensions had to be made at once. He tried to wriggle out of it, but ran out of excuses, and I handed to him our illegal's passport, and picked it up, duly extended, half an hour later, by visiting the Afghan embassy my-self. 'Ram' of course was well paid for this operation. When he left Iran shortly afterwards, it was like a weight falling from my shoulders.

The main task of N line at that time was to work with our illegals 'Konrad' and 'Evi', who were using West German documents. Contact was made once every six weeks, mainly by dead letter-box operations. We chose the places beforehand, and informed the illegals of their whereabouts through the Centre. Anything you choose can serve as a location for a dead letter-box – a hollow in a brick wall, a space between a pole and a wall, or behind a drainpipe, and so on. The basic requirement is to find a place which is not overlooked from anywhere within what is known as 'the dead zone'. The idea is that at the precise moment when the dead letter-box is being cleared or filled, the intelligence officer doing so should disappear from the field of vision. Even if he is under observation, the surveillance must not observe that very instant of the operation. In illegal intelligence work, a site is used only once, after which nobody returns to it again. For that reason finding new locations was a continual task for us.

Dead letter-box operations were mounted in the following way. In the course of a routine radio contact, the Centre would instruct the illegals to prepare a message and then to pass it to the Residency through a dead letter-box at a given time and on a given day. When they had received these instructions, the illegals would exhibit a visible signal indicating 'the reception of a radio message', thus confirming that they were ready to carry out the operation. We would register this signal and inform the Centre about it. The Centre then informed the illegals that the Residency was ready and gave us the green light to go ahead.

On the day of the operation, once he had checked for surveillance, the illegal would go to the location and place a container with the information in the dead letter-box. Anything could be used as a container. The main thing was that it should not attract attention in itself. 'Konrad' preferred to use empty crushed toothpaste tubes. After he had put the container in the dead letter-box, the illegal would leave the area and put in a pre-arranged position a visible signal indicating that the box had been 'filled'. When we had received this signal, we collected the container, then put in place our own signal, indicating to the illegal that the container had been collected. Once he had received our signal, the illegal went back home, and we returned to the embassy.

Back at the embassy, we sent an immediate telegram to the Centre reporting the operation as completed and stating that the material received would be sent to the Centre on the 'Volna' or 'Wave' channel.

'Volna' is the most rapid channel for transmitting material of substance to the KGB Centre from abroad. The container received from an illegal is packaged up unopened and delivered by a consular official of the embassy (in this case by me) on board the earliest scheduled Aeroflot flight. The second pilot of every flight abroad is in the confidence of the KGB and he knows for whom the packet is intended. It always bears the same address – 'To Vasily Ivanovich 101' – meaning the KGB. When the aircraft arrives in Moscow, the pilot hands over the package to the commander of the frontier detachment. He in his turn delivers it to an officer of 'S' Directorate, who is already waiting at the airport. At that point we did not know anything of what the illegal had reported. The Residency was only told later of those parts which had a direct bearing on our work with them.

The failures in the Tehran Residency, and resultant enforced inactivity of PI line operational staff, led to a sharp drop in the supply of useful intelligence arriving from Tehran. According to rumours that reached us from the Centre, the blame for this was unofficially laid on the weak leadership of Gennadi Kazankin, who still remained as acting resident. As a result of this, Kazankin was not confirmed in the post, and Lieutenant-General Ivan Anisimovich Fadeikin, a legendary figure in the KGB, was sent to Tehran as resident, in order to strengthen the Residency. When he arrived in Tehran in March 1978, using the surname of Fadeev, Fadeikin was just over sixty. He was tall and lean, with black hair receding to the top of his head but thick at the sides, and with eyes which looked out sharply from behind metal-rimmed spectacles. His whole appearance gave a martinet impression.

Ivan Anisimovich Fadeikin was born in Moscow. Just before the Second World War he completed his studies in the Faculty of Journalism in Moscow State University and was accepted for work in intelligence. During the war, he played an active part as deputy commander of one of the partisan units in Belorussia. After the war he continued his work in intelligence, and became first an officer and then the chief of 'V' Department, which mounted direct actions (sabotage, diversions, and the physical liquidation of enemies of the Soviet regime). It was in this capacity that Fadeikin first visited Iran.

Following the CIA-organized coup in Iran, American influence proliferated. The Shah was becoming a personal dictator, and in the conditions of the cold war, the Soviet leaders saw with apprehension that should an armed conflict with the United States break out, Iran would be converted into a springboard from which to attack the Soviet Union from the south. Efforts to improve relations with Iran after Stalin's death had failed. The Shah became increasingly anti-Soviet. He recalled how, during the Second World War he, the monarch, had had to attend the Soviet embassy in Tehran in order to have talks with Stalin. Such insults are not forgotten.

All these apprehensions and deliberations brought the Soviet leadership to decide that the Shah must die. He had no heir at the time, and after his death the pro-Western type of government that would probably be set up would be much easier to influence than the 'foolish dictator and anti-Soviet'. The fate of the Shah was thus sealed.

'V' Department, whose head at that time was Fadeikin, was entrusted with the planning and mounting of this operation. Like all other operations of this nature, it was to be carried out solely on the instructions of the Politburo. In the KGB these were called simply 'special Central Committee tasks'. They were shrouded in the strictest secrecy, and only those directly involved knew their true essence.

In the Centre, Fadeikin worked by himself on developing the operation. Then in 1961 he arrived in the Soviet Embassy in Tehran under diplomatic cover, with full powers to use whomever he wished to help him to prepare and then to carry out the action. Fadeikin picked a KGB illegal who was in Iran at the time, and an officer from the Residency who blended in with the locals both linguistically and in personal appearance.

At the same time yet another remarkable event was taking place in Vienna. Khrushchev, the then Soviet leader, was meeting there with John Kennedy, the United States President. During a discussion on regional problems, and particularly on the situation in Iran, Khrushchev, with characteristic indiscretion, spoke frankly and disparagingly of the Shah of Iran, saying that 'Iran is a rotten fruit which will soon fall at the feet of the Soviet Union. Disturbances will soon begin in that country.' He hastened to add, considering apparently that he had said too much, that 'the Soviet Union however will not have any connection with these events, and has no intention of intervening in them.' I do not know how Kennedy reacted to this attack of frankness. He must have considered it to be one of the Soviet leader's usual propaganda thrusts. But Khrushchev knew very well what he was talking about, for the plan that Fadeikin worked out had been approved precisely by Khrushchev after discussion with members of the Politburo.

The operational plan was not distinguished by its originality, but it was simple and safe. Fadeikin intended to use existing agent resources to establish the route most often taken by the Shah's car, and to select a place at which to leave a car filled with explosives. The bomb would be detonated by remote control as the Shah's motorcade passed the spot. That is all there was to it.

It sounds simple, but a great deal of time, nearly a year, went by in preparing it. A Volkswagen 'Beetle' was selected and purchased by third parties. When the routes used by the Shah had been studied, a day was picked when he would be paying one of his visits to the Majlis, the Iranian Parliament. The explosives had been delivered in small amounts through the diplomatic bag to the Soviet embassy in Tehran. Our illegal made several secret visits to the embassy, where he and the Residency officer did shooting practice in the deep cellars. This was to provide against the eventuality of the victim surviving the explosion. The illegal was to carry out this part of the action should the need arise.

The operation was fixed for February 1962. On the appointed day, the Volkswagen, packed to the roof with explosives and with its detonating mechanism primed, was parked on one of the streets along the Shah's route between the Majlis and the Niavoran Palace. The illegal, holding the remote control, had a direct line of vision to the car bomb. Finally, the Shah's motorcade appeared. The cars came alongside the Volkswagen and the illegal pressed the button. But there was no explosion. The Shah of Iran passed safely by and out of sight.

The illegal naturally did not risk approaching the car, but set off immediately to meet the Residency officer. He reported that the bomb had not worked, and handed over the remote control mechanism. Then, looking like an ordinary local, he departed for the city, while the officer returned and reported everything to a distressed Fadeikin, who had not heard any explosion at the time when it should have gone off. The situation was very serious. The operation had failed, the Shah was alive, and the primed bomb was still in the car. If it went off now, it would be clear to everyone for whom it had been intended. God alone knew what consequences that would bring. Fadeikin took a decision. The bomb had to be rendered harmless by removing the detonator. So who was to do it? The illegal was not reachable, and Fadeikin was the boss, so this honour naturally fell to the Residency officer. It is not worth trying to guess the officer's feelings as he defused the bomb.

Fadeikin and the Residency officer flew back to Moscow on the next available Aeroflot scheduled flight. The detonating mechanism, along with its remote control device, were sent to the Centre for expert examination, and this is what came out. The illegal had indeed pressed the button of the remote control device, but he should have held it in the depressed position for about three seconds. Instead he had pushed it and then let go instantaneously, so the signal had not reached the detonating mechanism. It was a technical hitch like this that saved the Shah's life. But not only *his* life. Exceptionally powerful explosives had been used in the operation. Had they gone off, not only would the Shah and his entourage have been annihilated, but the entire area round about, within a 500-metre radius, would have been reduced to rubble. The KGB illegal, with his direct line of sight to the car, would have stood no chance at all of surviving. That is the sort of operation that Ivan Anisimovich Fadeikin devised and carried out in Iran. Its failure had no effect on his career. Who could be blamed for having been let down by a technical device?

Fadeikin's subsequent career developed like this. At the end of the Sixties he was appointed chief of the KGB station in Karlshorst, East Berlin, with the rank of lieutenant-general. This post was important to the coordination of KGB and East German illegal intelligence. The partition of Germany after the Second World War offered a splendid potential for documenting illegals. As he was a tough, disciplined man, Fadeikin established a regime of strict discipline inside the KGB representation. Since he was an enemy of alcohol he forbade the sale of even beer in the canteens of the representation. This mistrust of alcohol would be unhappily vindicated. In 1974, he was appointed chief of the First Chief Directorate of the KGB, in charge of the whole of KGB intelligence. This was a significant and, everyone thought, well-deserved promotion.

To mark his appointment, and just before he left for Moscow, Fadeikin gave a great banquet in the KGB headquarters in Karlshorst. It was at this banquet, after he had allowed himself to take a little strong drink and loosen up, that he spoke in a circle of intimate colleagues about his 'service in the KGB'. In the course of this excursion into history, he mentioned the name of Semyon Tsvigun, who was then first deputy chairman of the KGB. He recalled that Tsvigun had been under his command in a partisan unit, and spoke unflatteringly about Tsvigun's intellectual capabilities. He said no more than that.

Shortly afterwards Fadeikin returned to Moscow, where a painful disappointment awaited him. His appointment to the post of chief of intelligence had been cancelled. He was in effect removed from the active life of the KGB, and was appointed instead to the post of deputy minister of Medium Machine Construction (the code name for the atomic industry of the Soviet Union), responsible for security in this branch of industry. It turned out that someone who attended that ill-starred banquet had immediately reported to Tsvigun about Fadeikin's uncomplimentary remarks. Tsvigun was married to the sister of Brezhnev's wife. He had no difficulty in convincing Andropov, the KGB chairman, who was himself a distant relation of Brezhnev's wife, that he should punish the KGB general who had overstepped the mark. But at that time, Fadeikin could not be destroyed completely, since he already belonged to the nomenklatura, the Party establishment. As the Russian proverb truly has it, 'One raven never pecks out the eyes of another.'

Fadeikin's mishap left vacant the post of chief of intelligence, and the decision was taken to appoint Kryuchkov, then Andropov's deputy for cadres, who has already been mentioned. Andropov apparently decided that it was better to have his own man in the job than an arrogant professional holding general's rank like Fadeikin.

Ivan Anisimovich Fadeikin changed completely into an official of the ruling establishment. A very high salary, a personal car with a driver, Kremlin rations, special medical care – what more could a man want? Just sit quietly and wait for your pension. But the professional in him could not bear to sit quietly. After all, he had spent practically his entire career in the front line – the partisan war, 'V' Department, and directing several hundred illegals within East Germany. So Fadeikin plied Andropov with requests to be allowed back into active intelligence work, and in the end Andropov took pity. For Fadeikin, the Tehran appointment was an incredible demotion and a clear slap in the face, but he did not think twice. All he wanted was to return to active work. So in March 1978 he again appeared in Tehran. Lev Petrovich Kostromin, the former resident, came with him, to help him learn the ropes more quickly.

But troubles never come singly, they say, and troubles were pursuing Fadeikin.

This is what happened barely a few days after he arrived in Tehran. In broad daylight, a man walked past the main entrance gates of the Soviet embassy and surreptitiously threw a screwed-up ball of paper through the grille and into our grounds. The guard on duty saw this from his post in the guard-room, but he did not rush out to pick it up. Obviously having some instinct about it, he waited a little before sending out a colleague to collect it without drawing the attention of the SAVAK observation post. It so happened that I was walking past the guard-room at the time, and the guards told me what had happened. We unscrewed the paper. It turned out to be a sealed blank envelope. I questioned the guards about all the details, including the man's appearance. They said he was old, and that he looked like an Iranian.

I took the envelope and set off for the Residency. The envelope was opened in the resident's office. It contained a note written in Farsi, requesting a meeting and indicating a time and date, but not a place. The note was signed with the single letter 'D'. I reported to Kostromin and Fadeikin the details of what the guards had told me. At first no one could tell whether the note was genuine, or a provocation by SAVAK, or whether the man who had thrown the envelope was simply mad. At last it dawned on Kostromin.

'Of course!' he said. ' "D" is our agent!', and he mentioned his pseudonym. 'He always used to sign his messages with the letter "D".'

Naturally, no one asked any questions as to who in fact 'D' was. You do not ask such questions in intelligence work. Now that the source of the note had been established, it had to be decided what it meant. Was it a provocation by SAVAK? If not, had the SAVAK observation post seen the envelope being thrown in, and didn't that possibly jeopardize the proposed meeting? Opinions were divided. Some said that it was not worth it to go to the meeting, since SAVAK had certainly seen the message being thrown in and had since arrested 'D'. Obviously there would be an ambush at the rendezvous. I shared this opinion. Others suggested visiting the agent at his home, but after the date which had been given; no one should go to the meeting on the stipulated day. The duty guard who had observed the paper being thrown was again questioned. In his view, the throw had been a very accurate one, and he had not noticed any reaction in the SAVAK observation post. Finally Fadeikin, who had been silent until then, had his say.

'We will go to the meeting on the appointed day. There will be a meeting in two hours to set up the operation.'

Fadeikin's tone did not invite objections. He adduced no arguments to back up his decision. We had never been accustomed to such methods in the Residency. For better or worse, everything was discussed, and we could even argue with the resident. Fadeikin chilled us on that occasion with his peremptory intervention – the fiat of a highly placed member of the ruling establishment.

The following operational plan was worked out. Viktor Kazakov, a young officer of the PI line, would go to the meeting. He would use a car bearing ordinary Tehran number-plates which belonged to Shamirov, an officer of ours who worked in one of the Soviet–Iranian companies. Shamirov was to leave the car at an agreed place in town, and then go to the cinema for the duration of the operation. He himself could not be sent to this meeting, since he did not have diplomatic cover and so could be arrested by the Iranian authorities in the event of his being detained. Igor Minin, an operational driver of the Residency, would pick up the car in town, and then drop Kazakov at an agreed place. After checking for surveillance, they then had to move into the area where the meeting was to take place.

Here came the crux of the plan. For fifteen minutes before the meeting was due to occur, Kazakov had to drive through the vicinity of the rendezvous with 'D' in order to assess the likelihood of an ambush. Then he had to meet a second Residency car which would contain Kostromin, the head of the CI line, the head of N line and the operational driver. This second car would take up a position not far from the meeting zone. Kazakov would report on the situation, and at this point the operational group headed by Kostromin had to take a final decision as to whether to proceed. So, in the event of an ambush, the Residency would blow its entire leadership. But as I have said, there was no point in arguing.

On the day of the operation, everything went according to the plan. Shamirov left the car in the agreed place and went to the cinema. Kazakov, accompanied by Minin the operational driver, went to the rendezvous area. It has to be said that the usual place for meeting 'D' was not far from his home, since he was a very old man, approaching eighty, and not in the best of health. Boris Kabanov had previously worked with 'D', but following his expulsion from Iran and the lull that followed it, contacts had ceased.

When they drove along the street where the meeting was planned, Kazakov and Minin noticed that one side of it had a ditch dug across it, which barred the way to any movement. What was more, they noticed not far from the meeting place a suspicious car which was very similar to one used by SAVAK surveillance. They reported all this when they met Kostromin's group, and recommended calling off the meeting. Kostromin, however, called them cowards and ordered them to go ahead.

The meeting took place. 'D' was unable to say anything intelligible. His head and his hands were trembling, and all he would ask was what had happened to Kabanov. Seeing that he could get no sense out of the old man, Kazakov got into the car and drove off. As they passed by 'D' 's house, a young Iranian emerged from the gates, looked at the car, and wrote down its number.

The original set-up, the old man's behaviour, and the Iranian writing down the registration number of the car, led to some very unpleasant thoughts. What did it all mean? We did not have to guess for very long. Three days after the excursion from the Residency to meet 'D' an incredible scandal erupted in the press. The headlines screamed once again. 'Another KGB Spy Network Uncovered in Iran! General Darahshani Arrested. Worked Thirty Years For KGB! KGB Works Only With Generals!', and more in the same vein.

Everybody learnt at this point who 'D' was. General Darahshani had been recruited by Soviet intelligence during the Second World War. His only service to the Soviet Union was that in 1947, during the Iranian civil war, when he commanded the troops of the Tabriz Military Garrison, he surrendered without a fight to the forces of the People's Democratic Party of Azerbaijan. He was then just over fifty. He retired with a pension shortly afterwards, and produced practically nothing in the intelligence field thereafter, but the KGB went on seeing him and continued to pay him his pension, which had been given him for life. Kabanov's arrest had stopped the payment of Darahshani's pension. Although it was not a lot of money, the loss apparently undermined the former general's finances, and it was his desire to restore his pension that had brought him to the gates of our embassy.

Even though we had been convinced of the contrary, the SAVAK observers had noticed what Darahshani did at the embassy gates, and he was later arrested. They persuaded him to go to the meeting, where an ambush had been laid, but the appearance and subsequent disappearance of the Residency cars at the rendezvous fifteen minutes before the meeting was due apparently led SAVAK to conclude that they had been spotted. They lost their nerve and stood down the snatch teams. The second appearance of our car at the meeting place came as a complete surprise, and all SAVAK could do was to write down the registration number.

But the funniest thing in this entire tragedy was that the Iranian press attributed everything that had happened to our officer Shamirov, who had sat in the cinema while the operation was going on. It was his expulsion from the country that the Iranian Foreign Ministry demanded several days after the publicity. Shamirov was beside himself with rage.

'They're throwing me out for nothing! I wasn't even in the operational area, they wouldn't let me near the place. Bloody fools!' he shouted, clearly aiming his abuse at the heads of the Residency. He no longer had anything to lose.

'They've ruined my whole career for nothing, the swine! Now I can only go to socialist countries. And who the hell needs them?' He was inconsolable.

'Okay Shamirov,' the Residency officers teased him. 'It's a shame that they're throwing you out. But tell me, that film, is it worth seeing?'

Darahshani was not tried. Soon after his arrest, the Iranian press reported his demise from a heart attack during questioning. SAVAK had tortured the old man to death.

It was quite difficult to work with Fadeikin. The atmosphere of human contact with the resident was replaced by one of severe officialdom. It was no longer possible to go into the resident's office without making a prior appointment by telephone. Ask him for a meeting, and you might hear, 'I'll see you in three and a half minutes,' or 'Stand by your telephone, and I shall ring you when I am free.' Then you were stuck to your telephone indefinitely.

Once he had familiarized himself with the conditions on the ground in Tehran, Fadeikin realized how little chance he had of changing anything, the more so since he took over as resident right on the heels of failure and scandal in the press. Accustomed to working on a grander scale, his position oppressed him, and his grumbling spilled over on to the operational staff.

'Some damned Residency this is,' he would snarl, 'with only one and a half agents!'

Sometimes he was just irritable. I once brought him an information telegram for his signature. After skimming through it, Fadeikin threw it down on the table in front of me, saying that he had no intention of signing off such rubbish. He ordered me to rewrite the telegram, though without making any specific comments. When I got back to my office I reread what I had written several times, but could find nothing wrong. Two hours later, having changed absolutely nothing, I placed the same telegram on Fadeikin's desk.

'Now this is quite another thing,' he said as he signed it.

With all his brutality and heavy-handed character, Fadeikin did have one valuable positive quality. He hated corruption and dishonesty. In this of course he did not see eye to eye with Vinogradov, our ambassador, who protected swindlers of all shapes and sizes in Tehran, and whose own hands were not clean. Fadeikin and the ambassador were equal in status in their respective positions. Both had been deputy ministers. The ambassador therefore could not put pressure on the new KGB resident, as he had done previously. We in the Residency ceased to feel coerced by Vinogradov. We no longer heard our resident saying such things as, 'The ambassador won't allow it,' 'The ambassador wouldn't like that,' 'The ambassador demands,' and so on.

Ambassador Vinogradov was by nature a petty-minded man. He poked his nose into every domestic matter in the embassy, and intervened personally on such things as the allocation of flats, always trying to score off both the KGB and the GRU. A stop was put to this when Fadeikin arrived. For example, after the families of two Residency officers had exchanged flats in the embassy dwelling block on Fadeikin's decision, the ambassador rang him up and demanded to know why this exchange had taken place behind his back. Fadeikin's answer was brief.

'Because I do not consider it necessary to seek your advice over such matters,' he said, and hung up.

At 9 o'clock every Thursday morning, a meeting for the entire diplomatic staff was held in the ambassador's office in the embassy. At these meetings, one of the diplomats would deliver a pre-arranged report, which was then discussed by everybody. This practice had been started by the ambassador, and its aim was somehow to fill the time of the straight diplomats who made up the main audience at these meetings. The subjects of these reports were sometimes issues of current Iranian policy, and sometimes aspects of the country's history. The reports delivered by the straight diplomats, which were based on familiar material from the press, were of little interest to KGB and GRU officers. On one occasion it was announced that at the following Thursday meeting the ambassador would deliver a report on his time in Egypt. This sounded quite interesting. I do not know whether the straight diplomats were aware of the ambassador's role in the Egyptian fiasco, but most KGB and GRU officers knew these details. Why did the ambassador have to stir up the past, the more so since his actions had been so far from positive? He wanted of course to justify himself, at least in his own eyes.

When the day came, the room was full to capacity. Everybody wanted to hear how Vinogradov would account for what had happened. The report itself was dull. The ambassador enumerated his meetings with Sadat, trying to emphasize the influence that he had exerted on this man. I shall not recount its content. But then as the report proceeded, Fadeikin began to put questions. Could the ambassador tell us what had happened to this or that Egyptian politician after the Soviet military advisers had been expelled? The ambassador ignored Fadeikin's questions. Fadeikin then named the pro-Soviet politicians who had been liquidated by Sadat after the Soviet departure. Finally, the ambassador cracked. He threw his pencil on the table and shouted hysterically that he could not deliver his report in such an atmosphere.

'Yes, and what sort of a report is it?' asked Fadeikin. 'Complete and utter nonsense. You ought to be ashamed of yourself, Vladimir Mikhailovich, bragging about your part in something you yourself made a mess of!'

That was all. It was a clear declaration of war. The ambassador and Fadeikin had become mortal enemies.

One day we found a copy of Aleksandr Solzhenitsyn's book *The Gulag Archipelago* lying in the consular department waiting room. No one knew who had left it there. Whether some bungler from among the Soviet specialists had forgotten it, or whether someone had specially placed it there surreptitiously 'for the purposes of ideological subversion', I do not know. It was the first volume of *The Gulag Archipelago* in the Russian language. None of us was exactly filled with indignation at this 'provocation' and no one hastened to destroy the book. Quite the contrary, in fact. A queue quickly formed to read it, and after passing from hand to hand, it finally came to me. 'It's terrible,' said one of our officers as he passed me the book, sadly shaking his head. 'Can all this really be true?' He heaved a deep sigh, and then quoted some lines of Vladimir Vysotsky:

> 'If what they say is true,
> Or even one third no lie,
> There's one thing left to do,
> And that's lie down and die.'

After reading Solzhenitsyn myself, I understood his response and agreed with it completely. The book had left a dismal impression. It was hard to believe what I had read, but impossible not to believe it, for every Soviet person knows of individual cases of horrors that happened in Stalin's prisons and camps. One had relatives there, another had friends and acquaintances who had relatives there, while somebody else again had been there himself. In separate instances, the stories were terrifying enough; here in this book of Solzhenitsyn's all that horror of torment, suffering, tragedy, torture, brutality, death, the inconceivable atmosphere of the camps, name after name of people whose destinies had been destroyed, were brought together in such numbers that at times it became simply unbearable to go on reading. A lump rose in the throat, and nightmares came.

The content of *The Gulag Archipelago* continued to grip me long after I had finished reading it. The painful episodes played on my mind. Finally, after long and candid reflection, I realized what was gnawing at my spirit most of all. It was that I myself now belonged to the organization which was the direct perpetrator of all that terror which had reigned in the Thirties and Forties. The instigator and inspirer of all these horrors was the Party. It was not just Stalin alone, as they had tried to tell us at the time, but the entire leadership of the Communist Party of the Soviet Union. The NKVD only carried out instructions from above. But that did not make it any easier for me.

The picture from my childhood came back to me, of Andrei Dimitrievich, the butcher from the NKVD, who lived in our block of flats, who could break the collar-bone of a grown man with one blow. People like him were alive and many of them still working in the KGB. And now here was I, with them. Nor did the thought help that 'Times are different now, legality has triumphed and the guilty have been punished.' Who could guarantee that some Georgian ruler would not come to power again tomorrow and put everything back on to the old footing? What then? For corruption in the Party had by now grown to such dimensions that it would soon be possible simply to buy the post of secretary general.

All these thoughts gave me no rest for a long time. But nothing lasts. The state I was in did not last either, but it did not disappear completely. It went deeper into my subconscious, and surfaced every time I came up against the usual cases of corruption and illegality.

CHAPTER 11

Each officer in the KGB Residency is given leave once a year. Most officers prefer to take their leave during the summer months and spend it at home in the good weather. Leave is planned and agreed with the Centre in advance, so as not to leave the sections in the Residency short-handed. In practice, the officer himself has the right to choose, within reasonable limits, when he takes leave.

My leave was fixed for July, but I had to start preparing in advance. This preparation consists mainly of writing a comprehensive report about your work over the year. For those officers who work conscientiously and have results to show for it, these written reports are not particularly difficult to write. But for those who simply spend their time sitting around the Residency, it is a very hard job. They have to invent non-existent achievements, and justify their failure to fulfil some point or other in their brief. In my time most reports were of this type. The CI line officers were the hardest-pressed, for they had no practical results at all to write about.

Writing my report was not difficult. I had something specific to say on every point of my brief. By the summer of 1978, I had several promising cultivations going, one of which had in practical terms approached the point of recruitment. Here I shall mention no names, nor give any other details about my contacts, since they are all real people and I have no intention of causing any of them any trouble.

The report must reach the Centre approximately one month before the officer is due to arrive there on leave, so that those in charge can acquaint themselves with what it says and be able to discuss it with the officer when he appears. Those officers whose reports consist of verbal waffle do everything possible to delay their dispatch, hoping to arrive at the Centre before the reports do, and so to avoid an immediate blowing up by the chiefs, and a spoilt leave. The furious reaction may have cooled down by the time the leave is over, allowing them to get away with just a 'mild fright'.

Just before your leave begins, 'friends' begin to besiege you with requests to take 'a little box' to Moscow for them. These are mostly Residency and embassy officials who do not hold diplomatic passports, and are therefore liable to customs examination when crossing the frontier. What the diplomats take with them is 'strategy' – in the slang of the Soviet community in Tehran, 'strategic goods of Iranian manufacture, from which maximum profits may be made when sold in the Soviet Union'. These goods included synthetic fabrics produced by the Iranian textile industry, which came in different colours and were very cheap in Iran. One metre cost the equivalent of one rouble in Soviet money in the Tehran bazaar, and sold for thirty-five roubles in the commission shops in Moscow. So there you had 3,500% true strategic profit.

All Soviet people bought these fabrics in rolls, not of dozens but of hundreds of metres. Then at home the rolls were cut up and packed into whisky cartons and sent to the Soviet Union by the method just described, to be sold for a minimum of thirty-five roubles a metre. Fifty metres of cloth could be folded into one box. Take two boxes and you already had 3,500 roubles profit for an outlay of 100 roubles. Everyone without exception was involved in this business. That is why each person going on leave was laden like a pack-mule with luggage, two-thirds of it other people's 'strategy' boxes. The income obtained from this business was so great that anybody who managed to send fabrics to the Soviet Union regularly could buy a dacha or co-operative flat within a year. The main thing was that this material was sold perfectly legally and without any speculation in the State commission shops in Moscow, where it had only to be displayed to disappear. So it was profitable for everyone.

Here is the answer to the question as to why Muscovites are quite well dressed when fashionable Western clothes are totally absent from the shops. The answer is, thanks to the Soviet diplomatic corps. And it should not be thought that this business was unique to the Soviet community in Iran. From the Soviet point of view practically every country in the world has its 'strategic goods'.

Moscow had changed a lot during my year's absence from the capital, or perhaps it was only my eyes that had been changed by the contrast to Tehran. I only saw that the people had become more unfriendly, and the shops, particularly the food stores, were half empty. Queues everywhere. A year before, you could always buy frankfurter sausages in the grocery store not far from where I lived. Now you couldn't find them in a month of Sundays. People crowded round the counters waiting for the meat and sausages to be dumped on the shelves. The air was so electric with exasperation that rowdy scenes flared up here and there, especially in the shops. People took out their frustrations on each other.

In the Centre, I quickly did the rounds of the chiefs. Nobody kept me very long, since there were no problems over any of my work. By way of gratitude for my successes, they helped me obtain a place in the Livadia holiday resort on the Black Sea coast of the Crimea. Usually such privileges are only granted to senior officers.

Many people, both in my own department and in the Eighth Department of the First Chief Directorate, asked about the political upheavals which had begun to shake Iran. I answered that in my opinion they had to be taken seriously, but in response I heard the old refrain about the strength of the Shah's regime, which would not permit any changes in Iran.

I met up with my friends from the various departments and we naturally exchanged impressions about different countries. It turned out that, when it came to corruption, the Soviet community in Iran was by no means unique. In every country our ambassadors, Party leaders, domestic managers, were involved up to the eyes in corruption. The stories were different, but the result was the same. All these rogues went unpunished. A corresponding malaise was affecting the work done in the residencies. Most officers simply sat out their time, avoiding doing anything that might have them thrown out of the country. The same opinion was held everywhere – 'For whom and for what should I stick my neck out? For this mafia? No thanks!' Our position gave us the perspective to see that corruption in high places was not just a series of isolated cases, but had grown into an incurable epidemic.

This infection had even begun to spread inside the KGB intelligence service. It was a long-standing tradition to bring small gifts when coming on leave. These were marks of consideration rather than corruption, the more so since an officer could bring presents only to colleagues on his own level – they were not given to the chiefs. The presents were mainly items for office use produced in the West, such as pencil holders, rubbers, and correcting substances for typewriters. Close friends were usually given a bottle of whisky or French cognac.

While I was on leave, I was told of something which had recently happened in the American department of 'S' Directorate. The head of this department asked for presents from an officer who had arrived on leave. When the officer replied that he had nothing to give, his chief made threats, saying that such indifference could affect his career. Without hesitation the officer reported this incident to the Party leadership in 'S' Directorate, and the head of the American department was spectacularly sacked from the KGB. Here at least justice still triumphed.

My section in the Centre was in a room at the end of a corridor on the sixth floor, just opposite the staircase. When I arrived on leave, I noticed that this wide staircase was blocked off by a strong metal grille between the fifth and sixth floors. A similar grille was visible between the fourth and fifth floors. When I asked why the grilles were there, this is what I was told.

Several months before, when it was still winter, a meeting attended by officials of the Central Committee of the Soviet Communist Party and representatives from some ministries was held in the fourth-floor office of Yuri Andropov, then chairman of the KGB. When the meeting ended, the guests left the office and went to put on their warm coats and hats. It was then discovered that six expensive musquash hats were missing. They had been stolen. This naturally was an unspeakable disgrace for Andropov. The most senior big-shots of the Party ruling establishment had been robbed in the holy of holies of security and in the very waiting room of the chairman of the KGB himself. Andropov's anger found expression in the appearance of the grilles between the floors. It was later alleged that a 'hardened thief' had got at the establishment head-gear through a back staircase. The hats were never found.

It was during that leave that I learnt the details of the military coup in Afghanistan which had taken place on 27 April 1978, while I was still in Tehran. President Daud's government was overthrown by air and tank units of the Afghan army, and a communist government put into power. I shall deal with the Soviet involvement in Afghanistan in a later chapter. Here I will only remark that no one in the KGB Residency in Tehran had the slightest inkling of the future course of our country's policy towards the people on Iran's eastern border. Our reaction to the coup when it was reported in the Tehran media was largely one of indifference. Everybody knew that Afghanistan lay within the Soviet sphere of influence, although it was considered to be a non-aligned country. Relations between the two governments were friendly, the Afghan army was full of Soviet advisers, and we saw the coup as merely adding another greedy mouth to the pack of socialist communities that fed upon the Soviet economy. KGB friends and acquaintances filled in the background to these events while I was in Moscow, but they made no deep impression. It was just one more piece of evidence to confirm the mindless policy of the Brezhnev–Suslov leadership. I was far more concerned about what was happening in Iran, where events were developing at a dramatic pace.

PART THREE

'Khomeini Rakhbar!'

CHAPTER 12

I returned to Iran from leave at the beginning of September 1978. During my six weeks' absence, the political situation had changed beyond recognition. Of my quiet and peaceful Tehran, not even a trace remained. Demonstrations were now taking place almost every day, and they were constantly growing in strength. Right from the beginning of the disturbances in December 1977, the Shah's regime showed indecision. The attitude of the Americans, and of President Carter in particular, contributed greatly to this. Since he was a devoted defender of human rights, he did not advise the Shah to take tough measures. Nor was the Shah himself, it must be said, inclined towards ordering repression. Sensing this weak spot in the regime, the opposition stepped up its activities. In addition to the demonstrations, strikes by manual and office workers began to break out all over the country. The largest was the strike of workers employed in the oil reprocessing industry. In Iran interruptions began in the supply of petrol and foodstuffs.

In Tehran and throughout the whole country, cassette tapes were being circulated bearing the recorded speeches of some ayatollah called Khomeini. In these speeches the mullah called for the overthrow of the regime of the Shah, whom he roundly denounced in particularly uninhibited language. The name of Khomeini meant nothing to us, not even to the longest-serving officer in the Residency. The Centre's records produced the following: 'The Shah's reforms of 1962 led to agitation stirred up by organized Islamic clergy. One of the leaders of this agitation was Ayatollah Khomeini. After the agitation had been suppressed he was deported from the country to Iraq, where he has been living ever since.'

In order to understand the conflict that was surfacing in Iran, some historical perspective is essential. The political upheavals that shook Europe in the late nineteenth and early twentieth century did not bypass Iran, which had its own middle-class nationalist forces. Historical processes of this nature always throw up strong personalities, and here it was Reza Khan, the father of the last Shah of Iran. From being a captain in the Iranian Cossack division, he rose to become Minister of War by 1924, and the following year he organized a military coup that overthrew the Qajar dynasty which had ruled Iran since 1737. Reza Khan declared himself supreme ruler under the name of Reza Shah Pahlevi – the Pahlevi element implying that the new Shah was a descendant of the Achaemenid dynasty that had ruled the country in the distant past, before the advent of Islam.

The new Shah was trying to show that he was no devotee of Muslim traditions, and wanted to look further back towards the ancient greatness of Zoroastrian Persia. His intention was to modernize on the European model. He started to develop the economy, and introduced reforms, including a prohibition on women wearing the chador, as well as more rights and liberties for women. His target was what he saw as the excessive influence of the Islamic clergy, and when the mullahs stirred up discontent among the Muslim population, Reza Shah repressed them ruthlessly.

Reza Shah's idol was Nazi Germany, with its great economic prosperity in the 1930s, so when the Second World War was under way it was inevitable for Britain and the Soviet Union to send in troops against a possible ally of Hitler. Reza Shah was exiled to South Africa, where he died in 1944. The allies put his son, the young Mohammed Reza Pahlevi, on the throne, but after the war, and after the rout of the opposition in 1953, he ceased to be a puppet and began to gather strength. His father had taught him to look towards Europe, and he wanted to see his country take the path of economic development. His solution was what he called the 'White Revolution' – bloodless reform, coming from the top. Its six principles were:

nationalization of the country's forests;
workers' participation in company profits;

a new electoral law;
the sale of some State undertakings to private ownership;
the creation of an education corps from among Iran's military conscripts, to set up schools in remote areas and teach literacy;
land reform.

The most important principle was land reform. The land was to be transferred in perpetuity to the country's landless peasants, making them productive farmers. But the land was divided among three main groups: the Shah's family, the landowner class, and the Muslim priesthood. The first two were untouchable – the landlord class was his main support – but the clergy disliked the Shah, whom they saw as the son of an anti-Islamic imposter and a Western puppet. The Shah shared his father's view of the clergy as the cause of national backwardness. The problem solved itself. He secularized many of their lands and bestowed them on the peasants free of charge.

The Education Corps was undermining the clergy's role as teachers. They had lost a fairly large part of their lands. They responded by organizing mass protests and disorders, starting in the holy city of Qom in 1962. One of the organizers was a theologian of that city, Ayatollah Khomeini.

Ruhollah al-Mussavi Khomeini was born not far from Qom in 1902. He lost his father when he was only five months old, killed during a land revolt, and he grew up in the unshakeable conviction of the Shiite priesthood that it alone was the true authority in Iran. From childhood, his own character was radical and uncompromising. The higher he rose among the clergy, the more he was bound to clash with the Shah. He was frequently arrested for his attacks on the monarchy: he would promise to stop delivering political sermons, only to start again after his release. In June 1963 he stepped up these attacks. 'They are throwing us into prison, torturing and killing us for the benefit of the Jews, the United States and Israel, sacrificing us to the Great Satan,' he would cry. Massive unrest in Tehran was brutally repressed by the army and SAVAK, with several thousand people killed. Khomeini was arrested and held in prison without trial until April 1964, when he was released.

The SAVAK Third Directorate worked hard against subversive

elements among the priesthood, which became relatively quiet after 1963. At the same time oil-rich Iran was drawing more and more foreign investors, and particularly Americans, who were to be seen in all walks of life. A bill in the Iranian parliament in 1964 allowed Americans to be tried in their own law courts, not those of Iran, for alleged offences inside Iran, and this further incensed Khomeini, who called upon the army to overthrow this slave regime. That was going too far. He was arrested and deported to Turkey, an awkward guest who soon moved on to neighbouring Iraq, where he settled in the Shiite pilgrimage town of Najaf. There he went on attacking the Shah's regime, while remaining in constant contact with the Iranian clergy.

Iran continued to develop rapidly. Industry and business, trade and agriculture flourished, the national health service improved, schools and hospitals were built. These and other reforms had the backing of the Europeanized middle class – some 20 per cent of the population. The rest were peasants, who benefited from the reforms but remained under the influence of the Islamic clergy. Khomeini was by no means the sole opponent of the Shah. Many of the country's mullahs preached that he and his servants were atheists, the seed of Satan, and his reforms a deviation from Islam. His lavish celebration of Iran's pre-Islamic past on the occasion of the 2,500th anniversary of statehood in 1971 played into their hands. The fact that the Iranians were Indo-Europeans, not Arabs, was constantly harped upon. A special Farkhangestan Institute of Iranian Culture was set up in Tehran with the main purpose of ridding the Farsi language of its Arabic borrowings. To the clergy, these were attacks on Islam.

The disturbances that began at the end of 1977 were inspired by both the mullahs and left-wing organizations. They spread in the face of inaction by the Iranian authorities, and by the summer of 1978 they embraced practically the whole of the country. Continual strikes were virtually paralyzing the economy. Petrol supplies were interrupted, with enormous queues outside the petrol stations, and frequent brawls.

The Iranian Ministry of the Interior issued petrol coupons specifically for the diplomatic corps, since petrol prices were out of control. But even with these coupons our drivers had to spend hours, and even nights, standing in queues. A petrol pump with a storage tank was installed in our embassy grounds to meet emergency needs.

By the summer of 1978, the wealthy sector of the Iranian population was already in a state of incipient panic. The banks in Tehran were besieged by people who wanted to transfer their capital abroad. Astronomical sums in hard currency flowed out to Switzerland, Paris, London, New York and other places. According to reports we received, the Shah's family alone transferred about two and a half billion dollars abroad. Suddenly all that stopped. The employees of the Central Bank of Iran went on strike, refusing to stand by and watch this exodus of capital.

It must be said that the most far-sighted individuals began to remove their capital from Iran even earlier. The Shah himself took precautions. At that time I got to know a Swiss national who proved to be one of the personal pilots working for the Shah's family. This man was sure even then that something serious was coming. He based his conclusions on the fact that, if the Shah himself was afraid of the opposition, the regime was finished. The Shah had begun to transfer valuables in secret to Switzerland at the end of 1977. My acquaintance had taken part in these flights.

'Political unrest will soon begin with you too in the Soviet Union,' he told me in conversation.

'Where did you get that from?' I asked him, puzzled.

'From the same thing,' he answered calmly. 'Your top leaders are also transferring capital and valuables to Swiss banks. But all that is being done very much on the quiet.'

'But if it is being done very much on the quiet, then how do you know about it?'

'It's like this. Your bosses use special Swissair flights for these operations, and I have many friends among the pilots.'

I began to try to find out whether he knew the names of the Soviet leaders involved in these operations. Naturally, he did not. I did not doubt that my acquaintance was telling the truth for two reasons. First, I knew the nature of our leaders. Second, when my acquaintance realized that he had said too much, he began to beg me not to report what he had said to the embassy. It was enough for him, he said, that SAVAK would not let him out of its sight; the last thing he needed was to have the KGB after him as well.

He did not suspect with whom he was sharing his secrets. But even without his pleas, I had no intention of reporting what he had said to the Residency. Information of this nature would have brought me nothing but trouble.

When the disturbances began, the demonstrations were held under purely religious slogans, the main one of which was 'Allah o Akbar', or 'Allah is Great'. Then political slogans began to appear. The name of Ayatollah Khomeini as the leader of the movement was mentioned with increasing frequency. 'Allah o Akbar! Khomeini Rakhbar!' – Allah is Great, and Khomeini is our Leader! All the slogans of the demonstrations were in rhyme, and they sounded poetic and beautiful, in the best traditions of Persian poetry. These rhythms were easy to remember, and they sank indelibly into people's minds. The name of Khomeini as leader was on the lips of Iranians throughout the country.

Right from the outset, the Mujahidin and Fedayin left-wing groupings took an active part in organizing demonstrations and strikes. However, in order to enlist the support not just of the student youth, but of the ordinary people as well, they chose the already well-known 'Allah o Akbar! Khomeini Rakhbar!' as their main slogan. In this way they acknowledged his leading role.

Still the Shah did nothing, trying to find a way to bring the disturbances to a peaceful end. In an effort to do this, he went as far as deciding to sacrifice some of his closest supporters. The most unpopular personages in the country at the time were Hoveida, the prime minister, and Nasiri, the head of SAVAK. They were arrested on the Shah's orders. But this measure in no way calmed down the demonstrators, since they were already demanding the blood of the Shah himself. It was said that, apart from purely political reasons, Khomeini also had a personal reason for hating the Shah. In 1977, Khomeini's eldest son Mustapha, then living in Iran, was killed in a road accident. Khomeini blamed SAVAK, acting on the Shah's orders. He allegedly vowed vengeance in blood on the Shah for the death of his son.

The attitude in the KGB Residency to the events which were

taking place in Iran was twofold. On the one hand we could not ignore the manifest threat to the existence of the Shah's regime. On the other, we could not rid ourselves of the belief which had grown up over the years that the Shah's regime was the strongest in the area, with its modern army, police, SAVAK and the support of the West. I have already said that we had no contacts with the opposition, while sources close to the regime continued to assert that the Shah was preparing to deal a crushing blow at his enemies. Meanwhile we all sat day after day, and expected that 'now he will give it to them!' But the Shah did not give them anything, while the strength of the opposition went on growing.

In face of this situation, Moscow organized a secret approach to Khomeini in Iraq. It was done with great care, for fear of the Shah's reaction. A meeting took place, and Khomeini was given vague promises of support in the event of his coming to power. For his part, he gave evasive answers, but it was clear that he did not burn with a desire to throw himself into the Soviet embrace.

In the course of this visit to Khomeini's camp, our representatives were struck by the fact that there were many Iranians in his entourage who until then had been living in the United States and Britain. Our analysts used these circumstances, and various other facts, to put together a new theory, and this is what resulted. In the analysts' opinion, the Americans had reached the conclusion that the Shah's regime had become obsolete. In his domestic policy he was incapable of anticipating or containing the disturbances. In foreign policy he had come to show considerable independence, having begun to play with the Soviet Union and other socialist countries while following a policy of balance between East and West. The Shah was thus milking two cows. The United States government, which attached great importance to the strategic position of Iran in relation to the Soviet Union, did not wish to lose influence in this area. When the disturbances, organized by the clergy, began in Iran, the Americans saw the chance to get rid of the redundant Shah and to establish good relations with the new regime.

The clergy, according to all the Soviet theories, and especially the Iranian clergy, had always been reactionary and stood in the service of CAPITAL. As the well-known saying has it, 'Under the beard of every mullah, there is a stamp saying "Made in

Great Britain".' Khomeini, in the Soviet experts' opinion, was a natural ally of the West. That was why President Carter restrained the Shah while he held forth about human rights. That was why Khomeini was surrounded by Iranians who had spent a long time in the United States and now no doubt had been dispatched by the CIA into Khomeini's entourage. The conclusion that suggested itself was that the Americans were playing a new Iranian card. At that stage, the Soviet leadership began to look upon Khomeini as a protégé of the United States.

Meanwhile the demonstrations went on spreading, and had by now assumed a menacing character. Now the slogan 'Death to the Shah' rang out unceasingly. Troops were deployed on the streets of Tehran, but they did nothing, apart from performing the functions of guards at government buildings and some foreign embassies, including our own. During demonstrations that went past the Soviet embassy, the demonstrators insulted the soldiers and openly spat on them. The soldiers did not react, as they had no orders to oppose the crowd. Finally, the officer in charge of the unit guarding our embassy asked our permission to deploy his soldiers in the grounds, in order not to provoke the crowd with their presence on the street. After some vacillation, the ambassador agreed.

At first the soldiers adopted a very chilly manner towards us, most likely expecting the KGB to begin recruiting them all. The ice was broken by the children of the embassy officials. At first they only talked with the soldiers, but soon they began to play with their guns, and finally football matches were taking place between them. Gradually we succeeded in conversing with the soldiers and their officers. There was only one subject of conversation – what was happening? They said that they had strict orders not to enter into conflict with the demonstrators. Some soldiers were in agreement with this, while others, the officers especially, favoured tough measures.

The Shah's regime was beginning to lose control of the situation. In the end, the advocates of tough measures convinced him to make a show of strength. On the morning of 8 September 1978, a demonstration of many thousands strong began to gather in Jaleh Square, in the eastern part of Tehran. By midday, the square was full to overflowing with demonstrators. It was then that the troops appeared. The square was quickly cordoned off, and all approaches to it blocked. It was quite easy to do this. The square was in the form of a circle with four streets in all leading to it. By cutting them off, the soldiers could shut the people into the square. Now they opened fire. The purpose in taking this action was not to break up the demonstration, but to eliminate those taking part in it. The troops moved in to the square from all the adjacent streets, steadily firing straight into the crowd with automatic weapons. Military helicopters flew overhead, machine-gunning the demonstrators.

Jaleh Square was about four kilometres from the Soviet Embassy, so we heard the shooting clearly. It continued from noon until somewhere around 11 o'clock at night. People outside the square could only guess what was going on inside. The soldiers kept it cordoned off until the following morning, by which time practically no traces of the carnage remained. All the corpses had been removed somewhere during the night. Fire engines hosed away the blood from the road surface. Nobody knew the exact number of those who died, but rumours said that several thousand people had been killed.

The massacre in Jaleh Square did not have the effect desired by the hard-liners, since the Shah opposed the next step to be taken in suppressing the disorders, which was to arrest all opposition leaders, lists of whom had already been drawn up. The indecisiveness of the Shah thus played into the hands of the opposition. The spilt blood excited the people still further, the mullahs declaring those who had fallen to be martyrs in the name of Islam and Allah, and calling for revenge. And the never-ending funeral wakes for those who had died set off further waves of demonstrations.

The Shah's regime kept quiet about the events of Jaleh Square. No one wanted to take responsibility upon himself. Rumours circulated in Tehran, apparently spread by the military, to the effect that the gunning down of the demonstrators had not been done by Iranian soldiers at all, but by some foreigners wearing uniforms without identifying insignia. They said that they were Israeli commandos brought specially to Iran in order to carry out this operation at the request of the Shah himself. The military were thus trying to dissociate themselves from what had been done. According to intelligence material held by the GRU Residency, there had been no foreigners in Jaleh Square. The entire operation was carried out by commandos from the Iranian division of special purpose troops.

Reaction to the slaughter in Tehran itself was varied, and sometimes quite surprising. We in the KGB Residency expected to hear condemnations of the authorities' actions, but the real responses were quite different. The supporters of the Shah's regime welcomed the action taken, complaining only that force of arms was long overdue and should have been used from the very beginning. 'They killed five thousand? Ten thousand should have been shot, and much earlier, in order to stop this black plague! You Europeans don't even begin to understand the horror that faces Iran in the power of the priesthood. The Shah's repressions will turn out to have been child's play in comparison.'

Nor did we find any special sorrow for the dead even among the opponents of the regime. Revolutionary-minded young people who came to us in the consulate, and who looked up to the Soviet Union, spoke triumphantly. 'We want to build a society in this country like the one you have in the Soviet Union! One must not worry about the spilt blood. The more blood, the more vicious the masses, and the quicker they will overthrow the Shah's regime. One must not grieve for those killed. The Shahidi [those who die in the name of Islam] go straight to paradise and they are only to be envied.' I wanted to warn these naïve zealots about the dangers of their delusions, and to tell them about the falsity of the whole Soviet system, but that was something I could not do. In any case, blinded and deafened as they were by communist and Islamic propaganda, they would never have believed me.

The noble enterprises set in train by Ivan Anisimovich Fadeikin, the KGB resident, were suddenly interrupted. He contracted severe hepatitis and was sent semi-conscious to the Soviet hospital in Tehran. Although the doctors agreed unanimously that Fadeikin could be cured on the spot, the ambassador insisted upon his being sent to Moscow immediately. 'We can't take risks with the life of such an outstanding servant of the Soviet State,' Ambassador Vladimir Mikhailovich Vinogradov pronounced with feeling. Fadeikin could not make the decision himself, and nobody argued with the ambassador. Fadeikin was sent back to Moscow on the next available plane, early in 1979.

With a specious pretext, the ambassador had got rid of his worst enemy. But it is one thing to send the KGB resident back to Moscow, and quite another to ensure that he does not return. Our ambassador found a way. With Fadeikin gone, he wrote a mud-slinging letter to Yuri Andropov, then KGB chairman, accusing the resident of every possible sin, including making statements against 'the leading role of the Communist Party of the Soviet Union'.

Fadeikin spent about seven months in hospital. When he was discharged, Andropov promptly summoned him to his presence, gave him a fearful dressing down, and informed him that his career was finished. Fadeikin could not take such injustice and it broke him completely. His illness broke out once again, and shortly afterwards it took the form of cancer of the liver. Fadeikin died in December 1979. He was given a funeral corresponding to the rank of KGB lieutenant-general, and as a farewell gesture, his body was laid out in state in the Central Club of the KGB.

Thus a self-serving crook of an ambassador destroyed a general of the KGB. There could hardly be a better example to show to whom the power in the land belongs.

During my absence from Tehran, a new head had arrived to take over the consular department of the embassy. He was Vladimir Ivanovich Dyatlov, supposedly a straight diplomat. The post of embassy consular department chief traditionally belonged to KGB intelligence, but after the expulsion of Boris Kabanov, the intelligence officer who had held the post, following General Mogarebi's arrest, the Centre took a decision, for reasons of cover, to give it up for a couple of years. Soviet Foreign Ministry people do not like these posts – they think that the local counter-intelligence might 'stage a provocation' – so instead of a professional Iranian specialist we received Dyatlov, who was not even a diplomat in the usual sense of the word. He had been a small-time Party functionary somewhere in industry, and although I had no idea why he had been moved into diplomatic work, it seemed to me that, wherever he was, everyone would long to get rid of him. The fact was that Dyatlov was a complete idiot.

Short in stature, broad-shouldered and solidly built, he gave the impression of a lout. He had done free-style wrestling when he was young and had been well-developed physically, but now he had put on weight, and when he walked he waddled along with his arms stuck out at his sides. He had no neck, and his raised head sat directly on his shoulders. His round, fat, constantly smiling face was the embodiment of giggling stupidity, and perfectly in keeping with his stream of feeble jokes.

By the time I returned, Dyatlov had already spent about six weeks in the consulate, and had acquired the reputation of an absolute layabout and a blockhead. His duties included receiving both Soviet and foreign visitors, dealing with the correspondence with the Soviet Foreign Ministry, and visiting the Iranian Foreign Ministry to discuss visa and other matters. Instead, he did not work at all, pleading at first that he did not yet know the situation and that he was still learning the ropes.

Until then, all of us in the consulate had been KGB officers, each with his main work to do in the Residency. Our consular duties were a nuisance, but we shared them out equally, irrespective of rank. Now we had the spectacle of a man who had nothing to do but his consular duties, yet had no intention of performing them. Soon it began to irritate us. Dyatlov either sat for days on end in his office, gawping at the local English-language paper, although his knowledge of the language was rudimentary, or else he would disappear for days at a time, always 'on consular business'.

It soon became clear what business was accounting for Dyatlov's day. He would visit the heads of the different Soviet organizations in Tehran and, in essence, invite himself to meals. What head of an organization does not dream of having in his pocket the head of an embassy consular department, who holds all legal authority in his hands? A moment finally came when one of our officers ran out of patience and asked Dyatlov straight out when he intended to start doing his job. The question was put so directly and sharply that Dyatlov was unable to divert it with a joke, as he had done previously. When he revealed his real nature, he spoke with the authentic voice of the nomenklatura.

'I didn't come here to work,' he sneered, 'but to give orders to you and others like you! Try to put pressure on me again, and I'll cover you in so much mud that you'll never wash it off with the Chief. I already know all about the lot of you.'

The 'Chief' was what Dyatlov always called the KGB resident, whom he considered to be his guardian. Dyatlov was a KGB informer, with the cover name of 'Aleksandrov'. It is interesting how all these 'knockers' would choose noble-sounding pseudonyms, as if in an attempt to compensate for the meanness of their character. Like all 'knockers' he regarded himself as influential. Here he was mistaken. 'I don't want to see that oaf of an informer again,' said Fadeikin after he had met him on one occasion, and he handed him to a security officer to run. Our officer reported Dyatlov's behaviour to the resident but he simply spread his hands in a gesture of help-lessness, although he promised to reprimand Dyatlov as curator of consular affairs.

It must be said that while Dyatlov was a complete idiot in the intellectual sense, in daily life he possessed an animal cunning and the insolence of a thief. Working in the Party machine had taught him that in Soviet society, anything goes. It is not strictly true to say that Dyatlov ignored consular matters. He studied the financial machinery very thoroughly, and I began to notice strange things.

Like any consulate, ours required applicants to fill up visa forms, which were always issued free to callers. They lay on the security guards' table, and anyone could take them. Suddenly these forms disappeared. I needed some on one occasion in order to register a visa for one of our contacts to make a secret trip to the Soviet Union. They turned up, under lock and key, in the desk of the duty security guard. He had put them there on Dyatlov's orders.

All the forms were now ordered in batches of 100, and a log-book had been opened to keep track of their distribution. But the most inconceivable thing was that these forms were now being sold to callers for money: Dyatlov had ordered the security guards to charge the equivalent of two dollars apiece. Two forms had to be filled in to apply for a visa, which meant that each applicant had to pay four dollars. The security guard said that the log-book had been opened, not to keep a record of the forms, but to register the money received. Dyatlov and his wife would make up the forms into batches in the evenings, and then issue them to the security guard against a signature. At the end of the day he counted the forms again, and the profits made, and gave the security guard a dressing down if he had given any forms out free of charge.

When I asked him the reason for this innovation, Dyatlov replied, without batting an eyelid, that the consular department was going over to a system of financial self-sufficiency, and that this had already been agreed with the ambassador. The money made would be spent on stationery and other office materials. Knowing our ambassador's attitude to the financial independence of whomever it might be, I did not believe Dyatlov. My suspicions were confirmed two years later when one of our officers conducted a personal investigation into Dyatlov's malpractices and worked out that our titular chief had pocketed a sum in Iranian currency equivalent to $50,000 from the sale of these forms alone.

Dyatlov would stop at nothing to enrich himself. An old woman, one of the local White Russians, used to keep coming round to the consulate to see us. She was somewhere about eighty years of age, all her relatives in Iran had died, and she was living entirely alone. What she wanted was to take up residence in Russia, in order, as she put it, 'just to die on my native soil', but because of her age and because she had no living relatives, we knew that the Soviet Union would not accept her for residence. Although we explained all this quite bluntly, still she kept coming in to the consulate and imploring us all. It was such a pitiful spectacle that, had I had my way, I would have paid for her myself, but Soviet law is inexorable. Then, suddenly, everything changed. Whereas before our elderly lady sat in the waiting room being looked after by the security guards, she now went straight into Dyatlov's office, and stayed there for an hour, and sometimes two.

One morning I saw our constant visitor in the waiting room. She was no longer crying. On the contrary, she looked happy and full of the joys of life. I invited her into my office and she agreed to have a chat, saying quite proudly as she did so that she was now being dealt with personally by Consul Dyatlov, who had told her that she must not go to anyone else but him.

'And you were all telling me,' she began, looking at me with her kind eyes, 'that they wouldn't accept me for residence in Russia! I was old, you said, and I have no relatives. But now your consul, God bless him, has fixed everything. He has already sent all my papers to the Supreme Soviet in Moscow, and he says that he has had a preliminary favourable reaction already. My mind is now at rest, I know that I shall soon be in my homeland. I have already begun to get ready for the move. I have withdrawn all my savings and have taken out my valuables from the bank, and have handed them over for safe keeping to Vladimir Ivanovich, God bless him. He said that the banks were now unreliable and I agree. Oh, I've been talking too much to you,' she said, standing up. 'It's time for me to see Vladimir Ivanovich. Today I'm going to discuss the sale of my house with him.'

Immediately after that conversation, I went into our registry and looked at the files dealing with resettlement cases in the Soviet Union. There was no mention of the case of this old Russian lady, and the secretary who handled all cases and correspondence knew nothing about it either. Now everything was obvious. Dyatlov was trying to get his hands on the old woman's fortune, by duping her with promises of resettlement. He was counting on her not having long to live.

How low a man must be, to play so coldly with the life and trust of a defenceless old woman. At that moment my only wish was to go into Dyatlov's office and beat the life out of him, but that I could not do. I did report the whole thing to the resident, and he in turn reported it to the ambassador. Dyatlov was ordered to return everything to the old woman. As always, he made excuses and played the gormless idiot, but he promised to give everything back. Incidentally, all the valuables, excluding the money, fitted into a small sack. They included two gold bars, gold coins and some fairly large diamonds.

Dyatlov reported later that he had returned the valuables and the money, but nobody saw him do so, and there were no witnesses. The old woman herself disappeared and was never seen in the consulate again. I do not know what became of her, but her sudden disappearance inspired some sinister thoughts. A scoundrel like Dyatlov was capable of anything.

The case of the old woman was not the only one of its kind. The same thing happened with an Iranian Azerbaijani who had relatives in the Soviet Union and who wanted to move to Soviet Azerbaijan to settle there. Dyatlov 'handled his case', promising him the earth in his homeland. As a result the Azerbaijani divorced his wife, who did not want to go to the Soviet Union, sold his house and gave up his job in the expectation that he was about to receive his visa. It turned out in the end that he could not have a visa, since Dyatlov had not even thought of sending his papers to Moscow, while he went on feeding the Azerbaijani with promises over a period of eighteen months. This affair came to light by chance. Dyatlov was on leave in Moscow and a new consular official who received the Azerbaijani in his absence explained perfectly honestly and openly to him that he could not find any papers on his case. When he realized he had been duped, the Azerbaijani flew into a murderous rage. Later he submitted to the ambassador a written complaint, in which he said among other things that he had paid Dyatlov ten thousand dollars to speed up his case. As we knew Dyatlov, we all believed the Azerbaijani. The ambassador preferred to call it a provocation.

Everybody in the Soviet community drank. But alcohol affected Dyatlov in a way peculiar to him. After a few glasses of vodka, his eyes would glaze, the inane smile would fade from his face, and he would silence anyone else who might be speaking. At the same time he would begin to swear foully, irrespective of the presence of women. It seemed that he became another person, who in no way resembled the usual Dyatlov, the fool. His monologue was always the same: 'Nobody here can tell *me* what to do! Neither the KGB nor the ambassador! I am so well connected that I can destroy the lot of you!'

Embassy officials stopped socializing with him, but that did not isolate Dyatlov. He was taken up by the heads of the various Soviet economic organizations, for whom it was a rare success to number among their friends a person with consular authority, no matter what a dung-heap he might be. He also made a name among the diplomats of the consular corps in Tehran. He was famous for always being late for all consular functions without exception, be it a reception, a cocktail party, or a dinner. Sometimes he appeared when the dessert or coffee was being served. He would sit down at table, unabashed, and demand to be served with the courses he had missed. For him, anything went. He had no manners, no tact, no idea how to behave socially, and spoke practically no English. Even if he had done so there was absolutely nothing to talk to him about. Of politics he was totally ignorant.

We in the Residency, as well as the straight diplomats and GRU officers, were at a loss to understand how Dyatlov was able to get away with what he did. Anyone else would have been thrown out of Tehran and the Foreign Ministry long before, but he blundered on. We could only assume that he must have very high connections in the Party machine. No one knew exactly who they were, but it was said that he had relatives somewhere at the candidate membership level of the Party's Politburo. Certainly he was swinish enough to remind one of somebody up there at the top.

By the autumn of 1978, Khomeini's activity in Iraq had intensified to an incredible extent. The Iraqi town of Najaf, where Khomeini was exiled at the time, had become a centre of Iranian opposition. Iranian emigrants of all types and political convictions flocked there from all over the world in order to make contact with the new and now undisputed leader of the future Iran.

Khomeini's activities were not much to the liking of the Iraqi government, since they were taking place in areas which were populated predominantly by Shiites, a numerical but not a political majority in Iraq. The authorities there had enough problems of their own, so they had no hesitation in agreeing to an Iranian proposal that Khomeini and his supporters should be deported, and in October 1978 the Iraqi authorities ordered him to leave Iraq. Not all that many countries wanted to see this trouble-maker on their territory, particularly those Muslim countries which, even without Khomeini, already faced the problem of Islamic fundamentalism.

According to information that we held, the Shah played an active part in Khomeini's removal. It was said that he had even tried to persuade the Indonesian government to accept Khomeini, and promised to pick up the bill for Khomeini's upkeep himself, if only his worst enemy could be sent as far as possible from Iran. Finally France agreed to take the Ayatollah as a tourist, but issued him with a visa valid for only three months. The Shah made no objection when consulted, as he calculated that Khomeini would be a far greater threat if based in Libya or Syria. Events disproved this view. By settling in Neauphle-le-Château, a village not far from Paris, Khomeini obtained access to the world press. Or more exactly, the world communications media obtained access to this new sensation which was Khomeini.

The name of Khomeini now became known not just in Iran, but throughout the world. His protests against the Shah's regime, spread by the mass media, rang round the globe. Since the Shah was unable publicly to answer these accusations, world public opinion tilted in favour of the Iranian opposition. Foreign radio stations like the BBC and the Voice of America informed the Iranian population of what was going on around Khomeini in their broadcasts in Farsi to Iran. Contact like this was far more profitable for Khomeini than the distribution of tape cassettes with his speeches. Now everything he said or did became known immediately in Iran. These broadcasts also performed an enormous service for us in the Soviet embassy, since we did not have to run around town looking for information on what the opposition was doing.

Finally, as events continued to unfold in Iran, the crunch came. On 5 November 1978, following Khomeini's orders from Paris, throughout Tehran groups of people who had been specially prepared and briefed in the mosques began simultaneously to smash up banks, hotels, cinemas, restaurants, cafés and shops that sold alcoholic drinks. Crowds joined in, and the chaos assumed mass proportions when neither troops nor police intervened. The underlying purpose of this action was purely Islamic. It was to destroy and smash up everything that ran contrary to the Muslim faith, everything connected with the use of alcoholic drink, charging interest on money, and depicting the human image, either on the screen or on paper.

We in the embassy had a good view of the unfolding tragedy. Plenty of establishments hateful to Islam were located in this central part of town. Frenzied groups of young people rushed at the shops and cafés, tore down the sliding metal shutters, dragged beer cans and bottles of spirits out on to the streets and smashed them on the roadway. Some of them also tried to set fire to the premises. For many Russians observing what was happening through the grilled embassy gates, and whose Christian religion certainly did not ban the use of alcohol, what was taking place was sheer blasphemy. 'What a lot of stuff you've wasted, you Muslims!' Several cans of Carlsberg beer were hurled at us over the wall by the ravening crowd as it surged past the embassy. One can hit an officer of our Residency right in the back. He picked it up and looked at it. 'God has sent it,' he said. 'And it might be the last one.' He then toasted Khomeini's health and drank it.

Next morning, one of our officers and I decided to go into town and see the results of the riot. A stench, the suffocating reeking smell of alcohol, hung over the centre of Tehran. We saw in the rows of buildings the yawning black gaps where there had been shops and restaurants, now burnt and destroyed. Standing aimlessly around them were people with lost expressions on their faces, apparently the owners of these establishments. Hotels and banks, destroyed and burnt. Not one cinema in town remained undamaged. On Lalezar Street, famous for its small cafés and tiny restaurants, they had all been destroyed and burnt down to the last one. In one place, a large expanse of street was covered with a thick layer of the melted metal of beer cans. The stench of alcohol here was intolerable.

For the first time, we had all had a purely physical experience of what the forthcoming Islamic regime would bring. In carrying out that assault, the opposition had gone over from peaceful protest demonstrations to open confrontation. A few days later, Khomeini announced that it had been an act of revenge on the atheists for the killing in Jaleh Square. Open war was declared on everything Western in Iran.

The peaceful stage was over. Delegations from the most senior ranks of the military went to the Shah to demand the introduction of martial law, and the Shah agreed. The military wanted the post of prime minister to go to General Oveissi, the commander of the Tehran Military District. He was a tough, decisive man who reckoned that the disturbances could still be put down by arresting the entire opposition leadership. But the Shah vacillated over Oveissi's appointment, and in the end he declined to accept it. Instead of Oveissi, he appointed General Azhari, a soft man opposed to using force. According to reports we held in the

Residency, his appointment was promoted by the Shah's American advisers. Azhari planned to placate the mullahs by means of negotiations.

With the introduction of martial law in November 1978, a curfew lasting from 9 p.m. until 5 a.m. was imposed on Tehran. This curfew however was constantly infringed. Evening prayers in the mosques were intentionally prolonged by the mullahs until 10 p.m., and after the crowds left the mosque, clashes began with the troops. The soldiers opened fire, mostly into the air. The crowd usually scattered, but only in order to regroup elsewhere. It went on like that almost every evening. The military prime minister made frequent television appearances to give a 'last warning', but this did not help.

At that time I was living in town, not far from the embassy. In the evenings we used to go up on to the roof of the house in order to see what was going on, or rather to listen to what was taking place in the eastern part of the city, where many mosques are concentrated. The rumbling wail of 'Allah o Akbar' would begin shortly after 10 o'clock, to be followed by shooting, accompanied by the wilder cry of the crowd. We soon learnt to tell from the sound which weapons were being used. They were usually the standard semi-automatic rifles of the Iranian army, but sometimes the air was torn by the more rapid crackle of a Kalashnikov automatic rifle, with which I was well acquainted. The Iranian army had no Kalashnikovs. Evidently the opposition had begun to put up armed resistance.

Our vigils continued until one occasion late at night when we heard strange sounds just above our heads, 'zzzz, zzzz', reminiscent of the buzzing of bees. But bees do not fly at night. At that point I realized that the sound came from ricocheting bullets. We quickly came down from the roof and never went back.

The pace of events was accelerating. Attacks on SAVAK premises were increasing throughout the country. The SAVAK observation post opposite our embassy closed down in December, and we stopped seeing and hearing their surveillance teams at work. Not that we were doing anything for them to observe, for even without what was going on, the small KGB agent network in Iran had to all intents and purposes collapsed, and most agents and contacts had left the country.

The military situation was not working out. Azhari resigned, and the Shah proposed to Shahpur Bakhtiar, a representative of the National Front Party, that he form a government. Demonstrations continued all over the country. There was now but one demand – 'Death to the Shah.' It was announced on 9 January that the Shah would shortly leave 'for a holiday' abroad. On 14 January a regency council was formed for the duration of his absence. On 16 January 1979 the Shah and his family left Iran aboard an aircraft bound for Egypt.

Tehran Radio broadcast this news at 2 p.m., and the immediate response was unimaginable. Vehicles moving through the city switched on their headlights and ceaselessly sounded their horns. Hands stuck out of windows giving the victory sign. People on the streets laughed hysterically, danced and sang. 'Freedom, freedom,' was the constant cry which hung in the air. Everywhere portraits of the Shah were being torn up and burnt. His numerous monuments were overturned and smashed. Special newspaper editions came out bearing the headline in huge letters, 'The Shah Has Fled', printed upside down. And much more in the same vein.

The Iranian army declared its support for Shahpur Bakhtiar, the new head of government, and in order to cool the ardour of the excessively democratically-minded Iranians, it organized a show of force on 23 January. That day a motorized division of the Shah's guards passed through Tehran. We all went out to see this spectacle. Gleaming light tanks and armoured vehicles. The clean, smart, well-fed guardsmen with inscrutable faces. The endless column of vehicles passed through the crowds in almost total quiet. The noise of the engines was all that could be heard. The people looked on in silence, not knowing how to interpret this act by the army. The chill of a possible military coup was felt by everyone.

But nothing happened. Having displayed their strength and devotion to the Shah, the guardsmen returned to barracks and life resumed. That is to say, the demonstrations flared up again. Now that the Shah was no longer in the country, the demonstrators demanded the return of Khomeini. For Khomeini himself, who had previously stipulated the Shah's departure as a condition for his own return to Iran, only a single obstacle remained. There were persistent rumours that enemies of the Ayatollah in the Iranian armed forces were threatening to destroy his aircraft as soon as it entered Iranian air space.

One of the most noticeable changes that had followed Bakhtiar's appointment as head of the government was the removal of press censorship. Now the newspapers printed everything they wanted, both the truth and invention. It became no longer necessary for us in the Residency to run around town collecting information about what was happening and meeting with contacts. In any case, there was hardly anybody to meet. With every day that passed, the number of the Residency's contacts dwindled, in inverse proportion to the growing numbers of the Shah's supporters who were leaving Iran, for among these were most of our contacts. We still continued to be cautious towards the opposition, in accordance with the fine Soviet tradition of keeping our heads down in case something happened. Meanwhile, the resident's main concern was to keep up a stream of information to the Centre. It did not matter where it came from, provided that it was reliable. All our officers had to do was to compare the various newspaper reports on the same subject, add radio and television reports, remove inventions and arrive at the required information.

Meanwhile rumours about Khomeini's return intensified and were spread by the newspapers. The date was even given for his planned return – 25 January. On 24 January, as a precaution, the military authorities closed the airport to all flights. Demonstrations in support of Khomeini gathered strength. Shahpur Bakhtiar recognized the influence that Khomeini had over the Iranian population, and he tried to establish contact. He even planned to call on the old man in Paris. But Khomeini sensed victory; he stipulated that the Bakhtiar government should resign as a condition of any negotiations. Naturally this was unacceptable. No contacts took place.

All this was reported openly in the Iranian press. The government's reluctance to allow Khomeini to return gave rise to more anti-government manifestations. Clashes between troops and demonstrators were occurring all over the country. Bakhtiar finally lost control. Now there was nothing left for him to do but to allow Khomeini to return, but this would be an admission of defeat. A compromise was found in the end. The Iranian authorities opened Tehran airport on 31 January, saying nothing either for or against Khomeini's return. On the same day the newspapers announced that Khomeini would return to Iran on 1 February.

That is what happened. On 1 February 1979 Ayatollah Khomeini returned to Iran after a fourteen year exile. A special Air France flight brought him from Paris to Tehran. Apparently aware of the threat to him from the Iranian armed forces, Khomeini did not venture to fly by an Iranian aircraft, and preferred a French one. Bakhtiar would be unlikely to shoot down a French plane in Iranian air space.

That day Tehran was full to overflowing. It seemed that all its four million inhabitants had poured out on to the streets and had set off for Mehrabad airport. Khomeini's arrival was transmitted by television from the moment his aircraft touched down. A door is opening. He begins to descend the gangway, with a French airman taking his arm. Halfway down, one of the backless slippers he is wearing comes off, and he gropes clumsily to find it. Now comes the chilly meeting with representatives of the authorities. Around the aircraft, all is quiet. No crowd, no enthusiasm.

At that moment there were many supporters of the Shah's regime who still cherished the hope that the military would arrest Khomeini and settle accounts with him. Neither Khomeini himself nor his entourage knew what to expect from the Iranian authorities. They looked very tense and apprehensive. But nothing happened. The representatives of the clergy who had come to meet him put Khomeini in a Land-Rover, and the vehicle left the confines of the airport. Here the conditions were entirely different. When it saw the vehicle carrying its new spiritual leader, the vast crowd, heaving like the sea, grew more agitated and began to shout still louder. The road was crammed to overflowing with people, and the vehicle inched its way forward.

The events that followed Khomeini's return unfolded with incredible speed. Khomeini rejected the negotiations proposed by Bakhtiar, the prime minister, and instead declared that he was appointing Bazargan head of the government of the Islamic Republic. He also called on the population to ignore all orders coming from Bakhtiar and to place themselves under the government of the new Islamic Republic and no one else. In effect a dual authority, with the balance favouring Khomeini, was established in the country. Demonstrations throughout the land supported the Islamic Republic. Many ministries and institutions declared their recognition of the Islamic Republic government.

The armed insurrection began on 9 February. An armed clash took place between the Shah's guards and technical personnel at the Doshan Tappeh air base in Farahabad, situated in the south-east part of Tehran. Both sides suffered heavy losses. The insurgent air technicians appealed to the people for help. This appeal was immediately answered by armed formations of the Mujahidin and Fedayin organizations, consisting of young people, mostly students, who had been hoarding arms for some time for precisely such a moment. The members of these organizations did not just join in the fighting at the Doshan Tappeh base. They also began to attack troops and police stations throughout Tehran. The Bakhtiar government declared a curfew from 4.30 p.m., but only foreigners observed it. We preferred to sit in our homes and not to interfere.

We in the KGB Residency knew virtually everything that went on from the beginning of the uprising. We knew about it, not because we had a circle of agents, but simply because we were monitoring almost all radio conversations in Tehran – army, police, fire service, first aid service, everything. Round-the-clock duty was set up in the Impulse interception station in order to keep track of events.

Thus we knew that police stations were falling one after the other into the hands of the rebels. The mood of the police was one of panic. Many did not want to open fire on the people and preferred to go over to the rebel side. Soldiers went over to the opposition and surrendered their weapons. Thus the soldiers who were protecting the British embassy surrendered their weapons to the opposition without resistance. Members of the Mujahidin and Fedayin attacked arms storage depots belonging to the army and distributed the weapons to the populace. The rebels attacked the prisons and opened them, releasing everyone indiscriminately, both political prisoners and criminals, and even those who were the worst enemies of the opposition. Thus, for example, General Nasiri, the former head of SAVAK, who had been put in prison by the Shah, was also nearly released. His cell door was opened, and he was almost outside the prison grounds when he was recognized as the former head of SAVAK and once again placed under lock and key, after a thorough beating.

Control of the city gradually passed into the hands of the opposition. On 10 February I was on duty at the radio interception station, checking on what was going on. There was chaos on the air-waves. Some of the radio networks were still held by the authorities, but others had fallen into the hands of the insurrectionists. Practically nobody could connect with anyone else. Suddenly I heard two police stations establish contact with each other. At one end was a government policeman, on the other a representative of the rebels. When it dawned on them who was who, each decided to deluge the other with his political credo, and in the foulest language.

'You rebels,' the policeman began. 'I've fucked your mother in the mouth, and your Khomeini, Lenin, Marx, Brezhnev!'

'Aaah,' bawled the rebel's representative in fury. 'Your Shah, and Carter, and aaah' (he was unable to bring any more names to mind) 'I've fucked them in the mouth as well!'

They were still slanging one another when their conversation, which was most unusual for the very polite Iranians, was interrupted by a third voice, that of an elderly educated man.

'Stop this filthy squabble immediately! You are both Iranians and representatives of a great culture. Don't you understand that your conversation can now be heard by the whole world?'

Strangely this intervention had the effect of a bucket of cold water on both, and they ended their exchanges abashed. It was strange that I too felt ashamed for having been amused by their wrangle.

At 3 o'clock in the afternoon of 11 February, the Bakhtiar government resigned and a new government took power. Everything of the Shah became the opposition! Just like that!

The last monolithic bastion of devotion to the Shah's regime were the barracks of the Shah's guards. They resisted to the last and finally, after suffering enormous losses, they surrendered to the will of the victors on 12 February. On the same day the Iranian army, 'in order to avoid bloodshed', withdrew to its barracks and declared itself outside politics. Authority passed completely into the hands of Khomeini's supporters.

Now the soldiers were no longer visible on the streets. Cars and armoured carriers, with armed youths who were members of the Mujahidin and Fedayin organizations, no longer underground, sped through the city. They continued to seize various government establishments and to arrest known officers of SAVAK and the police. Armed representatives of the clergy were nowhere to be seen.

On 14 February, there was no longer any doubt that the Shah's regime had been overthrown completely. Fighting in Tehran had largely ceased, but for a few isolated bursts of shooting.

We who until that day had been sitting either in the embassy or at home now felt that we could go out on to the streets without being cautious. The KGB Residency had had no contacts with the anti-Shah opposition. The situation now changed. We had to recover lost ground, and this was the strategic moment. A firm authority in the country had not yet been established. SAVAK was out of action. The young people holding the weapons were mostly pro-Soviet. On 14 February all Residency officers were ordered to go out into town and to begin to 'fish in troubled waters' until the new authorities had collected themselves and were putting us back under pressure. That this would happen, we had no doubt whatever. So early in the morning on 14 February we set off for town. Most of us went to Tehran University, where the headquarters of the Mujahidin and Fedayin were now installed.

The grounds of the university were literally filled to overflowing with people, most of them young, in appearance students and representatives of the middle class. They crowded round the headquarters of the Mujahidin and Fedayin, which were located in separate buildings not far apart. It was very easy to distinguish the Mujahidin members from those of the Fedayin. Both organizations had been underground and clandestine in the time of the Shah; now they had divided opinions about the new authorities. The Mujahidin, who believed Khomeini's promise that different political parties would function freely and openly in the Islamic Republic, decided to cease completely to be clandestine and to uncover their faces. Their members were now distinguished only by a white band round their heads. But the Fedayin considered that it was still too early to trust the new authorities. They wanted to wait and see whether they would keep their promises about democracy: it was entirely possible that the clergy would intentionally encourage the legalization of political parties and groups in order to bring all their members into the open and then pounce at a suitable moment. This was prophetic! The Fedayin therefore continued to keep their faces covered, which they did by wearing checked Palestinian headscarves and sunglasses. When socializing, they used pseudonyms only.

To my surprise, that day in Tehran University I met quite a number of young Iranian acquaintances whom I had got to know when I was working as an interpreter (before the KGB) both in Moscow and in the course of my first tour of duty in Iran. Most were among the sympathizers of one or the other organizations. This suited me down to the ground, since in terms of illegal intelligence I looked upon them as potential recruits. The rules laid down that such recruits must not be active members of any political party or group. Such organizations are always under the close attention of the authorities.

In this favourable situation I planned to make as many contacts as I could, and then work out at leisure who was suitable for serious work and who was not. Pearls are not found in every oyster shell. The climate was favourable at the time since, although they were Muslims, the members and supporters of these organizations were still Marxists, with a sympathetic attitude towards the Soviet Union. Therefore as soon as they learnt that I was a Soviet Russian, friendly conversations at once started up. The fact that when the Shah was in power, social contacts with Soviets could easily land Iranians in serious trouble with SAVAK also helped this process along.

I spent that entire day in the university, talking both to members of Mujahidin and Fedayin fighting detachments and to their supporters. For the members of these fighting organizations, I was the Soviet government, for whom they had but one request – 'Give us weapons while it is still possible to seize power. Later will be too late.'

'But you are already armed,' I said.

'All this is nothing. It will only last a few days. We need continuous supplies.'

Some sceptical Mujahidin and Fedayin members had learnt from the bitter experience of appeals for Soviet help before the overthrow of the Shah. They wanted no contact at all, saying that 'When we were underground, you didn't want to know us, and now you come when it's all over! No, dear comrades, we can get on very well without you.' In my heart, I agreed with them completely.

Somewhere around 6 o'clock in the evening, an armed personnel carrier, with young lads in Palestinian field uniform, their faces
covered with their headscarves, literally clinging to its sides, raced
up to the Fedayin headquarters. They were all very excited. From
a brief conversation with one of them, I was able to discover that
their fighting groups had just seized the American embassy and the
diplomats inside it.

'We wanted to take the head of the CIA Station and learn from
him all their secrets and the names of American agents in Iran,' a
fellow with a covered face and dark spectacles said excitedly. 'But
a representative of the new authorities, someone called Yazdi, gave
us an order from the new government to do nothing of the kind and
to leave the embassy territory. And who are you?' he asked suddenly,
eyeing me with suspicion. 'An American?'

'No, no,' I hastened to assure him. 'I'm a Russian from the
Soviet Embassy.'

'Oh, that's all right then. Incidentally, we have a Russian among
us,' he said, and introduced me to a tall man with his face covered.
My new acquaintance and I moved to one side. He turned out to
be a third-generation White Russian, from a family who settled in
Iran after 1917. He spoke Russian almost without an accent, but
in the style of before the Revolution. After a brief conversation he
uncovered his face. He was an agreeable fellow with serious blue
eyes.

'We don't uncover our faces because we're sure that the new
authorities are not to be trusted. Just look how they've reacted
to the seizure of the American embassy. What we wanted to find
there was a tunnel leading to the main SAVAK building. There
are quite a few of these SAVAK tunnels around town, and we're
trying to locate them.'

We ended our conversation after it got dark, and agreed to meet
next day.

I reported my new contacts in the Residency, dwelling particularly on the Russian. I suggested that we might be able to
get at the leadership of the Fedayin through him. The resident, Kostromin (who had again been sent to Tehran by the
Centre in order to reinforce the Residency), said that there was

no need to do that, since contact had already been made that day.

It turned out that on 14 February, acting on direct orders from the Central Committee of the Soviet Communist Party, the Residency had established contact with the leadership of both the Mujahidin and Fedayin organizations. This was done by Vladimir Fisenko, an officer of the PI line, who was also an intelligent officer and an able Iranian specialist. He looked like an Iranian, with his black hair and dark brown eyes. Fisenko went straight to the buildings housing both the Mujahidin and Fedayin headquarters and presented himself as the official representative of the Soviet Union, at the same time producing his diplomatic passport. After some hesitation (they were afraid of a provocation on the part of the authorities), Fisenko succeeded in having a talk with the leaders.

There was only one proposal from the Soviet side: 'We should like to keep in touch with you.' The answer from both organizations was: 'No. In the present circumstances the authorities could use our contact with Soviet people to stage a provocation, and represent us as "the red hand of Moscow".' Agreement was reached to maintain contact in Europe. Both Mujahidin and Fedayin asked for immediate deliveries of weapons. Fisenko of course could say nothing in reply to this, but promised to report to Moscow. In the event of an emergency contact being needed, the Mujahidin gave us the telephone number of a safe flat in Tehran. The Fedayin preferred not to become involved.

The story from my recent Russian acquaintance whom I had just met, that they were frantically looking for SAVAK tunnels, led Kostromin to a very interesting idea. He suggested that at my next meeting with my Russian, I should let him know in a very casual way that opposite the Soviet Embassy there was a whole house which had been entirely occupied by SAVAK, and that a tunnel was supposed to have been dug from this house to beneath the embassy, and used for eavesdropping on our conversations. It did not matter whether such a tunnel did in fact exist. The idea was that Fedayin fighting groups should destroy the SAVAK surveillance centre that we hated so much.

The following day all newspapers announced the first executions of members of the Shah's regime. Generals Nasiri (head of SAVAK),

Khosrodad, Rahimi and Naji were all shot at dawn on 15 February. Their pictures, and the pictures of their bullet-riddled corpses, were published in newspapers all over the country. This was only the beginning.

I met my Russian that evening and told him about the SAVAK house close to our embassy. He received what I said with great enthusiasm and said that it would be razed to the ground that very night.

Back in the Residency we were as happy as children, but as it turned out, our raptures were premature. The following morning the house was still there untouched, and members of the fighting groups were nowhere to be seen. The next meeting with my Russian contact explained what had happened. He said that he had reported the information at once to his leadership, who in turn had got in touch with representatives of the new authorities. These authorities had forbidden them in the strictest possible terms to undertake any actions whatever against the SAVAK building in question, or against any other objectives around the Soviet embassy.

Everything was clear. We should not expect any changes in our situation under the new authorities. They would go on tracking us, and perhaps even more closely than before. In view of this situation, I stopped the meetings with my Russian, so as not to bring trouble upon him.

CHAPTER 13

On 17 February 1979, the Bazargan government announced the legalization of all political parties in Iran, including the Tudeh Party, which is the Iranian Communist Party.

The Iranian Communist Party (ICP) was set up in 1920, with the help of the young Soviet State and under its influence. With the coming to power of Reza Shah in 1925, the ICP was banned and its members had to go underground. Reza Shah's rapprochement with Nazi Germany led to the party's complete destruction, and its remnants fled to the Soviet Union. When the Soviet Union and Britain sent their troops to Iran in 1941, the northern provinces, including Tehran, were occupied by the Soviets, while the British held the south. A revived ICP now called itself the People's Tudeh Party (Tudeh means 'Masses'), and under the protection of the Soviet occupiers it set out to recruit as many members as it could and to liquidate its enemies.

After the Soviet troops had been withdrawn, the Tudeh Party tried to organize a coup. In 1949 some Iranian officers who were Tudeh members made a botched attempt on the life of the young Shah, Mohammed Reza Pahlevi. Several shots were fired, but he survived. The authorities now set out to destroy the Party. Its members were arrested and the survivors fled once again to the USSR. From there they worked against the Shah's regime right up till 1979. Tudeh activity in the Soviet Union consisted in effect of their members making radio broadcasts in Farsi to Iran. Many of them worked in various universities throughout the country, teaching the language, literature and history of Iran. They were even to be found among my teachers at university. Some Tudeh members lived in East Germany, doing the same as their fellow party members in the Soviet Union. Between 1949 and 1979, the Tudeh Party was virtually inactive in Iran, where its members were either in prison or had renounced their communist ideals.

The first members of the Tudeh Party began to arrive back from the Soviet Union and the GDR at the end of January 1979. Among them was their secretary general, Iraj Eskanderi. Eskanderi was by then seventy-nine years old, and had led the Tudeh Party since 1944. Soon after returning to Iran, however, he was replaced as secretary general by Nureddin Kiyanuri. The official story of this substitution was that Eskanderi was by then quite old. But the true reason was quite different. The fact was that Kiyanuri, who had been a member of the Tudeh Party since 1942 and on its Central Committee since 1944, was a relative of Ayatollah Khomeini, and it was Moscow's plan that his appointment as leader should strengthen the Party's position under the new regime. Kiyanuri himself only returned to Iran in 1979.

Meanwhile Islamic reforms had begun in the country. In March, Khomeini banned the consumption of frozen imported meat from Australia and New Zealand. Cattle in these countries were allegedly not slaughtered according to Muslim traditions. In another order from the leaders, it was made obligatory for all women in government service to wear the chador. From then onwards, women announcers on Iranian television never appeared without veils. Attacks on women who ignored this instruction increased in frequency. Fanatics poured acid over them.

Islamic courts were set up in March, and immediately began to operate with ferocity. A married woman caught with her lover was publicly flogged for adultery, but a couple like that were getting off lightly. The basic sentence handed out by Islamic courts was to be shot. And the sentence was carried out immediately. Judgement was pronounced by a single mullah after a brief hearing of the charge. No lawyers, no defence.

Revolutionary Committees operated throughout the city. As a rule, a committee was a group of youths who had seized weapons in the first days of the revolution. There were many criminal elements among them who had been released from prison. The authorities were not up to controlling the committees; they simply let matters drift, and gave them the right to arrest 'counter-revolutionary elements'. Practically every quarter and every street had its own committee, which interfered in everything and made their own sometimes quite senseless rules. One of their favourite occupations was directing the traffic, since the traffic police had not yet returned to their duties in the new conditions, so the already chaotic traffic in the streets of Tehran turned into even greater chaos. Although the curfew had already been lifted, members of the committees patrolled the streets at night on their own initiative, arresting people indiscriminately and shooting at their own discretion.

One of our technical specialists was killed in such an incident. He was returning home one evening at 11 p.m. from the embassy to his flat in town. Shortly after he had left the embassy, a cry of 'Stop!' rang out from behind his car. As our man slowed down, a shot was fired. The bullet pierced his neck and he was killed on the spot. A young boy with a rifle had simply decided to have a little practice shooting at a moving target.

I had to pay several visits to the main Tehran mortuary over this incident. Usually clean and orderly, it now presented a dreadful spectacle. Most bodies were no longer kept in the special refrigerators, which were all full. The corpses lay in corners on the floor, on occasions one overlapping another. In the past I had had to go to the mortuary from time to time on consular business, so I had acquaintances there. I asked one of them why the place was in such a state. He answered that they could no longer cope with the number of bodies arriving. There were very many unidentified corpses killed by bullets. 'These committee small-fry are settling scores with their personal enemies,' he said. 'They've let the big criminals out of jail, and here they are, they've taken power! Just wait and see what's coming!'

Soon after the Islamic Republic of Iran had been declared in Tehran in April 1979, Amir Abbas Hoveida, the former prime minister, was shot, as were many others who had held high rank in the Shah's regime. This served as a signal for similar actions to be taken throughout the country. Every day the newspapers were full of pictures in sadistic detail – the condemned tied to posts while still alive, and then their strung-up, bullet-ridden bodies. The very instant of shooting was caught in one of these pictures under the caption 'Moment of Death'. It showed the hooded head and shoulders of the marksman taken from behind, the cartridge case flying from the rifle at the instant of firing, and in the distance the victim of the execution, tied to the post, his legs just beginning to buckle. The Islamic regime was liquidating its worst enemies – those representatives of the Shah's regime who would have been capable of organizing resistance to the new authority. But this was only the beginning.

The establishment of relations with the Mujahidin organization continued to make progress, in spite of Mujahidin misgivings. Through its officer Fisenko, the KGB Residency had succeeded in convincing the Mujahidin leadership that, provided we maintained contact clandestinely, and observed all precautionary measures, then the authorities could not uncover our liaison. So far everything had been going quite well, and some interesting information had come in from the Mujahidin. For example, the Residency learnt that, during the seizure of power, the SAVAK archives had fallen into their hands. The Centre's reaction was immediate. The telegram read, 'Get in touch with the Mujahidin immediately and obtain from them the SAVAK file on General Mogarebi.' This was the greatest failure the KGB Residency had had in Iran, and it was not surprising that the Centre was impatient to learn the reasons behind it.

Gennadi Kazankin, the head of the PI line, was again acting resident at the time. Lev Petrovich Kostromin, deputy head of the Eighth Department of the First Chief Directorate, who had been sent to reinforce the Residency during the revolution, had already gone back to Moscow. It was he who was pressing for information on the Mogarebi case. Kazankin immediately summoned Fisenko. He showed him the telegram, and ordered him to get in touch with his contact immediately. I happened to be present when this conversation took place. Fisenko said that he would go out into the town at once, and after he had checked for surveillance he would give his contact a ring. This did not suit Kazankin.

'That's a pointless waste of time,' he said with irritation. 'Ring directly from the embassy.'

'But that's dangerous,' Fisenko objected.

'There's no danger here,' insisted Kazankin. 'SAVAK has been destroyed, and there's nobody listening to our telephones. Go and ring immediately from the embassy.'

Fisenko rang his contact from the embassy, and after he had told him in essence what it was about, arranged a meeting.

Fisenko's contact was Saadati, one of the leaders of the Mujahidin organization. Meetings with him were held in a Mujahidin safe flat which was in a block somewhere in western Tehran. On the appointed day, accompanied by an operational driver and Aliev, another Residency officer, Fisenko set out for the meeting. After checking for surveillance in town, the car drove into the quarter where the operation was to take place. The Residency car had diplomatic number plates, so Fisenko left it, with the operational driver, about a block away from the actual place of the meeting. Aliev had to keep watch from the street on the block that housed the safe flat, and give Fisenko the danger signal if need be.

Everything seemed quiet. Fisenko rang, and when the main front door of the block opened, he walked along the corridor and rang the door-bell of the ground-floor flat he had to visit. The door opened and he went casually inside. Behind a desk stood Saadati. He was unusually pale. A bulging file full of documents lay on the desk.

The door behind Fisenko suddenly slammed shut, and he looked round. Another four men had come into the room and were holding pistols on himself and Saadati. It was a trap. One of the strangers came up to Fisenko, poked him in the chest with his pistol, and asked who he was. Fisenko tried to talk his way out of it by saying that he had come to the wrong flat, but the stranger interrupted him, called him by his name, and said that he had come there for that file which was lying on the desk.

There was no longer any sense in stalling, so Fisenko invoked his diplomatic immunity. A second stranger came up, pointed his pistol at him and told him, 'Run!' Such an order could mean only one thing – killed while attempting to escape. Fisenko refused. 'Run!' the gunman repeated in an even more threatening tone, and began to move closer to Fisenko. The door behind him was now open, and through it another armed man was visible, standing at the main entrance door to the block.

At this point something that may be called luck intervened.

Someone began to knock loudly at the main entrance door. The guard opened the door slightly and unceremoniously pushed a man away. The man then began to knock even louder, and shout that he lived in that block and that nobody had the right to keep him out. The row flared more and more intensely until the guard just had to let the intruder in. This proved to be a man with his daughter, and he went on shouting even after he was in the entrance hall. Confusion ensued, and Fisenko took advantage of it to get out of the flat and away from the block itself, hoping that, in the presence of witnesses, his captors would not open fire. And so it happened. He reached the car safely, collapsed on to the seat, and ordered the driver back to the embassy at full speed.

Once in the quiet atmosphere of the embassy, Fisenko reflected that the people who detained him had been nothing like the members of the revolutionary committees. They looked very respectable and were expensively dressed. We had no doubt at all about their identity – they had to be SAVAK. This incident shattered the illusion that the Shah's secret police had been totally destroyed and that our embassy telephones were no longer tapped. But what a price we had to pay for that information!

When it learnt of what had happened, the Centre immediately ordered Fisenko to leave Iran, in case of provocation. That is how we lost yet another able intelligence officer. A trial of Saadati was held soon afterwards and he was sentenced to ten years' imprisonment for espionage. This sentence surprised us. At that time in Iran, people were being shot for much lesser offences. But in the end the Islamic authorities lived up to their reputation. Several months later, a second trial took place, and this time Saadati was shot. That was the end of our contacts with the Mujahidin.

So SAVAK continued to exist. And not only to exist, but also to operate. A flow of information from various sources saying that SAVAK had been completely destroyed was nothing more than wishful thinking. Like the Iranians, we wanted to believe it, so we did.

True, the main SAVAK building at Saltanatabad in north-east Tehran had been seized and was now in the hands of the new authorities. But the building and everything in it was empty when they took it. SAVAK's officials knew perfectly well what their fate could be, and they went to ground, but the hatred of the new authorities was by no means indiscriminate. Their vengeance was mostly directed at the Third Directorate of SAVAK, which was responsible for countering subversive elements. The intelligence, counter-intelligence and technical directorates were left alone for the time being – that is, they were neither arrested nor persecuted. But this state of truce dragged on, and SAVAK officials were still without work and without pay. So an unusual event occurred in April 1979: SAVAK officials organized a demonstration in front of the Prime Minister's offices in Tehran. They claimed that those officials present at the demonstration had played no part in the punitive measures taken against the Iranian people, but had been working to ensure the country's security, and demanded that they be given work. No punishment resulted for those who had taken part in the demonstration. Their spokesmen were even received and heard by the authorities.

By May everything had come full circle. The SAVAK surveillance radio station, silent until then, went back on the air, and surveillance team vehicles were again parked around the embassy. I was the first official of the embassy to be taken under surveillance on that first day. What an honour!

Leaving the embassy that morning with my car radio as usual tuned in to the surveillance frequencies, I suddenly heard the familiar signal transmitted from the observation post opposite our gates to the surveillance cars. It was still the same official on duty in the observation post. We had long been used to his voice, and it would have been difficult to confuse it with another. Shortly afterwards I noticed a surveillance car on my tail, and then another. The cars too were the same ones as before. Excited at having discovered them, I returned to the embassy, without even bothering to go through with my cover story. The operator on the KGB Residency's Impulse radio interception station had also noticed the return of external surveillance and said that the voices of the officials were the same as before.

For us, the reappearance of surveillance was a relief. It was far better to know that they were at work and to take the necessary precautionary measures, than to be wondering all the time whether surveillance was there or not.

The new authorities were using the old SAVAK resources because they had to, since they were still without a security organization of their own. And they would go on using them for as long as they could be of assistance in training new cadres. This was exactly what happened after the revolution in Russia, when the new VChK took over the Third Gendarme Directorate almost in its entirety. But now there was one essential difference for SAVAK officials serving the new regime. Whereas before they were all devoted heart and soul to the Shah's regime, they now worked not from conviction but from fear. The new authorities naturally distrusted them, and kept them under constant control by appointing their own people, mostly mullahs, to all the leading posts. The slightest suspicion of dissatisfaction or disloyalty, could mean only one thing – death. This was something which made them all the more dangerous for us.

Soon the kiosk just opposite the embassy gates, the one that sold non-alcoholic drinks, opened again for business. From it the same SAVAK officials continued as before to keep our comings and goings under observation. We knew all these people and they knew all of us, but now they tried to avoid looking us in the eye. On one occasion, and without any ulterior motive, I went up to the kiosk to buy a few bottles of fruit drinks. I said hello. The man in the kiosk answered, without raising his eyes.

'How's life?' I asked him, with a tone of natural sympathy in my voice. He said nothing in reply. He just raised his eyes to me, shrugged his shoulders, smiled guiltily and sighed deeply. That glance said everything. An apology for having lost, and for now having to serve a new regime which was hateful to them. It was as though he was whispering, 'Our generals are now in America and Europe. But what are we, the rank and file, to do now, die of hunger? We've got families to feed.'

When the Soviet leaders realized that the new regime which had come to power in Iran was stabilizing, they began to make up for lost ground. The ambassador received instructions from Moscow telling him to see Khomeini and announce to him the Soviet Union's recognition of the Iranian Islamic Republic. As Khomeini had left

Tehran on 1 March 1979 and moved to Qom, thereby demonstrating his faith in the stability of the new authority, Ambassador Vinogradov had to make a 120-kilometre journey by car in order to see the Iranian leader. He took along with him a young diplomat as interpreter, together with Viktor Kazakov of the PI line. He needed Kazakov in order to provide consular assistance in the event of trouble. The ambassador was clearly nervous. The new authorities were not preaching any special love for foreigners.

Khomeini received the Soviet ambassador with reserve. He heard him out, and then having said practically nothing, ended the interview. Kazakov was not present at the meeting, but the ambassador's interpreter was a KGB informer, and that same day he reported everything to the resident down to the last detail.

After the Soviet ambassador's first meeting with Khomeini, Moscow was not reassured. They wanted something specific from Khomeini, not just a few protocol courtesies, and Vinogradov was instructed to set up another meeting. The Iranian leader received him once again, and again made no specific replies. The Soviet proposals were the usual ones – good neighbourly relations, an extension of economic development aid, and the widening of trade and cultural links. So Moscow ordered the ambassador to meet with Khomeini yet again, and elicit his reaction to our proposals. Khomeini received the Soviet ambassador for the third time, with exactly the same stonewalling result.

Yet again the ambassador was dispatched to Qom. It must be noted that these meetings took place at weekly intervals. The Iranians were signalling that they did not want to accept the Soviet helping hand. This was quite evident. The ambassador however drew no such conclusions in his reporting to Moscow. He smoothed over Khomeini's negative reaction so thoroughly that the Iranian leader might almost have had some regard for the Soviet Union. Then for the fourth time in three weeks came instructions for the ambassador to go and see Khomeini. The straight diplomats in the protocol section felt embarrassed by then at having to ring Khomeini's office and thrust another manifestly unwelcome visit upon them. We in the Residency could laugh about the situation, but only among ourselves. Our man Kazakov merely suffered physically, for the departure time for every visit to Khomeini was 4 a.m.

The Soviet ambassador's fourth visit to Khomeini finally did bring specific results. The guards stopped his car at the barrier controlling the access road to Khomeini's offices, and a bearded young official informed the ambassador that Khomeini would meet with him no more, and that the Soviet embassy must henceforth address itself exclusively to the Iranian Ministry of Foreign Affairs. This statement was made through the open window of the car. After that one of the guards gestured to the driver with his automatic weapon that he had better turn the car round and go back the way he had come. This was a calculated faceful of spit for a representative of the Soviet Union. On the return journey Ambassador Vinogradov ground his teeth while all the others, the interpreter, Kazakov and the chauffeur, did their best to stifle their mirth.

Some time later, the KGB Residency succeeded in learning, through its sources, what Khomeini's true reaction had been to our ambassador's visits. His political advisers had persuaded the Ayatollah that it was not advisable to make an open display of his native hostility towards the Soviet Union. It was best to do that by making use of diplomatic methods. However, when he heard that the ambassador was insisting on a fourth meeting, the Iranian leader lost his patience. 'I don't meet the American or the British or the French ambassador. So why must I see the Soviet ambassador? No, I have no intention of seeing him again.'

Right from the outset, disagreements began to appear both between the various political groups and the new authorities, and also between individuals within the new authorities. Thus it was that, just one week after the 11 February revolution had triumphed, Khomeini publicly condemned the members of the Fedayin organization for still keeping their faces covered. And this condemnation was expressed in spite of the fact that Fedayin fighting detachments had played a most active part in overthrowing the Shah's regime.

No representatives of either organization, the Fedayin or the Mujahidin, were admitted to the centre of power. They were made legal, but neither of them ever occupied any posts of responsibility. These were the organizations that opposed the establishment of an

Islamic Republic in the form envisaged by the clergy. But their opinion was ignored.

There was however one man at the top level of the clergy who considered that the Mujahidin and Fedayin had been unjustly treated and who tried in every way to support their demands and opinions. He was the Ayatollah Taleghani of Tehran. Taleghani was enormously popular not just in these two organizations but with the people in general, particularly in Tehran. Every Friday in the University, his sermons could be heard calling for mercy, for love of fellow men, and the need to follow pure Islam. He was clearly hinting that the authorities were abusing the death penalty and that the priesthood was interfering excessively in politics. Even his appearance was prepossessing – a grand-fatherly face with soft features. Taleghani had actively opposed the Shah's regime all his life. For this he was repeatedly imprisoned. The last time he was released from jail was during the days of the revolution. His children were Fedayin members who took an active part in the conflict with the Shah's regime.

It soon came out that Khomeini was complaining about Taleghani's peace-making sermons and was trying to pressurize him to stop censuring what the authorities were doing. In reply to this, Taleghani preached a sermon in which he openly told of the pressure he was under. This caused a wave of dissatisfaction, particularly among Fedayin and Mujahidin members, and they organized mass demonstrations in support of Taleghani which lasted four days. Both organizations declared in the end that they would place all their armed formations at his disposal. It was quite evident that they were prepared to move against Taleghani's enemies at the first sign from their new spiritual leader. He did not take this opportunity. It was against his nature to do so. The authorities, alarmed by this turn of events and sensing a real threat of civil war, left Taleghani alone for the time being.

On 1 May 1979 Ayatollah Morteza Motakhari was murdered by terrorists in Tehran. Something that called itself the Forgan organization claimed responsibility. The authorities said that Forgan was extreme left-wing and that its main aim was to fight the Islamic Republic and liquidate prominent members of the clergy. This sounded quite odd to us. First, Motakhari had not been a fervent supporter of Khomeini's policies. He tended to side with Ayatollah Taleghani in complaining about the excessive brutality used against the opposition. To kill such a progressive (from the standpoint of the forces of the Left) mullah could only have led to one thing, namely the weakening of their own positions. Second, no one among our contacts on the left either knew or had heard of the Forgan organization. This too was very odd, since organizations of this kind, even if they do not fraternize, at least know of one another. Forgan seemed to fade away after Motakhari's murder had been committed.

The mystery surrounding this Forgan phantom was explained for us in the KGB Residency shortly afterwards. At the end of May the authorities announced that an attempt had been made on the life of Hojatolleslam Hashimi Rafsanjani in his own home. Responsibility for this action was again claimed by Forgan. Some days later however the Residency obtained through its sources reliable information on what had really happened. Two old friends from the Shah's time came round one evening to see Rafsanjani. The guard, on Rafsanjani's orders, let them in. At the beginning of the evening everything went smoothly, but as the conversation turned to the policies of the new authorities, passions flared and a fight broke out. As a result of the scuffle, an accidental shot was fired from a pistol belonging to Rafsanjani, who was slightly wounded. Rafsanjani's bodyguards pulled the fighting men apart, and no one would have known anything about it had Rafsanjani not come out of it with a huge black eye. This had somehow to be explained to the people, and again the Forgan organization comes on the scene. The same organization later perpetrated two more terrorist acts. Their victims, as before, were people who were in disagreement over something or other in the policies of the priesthood.

The Forgan phenomenon was used officially to put into operation a corps of special bodyguards to protect priests and politicians from attempts made against their persons. At the beginning of May 1979, yet another serious step was taken towards reinforcing the position of the ruling clergy. Khomeini ordered the formation of the Corps of Revolutionary Guards ('Pasdaran-e Engelab'). It was to become the personal guard of the new authorities, and would carry out the policies of the clergy with an iron hand.

This step was quite unavoidable, since those who had been the allies of the clergy in the overthrow of the Iranian monarchy had now become their opponents. The forces of the Left, with their armed formations many thousands strong, were not admitted to power and they now posed a threat to the regime. In the army there were still many pro-Shah elements. Khomeini needed his own loyal armed formation. Like the Cheka under Lenin, it would be the armed detachment of the Party. The Corps of Revolutionary Guards became just such a force. It was placed under the command of the Islamic Revolutionary Council.

The Revolutionary Guards recruited mainly young people from among devout Muslims and those devoted to the new regime. Iran has always produced more than enough young fellows who were not only devout, but physically well developed. The traditional Iranian athleticism and wrestling, which have been cultivated from time immemorial in *zurkhaneh* ('houses of strength'), were directly connected with Islam and the Koran. Limbering up, physical exercises, weight lifting and wrestling would be ritually accompanied by a reading of some lines from the Koran. It was like a simultaneous development of body and mind and contributed to the attainment of the best results in sport. From time immemorial, the *zurkhaneh* have been under the influence of the Iranian clergy. These sportsmen felt that the power of the clergy in Iran was now close to them. The ideology of Islam was their ideology.

At the same time, a fairly high percentage of yet another religious-minded stratum of Iranian society was enlisted into the Revolutionary Guards – the criminal element. I do not know why, but in practically every country the representatives of the criminal world tend to be deeply religious people. Take for example the Italian mafia in the United States or criminals in the Soviet Union. They are mostly believers. Iran was no exception to this rule, and now the criminals saw their chance to change from being antisocial elements into armed defenders of the new authority. This situation could be exploited at the same time for settling old scores.

In addition, the left-wing Mujahidin and Fedayin, foreseeing against whom the Revolutionary Guards would be used, infiltrated their own secret members into the new formation. Part of their task was to keep their organizations informed about official plans to move against them. Members of several of the self-appointed revolutionary committees mentioned earlier were also brought into the Guards. Thus the composition of the first recruitment levy was ill-assorted. All the same, they looked more respectable than the members of the revolutionary committees. They all wore a uniform field service dress, and most of them had beards. Their heads were either completely shaven, or they had closely cropped hair. During the cold season they wore khaki-coloured NATO-type jackets. In the early days they were armed only with automatic rifles, but in time it was planned to arm them to the teeth, and even to create tank and aircraft formations manned by Revolutionary Guards.

At the outset, a Department for the Propagation of the Islamic Revolution Abroad was formed within the structure of the Corps of Revolutionary Guards. But this title so directly and openly expressed the intentions of the Mosque in foreign policy, that it was quickly changed to the Foreign Department.

From their earliest days, the Guards became the real power in the land. They had their fingers in every pie. They could be seen with the army, the police, the administrative bodies, and the Iranian Foreign Ministry. They were in the new security service, gaining experience and at the same time keeping an eye on former employees of the old regime. Revolutionary Guards stood about at railway stations, at the airport, in the customs . . . They interfered and wormed their way into everything, whether or not they had the slightest understanding of the issues.

For us, as for all other foreign diplomats, it was issues of diplomatic immunity that always gave rise to friction with the Guards. In the post office, in the customs, on the street, you were stopped by some brawny young man who wanted to search either you or your car, and just you try proving to him, who had no conception of international relations, that he had no right to touch a diplomat. For there was his right, in his hands – an automatic rifle! The best way to fortify the nervous system was to avoid any contacts whatever with the Guards. But this was not always possible. For example, by virtue of my consular duties I frequently had to go to see the Foreign Ministry or the police. Now on every visit a Guard was present along with the usual official, to make sure that there was no spying going on. It would have been funny had it not been so sad.

With the creation of the Corps of Revolutionary Guards, spy

mania was whipped up to incredible heights. In propaganda every foreigner was declared to be doing all he could 'to strangle the young Islamic Republic'. It was just like the Soviet Union in Lenin's time. The people were constantly alerted. Radio and television broadcast special telephone numbers to be called by the witnesses of suspicious activities on the part of foreigners, or when vehicles with diplomatic number-plates appeared in town. This new environment rendered intelligence work incredibly difficult. While in the Shah's time only SAVAK was against us, and we knew where to look for its traces, now danger lurked behind every corner. Previously the population did not meddle in these espionage games. Now they were called upon openly to keep an eye on diplomats and to inform on them. And there are plenty of people to be found in any country who are ready to play at counter-espionage.

The Islamic Republic continued to tighten its grip. Most women, including non-Muslim ones, were compelled to wear headscarves and stockings even in the hottest weather. Khomeini announced a change in the marriageable age. Now boys were allowed to marry at fifteen, and girls at thirteen. That is what the Koran laid down. Khomeini's promise that the rights of religious minorities would not be encroached upon remained empty words. The authorities were now enjoining the Armenian community to put an end to mixed teaching of boys and girls in their schools. The wearing of ties by men was abolished. Before they left embassy territory, our straight diplomats took their ties off, and put them on again when they got back. How cowardly can one be? For the rules about ties were never extended to foreigners.

Revolutionary courts continued to function throughout the country. They were now headed by Ayatollah Khalkhali, a nervous, irascible individual who was quick to mete out punishment. There was something maniacal in his appearance. It was said that in the Shah's time he had been in a clinic for the mentally ill, although it is common knowledge that there is no shortage of healthy patients kept in such institutions under dictatorships and totalitarian regimes. With Khalkhali in office, the procedures of the revolutionary courts were considerably speeded up. Now only the charge was heard before the mullah judge pronounced sentence, and there was only one sentence – shooting. In one case, Khalkhali passed the death sentence on a young fellow who was weeping and swearing that he was innocent. 'What are you crying for?' Khalkhali said to him. 'In two minutes' time, you'll be shot. If you're telling the truth and are really innocent, then you'll go straight to heaven. If I'm right and you're guilty, then you'll go to hell. So you are worrying for nothing.' Announcements of shootings were now appearing continuously in the newspapers – 27 executed here, 35 there, 19 somewhere else, and so on every day.

During this period, Elganyan, the leader of the Jewish community in Iran, was executed on a charge of spying for Israel. Immediately afterwards, representatives of the Jewish community went to see Khomeini, and in spite of the Iranian leader's attitude to the Jewish question, no more was heard of executions of Jews. Evidently economic levers were pulled. The position of the Jews in the Iranian economy and in its trade was very strong. But the attitude of the clergy to Israel did not change in the slightest. The Israeli embassy in Tehran was seized in the first days of the revolution. Apart from the building itself, the new authorities got nothing out of it. All the Israelis had seen what was coming and got out of Iran well in advance.

In order somehow to sting the Israelis, the new Iranian authorities placed their embassy building at the disposal of the representative of the Palestine Liberation Organization (PLO), which had come to Iran immediately after the revolution. The Soviet Union's relationship with the Palestinians has always been good, so contact was immediately established on all levels – embassy, KGB, GRU. But the Palestinian representatives were not conversant with these separated powers, and when they dealt with people from the various divisions they were puzzled, saying that they had already discussed this question with another Soviet official, so why go over it again? They still did not know about the Soviet bureaucratic machine.

When they visited the Palestinians, our officers naturally inspected the premises of the former Israeli embassy, and could only admire the Jewish genius. Although Israel had been one of the Shah's closest allies, safety came first. While collaborating fully with SAVAK, the Israelis preferred to hide the contacts they had in Iran from their colleagues. So an underground tunnel had been built between the guard-room at the entrance to the embassy grounds and the embassy building itself. To an outside observer, a person visiting the Israeli embassy did not leave the guard-room, while in fact he might have gone through the tunnel into the main embassy premises. What is more, a collapsible ladder had been fitted on to the roof of the main embassy building. This ladder could be extended horizontally across the street to the roof of a neighbouring house that stood outside the territory of the embassy. It enabled a private visitor to leave the embassy surreptitiously, and perhaps also to enter it, should the need arise.

At first, the PLO had the best of relations with the new Iranian authorities. Every member of the Palestinian mission in Iran was allowed to carry a weapon. Each was issued with a special certificate, instructing everyone to cooperate fully with the holder. The Revolutionary Guards used the same certificates. But this love affair did not last long. First, the Palestinians' extensive contacts with Soviet diplomats were not to the liking of the Iranian authorities. Efforts to persuade the Palestinians to break contact had no effect. Second, soon after the Corps of Revolutionary Guards had been formed, the Iranian authorities asked the PLO to organize combat training for its fighters. To the question, against whom will the guards be used, the Iranian authorities frankly answered that it would be in the next stage against the left-wing forces of the Mujahidin and Fedayin. The Palestinians answered with a refusal. They had very close links with both groups, who had undergone training in their camps. Now they had no intention of betraying their friends by training formations to eliminate them. The Mosque's reaction was sharp. The Palestinians were stripped of their privileges and put under surveillance. Some Palestinians who had particularly active contacts with the Soviets were thrown out of Iran.

CHAPTER 14

Gennadi Kazankin was still acting KGB resident in Tehran, but the Centre had no intention of confirming him as permanent. On the contrary, there were persistent rumours that a new resident was due. No one knew him, and it was said that he would come from somewhere outside.

So in May 1979, Leonid Vladimirovich Shebarshin took over as the new KGB resident. He was youthful-looking, with an intelligent face, wise eyes, and carefully cut dark hair combed with a parting. Occasionally he would force a smile. His manners were restrained, his voice deliberately quiet, which compelled attention. He always wore a suit, as a rule dark grey in colour, and a tie. Overall, he was a man of pleasant appearance and with good manners.

Shebarshin was introduced to the officers at a meeting that was held in the Residency immediately on his arrival. He spoke with reserve, and went to the heart of the matter, with no hot air. This is what he said when he introduced himself.

'I worked in the Centre in the Seventeenth Department of the First Chief Directorate [which runs political intelligence in the Indian sub-continent]. I was head of a section, a colonel. Then, on the decision of the First Chief Directorate heads, I was transferred to the Eighth Department [Iran] and posted as resident to Tehran. Yuri Vladimirovich Andropov received me before I left. He expressed his anxiety over the state of affairs in Iran, seeing that the Residency has lost almost the whole of its agent network as a result of the revolution which has taken place. He has given me two years to rebuild this network. Two years is quite a long time, and I think that it can be reduced, so I'm giving you only one year to fulfil the task set us by the Chairman. I understand that both work and efficiency will have to be stepped up to achieve this, but that's what we're here for, and what the State is paying us for. That is all, for the time being. I shall get to know each one of you in the course of work.'

The new resident's speech made two main impressions on our officers. For the more conscientious, nothing had changed. For the time-servers, it was the moment to start worrying. As I have said, a large part of the Residency had been doing nothing since mid-1977, following the agent failures and then the revolution. The PI line, which had lost its main source of information in General Mogarebi, was mainly doing analytical work and collecting gossip from casual sources. Not one new agent was recruited during this time. The CI line, since it had no contacts at all among foreigners, concentrated on 'guaranteeing the security of the Soviet community'. Line X, which dealt in scientific and technical intelligence, never achieved any results in Iran. The N line alone continued to work as before. We had illegals with whom work did not cease no matter what the circumstances were. By the time the new resident arrived, I had almost completed the important recruitment of a new agent, and we had other promising contacts both among the locals and among foreign nationals. So the new resident's policy did not worry us unduly.

The attitude towards Shebarshin was noticeably negative, especially among the PI line officers. Until that time, Tehran had for years been the preserve of the Eighth Department of the First Chief Directorate, and all the residents had been reared in the milieu of this department's Iranian specialists. There were conventions, definite traditions, and a fixed pattern in its work. Now all this had been breached by Shebarshin's appointment as resident in Tehran. Quite obviously the leadership of the First Chief Directorate had lost confidence in the older officers of the Eighth Department, and was making them indirectly responsible for the failures in Iran. Shebarshin's appointment was intended to galvanize a stagnant state of affairs. It was natural that the officers of the Eighth Department took this as an insult. Therefore it was difficult for Shebarshin to count on their support. He had become the physical embodiment of their damaged interests. Of course, nobody disputed the decision of the First Chief Directorate heads, but they might use Shebarshin as a scapegoat. As always, everything was very decorous on the surface. But behind his back it was said that he was an upstart and an opportunist who had no experience of work in the prevailing conditions. There was a spate of gossip, especially at the beginning, and gradually an outline of his biography began to appear.

Leonid Vladimirovich Shebarshin was born in Moscow in 1935. In 1956 he completed studies at the Moscow State Institute of International Relations and was sent to work in the Soviet Foreign Ministry. Shebarshin made Pakistan his special subject, and he studied Urdu and English at the Institute. In 1958 he was posted for four years as an attaché to the Soviet embassy in Karachi, and in 1966, after a spell in Moscow, he was sent back to Pakistan with the rank of second secretary. This tour of duty lasted only two years. Then his career changed abruptly. Ever since his days at the Institute, Shebarshin had been a KGB informer. Even after he began to work in the Foreign Ministry he kept up his contact with the organs of State security. While he was in Pakistan, the KGB Residency there used him as an agent informer. During all this time he was run by Medyanik, the KGB resident in Pakistan, who suggested to Shebarshin that he transfer permanently to the KGB intelligence service. Medyanik had been attracted by this young diplomat's capacities for analysis.

In 1958 Shebarshin returned to Moscow, and after undergoing a year's training at School 101, he was sent to work in the Seventeenth Department of the KGB. In 1971 he went to the Soviet embassy in Delhi as a PI line officer in the KGB Residency there. He now held the post of first secretary. While in India he was promoted, and became chief of the PI line and deputy resident. He returned in 1977 to Moscow Centre, where he was given the post of head of the Indian section of the Seventeenth Department. Meanwhile his patron Medyanik had gone higher and was now deputy chief of KGB intelligence. It was he who recommended Shebarshin for the KGB resident's job in Tehran.

The fact that Shebarshin came into the KGB from outside, and particularly that he had been a KGB informer before that, incurred the especial enmity of the Eighth Department officers, who didn't like knockers. What caused even more indignation was that Shebarshin had had virtually no experience of agent work. But what could the carpers do when he had the backing of so highly placed a patron as

Medyanik? All they could do was to whisper behind his back, pull faces, and hope that the inexperienced Shebarshin would soon shoot himself in the foot in the complex environment of Iran. It must be said that Shebarshin was no more popular in his old Seventeenth Department, and for the same reasons.

In the early days Shebarshin kept very quiet. He spent most of his time sitting in the resident's office with Kazankin and briefing himself. Not that there was anything of importance to take in. As Fadeikin, the former resident, had remarked, 'The Residency has one and a half agents.' Kazankin behaved very patronizingly towards Shebarshin, always trying to show his superiority, and hence encouraging Residency officers to cold-shoulder the new resident. Shebarshin behaved calmly and did not go looking for a fight. His KGB career had already accustomed him to accept that he could not count on people liking him.

Finally Kazankin departed, and Shebarshin remained as sole master of the Residency. But nothing much changed. He continued to spend most of his time in his office, where he either read or wrote. In spite of the difficulties caused by the revolution and the change of resident, the Centre never lessened its demands, and every day the Residency had to send a minimum of two information telegrams on topical political subjects. In the early days Shebarshin practically wrote these telegrams himself, or else rewrote what had been written by others – he was a good stylist.

As he spoke Urdu, it was not too difficult for him to master Farsi, and soon he was able to read newspapers written in Farsi acceptably well, although he did not bring himself to speak the language. He took to reading the open press very seriously, rightly calculating that reliable analytical conclusions could always be arrived at from a continuous close analysis of the press. If some important event happened, Shebarshin would cut out the headline from the newspaper and stick it on the wall opposite his desk. This wall was soon covered with cuttings. It was a good method, since food for thought was always right in front of him, and there was no need to delve into files in order to refresh the memory about an event.

Shebarshin lived a modest personal life, and this distinguished him quite sharply from his predecessors. He spent most of his time in the Residency, working on information. The rest of the time he was at home, reading a book. Shebarshin was widely read, and he was also what we in the Soviet Union call a 'bookman', a collector of rare books. He had no friends among the Residency officers, not because he stood intellectually above the rest – there were bookmen among us too – but because he sensed full well what the situation was, and expected dirty tricks. The wisest thing to do was to keep his distance.

The first members of the Tudeh Party began to turn up in the embassy very soon after Khomeini came to power. Those who had returned from the Soviet Union handed over their Soviet documents to us. These were not passports, but certificates for return. Most Tudeh members who had been living in the Soviet Union were stateless persons. Sometimes these return certificates were brought to us by the holders themselves, but mainly we received them through one and the same person. He was the Armenian liaison courier who came to us from the Tudeh Party Central Committee, an old Party member who had spent twenty-six years in prison and had only been released after the revolution.

At first this courier brought only documents, and the guards on duty sent them to me, since I received most of the callers. But soon he began to hand over little notes along with the documents. These notes were written on small sheets of paper, tightly folded into ever-decreasing squares. He extracted them from under his trouser belt and handed them over without saying a word, but giving me a meaningful stare. He was always very careful. When he was in my office he said practically nothing, preferring only to stress the significance of one thing or another by means of the expression in his eyes. He had probably been given instructions that our consulate might have been bugged by the Iranian Security Service.

When the liaison courier placed the first note in front of me, I did not touch it, as I was accustomed to provocations, but asked him what it meant. The courier put his fingers to his lips, and explained by gestures that it was for the embassy from the leadership of the Tudeh Party. For whom? I asked. He mimed that they would know there. Well, whether they knew or not, I naturally took the note to Resident Shebarshin. 'So they've decided to liaise with that muck!' he complained, when he had heard me out. Although he did not name them outright, it was clear about whom he was speaking. The decision to maintain contacts with the Tudeh Party could only have been made by the International Department of the Central Committee of the Soviet Communist Party.

Unable to establish good relations with the new Iranian regime through direct contacts with Khomeini, the Soviet leadership had decided to use the Tudeh Party as a Trojan horse. As has already been said, Moscow replaced the Tudeh Party secretary general with Nureddin Kiyanuri, Khomeini's relative. This step was meant to bring the Tudeh Party closer to the regime. Kiyanuri returned to Iran only in April 1979. In the interval, from January onwards, he had been undergoing special training in the International Department of the Soviet Communist Party's Central Committee. He was trained there to organize future work in Iran. This probably sounds odd. People are used to identifying the expression 'special training' with organizations like the KGB, the CIA and the GRU. But it is the Soviet Party's International Department that I mean.

The International Department runs the contacts with communist parties all over the world. These contacts may be either legal, in countries where the communist parties exist openly, or illegal, where they have gone underground. Direct and open contacts with communist parties are run by International Department officials. There is no risk here. Contacts with underground parties are carried out clandestinely, by using resources at the disposal of the International Department. These resources include both the KGB and the GRU but no longer, of course, their equivalents in the countries of the Eastern bloc. Even so, the KGB for example does not direct this work, but is only used to carry it out. In the KGB, work of this kind is referred to as 'executing a special Central Committee task'. To perform it, the International Department may ask for an illegal from 'S' Directorate of the KGB First Chief Directorate. When this happens, the nature of the task will be known only to the illegal, and since he is a KGB officer he has to give a signed undertaking not to reveal it. All reports from this officer are sent straight to the International Department; the KGB does not know what they contain.

The International Department may also use KGB officers for

training members of foreign communist parties, but while this training is going on, they remain subordinate in every way to the International Department. That is why that department's senior Party School has a section which trains illegals, or more simply secret members of foreign communist parties. This work is performed on the basis of the theory of international communism, unshakeable and now axiomatic, namely that each communist party in a non-socialist country, even if it has a completely legal existence, must have its secret members.

This practice has two objectives. The first is that should the authorities in a country suddenly decide to ban the communist party's activities and destroy its legal wing, then the secret members can carry on the party's work underground. The second is that in peacetime these communist parties send their secret members into various establishments of their country in order to collect information in areas which are closed to communists, and to exert influence on the country's political life. For example, in developed capitalist countries such areas might include defence, the secret services, the political parties, including the party in government, and the trade unions. Information gathered by secret communist party members is kept in the International Department. It is impossible to overestimate the importance of this information. Compared to it, the information obtained by the KGB is peanuts. That is why the Soviet Party's Central Committee categorically forbids the KGB even to go near communist parties, let alone to recruit their members. It also explains why the Soviet leaders intentionally do not protest at the vilification of the KGB by the Western press.

The reality is that while the Western counter-intelligence services go chasing after the KGB and the GRU, the International Department is receiving top-secret information obtained by the secret members of the communist parties of these countries. In Western countries, the International Department can spark the organization of mass strikes, again through the infiltration of secret party members into the trade union leadership. In the democratic countries of the West, communist parties are legal, and no one can stop them having overt contacts with the 'fraternal' Communist Party of the Soviet Union. It is natural that counter-intelligence in Western countries should keep an eye on their own communist parties, but they are looking for contacts between these and the KGB. There are no such contacts, nor can there be.

The names of secret communist party members are held in the strictest secrecy. They are unknown not only to the ordinary party members, but even to the majority of members of the party's Central Committee. As a rule, they are run by the member of the Central Committee who is responsible for party control. He is usually an undistinguished shadowy figure in the party, who does not aspire to wide publicity. It is to him that all information comes, and it is through him that it goes to Moscow. Secret members are selected with particular care, not from among party members, but from among sympathizers. This is because Central Committee members always assume that counter-intelligence agents might be present in their entourage and they might therefore know the names of the party members. The names of those selected for a secret member role are never entered on any lists.

Once everyone is satisfied with the loyalty of the candidate, he is sent to the Senior Party School in Moscow. This journey is made clandestinely through third countries, in order to conceal the fact that the individual concerned has been in the Soviet Union. Once in the Senior Party School, the secret member is given thorough training in ideology, politics, but above all in how to work clandestinely. Plans for his future career are discussed with him, and also methods by which he can achieve rapid advancement. After completing his training the secret communist party member returns by a roundabout way to his home country. From that time onwards, he must change himself into an 'enemy' of communism in order to penetrate the targets that interest Moscow. His life is now full of romance and electricity. Contacts with him are effected by the Central Committee member responsible for party control. These contacts are rare, and are made with particular care. No KGB agency is involved, and no espionage in the customary sense of that word.

In the foreign country concerned, the chairman of the department of party control in the Central Committee, along with other Central Committee members, maintains overt contacts with the Soviet side. These may take place in the following way. In almost every Soviet embassy there is a representative of the Soviet Party Central Committee's International Department. Officially his post does not carry this title, and he is known to foreigners as a counsellor in the embassy responsible for maintaining contacts with friendly parties, including the local communist party. Among his other contacts, this 'counsellor' may meet officially with the local communist party's chairman of party control and be given information about him. Meetings with the party control chairman may be set up either in a third country or in the Soviet Union. Such methods are used in the conditions prevailing in the Western democracies where communist party activities are protected by law.

The situation that existed in Iran immediately following the revolution was entirely different. Although Prime Minister Bazargan legalized all political parties a few days after the regime came to power, and these included the Tudeh Party or Iranian Communist Party, Moscow doubted whether the new authorities would look benignly upon Tudeh contacts with the Soviet Embassy. So would it be possible to hand over the Tudeh Party to be run by professional intelligence officers from the KGB Residency in Tehran? Resident Shebarshin had been warned about this possibility before he left for Tehran, and it clearly did not impress him – nor incidentally did it impress anyone at all in the leadership of KGB intelligence. Maintaining contacts with a local communist party in hostile conditions is regarded by the KGB as digging a grave that sooner or later will receive the body of the man who runs the contact. The KGB is certain, and not without reason, that foreign communist parties have been penetrated by counter-intelligence agents and that in the end failure is inevitable. That is why Shebarshin reacted so negatively to the contact made with us by the Tudeh Party's liaison courier.

The KGB's hostile view of this matter cut no ice with the Party Central Committee. The decision had been taken, and the KGB would have to carry it out and ask no questions. When the resident reported to the Centre about the first contacts with the Tudeh Party's liaison courier, the reply from Moscow was signed, not by the head of the Eighth Department with his usual pseudonym, or by the head of the First Chief Directorate or even by the Chairman of the KGB himself, but by Ulyanovsky, one of the chiefs of the Party's International Department. The telegram stated that the Residency must continue to accept messages from the Tudeh courier, and convey their content immediately to the International Department.

Thus began our contacts with the Tudeh Party, and it fell to me to run them, because I worked in the consulate. This assignment did not suit me at all. I was already up to my neck in N line work, while the Residency at that time was full of officers without any contacts at all. I expressed my objections to the resident, but without effect. He did not like to be contradicted. Since he could find no logical arguments to induce me to do it willingly, Shebarshin invoked his authority as resident and ordered me to carry on. I requested him to inform the Centre about this, knowing that 'S' Directorate would never agree to my having contacts with a local communist party. Shebarshin refused. It was pointless to argue, but I reserved the right to report this to the leadership in the Centre when I was next on leave. Meanwhile I had to carry out the order.

The Tudeh Party courier was now appearing at the consulate almost every two weeks. He continued to bring the documents belonging to Iranians who had returned, but these were only a cover. His main purpose was to hand over information from Kiyanuri, the Tudeh secretary general, still in the form of tightly folded notes, written out in Kiyanuri's own fine clear handwriting. Their contents dealt mainly with organizational matters, and in many cases were unintelligible to us, since Kiyanuri used code-words known only to the International Department. The Residency was instructed to make exact translations of the content of these reports, and send them immediately to Moscow. The originals were to be sent to Moscow by diplomatic bag. I had to translate these notes fairly frequently, and without knowing the meaning of the code-words I was left in the dark by messages that might say something like, 'Gaimar project successfully begun. We shall report on results later.'

In each of his reports, besides dealing with organizational matters, Kiyanuri would devote some attention to the political scene in Iran. He was quite objective about the general situation. It was only when he got to the position of his own party that his objectivity disappeared completely, and he would invariably present it as a heavyweight political force, close to the governing summit and exercising influence on the course of events. He often used in his notes expressions like 'sources close to Khomeini' or 'sources close to the President', but he never gave names even when we asked him to. Kiyanuri presented the Tudeh Party as a leading and guiding force on the left.

He said that its popularity was growing among the young and that new members were constantly joining. The Mujahidin and Fedayin organizations, according to him, looked up to the Tudeh leadership as experienced, hardened fighters and always listened to their advice.

In reality however the Tudeh Party's position was quite different. Immediately after Kiyanuri returned to Iran in April 1979, a Tudeh Party Congress was held. The final document it published amounted to almost total support for the Islamic Republic. It even attempted to provide a theoretical basis for a possible rapprochement between Islam and Marxism 'at the present stage of historical development'. This voluminous document was handed over to us for transmission to Moscow, and one of our officers had to spend much time poring over its translation. The clumsy prose was exactly reminiscent of the language used in the newspaper *Pravda*.

By declaring its support for the Islamic Republic, the Tudeh Party was expressing a wish to be closer to the ruling summit. That was what had been planned in Moscow. But it did not happen. No one in Iran took Tudeh seriously. Numerically it was tiny, with no more than 2,000 people, most of them either Party veterans or members of their families. The Party had no armed formations of its own, nor did it enjoy support among any section of the population. For the authorities, the Tudeh Party presented no threat, apart from its being a protégé of Moscow, which was only a potential problem. The Iranian authorities did not touch it: they neither fought it as an enemy, nor praised it as an ally, but simply ignored the Party's existence.

Nor were the Tudeh Party's relations with the forces on the left as affectionate as Kiyanuri tried to show in his reports. The Mujahidin and Fedayin organizations looked upon Tudeh as 'the red hand of Moscow', a party which had played no part in either the preparation or seizure of power, but simply sat it out in the Soviet Union. They flatly rejected Tudeh's bids for the leadership of the Left, and condemned the Party for blindly and completely supporting the clergy in its scrabbling for political advantage. Nor did they welcome Tudeh's unsuccessful attempts to win over members of other left-wing organizations to their side. The Tudeh Party, for its part, repeated Khomeini's accusations, and accused the Mujahidin and Fedayin of distrusting the authorities – an attitude proved by their reluctance to subordinate themselves and to surrender their weapons. This policy divided the Left and played right into the hands of the Iranian authorities.

But why did the Tudeh Party have to misrepresent the facts in its reports? Why not describe the situation as it was? The answer is that the true situation ran counter to the Moscow line. There the plan was to unite all the forces of the Left in Iran under the aegis of the Tudeh Party, thus creating a strong leftist front which could form the real opposition to the regime of the Mosque. Moscow planned to give aid in arms and money to the leftist front, and finally to bring its forces to power, even if it meant civil war – quite a familiar blueprint for the Soviet authorities.

What wrecked this prospect was the impatience, arrogance and conceit of the Tudeh Party leaders, who considered that it was beneath their dignity to pander to the young Mujahidin and Fedayin leaders. Thus it was not just that the leftist front failed to materialize. A state of open hostility grew up between the Tudeh Party and the other forces of the Left in Iran. The KGB Residency later received reports that, when the Iranian authorities began the physical extermination of the Mujahidin and Fedayin organizations, the Tudeh Party played an active part, helping the authorities to find the safe flats they were using.

But reality is one thing. What to report to their Moscow masters was another. During the decades they spent in the Soviet Union, the Tudeh old guard had mastered to perfection the rules of Soviet society. One of these has always been, 'The authorities want to hear what the authorities want to hear.' This precept was particularly highly developed in Brezhnev's time. Why upset the old man? He might fly into a rage, and who knows, he might even cut the Party's subsidies. Because it is a fact that the Tudeh Party was being fully maintained by the Soviet Union, or more exactly by the International Department. All the members of the Tudeh Party Central Committee were on Moscow's payroll. All the means needed to finance Tudeh Party activities were also provided by Moscow.

I first stumbled across this financial angle when the Tudeh Party courier handed over a packet of used airline and railway tickets and explained that they were to be sent to Moscow for a refund of expenses incurred by members travelling on Party business. The packet contained tickets for journeys made both in Iran and abroad. We forwarded the tickets to Moscow, but to my surprise the Residency was given no instructions to pass on any money. When the courier was making one of his routine visits to the consulate, I asked him whether they had received the refunds for their travelling expenses. When he told me that they had, I realized that there must be another channel of communications to the Tudeh Party of which I knew nothing. Through personal curiosity, I tried to find out how this was done, and eventually I succeeded in learning the following.

In addition to the embassy, the Tudeh Party was also in touch with the Soviet Trade Delegation in Tehran. The tried and tested system of financing foreign communist parties developed by the International Department over the years was used in this case. A trading company was set up by secret members of the Tudeh Party. It did business with the Soviet Trade Delegation, and it was through this channel that the Tudeh Party was chiefly financed. They received both hard cash and goods free of charge to sell on the Iranian market. Everything in this was legally above board, and there was no chicanery. It was normal business. And dozens of companies were doing business with the Soviet Trade Delegation. It was through this channel that those travelling expenses were paid off. The matter had reached the stage where newsprint from the Soviet Union was being delivered through this straw company to enable Tudeh to print *Mardom*, the Party newspaper.

There was yet another channel used to finance the Tudeh Party, and that was personal funds for Comrade Kiyanuri, which I was in a position to monitor because all communications with Kiyanuri were effected by means of notes through the KGB Residency. The courier brought us a note, we translated it, and sent it to the Central Committee. Shortly afterwards a reply would come back, which we translated into Farsi – often this chore fell to me – and then handed over to the courier. Kiyanuri was asked in one of these messages how he would prefer to receive his personal funds. This time his reply came in a securely sealed envelope, whereas before his notes had been tightly rolled up, and the courier could have read them had he wanted to. In the note in the envelope Kiyanuri gave a clear answer to the Moscow question: 'I prefer to be given money only person to person. On no account must these funds be mentioned or passed through the channels of the Trade Delegation or the courier.'

So the conclusion was clear. This money was not going into Party work and the building of communism in Iran; it was being spent on the personal needs of the secretary general of the Tudeh Party. Personal clandestine meetings were accompanied by a very high risk both to the Tudeh Party and the KGB Residency. The Iranian authorities could have used the fact of these secret payments to the head of the Tudeh Party either to destroy it or to damage relations with the Soviet Union. The Residency pointed out this danger in its report, but Moscow ignored it. Personal meetings began to take place at which Kiyanuri risked his own life and the security of his entire party for the sake of personal gain. In his next note Kiyanuri reported that he intended to visit West Germany 'on Party business'. We were charged by Moscow 'to ascertain from Comrade Kiyanuri in which currency he prefers to be paid the next sum from his personal funds'. The answer was very modest. 'In West German marks, please.' Shortly afterwards the Residency received through the diplomatic bag a bulging packet containing the usual personal funds for Kiyanuri, this time to the tune of 30,000 Deutschmarks. He could have not too bad a time on a two-week trip to the FRG.

Shebarshin involved various officers in the Tudeh Party operations at different stages, and therefore many people in the Residency knew about them. A feeling of disgust and revulsion took hold of all those who knew about Kiyanuri's personal funds. 'Like master, like man,' we used to say, as we saw the corruption among the Soviet Party elite spreading to foreign communist parties. It meant that the entire world communist movement was susceptible to corruption and that everything it did was being paid for by Moscow. One could imagine what sums of money were being paid out by the Soviet Union to support the world communist and national liberation movements and their allies.

In theory, of course, we had known all this for some time. But it is one thing to read about such facts in the Western press, and quite another to play a personal part in operations of this kind when you know everything down to the last detail. The incident in New Zealand, when the Soviet ambassador was caught red-handed by the local security service while handing over a briefcase full of money to a member of the New Zealand Communist Party, now appeared in a different light. This too must have been 'personal funds for Comrade . . . ' The tranquil environment of New Zealand was doubtless taken into account when contacts with the local communist party were effected at ambassadorial level without any intervention by the KGB.

Brought up in the harshness of Soviet reality, I never felt any love for communism. It always appeared false to me. Yet here I was having to take part personally in the machinations of this international mafia. The Iranian communists, who had spent more than thirty years in the Soviet Union, had an excellent understanding of Soviet society, and the people who ran it. Now they were aspiring to seize power in Iran, create a society similar to Soviet society, and deliver their country into the Soviet sphere. That was their affair, but I wanted no part of it. Whereas before my hatred for communism had been passive, I now began to examine my own involvement in this filth.

The Tudeh Party continued to operate in the spirit described. In May 1979 the Iranian authorities began a massive anti-American campaign. Mass demonstrations under the slogan of 'Death to America' marched through all the main cities. They were particularly strong near the American embassy. The Mosque demanded that the United States should hand over the Shah so that he could be 'given a just trial'. Beyond all doubt, the anti-American campaign had been initiated by the clergy, and perhaps even by Khomeini himself. For everyone knew how Khomeini viewed the United States. The aims of this campaign were to divert the attention of the local populace from the ever-worsening economic situation, to damage the standing of the United States in Iran, and to show people that the Islamic authorities did not fear even the strongest power. As the well known fable has it, 'Ah Moska, little dog, it seems so strong that it yaps at an elephant.'

But in its reports to Moscow, the Tudeh Party made out that the anti-American campaign in Iran had been begun and developed on its initiative and with its direct participation. Moscow rejoiced. But there in the International Department no one gave a damn who it was who began the campaign in Iran. The main thing was that they could claim the credit to the Politburo. The Tudeh Party's lie was profitable not just to the Party itself, but in this case to its Moscow backers as well. The International Department accepted all the bogus assurances that Tudeh stood at the head of a united movement of the Left, ignoring comments from the KGB Residency that 'Comrade Kiyanuri's information about the situation in the movement of the Left does not always reflect reality.' Moscow continued to pour more and more resources into the living corpse which was the Tudeh Party.

Meanwhile political contradictions in Iran continued to grow more acute.

After a mass campaign in the press condemning the Mujahidin and Fedayin, the Iranian authorities began to mount direct hostile actions. In July and August 1979, exchanges of fire redoubled between members of these organizations and the Revolutionary Guards. Taking into account the fairly strong Mujahidin and Fedayin armed formations, and their popularity among the young, the authorities acted subtly and with caution. The first attacks on their centres of power took place in outlying provinces. Then came a lull. The authorities were waiting for some reaction from the main leadership of these organizations. But this armed retaliation did not come. There were too many differences among their leaders over relating with the ruling regime. The authorities then made their next move, which was to seize Mujahidin delegates in towns close to Tehran. Again there was no reaction. Finally the Revolutionary Guards seized the Mujahidin and Fedayin headquarters in Tehran. No arrests were made; the leaders of these left-wing organizations were simply evicted on the pretext that their presence on these premises was illegal. As in the time of the Shah, both groups had to go underground again.

The authorities' actions against the Left also intensified the conflicts among the clergy. I have mentioned already that the children of the well-known Ayatollah Taleghani were members of the Fedayin. Now they were arrested by the Revolutionary Guards. Their car was stopped one night and found to be crammed full of weapons which they were taking to one of the safe flats. Taleghani was outraged and demanded his children's release. This was refused. The old man then relinquished all his posts and went off to his home town of Taleghan and sat down in the posture of 'best'. (This is the strongest form of silent protest in Islam.) Such a form of protest adopted by one of the most popular personages in the country could bring nothing but harm to the authorities, so a special representative from Khomeini was sent to Taleghani, and he begged the Ayatollah to return to Tehran.

Taleghani returned. Nothing was heard of him for a few days. Then he appeared on a television programme and delivered a penitential speech. With downcast eyes, he said that what he had done was mistaken, that he had inflicted damage on the cause of the Islamic revolution, that he was devoted with all his heart to Khomeini's cause, and so forth. All this was quite unlike Taleghani, and so humiliating that it was painful to watch. They had found some means to silence this free voice. This entire farce was familiar to me from history. The confessions of Lenin's comrades-in-arms sounded just the same at Stalin's show trials in the Thirties.

And so Taleghani was tamed. Yet here came Moscow perceiving him as a potential opposition leader among the clergy and, to be on the safe side, deciding to establish contact. Ambassador Vinogradov was instructed to meet Taleghani and test the ground. The meeting took place on 10 September 1979 and lasted almost two hours. When he got back to the embassy Vinogradov was very happy with the outcome, but the following morning every Tehran newspaper carried reports of the sudden death of Ayatollah Taleghani. Iranian reporters with an eye for detail described the condition of the body, and for people with medical knowledge their accounts clearly pointed to signs of poisoning. At the same time, all the papers unanimously stressed the fact that Taleghani had died immediately after meeting the Soviet ambassador. Nothing was said directly, but soon the city was alive with rumours that Vinogradov had pricked him with a poisoned ring while giving him a farewell handshake.

The story was drivel, of course, but Iranian society with its penchant for this kind of tale took the reports quite seriously. Vinogradov had not been seen in public during these days, and when he did go outside, he was then accompanied by an armed guard made up of duty security guards. In those days, a new witticism was popular at diplomatic receptions. 'And when does your ambassador intend to meet Khomeini?' foreigners would ask us.

We learnt the actual details of Taleghani's death only a few days later from our sources. This was the sequence of events. The meeting with the Soviet ambassador took place in the morning. After it had ended, Taleghani was cheerful as usual. But after supper that evening he suddenly fell ill. His personal guards rushed to the telephone to call a doctor, but the line was dead. They tried to give him water, but the water supply had been turned off. The old man did not have a chance. His opponents had thought of everything down to the last detail. Naturally, as always happens in such cases, all his differences with the authorities were forgotten after his death, and a prolonged period of mourning was declared. It was thus that the movement of the Left was deprived of its only support among the clergy. Now the authorities could declare open season on the youths who had overstepped the mark.

Sometimes telegrams of a general nature would arrive in the Residency from the Centre. They would give an assessment of the political situation in Iran, in the region, or in the world as a whole. These telegrams usually ended with the sentence 'all Residency personnel to note'. Usually telegrams of this type were boring and their reading a pure formality, since they were based on rehashed Residency material. However, on one occasion some time at the end of autumn 1979, at a general Residency meeting, Resident Shebarshin read us a telegram from the Centre which differed greatly from all other previous ones. In particular it stated:

> World conditions, which are steadily deteriorating, are approaching a situation where the world stands on the threshold of a nuclear catastrophe. The ruling circles of the United States of America are planning to deliver a massive nuclear strike against the USSR and its allies, and to this end at the present time they are increasing their military potential and stepping up their preparations to begin a military conflict. In this connection the leadership of the KGB of the USSR

directs all its residencies to change their basic orientation in acquiring intelligence. While continuing to pay due attention to obtaining political intelligence, you should focus your main attention on intelligence of a military-economic nature which would substantiate material on the preparation being made by the USA for an attack on the USSR. In order to obtain this intelligence, residencies must use all the resources they have at their disposal. Intelligence-gathering officers must step up their activities even more in their work to fulfil the tasks given them by the Centre, without thought of threat to their personal safety.

Signed – Sviridov (the KGB Chairman's pseudonym).

This telegram hit us like a bolt from the blue. What war? What preparations of the United States for a nuclear strike? What ravings! When Shebarshin finished reading the telegram, he looked a little embarrassed. We began to put questions to him, and he answered. Yes, in practical terms we would be duplicating the work of the GRU by concentrating our main attention on military-economic information, but there was nothing terrible in that. But wasn't it true that so far no signs had been seen of a deterioration in Soviet–American relations, to say nothing of preparations for an attack? For in Tehran we were not cut off from information and we knew very well what was going on in the world. That was not for us to say. The Centre knew best. It was our job to carry out this order.

It was quite clear that somebody in Moscow needed material about an American threat in order to begin the next campaign of struggle for peace and the prevention of nuclear catastrophe. And Soviet propaganda was indeed to launch such a campaign a few months later, directed above all at the Soviet people. The economic condition of the Soviet Union was continuing to deteriorate steadily. There was already a serious and permanent countrywide shortage of foodstuffs and consumer goods, and public discontent was steadily mounting. The Party was saying to the Soviet people through its campaign, 'Why are you worrying about butter and meat when the world is standing on the brink of general annihilation? All our strength and resources must now be directed at preventing a nuclear catastrophe, and after that we'll think about the material situation of the people.'

Thus the Party began yet another campaign to fool the Soviet people. It was interesting that in the Soviet Union the people remained completely unmoved. Nobody took seriously the usual chatter of the Party propagandists. Who wants to think about politics when all thoughts are taken up with where to find good food products? In the West on the other hand this latest upwards twist given to the struggle for peace was seized upon with unprecedented enthusiasm. In all capitalist countries, movements began for, among other things, the prevention of a nuclear catastrophe, and against cruise and other missiles. There were peace marches in all these countries. Western counter-intelligence services were run off their feet looking for the KGB agents who were organizing these demonstrations. But their efforts were in vain: the KGB had nothing to do with it. Having failed to obtain any response from the Soviet people, the struggle for peace campaign, to the surprise of its progenitors in Moscow, was taken up in the West. A good beginning like this must not be thrown away, the Moscow leaders decided, and placed the reins of the campaign in the hands of the International Department. It was from here that this campaign was co-ordinated. In countries of the West, the local communist parties acted as its conduits.

In Iran, mass anti-American demonstrations, whipped up by the authorities, continued to grow and finally took the form of a continuous demonstration that went on for several days outside the walls of the American embassy in Tehran. It was a real siege. Then on 4 November 1979 the embassy was seized by spokesmen for the demonstrators who called themselves 'students following the line of the Imam Khomeini'.

Details about the seizure of the embassy are already well known by way of the hostages themselves, as well as from other sources, so I have no need to repeat them here. I shall only say that we knew from our sources who it was who sanctioned and then carried out the seizure of the embassy. When it writes about these events, the Western press uses the word 'students' to describe the people who seized the embassy and held the American hostages. But according to material held by the KGB Residency in Tehran, these were no students. The seizure was sanctioned at the very summit of the Iranian leadership, and was carried out by a trained team that consisted exclusively of members of the Corps of Revolutionary

Guards. It is true that when the attack began, some zealous on-lookers who were or might have been students, and who belonged to different political groups, attached themselves to the raiders. But they were removed subsequently in the course of the lengthy detention of the American hostages.

The British embassy in Tehran was seized the following day, 5 November. Now this really was a spontaneous action on the part of fervent young hot-heads. But as their action had no official sanction, the intruders were thrown out of the embassy by Revolutionary Guards. The occupation lasted about six hours, but considerable damage was inflicted during this time. The block of flats in the Soviet embassy grounds is across the street from the British embassy building, which gave us such a good view of what was happening in our neighbours' place that we were able to stand on the balconies and photograph what was going on. Now the crowd is knocking down the metal gates. Now they are bursting into the embassy building and we see the flying glass splinters from the smashed window panes. Now smoke begins to pour from the corner room on the third floor – obviously the British are burning the contents of their registry. When the crowd left the British embassy and passed by ours, they saw us with our cameras on the balconies. They did not like this at all and began to shout that the Soviet embassy was next in turn for seizure.

On the same day the Iranian government unilaterally rescinded articles 5 and 6 of the Soviet–Iranian Treaty of 1921, under which Lenin's young government transferred free of charge to the Iranian government all concessions which had been made to Tsarist Russia in Iran. This treaty was without time limit. Articles 5 and 6 provided that either party might send troops on to the territory of the other in the event of any threat to the other's security. In other words, if forces hostile to the Soviet Union became active on Iranian territory, the Soviet Union had the right to send its troops into Iran. (No one of course took seriously the reverse possibility.) That is why these two articles were denounced by the Iranian clergy. The Soviet authorities did not react in any way to Iran's decision, thus showing that, for them, these articles of the treaty remained in force. It was evident that the Iranian leadership was rather afraid of its northern neighbour. That made us confident that they would not dare to touch our embassy.

The seizure of the American embassy in Tehran caused confusion in Moscow, which had previously viewed Khomeini as a pawn of American imperialism and calculated that his anti-American campaign could be discounted. Barkers are no biters, it was said. But this dog up and bit – and hard! Now Moscow's attitude must change, and the change was expressed in the reaction to the United States' military threat to Iran in which it was stated that the Soviet Union would regard any military action by the United States against Iran as a threat to its own southern frontiers. Although this implied the possibility of a direct clash between the super-powers, it was clear to us that the Americans would not start a direct conflict. This situation was advantageous for the Iranian authorities, since the Soviet Union was in fact taking them indirectly under its protection. It freed their hands in the case of the detention of the American hostages. But as it turned out, one can always expect surprises from the Iranians. And they came later.

American propaganda reacted to these Soviet moves with a massive press campaign directed against both Iran and the Soviet Union. It was said in numerous publications and in every possible way that the Soviet Union was behind the Iranian revolution, and was making massive arms deliveries to Iranian Azerbaijan and Baluchistan. The role and influence of the Tudeh Party, which was almost called the basic motive force of the revolution, were greatly inflated. It was said that the Soviet Union was continuing to make massive deliveries of the latest weapons to the Khomeini regime, and that the new security forces of Iran were undergoing training under KGB instructors. Everything that it was possible to invent, the US invented.

As we saw it, this kind of propaganda not only failed to bring any benefit to the United states, it worsened Irano–American relations still further and practically drove the new regime into Moscow's embrace. We in the Residency, who had hardly any agents at the time, derived great amusement from American fables about the omnipotence of the KGB in Iran. The Americans were again creating excellent publicity for us. But it must be said that the true state of affairs was known only to KGB officers, and we preferred to maintain silence on the subject. So it was that the GRU and the straight diplomats in the embassy believed, though perhaps not completely, in the KGB successes that were trumpeted in the American press.

CHAPTER 15

At the end of November 1979, Sadegh Ghotbzadeh was appointed Iranian foreign minister. Ghotbzadeh first appeared in the pages of the world press when he turned up from the United States to join Khomeini's entourage in Paris. However, certain people representing Soviet interests had got to know him much earlier. When he was a young lad in the early Sixties, Sadegh Ghotbzadeh followed the fashion of the time and went to study in the United States. There he was quickly attracted by left-wing ideas, which were very popular with Iranian students abroad. That is what he was doing when he came into the sights of the GRU, the Soviet military intelligence service, whose representatives at that time were 'fishing' among left-inclined students.

Ghotbzadeh's recruitment presented no difficulty. He was ready to help the Soviet Union, the bastion of world communism. But friction soon arose between Ghotbzadeh and the GRU. The GRU wanted their new ward to remain in the United States in order to live and work there after he had finished his studies. In this way the GRU would have resolved their problem of how to introduce their agent into the land of the main enemy. Ghotbzadeh had other plans. He wanted to go to the Soviet Union and continue his studies there. This took the GRU aback. They tried to persuade Ghotbzadeh that he had made a hasty decision, but he stood his ground. Then they began to bring pressure to bear, even going as far as to make threats. This caused a row with his GRU case officer, and as a result Ghotbzadeh refused to collaborate further. His romance with Soviet communism was over. After this, he continued to live as an eternal student in the United

States until the opportunity presented itself to join Khomeini's movement.

Ghotbzadeh's grudge against the Soviet Union appeared in full measure from his earliest days as Iranian foreign minister. Now he had the chance to get his own back for the insult inflicted in his youth. At a time when the clergy were waging a mass anti-American campaign, Ghotbzadeh began an anti-Soviet one. At first it consisted of attacks at the diplomatic level, but then, as his temper rose, Ghotbzadeh began to make quite serious statements in the press. Thus during his first days in office, he decided to review the status of all Soviet representatives in Iran. He wanted to know why the Soviet Union had so much property here. Why did we have two consulates? Why was the staff of the Soviet embassy in Tehran bigger than the staff of the Iranian embassy in Moscow? He was the source of initiatives to bring all this into balance. Moscow liked none of this, and negotiations began in the hope of taming the vindictive former agent, but Ghotbzadeh would not be brought to heel.

The Iranian foreign minister made frequent statements on Afghanistan, accompanied not just by protests but by threats against the Soviet Union, which he said was in touch with the Tudeh Party through the Trade Delegation. Finally, in July 1980, he bluntly demanded that the diplomatic staff of the Soviet embassy be reduced by thirteen. This was regarded by the Soviet side as a gross breach of good manners, but nothing could be done about it. After some haggling in the embassy between the Foreign Ministry officials, the KGB and the GRU, it was decided that the reductions must be equally shared. Ghotbzadeh's blow however did not quite achieve its desired result. The fact was that there was quite a number of unoccupied diplomatic slots in the embassy. These were the ones which were cut. The situation which had come about enabled the KGB Residency to dump some ballast by sending home dud officers who were just serving out their time.

What Ghotbzadeh was doing naturally vexed the Soviet authorities, who found this type of behaviour from the foreign minister of a small neighbouring country hard to swallow. So the Politburo gave the KGB an instruction to take steps to oust Ghotbzadeh. It happens that he was in fact suddenly removed from his post in August 1980, although the KGB had nothing to do with it. Ghotbzadeh disappeared from the political arena, but all that he had begun went on as before. The Soviet consulate general in Resht was closed in September 1980.

Although Ghotbzadeh had been dismissed, the Politburo's order to the KGB remained in force. Orders are orders, and active measures were taken. They consisted in essence in bringing to the knowledge of the Iranian authorities information that Ghotbzadeh was a CIA agent. This was done, among other things, by using the Tudeh Party. The authorities did not need too much convincing, since Ghotbzadeh had spent many years in the United States. Finally in April 1982 he was arrested and accused of preparing a plot against the regime.

When he was already under arrest the KGB made another move against Ghotbzadeh, which hammered a final nail into his coffin. A 'coded letter from the CIA to its agent in Tehran' was prepared in the Centre, using a quite simple code which any expert could decipher without difficulty. No names were mentioned, but it was clear from the text that this secret and highly valuable agent was Ghotbzadeh. A fairly large and conspicuous package of white paper became the container for this message. It was placed under a telephone box located right beside a petrol pump on Tabandeh Street in north Tehran. Our officer then rang the bomb disposal service, and speaking Farsi, reported that he had seen somebody placing something under the telephone box. Bomb explosions at petrol pumps were a frequent occurrence at the time. The package quickly disappeared from under the telephone box. Ghotbzadeh was shot in September 1982.

Soveksportfilm is a Soviet foreign trade organization that deals in sales of Soviet produced films. It has offices in many countries, and has always traditionally been used by the GRU as a cover for its officers, though what connection the GRU has with the art of the cinema is anybody's guess. Up until 1977, the GRU made great use of the Soveksportfilm offices in Tehran, but some time in the summer of that year, SAVAK laid a 'honey trap' for an officer of the GRU Residency who was

working there under cover, by floating a very attractive young
Iranian film actress in front of him. The GRU officer took
the bait, SAVAK caught him on Soveksportfilm premises with
his pants down, and the usual course of events then ensued.
SAVAK proposed that the GRU officer should collaborate. The
officer refused, and reported what had happened to the resident,
presenting it all as a SAVAK provocation. He was sent back to
Moscow on the next plane. These things are done very fast in the
GRU.

In order to take the steam out of the situation, the GRU
proceeded as usual in these cases and handed over this slot in
Tehran to genuine Soveksportfilm employees. A straight official
occupied it for two years, and another was sent to replace him
in 1979. I had some personal acquaintance with this replacement,
whose name was Aleksei Guseinov. An Azerbaijani by nationality,
but living in Moscow, he had worked as a teacher in my Institute
of Asian and African Countries, and lectured on the history of art in
Turkey. He was small, sharp-featured, neat in appearance, smiling
and polite. He was over fifty, but he looked younger.

At first no one paid any attention to Guseinov. So a new
Soveksportfilm representative has arrived. So what? Leave him
alone to get on with it. But then rumours gradually began to spread
that Guseinov was splashing his money around. This is always very
noticeable in Soviet communities abroad, where everybody's financial
resources are very limited. And here was our Guseinov, after no more
than nine months in the country, contriving to buy himself a Bang
and Olufsen music centre, and the most expensive one at that. Mink
for his wife, diamonds for his wife and daughter, various smaller
items – the cost of these acquisitions was several times in excess
of Guseinov's legitimate income, but that did not worry him. In his
stupidity he boasted about his purchases and the rumours went on
spreading.

Then a denunciation landed in the KGB Residency, not just
from anybody, but from none other than the military attaché's wife,
who worked as Guseinov's secretary. She reported that something
funny was going on in Soveksportfilm. Guseinov was not showing
her the contracts which had been concluded for the sale of films,
and he was making some sort of secret deals with foreigners. By

chance she had seen in his safe bundles of dollars and some other Western currency which had not been recorded anywhere. The resident assigned Levakov, the security officer, to conduct a careful investigation, without alerting Guseinov. This was the outcome.

After he had got to Tehran and had a look around, Guseinov had come across a gold-mine which had been lying there unnoticed, right under the noses of everyone. Stored in a dark room in the embassy club, he discovered that there was a large quantity of films which had been sent over the years to Tehran to keep the Soviet community entertained. Since these films were for internal use only, they were not liable to customs duty, and so were of no interest whatever to the Iranians. Nor were they of any further interest either to the people who had provided them. There was no requirement to send them back to Moscow, and so they simply lay for years in the embassy club.

Everything that went on in the club was under the control of the representative of the Central Committee of the All-Union Council of Soviet Trade Unions. This was a post without substance: all the representative did was to think up various kinds of amusements for the Soviet community and collect their membership subscriptions. The representative of the Trade Unions Central Committee at the time was Valentin Stepanovich Soloshenko, who had started his career as a full-time employee in the Komsomol, but became too old to work there and was transferred to the Central Committee of the Trade Unions. He was not suitable to work for the Party Central Committee, because he was too shallow-minded. Getting on for fifty years old, he behaved like a naughty boy of Komsomol age. His job there had marked him for life.

So Guseinov began to entertain Soloshenko. He invited him to showings of sex films, and kept him well supplied with liquor. Soloshenko never let a drink pass him by. After they had become close friends, Guseinov asked Soloshenko's permission to sort through the old films. When he asked this, so Soloshenko was to maintain later, he did not let him into the real reason for his request, but explained that there were scientific purposes behind his interest. As we saw it, however, they were partners in the affair. In the end, Guseinov, with Soloshenko's permission, was admitted to the room where the old films were kept. After rooting around among them, he picked out the good copies for himself, took them over to the Soveksportfilm building, and after touching them up here and there, he began to sell them to his clients. The unsuspecting Iranians bought the films in the usual way, paying for them in accordance with the rules laid down by the agreement. For them there was no difference. The only difference was on the Soviet side, since the money went straight into Guseinov's pocket. We never found out how many films he sold in this way. But judging from his income, a good number.

Quite unaware of the investigation, Guseinov carried on with what he was doing. By then he was intending to buy himself a Mercedes. All the results of the investigation were reported to Moscow, but they wanted more proof than the evidence of KGB informers. Soon Guseinov's leave fell due, and he left for Moscow, still suspecting nothing. This was the opportunity to obtain material proof.

It must be said that the ambassador and the representative of the Party Central Committee had known all about the investigation from the very beginning, but this time they did not stand up for the law-breaker, as they had done quite often in the past. The fact was that Guseinov was so stupid and greedy that he felt no need to buy himself protection. Now the ambassador invoked the law. 'Yes, we must stamp out this sort of thing,' he declared, and gave permission for Guseinov's safe to be opened in his absence, and its contents photographed. The security officer was worried that Guseinov might suddenly have hidden the money somewhere else. But his fears proved groundless. The safe was neatly opened in the presence of witnesses by a specialist technician from the KGB Residency, and inside were found bundles of American dollars and West German marks. The money was counted, photographed, and replaced. All the material, along with the statements of the witnesses, was sent to Moscow. The security officer was delighted that the law had caught up with one thief at least. He wouldn't wriggle out of it now.

Time passed and, still unaware of the investigation, Guseinov returned to Tehran as though nothing had happened. When the Residency enquired about this, a reply came in from Moscow saying that all the relevant procedural measures had been taken to terminate Guseinov's posting. However they were a little behind with them, and this had enabled him to return to Tehran. There's the one hundred per cent efficiency of the KGB!

What happened next? The reader doubtless thinks that Guseinov was grabbed by the heavy brigade of the KGB Residency, who tied his hands, shot him full of dope, and shipped him back to Moscow on the next flight. That is how the KGB works in the best-selling fiction of the West.

In fact nothing like that happened. Guseinov continued to toil undisturbed in his offices, and three months later he set off for Moscow under his own steam when he was summoned to attend a conference at Soveksportfilm headquarters. When he got to Moscow and finally learnt what the authorities knew, Guseinov was not at all rattled, but resorted to the well tried maxim that the best means of defence is attack. He began to hit out at everyone he could, especially the KGB, accusing the Residency of intentionally setting him up, and of having planted the money in his safe. He wrote to the Party Central Committee that he, a war veteran, was being traduced by the KGB, and much more besides. And what happened? In spite of all the incontrovertible proof, no criminal proceedings were begun against Guseinov, and he was left completely in peace. Either the penny had suddenly dropped or he had taken someone's proffered hint, for by now he had obviously greased some palm in Moscow.

In order to show any particularly sceptical reader that such things went on in other places besides Iran, I give as an example the case of Arkadi Shevchenko, former deputy to the secretary general of the United Nations, who decided to go over to the Americans. He describes in his book how he took special care to keep out of sight of the KGB. The fact is that the KGB's Residency in New York noticed his strange behaviour and reported it to Moscow six months before Shevchenko defected. Moscow did not react at all. For the resident, this meant only one thing – 'Leave Shevchenko alone.' And they left him alone. In vain did he drive his car around the streets of New York, trying to detect surveillance. He was never tailed, nor could he have been. The only thing that a KGB Residency could have done to a person of Shevchenko's rank was to inform Moscow of his behaviour, and nothing else.

I have first-hand knowledge of this case from General Drozdov himself, who was then KGB resident in New York. When he returned to Moscow he became head of the KGB's 'S' Directorate, where our conversation took place. He said that after they had told Moscow about Shevchenko and got no reaction, the Residency played safe and washed its hands of the affair. At least after Shevchenko's flight, nobody in Moscow was asking silly questions like 'What was the KGB doing?'

PART FOUR

'What would Comrade Lenin have done?'

CHAPTER 16

On 28 December 1979 the Soviet Union sent its troops into Afghanistan. My KGB contacts had kept me informed about the situation there, and the perspective from neighbouring Iran gave a view that was not available to Western observers. The Soviet invasion also had serious repercussions for the staff of the Tehran embassy, and for all Soviet nationals in Iran. For these various reasons, I may claim to have been a privileged observer of these events.

Owing to its geographical position, Afghanistan was for years a bone of political contention between the British Empire and Tsarist Russia. The mountains that make it such formidable fighting terrain also make the country economically negligible, but it was strategy that concerned the two great powers. Britain wanted Russia kept away from the frontiers of its Indian Empire; Russia wanted no British presence on the fringes of Central Asia. The Soviet government inherited that view, and developed good relations with Afghanistan, which was the first country in the world to recognize the Bolshevik government in Russia in 1919.

The Nadir Shah dynasty came to power in Afghanistan in 1929, and British influence increased. However, the Russians had the considerable advantage that they had never made war on the Afghans, whereas the British made several attempts to subdue the country by force of arms in the late nineteenth and early twentieth century. None of them succeeded, and the British eventually withdrew from the empire, leaving the Soviet Union to benefit from the relatively friendly attitude of the Afghan people. From the beginning of the 1960s economic agreements were signed and Soviet arms and military advisers provided. Mohammed Zahir Shah was a frequent

visitor to the Soviet Union. In these conditions the Afghan Communist Party (ACP) grew strong, as did left-wing influence in the
army. Afghanistan had no security forces of its own, and this gave
a free rein to the intelligence services of the KGB and GRU.

In 1973 a nephew of the King, Mohammed Daud, staged a military
coup with the help of left-wing forces in the army. His uncle left
the country; Daud became president of Afghanistan. The influence
of the ACP grew, and its members entered the government. But
Daud had different ambitions. He began to improve relations with
neighbouring Pakistan and Iran, and late in 1977 he approached the
Shah of Iran for a loan to build a modern trans-Afghan highway that
would run from the Iranian frontier to Pakistan. The Shah agreed,
and Daud was only too willing to accept his secret condition, which
was to get rid of the ACP.

In early 1978 all ACP leaders were arrested and jailed. Even
in prison, however, they kept in touch with events, and when they
learned that Daud had decided on their physical liquidation they
decided to forestall him with a military coup. An ACP emissary
informed the Soviet ambassador in Kabul about their plan. How
could they stage a coup from the brink of extinction? Moscow
shared the incredulity of the ambassador, and sent back a cautious
reply: 'Do not promise anything specific. Stick to generalizations. Let
them make their own decisions.' But despite this off-hand response
the coup proceeded: its leaders had nothing to lose. On 27 April
1978 the presidential palace in Kabul was attacked by tanks and
planes and was seized after a brief battle. Daud and his family were
arrested and shot. The communists were in power.

Here I should like to emphasize that not one Soviet organization,
the KGB included, played any part whatever in the coup.

Now the Soviet leaders had changed their tune, but they had a
problem. The ACP was not united. Some years previously it had
split into two factions, and each had its candidate for the presidency.
The Khalq ('People') faction had a pro-Soviet orientation and was
led by Noor Mohammed Taraki; the Parcham ('Banner') faction was
supposedly more Chinese-oriented, and was led by Babrak Karmal.

Since it was pro-Soviet, relations with the Khalq faction were
maintained at the level of the International Department of the
Central Committee of the Soviet Communist Party. The KGB

and GRU were categorically forbidden to recruit agents from among its members. On the other hand the Central Committee authorized the KGB to recruit Parcham members 'in order to keep their pro-Chinese activity under control'. This was an easy task, since the Parcham members were ready to collaborate with the Soviet side, and their pro-Chinese reputation was a label hung upon them by their Khalq rivals, in pursuit of privileged treatment from the Soviet Union.

All the leaders of the Parcham faction, including Babrak Karmal himself, had been recruited as fully fledged Soviet agents, and KGB intelligence obtained a great deal of information about the Khalq faction from their political rivals. The Soviet leadership persuaded the Afghans to set up a coalition government which representatives of both factions would enter, but the key question was who should head this government, and the Politburo ordered the KGB to produce a detailed report that would brief them on both Taraki and Karmal. It was the opinion of the KGB experts that Karmal was the more reasonable and disciplined of the two, that he had shown himself to be pro-Soviet in his dealings and would listen to advice. The same report described Taraki as stubborn, intolerant, irascible and shallow. Such a person would be very hard to manipulate.

The Politburo chose Taraki, on the ground that Karmal was an unknown quality whereas 'We know Comrade Taraki personally as a fighter with a pro-Soviet orientation . . . ' The 'personal' connection was Suslov, then in charge of ideology in the Party, and whose influence in the Politburo outweighed even Brezhnev's, the secretary general. Soviet advisers flooded into Afghanistan, entering the Party machine and government ministries. KGB and MVD missions were dispatched to help set up new police and security forces. Right from the start, Taraki ignored all advice and behaved like the inflexible zealot the KGB had described.

Taraki started with land reforms, and confiscated lands belonging to the Mosque and to feudal landlords, but instead of distributing them to the peasants for their personal use he ordered kolkhozes, collective farms, to be set up on the Soviet model. His Soviet advisers wanted him to learn from the Soviet Union's mistakes, but he was determined to 'build communism following the teaching of Marx and Lenin' and had no intention of 'making concessions to all sorts of bourgeois landowning swine'.

When Taraki also embarked on a countrywide campaign against religion, the Soviet advisers tore their hair. This was Afghanistan, where the entire population were Muslims, fanatically devoted to Islam. Taraki simply threw out any particularly zealous advisers, and complained personally to Brezhnev, to whom he had a direct line. The weak-minded Brezhnev would simply repeat, 'Comrade Taraki knows his own country best.' He said much the same when Taraki convinced him that the Parcham faction were 'hidden enemies of the revolution', and removed their leadership from the government. Those of lesser importance he threw into prison, the more eminent he dispatched as ambassadors to various countries. Babrak Karmal went to Czechoslovakia.

The People's Democratic Party of Afghanistan (PDPA), led by Taraki, had begun to carry out reforms that undermined the way of life of a patient people who did not mind who was in power as long as they were left alone. The first disturbances began among the Pushtu tribes who for centuries had remained independent of central authority. For them, authority was the head of the tribe and the Imam in the mosque. To change this was not easy, considering that traditionally all members of the tribe, children included, carried weapons, and were ready to use them. The Kabul regime's response to a series of outbreaks of armed resistance was to attempt to dis-arm the tribes, and this became the trigger for the insurrectionist movement in the country as a whole. When his Soviet advisers tried to oppose his hard-line policy, Taraki issued secret instructions to his officials telling them to listen and agree with what the Soviets said, but to follow only his own commands.

On 22 March 1979 the Pushtu population of Herat staged an uprising that killed many Soviet specialists and spared neither women nor children before the government repressed it in the most brutal fashion. It must be said that both sides shared this incredible brutality, both then and later. By the summer of 1979, out of twenty-eight Afghan provinces only four were quiet and the army was suffering a steady drain of soldiers into the ranks of the partisans.

A new personality now appeared in the Khalq wing of the

PDPA. Hafizullah Amin was a skilful organizer and recruiter who had returned to Kabul from the United States in 1965 to devote himself entirely to politics. It was said of him that he had little interest in the communist or any other ideology, except as a means towards the summit of power. He achieved this early in 1979, when President Taraki appointed him head of the government and he proceeded to uproot the remnants of Parcham from their posts in the State machine and to have them either jailed or executed. He put his own people into the vacant posts, and was more or less running the country, although he chose for the time being to remain in the shadow of Taraki.

The communist regime continued to deteriorate. Outside the large towns, the countryside was controlled by partisans, and the ring was tightening around Kabul. Moscow was baffled and apprehensive. So much money invested, and nothing to show for it. And if Kabul should fall, what kind of chain-reaction might begin in other countries where Soviet-backed regimes were being challenged by an armed opposition? One possible solution was to set up a coalition government that would combine the PDPA, the heads of the various tribes, independent non-communists and the priesthood. Taraki inclined towards it, but Amin was categorically opposed – it would spell the end of his own ambitions.

In September 1979 President Taraki was summoned to Moscow, where he agreed to pursue the coalition option, and decided that a first step towards it would be to remove Amin, his 'faithful pupil'. Back in Kabul he summoned a meeting of the government, which Amin was to attend. Several shots were fired at him as he entered the presidential palace, and it became clear that Amin had prepared himself for trouble. A large group of his personal guards broke into the palace, and in the ensuing battle with Taraki's men many members of the Cabinet and of the Khalq Central Committee were killed, and Taraki lost his life.

Amin was now the sole master, but he knew that the Russians would try to remove him, and he took steps to protect himself, appointing relatives to all the key posts and surrounding himself with a host of personal bodyguards. He tried to avoid meeting the Russians, and made sure that his bodyguards were present in force when he had to. The gulf between Amin and his Soviet allies was widening all the time, and he kept asserting that they were betraying the cause of the Afghan revolution.

The new president stuck in the throats of the Politburo, and the KGB was ordered to remove this troublesome leader. The task went to the Eighth Department of 'S' Directorate of the KGB's First Chief Directorate – the direct action department which had been dormant since 1973. Lieutenant-Colonel Mikhail Talybov, an active illegal documented as an Afghan citizen, was selected to carry out the order. He was sent straight to Kabul, where with the help of KGB resources he was infiltrated into Amin's entourage as a cook in the presidential palace. Talybov was given the job of poisoning Amin. But as Misha Talybov told me himself later, it proved to be no simple matter to do this. Amin was so suspicious that he never ate anything completely. He ordered several dishes and ate a little from each one. What was more, his food was tasted by his bodyguards. On several occasions Talybov added poison to the fruit drinks that Amin usually took. But Amin always mixed the drinks, thus reducing the possibility of poisoning.

'I couldn't poison everything in the kitchen,' Talybov exclaimed. 'The operation had to be discreet.'

Worrying reports began to arrive from Kabul in December. According to information from sources close to Amin, it was learnt that he had his own plan for solving the crisis in Afghanistan. Amin intended to enter into negotiations with the leaders of the armed opposition, enlist their support, and then make an announcement to the whole world containing a demand that the Soviet Union withdraw all its advisers from Afghanistan. Sadat did something similar in Egypt. Amin also intended to appeal to the United Nations for help. He calculated that, if he could trumpet all this to the whole world, the Russians would not dare to touch him.

These reports greatly disturbed the Soviet leadership. An urgent decision had to be taken, and the Politburo had two possible ways of solving the problem. The first, which was suggested by the KGB, was to carry out a raid by a special commando group on the presidential palace in Kabul, overthrow Amin and his supporters, put in place a government in Kabul that would be acceptable to Moscow, and then introduce a policy of national reconciliation. This would still have been entirely possible at that time. The second way, proposed by the Party machine and the military, was more radical – put troops into Afghanistan, liquidate Amin, occupy all the country's principal towns, speedily destroy the centres of partisan resistance, and then when the job was finished, withdraw the troops.

KGB experts were against sending troops into Afghanistan, saying that it was not Czechoslovakia and that the resistance movement would grow in proportion to the Soviet presence. The military claimed that they could put down the resistance fairly quickly. How could Afghan peasants with their antediluvian rifles really put up resistance to the powerful Soviet Army?

The whole world knows which option the Politburo chose.

Soviet troops had begun to concentrate on the Soviet–Afghan border as early as May 1979, shortly after the massacre at Herat and after partisan resistance had begun. Two divisions, consisting entirely of officers and soldiers of Tadjik and Uzbek nationality, were concentrated in border areas. They wore Afghan uniforms. In Afghanistan, no one could distinguish them from the Afghan army. These two special divisions had been trained against the contingency of the resistance growing in strength, and of an immediate threat arising to the Kabul regime. Some sub-units had been sent into Afghanistan to protect Soviet specialists there. Here the whole absurdity of the venture revealed itself. Their lack of discipline, their sympathy for the local people, but most important of all their devotion to Muslim religious teaching, all gave rise to doubts about the reliability of these Soviet troops. It was decided to use brigades of airborne troops alongside the special divisions when the command sent them in.

On 28 December 1979, the Soviet army moved into Afghanistan. The timing was calculated. Always afraid of the reactions of the West, the Brezhnev leadership considered that the unfavourable effect that the Soviet action would cause would be slightly softened during the Christmas holidays. The troops were moved in both by land and by air.

The first Soviet military transport aircraft to touch down on Kabul airport brought the task-group to seize the president's palace. This group was made up of Soviet commandos and Farsi-speaking KGB and GRU officers who had been seconded to them. These were volunteers mainly from the First Chief Directorate, and there were no special killers from the KGB among them. They had undergone a brief training in weapons and tactics. A battalion of airborne troops was attached to the special group, or spetsgroup.

After having disembarked from the aircraft, the task-group, travelling in vehicles and light tanks, set off for the presidential palace. As the column left the airport, an Afghan sentry barred its way. A bullet from a silenced pistol made a neat hole between his eyes. The column met virtually no resistance as it moved along the route to the target.

The presidential palace in Kabul is surrounded by a metal fence with three gates on its perimeter. According to the plan, three light tanks were supposed to knock down these gates and dash for the palace building. Two tanks did what they had to do, but the third hit the gates and then, in the true Soviet fashion, its engine cut out. The timing of the tank operation had now been lost. According to the plan the airborne troops were to eliminate the guards outside and then surround the palace. Immediately after that, the spetsgroup would storm inside and do its job. The order was precise. Not one Afghan witness was to survive.

When they saw the attackers coming the guards outside the palace opened fire, but they were quickly silenced by the guns of the airborne troops. Most of those killed were Afghans, but after the first brief battle there were also victims among the spetsgroup. One of those killed was a young 'S' Directorate officer who was already being trained as my replacement in Tehran. As the attack started he began to climb out of his armoured carrier and a round from a heavy machine-gun took his head clean off.

Once they had forced their way into the palace premises, the spetsgroup came up against heavy resistance from Amin's hand-picked personal guard, who were completely devoted to their chief. Amin had given them the order to fight to the last man, and it was an order that they meant to carry out. On the evidence of those who took part in the operation, both sides suffered losses in the stream of fire from automatic weapons and bursting grenades. Members of the spetsgroup had not expected Amin's guards to put up such fierce resistance. They had calculated that the guards would surrender quickly and that the whole operation would be over in a matter of minutes. But in fact it turned out to be not quite so simple.

The losses grew. Colonel Boyarinov, the group commander, ran out of the palace building to ask for reinforcements, but was instantly caught in automatic cross-fire from the airborne troops who were all around the palace. He must have forgotten in the heat of battle that they had been given the order to shoot anyone who ran out from the palace.

Eventually the group was given reinforcements and the resistance crushed. Amin was found in one of the rooms. He was not hiding, but had resigned himself to his fate, and was quietly awaiting his end. It came in the form of a long burst of automatic fire that riddled his whole body. The operation had been successfully concluded, and not a single Afghan witness remained alive.

Mikhail Talybov, our own illegal and Amin's former cook, was present during the attack on the palace. When the assault began he was carried away with enthusiasm and tried to encourage the attackers by cheering them on. Shouting in Russian, he ran out to meet the members of the spetsgroup as they reached the first floor. His gaze met stunned, uncomprehending eyes, and he realized that he could well meet his end right there and then, so without a moment's thought he took a flying leap down the stairs to the ground floor. There was nobody left alive, only corpses. Talybov took refuge under the stairs and sat there until the voices of the members of the spetsgroup began to sound human. Only then did he give voice in Russian and emerge from his shelter.

While the spetsgroup was doing its work, more and more transport aircraft were landing continuously at the airport. They were carrying airborne troops who immediately set off for town and took control of the key buildings and other targets.

That same day Kabul radio broadcast a speech, relayed from Tashkent, made by the new president of Afghanistan, Babrak Karmal. In it he reported Amin's death and the overthrow of his murderous regime, 'on whose hands is the blood of tens of thousands of our compatriots'. It was only a few days later that Karmal himself returned to Kabul aboard a Soviet military aircraft.

On the whole, the operation to put troops into Afghanistan was considered a success. No rumours ever trickled out to the West about what really happened to Amin. All the main Afghan towns were very quickly occupied by Soviet troops. Now the second part of the plan remained to be carried out – the rapid liquidation of the 'primitive' partisan resistance, followed by withdrawal from Afghanistan.

CHAPTER 17

On 1 January 1980, having spent most of the preceding night celebrating New Year, I went into the embassy. At that time, nothing much was happening. It was simply that it had become a habit to call in on the embassy, and on the Impulse station in particular, even on the morning of a day off. After spending about an hour in the embassy and chatting with friends – chiefly about how we felt after the previous night's celebrations – we began to disperse.

I was going down the stairs of the embassy office building, and had just reached the ground floor, when suddenly the alarm sounded. The ring was sharp and painfully loud. 'What a time for an alarm drill,' I thought with some irritation, and decided to tell off the duty guard, but the bell went on ringing. I had almost reached the door when suddenly embassy officials and guards came rushing through it. 'The embassy's being seized!' they were yelling. 'There's a demonstration of Afghans at the gates, and the crowd's got into the grounds!'

The duty guard was the last to rush in and he slammed the door behind him. Through the window we could see a stream of bearded faces – young men running past the building. There was no telling at that moment whether they were Afghans or Iranians. A stone smashed through a window-pane. The attackers were breaking windows and were already beginning to heave at the main door, trying to break it down. We prudently withdrew into the corridor. Suddenly shots rang out and we saw armed men who looked like Revolutionary Guards, chasing the assailants. Then more armed men popped up around the perimeter of the embassy building. We didn't know whether it was protection for us against the attackers, or whether it meant that we had been captured. When everything had more or less calmed down, and the uproar around the building had subsided, another Residency officer and I decided to slip cautiously outside and exchange some words with the armed men. It turned out that they really were Revolutionary Guards and that they had gone there as soon as they learnt about the attempt to seize the embassy.

We went up to the embassy gates. The intruders had already been thrown out of our grounds, but the crowd was still raging outside the gates. The Soviet flag had been torn from its flagstaff and burnt. A soiled white rag bearing the inscription 'Allah o Akbar' now fluttered in its place. The crowd chanted continuously 'Death to the Soviet Union', 'Russians out of Afghanistan' and various religious slogans. When I went nearer to the gates the crowd raged like animals. The Revolutionary Guards advised me to withdraw to the guard-room, so as not to inflame passions further. Inside it, nothing had survived. All the window-panes had been shattered, and the telephones and both the internal and external alarm signalling equipment had been smashed to smithereens. The furniture was in pieces.

A Revolutionary Guard suddenly came up to me. There was a fire in the embassy, he said, and the fire brigade would have to be called at once. I looked at the building and saw smoke pouring out of the registry windows. They must be destroying secret documents inside. Without batting an eyelid, I explained to the guard that the smoke was coming from the embassy kitchen, where they were just beginning to cook the dinner. The guard believed it.

The order to destroy the registry was given minutes after the attack on the embassy began. After what had happened to the Americans, no one could tell for a while whether it was a provocation or a real seizure of the embassy, so the ambassador and the KGB and GRU residents preferred not to take any risks and gave the order to destroy all secret documents and equipment.

The security rules laid down that everything in the registry had to be destroyed in thirty minutes. There are two ways of destroying secrets. All secret documents are burnt in incinerator boxes fitted with oxygen bases (there were only two of these in our registry); while all the secret equipment, and the coding machines above all, were broken up into small pieces by using an ordinary sledge-hammer. In practice, none of this proved easy to do. So many secret documents had accumulated in the registry that it took two hours just to burn them. What was more, soon after the burning began, one of the incinerator boxes developed a crack along the full length of its casing and had to be turned off. The registry filled with smoke, which meant that the coding clerks had to work in gas-masks.

As for breaking up the equipment, there was no time to do it until everything had almost quietened down completely, and that operation lasted, not two, or even three hours, but for almost the entire week following the attack. It showed up how imperfect our system for destroying secrets was. We had come nowhere near to being equipped with computers. All the secrets were kept on paper. We didn't even have shredding machines for destroying all this mass of paper. The whole job was done in the old-fashioned way, by fire and sledge-hammer.

It is one thing however to break everything up, and quite another to get rid of the fragmented machines. According to the security rules, everything which had been smashed had to be accurately classified and then the remains sent to Moscow by diplomatic bag. So soon afterwards, the quantity of material sent from Tehran to Moscow grew to incredible proportions. The diplomatic bag, which is not a single bag or pouch, but rather the total of bags and parcels sent at any one time, grew from its normal weight of around 120kg to 700kg. We dispatched huge crates containing mutilated teleprinters, coding machines, radios, and all sorts of small gadgetry – tape recorders, signalling devices – intended for the KGB's operational use.

The Iranians of course did not have the slightest idea that the registry in the Soviet embassy had been destroyed. When they saw the enormous crates going as diplomatic bags, they must have thought that the KGB was stealing something from them, and naturally they wanted to see inside. The Revolutionary Guards at the airport were always trying to make difficulties for us over the dispatch of the diplomatic bag, looking for an opportunity. Since the opportunity never came, they used any pretext to contrive somehow to feel and touch the crates. One could imagine their disappointment had they found out that what we were sending by diplomatic bag to Moscow was nothing but scrap metal.

But neither the Iranian security service nor the Revolutionary Guards were to have any peace, for no sooner had we got rid of our scrap metal than we began to receive huge crates containing the new equipment, hundreds of kilograms of diplomatic consignments arrived from Moscow every two weeks. The crates were rather long in shape and were reminiscent of the packaging for weapons. I do not know what the poor Iranians thought. Probably that the Soviet embassy was preparing a coup in Iran.

Soon after the attack, we looked on the contents of the KGB Residency itself with new eyes and came to the conclusion that we had absolutely no need for much of what was there. For instance that great map of Tehran on the wall of the general room in the Residency clearly indicated that it was used for espionage. A map in the office of a normal diplomat would not require that large a scale. Desks needed clearing of all unnecessary papers. It is difficult to imagine how much clutter was discovered.

When all the Residency offices had been cleared of rubbish, the head of the counter-espionage line personally checked the officers' desks. And here something quite improbable was discovered in the desk of our information service officer, Colonel Aleksandra Kuzina. Already past fifty, she had worked all her life in the KGB information service, and mainly on Iran. She was in her way a monument to the Residency. She knew everybody, and knew everything about everybody, and was an awe-inspiring gossip. Her dyed black hair and fleshy face made it impossible to determine her nationality. She could have been anybody. I always associated her with Rosa Kleb, that character in the well-known James Bond film, *From Russia With Love*. They had something in common. The Residency officers disparagingly called her Aunt Shura, which is what the cleaning ladies in big buildings are usually called.

When Denisov, the head of the CI line, was making his final check of officers' desks, he found over four hundred information telegrams, or parts of telegrams, in Aunt Shura's desk. They were carefully hidden, and it was only Denisov's persistence that led to their being found.

These telegrams went back several years, and legally this was a clear and flagrant breach of security regulations. The copy of every telegram must be destroyed after it has been sent to Moscow. At first Aunt Shura tried to laugh it off, and she might have got away with that in the time of previous residents, but not with Shebarshin. She was one of his most malicious detractors, constantly gossiping behind his back, and fearless about doing it, because she had connections of some sort back in the Centre. But now she had clearly been caught out, and there was no getting around it.

The investigation revealed the following. In recent years Aunt Shura had begun to lose her memory, and in order somehow to compensate for this, she began to collect KGB clichés and standard expressions, then sentences which appealed to her, and finally entire telegrams. Information subjects repeat themselves from time to time, and Aunt Shura had a ready-made version for every occasion. The matter turned out to be more serious than at first thought, since many telegrams bore dates that preceded Aunt Shura's present tour of duty. It meant that she had kept them somewhere, or given them to someone to keep. It was obvious that it was not only Aunt Shura who was involved in the matter. A great scandal could have blown up from all this. Resident Shebarshin did not want to cause one, so the matter was closed. Aunt Shura was told that she would be sent back to Moscow at the first opportunity. She put up no objection. Just so long as it was all kept quiet.

The entire staff of the Canadian embassy left Iran in January 1980. It turned out later that among them were six American diplomats who had been lying low there for three months. The Americans were issued with Canadian passports, and the whole operation was a success. The Iranian authorities only found out when the clamour broke out in the Western press. They began to threaten Canada, but were given a very reasonable answer: 'Canada no longer has any interests in Iran, and does not consider it expedient to maintain diplomatic relations with that country.'

We in the Soviet embassy applauded the courage and determination of the Canadians, and especially the kick in the teeth they had administered to the Iranian authorities. Well done, you Canadians, we said. It is not for nothing that your ice hockey is as good as the Russians'. So why could the Americans do nothing to free their diplomats? Why could this super-power do nothing with a wretched country like Iran? We honestly believed that the Soviet authorities, no matter who they were, would never have abandoned us in a situation like that.

Many people in Tehran, and many of us, believed in our hearts that one fine morning we should wake up to see American soldiers' helmets on the streets, and life in Iran would return to normal. In the first months of 1980, all sorts of information reached us about an imminent anti-Khomeini coup. In the end we ceased paying any attention to it. It was just wishful thinking. When the American morning awaited by all of us finally came, on 25 April 1980, nothing happened quite in the way we had imagined. The Iranian press reported the failure of an American military operation to free the hostages. We did not believe any of the Iranian reports until we had confirmation from the Western mass media. It seemed that the American 'Delta Force' was supposed to begin the operation with a lightning raid on Tehran. During a halt in the Iranian Tabas desert for refuelling and regrouping, they were hit by a sandstorm. A helicopter collided with a fuel-carrying transport aircraft when attempting to take off, and everything went up in flames. Eight American servicemen perished, and the operation was abandoned. Material proof, including a map of Tehran on which the American embassy and other targets were marked, fell into Iranian hands.

We experienced a feeling of shame and bitterness for the Americans. 'How can they attack the Soviet Union when they can't even deal with a country like Iran?' many people asked. But the question did not absorb us for long. We had received information that on 27 April, the anniversary of the Afghan revolution, Afghans would again make an assault on the Soviet embassy in a bid to take hostages.

This information reached us from various sources. First of all, we asked the Tudeh Party for help. The N line of the KGB Residency gave to an illegal the job of visiting Afghan emigration centres in Tehran to try to find out what they were planning. The GRU activated its secret sources. The same information came in from everywhere. This time the attack on the embassy would be better organized, and they were planning to take hostages. What was more, the Iranian authorities were adopting an approving attitude towards the enterprise.

Representatives from the embassy approached the Iranian foreign ministry. We told them that we were aware of the Afghan emigrants' plans, and requested the physical protection of our embassy. The surprised Iranians tried to elicit our sources, but our representatives only smiled modestly, as if to say that here we had a wealth of resources. The Iranians promised to give us physical protection, but we still kept on reminding them about it.

The most vulnerable target on embassy territory was the accommodation block, which during working hours was occupied only by women and children. We therefore decided on the day when the attack was to be made to remove all women and children from embassy territory and install them in flats in town. The security officer drew up a detailed plan which allocated duties to every diplomat. Everyone was given a sector to defend. I was given a forward position at the main gates of the embassy. In addition, two Residency officers were positioned outside embassy limits. In the event of the embassy being seized, they were to get in touch with the GDR embassy and ask them to inform Moscow.

As to purely physical protection, security measures had been stepped up after the first attack on the embassy. Now every embassy floor was sealed off by metal gates. Gas-masks and tear-gas grenades reached us from Moscow through the diplomatic bag. In addition each Residency officer was given a short piece of metal piping – it was all we had available – to be used as a weapon in the event of the assailants breaking into the embassy office building. The idea was to give the Residency as much time as possible to destroy their secrets. Although it must be said that, after the first attack on the embassy, not so much secret material had been accumulated.

On 27 April everyone was as nervous as on the eve of going into battle. A small detachment of Revolutionary Guards arrived at the embassy around 10 a.m., and we admitted them to the embassy grounds. Groups of Iranian and foreign television reporters had already begun to set up their cameras opposite the embassy gates. It was not a pleasant wait.

In spite of all we had done to prepare ourselves, the assailants caught us unawares. We expected first a demonstration, and then an attack on the gates, but something quite different happened. Messages from our outside observers reported that the demonstration was on its way, and we could already see movement far down the street. There was no need to panic yet. Suddenly we noticed young men sprinting down both sides of Stalin Street, which leads straight to the gates of our embassy. We did not know whether they were in any way connected with the demonstrators. While we were wondering, the group of runners rushed straight at the gates and had scaled them in an instant. Instead of opposing the assailants, the Revolutionary Guards scattered in various directions and let them get at us.

We did not wait for a clash, but ran for the embassy as fast as we could. I could hear the pursuers breathing down my neck. We dashed inside, and our uninvited guests began to hammer on the door. Splinters from shattered window-panes flew again. Suddenly we heard the crash of breaking glass and realized that the main entrance door into the reception hall had been broken down. At once we withdrew along the corridor into the embassy office building and closed the heavy steel door behind us.

Several minutes later came an attempt to force this door from the outside. As the attackers were now in a closed corridor, it was decided to throw tear-gas grenades at them. Two guards from the frontier troops put on gas-masks and flung open the door. On the other side of it there were just two young lads. When they saw big strong fellows in gas-masks with grenades in their hands, and men behind them armed with metal pipes, the assailants turned tail and tore along the corridor so fast that our guards did not even have time to throw the grenades.

I went up to the Residency offices to tell Shebarshin what had happened, and to express my view that an attack on the office premises was no longer likely. The attackers did not look ready to tackle the registry. The resident was sitting beside the field telephone which had been specially set up between himself and the registry, so that if need be he could give the signal to start destroying documents. He could see from his window the embassy's representational building, now occupied by the attackers. A figure approaches the window from inside, holding a heavy chair above his head. He throws it through the window. The pane is smashed to smithereens. Now you can discern the man. He is young and bearded, with a madman's eyes. I do not know for certain, but in Iran before enterprises of this nature it was common to smoke narcotics. This rampage had been going on for about forty minutes when our Revolutionary Guards began to appear. It was obvious that they had quite intentionally allowed the attackers to create their havoc.

Gradually, the commotion tailed off and we went out of the building. We were confronted by the results of the attack. The embassy's representational premises were badly damaged. The antique mirrors and crystal chandeliers were smashed, all the windows had been broken, antique tables damaged, ceremonial china and glassware smashed, not to mention such trivial things as telephones, and the kitchen destroyed. The commemorative marble plaque marking the meeting of Stalin, Churchill and Roosevelt at the Tehran Conference in 1943 was also smashed to pieces.

While the attack was going on, the Impulse station had continued to monitor the radio exchanges between the Revolutionary Guards. After the attack was over, the Guards counted up the number of assailants. They only got as far as eight. But there should be nine, they said. This was yet another proof that the Revolutionary Guards had known all about the attack in advance. What was more, the attackers looked like typical Iranians, and not like Afghans at all. In general, however, things had worked out quite well. None of our people suffered and nobody was kidnapped. The demonstration at the embassy lasted several hours, but we were quite calm about it. We were sure that the Iranians would not risk going any further, at least on that day.

Every cloud has a silver lining, so the proverb goes. That attack did a whole lot of good to someone. I mentioned that ceremonial tableware had been smashed during the attack. At first, no one was too concerned about it, but then reports from informers came into the Residency saying that a beautiful ambassadorial porcelain service and a very large set of cut-glass wineglasses had been falsely included in the list recording the broken ceremonial chinaware. An informer reported that fragments of the broken dishes had been piled into a large box in the embassy cellar, but there was no sign in it of any fine porcelain or cut glass. Reports like this did not interest the Residency. We had long been accustomed to the thieving going on around us, and paid no heed to mere details like that. But out of purely personal curiosity, our security officer decided to check the contents of the box containing the broken dishes, and was not at all surprised to discover that the informer was telling the truth. There was neither expensive porcelain nor cut glass to be found there.

Here I ought to explain why examples like the one just given no longer interested the Residency. It had always been interested in the past. What had happened?

Leonid Vladimirovich Shebarshin, the new KGB resident in Tehran, adopted a principled attitude towards what went on inside the Soviet community. Unpopular in the Centre, and friendly with no one in the Residency, he could be seen more often in the company of straight diplomats than with KGB officers. I thought at first that he was just fostering his cover, in conformity with all the rules, and trying not to show the local counter-intelligence that he belonged to the KGB. Well, that could only be welcomed. Soon he was on friendly terms with the counsellor Evgeni Ostrovenko, who was one of the most despised people in the embassy because of his blatant careerism and brazen servility to his superiors. This too was very easily explained. Ostrovenko was a KGB informer of long standing and was now being run by Shebarshin. Through Ostrovenko, who was close to the ambassador, Shebarshin soon became part of Vinogradov's entourage. This was unprecedented, since Vinogradov hated the KGB. There was nothing wrong with that, of course. Far better to live in peace with the ambassador than to be at constant odds with him.

None of this would have mattered, had it not been for Shebarshin's attitude towards corruption in the Soviet community. Every time the head of the counter-intelligence line or the security officer reported cases of this kind to him, he would frown in displeasure, not at the news but at the messenger. It was obvious that he had no intention of becoming involved. Most reports about corruption concerned the Soviet hospital in Tehran, where everything went on as before, but under Sirak the new director, on an even grander scale. Complaints came in all the time about the depravity and corruption practised by Sirak and his cronies. At first Shebarshin sent them to the Centre, but shortly afterwards the situation changed. The KGB Centre summarized all the material on the hospital and sent it to the Party Central Committee. There, apparently, they went straight into the wastepaper basket, since no reaction ever came back from the Committee, where Sirak had support.

In the end the Centre decided to take action against Sirak independently, without Central Committee approval. When Sirak learnt from his protectors that he was under constant observation, he chose not to go on leave to the Soviet Union, fearing that the KGB would not let him back. Meanwhile his wife was shuttling to and fro between Tehran and the Soviet Union. So the KGB decided not to allow Madame Sirak to return to Tehran, thereby gaining leverage on Sirak. Her exit visa was cancelled. No sooner had this happened than the telephone rang in the office of the KGB section concerned. The call was from the Party Central Committee, demanding an explanation as to why the hospital director's wife was being delayed. The explanation was given. Back came the order from the Central Committee: 'That's all rubbish. Let her leave!' The KGB officer asked for written confirmation of this order. At this the telephone exploded with such a stream of obscene abuse, punctuated by threats, that it was pointless to argue. Sirak's wife returned to Iran.

The Residency naturally learnt of all this, and it was now that Shebarshin's attitude changed. When the embassy security officer placed the next instalment of the hospital saga in front of him, he flung back the report without even reading it. 'I never want to see this filth again,' he said. 'And I don't want to hear any more about that hospital either!'

'What?' Levakov asked. 'Leave them alone? Let them rob you?'

'That's none of our business,' Shebarshin snapped. 'Our business is intelligence, not poking about in dirty laundry. We are not responsible for the morals of the Soviet community, that's a matter for the Party organs, so let them get on with it.'

'But you know very well, Leonid Vladimirovich, what relationship there is between the Party organs and the hospital.'

'May I remind you, Levakov, that this is not 1937.' Shebarshin was fuming. 'The KGB will never go back to the methods of those days. We shall never substitute ourselves for the Party organs again!'

It was hitting below the belt to accuse an old officer like Levakov, who had spent his whole career in active intelligence, of Stalinist working methods. He was an honest man, trying to fight against large-scale corruption, and any other suggestion was dishonourable. Of course, you could understand Shebarshin. He knew only too well that the KGB could do nothing against the Party and the people it protected. It was pointless trying to change anything. That was why

Shebarshin preferred to be on close terms with the ambassador. He might be a crook, but he was also a member of the Central Committee of the CPSU. That was why Shebarshin preferred not to bother the Centre with the problems of the hospital and other forms of corruption. What can one person do? You only bring trouble on yourself.

In order to make a good career anywhere in the Soviet system, including the KGB, it is essential to please the Party. And his career was important to Shebarshin. It was for the sake of his career that he transferred from the Foreign Ministry to the KGB.

Nor did our resident pay the slightest heed to what was going on in the Soviet Trade Delegation, where corruption was also rife. KGB Residency officers who worked there were always reporting it. The head of the Delegation himself, Viktor Konstantinovich Slovtsov, was a past master of graft. He would arrange auctions between Iranian companies tendering for Soviet Trade Delegation contracts. The contract was won by the company that offered Slovtsov the biggest bribe. He could accept these bribes with equanimity. Whom had he to fear? The ambassador and the Party Central Committee representative were his friends, and the KGB resident treated him well, as he was a KGB agent. He was protected on all sides.

Sergei Polyakov, a new CI line officer, came to the Residency in October 1978. He was the son of that very highly placed Party Central Committee official, Aleksandr Vasilievich Polyakov, who was responsible for everything that happened in Iran, and with whom I had had a conversation in the Central Committee before I left on my posting. For cover, Seryosha worked in the consular department. He was vice-consul, responsible for work involving Soviet citizens. It is no exaggeration to say that, from his first day in Tehran until the day I left Iran, in his capacity as an intelligence officer in the CI line, Polyakov did not do one stroke of work. He did not have a single operational contact, either with Iranians or third country nationals, and took part in Residency operations in a support capacity only. He devoted all his time to consular work on the Soviet community, just like a straight diplomat.

Need anyone be surprised that Seryosha was never reproached by anybody, the resident included, for doing absolutely nothing? How could they? For his Daddy had given instructions that Seryosha should not be exposed to any danger. A curious situation came about. When Shebarshin put pressure on officers to improve their results, he left Polyakov in peace. In the end, though, the resident found a solution. He invented a special job for Seryosha, which was to write a weekly telegraphic review about the condition of the Soviet community. This presented no special problems to Polyakov, since he could copy the entire content of similar reviews written by political intelligence.

As he was a counter-intelligence officer dealing with Soviet community issues, Polyakov had the most direct access to all information that the Residency received on corruption. He knew all about the ambassador and the Central Committee representative, the hospital and the Trade Delegation, and as it seemed to me, he was sincerely disgusted by it. Seeing that Moscow was doing nothing about corruption, he swore to tell his father the whole story when he went on leave. Maybe his father could change something. But after the conversation in which he said this, one of the senior officers in the Residency told me privately, 'Nothing will come of Seryosha's good intentions. You know who rang the KGB up that time from the Central Committee and gave the order for the hospital director's wife to be allowed back into Iran? It was Aleksandr Vasilievich Polyakov, Seryosha's Daddy.'

It was the same hand in the Central Committee of the CPSU that was covering up all the corrupt practices then going on in Iran. It would be interesting to know whether Sergei knew this.

Although I am not normally despondent, what was going on all over the Soviet community, and throughout our country, left me with a very depressing after-taste. I tried to lose myself in work, since we always had plenty of that in the N line, but the thought kept recurring with increasing frequency, for whom and for what are we doing all this? Who profits in the end from our labours? The Party mafia? What idea are we working for? For the idea of communism had proved to be illusory and false. We saw this every day in the country where socialism had already been built. So for what purpose were we risking ourselves, and not only that but exposing foreigners to mortal danger by persuading them to collaborate?

Suddenly a ray of light appeared in the general darkness. In the autumn of 1980 the Solidarity movement was set up in Poland, and Lech Walesa appeared. I recall the excitement and delight with which I followed events. It has begun, I thought. It was bound to begin. You can't keep the spring held down indefinitely. Historical associations came to mind. It was in Warsaw that the first unrest began before the 1917 revolution. And history repeats itself in the form of a spiral. Well, may it come true! The main thing was that they should not be able to suppress it at birth, for it would be too late afterwards. The Soviet authorities will exert pressure, I thought, but after their experience in Czechoslovakia they won't send in the troops. Most important for the workers is to gain time, so that they cannot be put down later.

I studied the newspaper pictures of events in Poland with great interest. When I looked into the gloomy faces of the young workers, I saw resolution. 'That's it – the beginning of the end,' I thought. 'A pity that it didn't begin in Russia!' I did not hide any of these thoughts from my friends. Most of us thoroughly approved of what was happening in Poland.

As a result of a new illegal being sent into the country at the end of 1979, the volume of work in the N line of the KGB Residency in Tehran increased considerably. Now, in addition to our ongoing work with the illegal couple 'Konrad' and 'Evi', we also had to work with 'Vagif'. This case however was considerably more complicated. Whereas 'Konrad' and 'Evi' were foreigners, 'Vagif' – I do not know his real name – had been documented as a citizen of Iran.

'Vagif''s training began long before he came to Iran. He was born in Baku, into the family of a political emigrant from Iran. With the passage of years, 'Vagif''s father had become a professor of Persian literature. Within the family the Persian language, Farsi, was cultivated on equal terms with Azerbaijanian, and for 'Vagif' it was a second mother tongue. After leaving school, he completed studies at the Baku Oil Institute and became an engineer. It was in this capacity that he came to the attention of the First Department of the KGB of Azerbaijan, whose officials are constantly talent-spotting candidates suitable for training as illegals. This is done in direct consultation with 'S' Directorate of the First Chief Directorate.

After preliminary training in Baku, 'Vagif' showed himself to be a very capable young man and he was transferred to Moscow for serious training in the subtleties of illegal espionage work abroad. For his documentation, an internal Iranian passport was used: its holder had died in infancy, but his death had not been registered. Later the parents and other relatives of the dead double went illegally to the Soviet Union, and in this way their documents came into the hands of the KGB's illegal intelligence. Their presence in the Soviet Union was unknown to the Iranian authorities, so far as they were concerned the family was still living somewhere in Iran, where there is no registration of domicile. This internal passport lay for years in the operational archives of 'S' Directorate, and was now used for 'Vagif'.

A cover life story was devised for 'Vagif'. It related that he had spent a great part of his life in Kuwait, where many Iranians had gone at the end of the Sixties to find seasonal work. 'Vagif', according to the story, would have returned to Iran illegally from Kuwait, by crossing the Persian Gulf on a fishing boat shortly after the Iranian revolution. In order to rehearse this part of his cover story, 'Vagif' was sent to Kuwait for six months as an official of the Soviet Trade Delegation. He devoted all this time to studying the Iranian community there, entering into his role and building up Iranian acquaintances. The Centre had to be convinced that the Iranian community in Kuwait would accept 'Vagif' as one of themselves. He passed this test, and made quite a number of 'friends'. When one of them learnt that 'Vagif' intended to return to Iran, he offered to take him across the Persian Gulf on board his boat.

It was an ideal début, and the new illegal agent was ready to be launched into Iran. Strictly speaking, 'Vagif' came into the category of illegal agent, because he was not a cadre officer of the KGB, and held no military rank. However henceforth I shall use the word 'illegal' for greater clarity.

Yuri Andropov, who was then chairman of the KGB, exercised personal control over all illegal intelligence activities. He had a preference for 'legal' launchings of agents abroad, in which the illegal travels to the country using his launch documents, then switches to his main documentation after arrival. This option however was not suitable for Iran at the time, since the only working frontier checkpoint not connected solely with the USSR was at Mehrabad airport, and we doubted whether it was quite safe for 'Vagif' to appear there and pass through all the control points. They might photograph him, or quite simply remember him by chance. Andropov was persuaded in the end that it would be safer to launch him under the operational option code-named 'Tourist', which requires the intelligence agent to be inserted clandestinely into a neighbouring country across a coastal frontier.

The Soviet steamer *Guriev* plied once a week across the Caspian Sea between the Soviet port of Baku and the Iranian port of Enzeli, carrying both Soviet and Iranian and other foreign passengers. Her captain had for many years been an officer of the Azerbaijani KGB, and naturally the *Guriev* was used in KGB operations, one of which was 'Tourist'. Under this operational variant, 'Vagif' was put on board the steamer when the crew was ashore and accommodated in a special place of concealment. Only the captain, the first mate and two other trusted members of the crew knew of his presence aboard. 'Vagif' remained in his place of concealment throughout the voyage from Baku to Enzeli, which lasted about fourteen hours.

On arrival in Enzeli and after completing all formalities with the Iranians, customs examination included, the entire crew of the *Guriev* was summoned to a meeting in the passenger lounge. Meanwhile 'Vagif' came out of his hiding place, and his place was taken by a trusted member of the ship's crew. So as far as the Iranians were concerned, the number of seamen had not changed. After this, 'Vagif', accompanied by the captain, the first mate and two other members of the crew, set off for the harbour gates in order to go into town as usual. There was a passport check-point at the gates where, in accordance with long-established practice, Soviet seamen handed in their passports and received in return an official pass allowing them to visit Enzeli.

This was the key moment of the operation. The group, consisting of five people, including 'Vagif', handed in only four passports at the check-point and were given four passes in return. Here the element of Iranian disorder was turned to good account. Since it all began, the official on duty at the passport check-point had never once left his office in order to count Soviets on their way into town. But had he wanted to come out on this occasion when the operation was going on, it would have been difficult for him to do so, for by a pre-arranged plan a Soviet KGB agent who worked in the Caspian Steamship Agency in Enzeli was already inside the check-point office. He had looked in 'by chance' at a stipulated moment in order to visit his Iranian friend and present him with a gift. In addition to this, the main group of seamen from the *Guriev* were already moving in on the check-point, thereby creating a crush. The official took the four passports, did not check the number of people, handed out four passes, and turned his attention to the crowd of Soviet sailors now pressing in on him.

Having left the port area, 'Vagif''s group followed the route usually taken by Soviet seamen – straight to the shops. Halfway there they turned down a sidestreet, where they were picked up by the car of a Residency officer who worked in the Caspian Steamship Agency in Enzeli. He took only three people into the car – 'Vagif', the captain and the first mate. The others went about their business. Their part in the operation was over. Our officer drove around Enzeli for a time to satisfy himself that he was not under surveillance, then he set down the captain and the first mate and was left on his own with 'Vagif'. He drove at once to Resht, 20 kilometres from Enzeli, and delivered 'Vagif' to a point near the bus station, where he handed him his Iranian documents and money.

'Vagif' then stepped out on to Iranian soil as a citizen of Iran. He set off for Tehran by bus, shadowed at a respectable distance by the Residency car, which followed the bus from Resht nearly all of the 350 kilometres to Tehran, just to be on the safe side. 'Vagif' was now on his own. His first night was spent in a small hotel in south Tehran. Next day we received his visual signal that everything was going well. Operation Tourist had been successfully concluded.

The first thing 'Vagif' had to do was to buy a good short-wave radio receiver in order to pick up radio messages from the Centre. (The Centre transmits radio messages in Morse code and the illegals receive them on a normal radio receiver. No specialized equipment is needed.) Buying a receiver was no problem, since Iran was still flooded with Japanese goods. Several days later, a dead letter-box operation was mounted, in the course of which 'Vagif' was given his one-time codes for deciphering radio messages from the Centre as well as some other materials. Everything with 'Vagif' was going according to plan. For us, the usual routine work with an illegal was only the beginning.

A festive mood reigned in the Centre, as it did in Baku. Everyone who had taken part in the operation began, as they say, to make little holes in their lapels to take the anticipated decorations. This time, however, the rejoicing was premature: the leadership announced that awards would be forthcoming only when 'Vagif' began to produce intelligence. There were long faces at this, for nobody was expecting anything useful in the short term. In spite of all his Soviet education, to go by his Iranian papers 'Vagif' was a nobody. Apart from his passport he had nothing – no educational certificate, nothing about qualifications. Of course we could manufacture all kinds of false certificates, but that was dangerous. In illegal intelligence the preference is to use authentic documents. In the Centre 'Vagif' had been taught the trade of refrigerator repair mechanic, but before he could start a good business it was essential that he should establish his cover story. So when he set out on his new venture 'Vagif' almost touched rock-bottom in Iranian society, spending his time hanging around with small-time artisans in south Tehran. What sort of intelligence could possibly come from there?

CHAPTER 18

After the second attack on the Soviet embassy in April 1980, the ambassador made an official protest to the Iranian authorities over their connivance at terrorist actions perpetrated by Afghan emigrants against Soviet representatives. Iran's reply was insolent and provocative. They threatened the Soviet Union directly, hinting at unspecified consequences to follow from the Soviet invasion of Afghanistan. Diplomatic language did not come easily to the Iranian clergy. The Soviet authorities then made another move. The Caucasus Military District carried out exercises in an area adjacent to a long sector of the Soviet–Iranian frontier. Barbed wire obstacles were removed from a stretch of frontier, and tank operations were carried out right up against the Iranian frontier itself. In one incident a couple of tanks even crossed over on to Iranian territory. This was a language that the Iranian leadership could better understand. After these manoeuvres their tone became considerably more polite.

Our relations with the Tudeh Party were going on in the same spirit as before. The liaison courier appeared, sometimes in the consulate, sometimes in the Trade Delegation, bringing reports from Comrade Kiyanuri, who kept up his old refrain about his Party's sound position under the Khomeini regime. But none of this was true, and the more he wrote the more his assessments of the political situation diverged from the real world.

Already there were signs that the authorities would soon begin a total offensive against the forces of the Left with a view to destroying them completely. We were sure that the authorities would deal first with the Mujahidin and Fedayin, and would mop up the Tudeh Party later. Exactly when that would happen it was difficult to say, but that it was certain to come, we did not doubt for an instant. We did not doubt either that if the Tudeh leaders were arrested they would tell everything about our contacts, with catastrophic consequences for the Residency.

The resident sent these thoughts and conclusions to the Centre, though without putting them so bluntly, but it seemed that they made no impression on the Party Central Committee. Instead of reducing contacts with the Tudeh Party, we had to act on Moscow's orders and extend them. We now supplied special equipment for sending signals to the embassy, special containers for the instant destruction of records, special tape recorders for recording lengthy conversations, and more besides. We might have been intentionally giving the Iranian security service as much incriminating evidence as we could. There was a feeling in the Residency that the Iranian authorities knew a great deal about our contacts with the Tudeh Party, and were only biding their time to deal us the most crippling blow possible.

Indeed, the Iranian foreign minister had said earlier that he knew all about the Tudeh Party's Soviet contacts through the Trade Delegation. When this happened, the Tudeh members who were in touch with us were surprisingly off-hand about observing the proper security measures. They thought for example that it was quite adequate just to turn into a sidestreet in order to be satisfied that they were not under surveillance. They had no idea how to conduct a full surveillance check.

In order to reduce our Tudeh contacts to a minimum, Resident Shebarshin devised quite a good system, under which the Tudeh man would throw his report over the wall of the embassy's summer residence in Zargande at an agreed point. Then at a previously fixed time he would ring the gate-house bell at the Soviet embassy. When the guard answered, the caller would say nothing, but simply place a transistor radio playing music against the mouthpiece. The guard on duty had been briefed about these calls, and immediately reported them to us in the Residency. Then one of us would drive out to Zargande and collect another message from the Tudeh Party.

It was interesting that our Impulse station never picked up any surveillance on Tudeh Party members. This meant only one thing. There was no need to follow them. There must have been an Iranian security service agent or agents in their ranks.

*

The interest of the Iranians in the Soviet embassy's diplomatic bag had grown considerably, especially after those enormous crates that we sent and received after the destruction of our registry. Now our diplomatic bag had become the centre of so much attention, and the Revolutionary Guards were putting so many obstacles in our way, that we had no doubt that they were simply seeking a suitable pretext in order to seize the bag. The seizure of the diplomatic bag would have been an utter disaster. It would have led to a serious deterioration in Soviet–Iranian relations, which even so were far from loving. In these circumstances, Moscow considered it expedient to stop the diplomatic bag service.

For all of us, this was no great tragedy. All the material that went by diplomatic bag to the Centre was photographed in the Residency, and only the undeveloped film dispatched to Moscow. Not very much documentary material was sent and usually it was of no great importance. All that the KGB Residency usually sent by bag could now quite easily be communicated to the Centre by telegram. It only had to be condensed. But even before all this happened, the Residency sent Moscow its basic material by telegram only. Most of the volume of the diplomatic bag, that is six or seven sacks each way, was taken up by the personal letters of Soviet specialists. There were just under 8,000 of our technicians in Iran at the time.

After the bag had been stopped, the Iranians grew worried and started to seek the new channels that the Soviet embassy was using to send its 'secrets' to Moscow. It never entered their heads that we were using telegrams. They decided that the diplomatic bag was now being sent in the Russians' personal luggage, and therefore the brutish behaviour of the customs service towards Soviet citizens leaving Iran intensified. A customs official friend of mine told me frankly that the the Revolutionary Guards were compelling them to check all Russians without exception and look for any documents. We had a good laugh at this. What naivety!

It was at this point that the tour of duty of Slovtsov, the head of our Trade Delegation, came to an end. Having learnt about the recent excesses of the customs, he came round to see us in the consulate before he left and asked us to be present at his departure. Slovtsov held a diplomatic passport, and under the regulations his luggage was not liable to examination, but as he said, you never know what to expect from the Iranians.

It was an accurate premonition. This time, along with the customs officials, there was a whole gang of Revolutionary Guards. As Slovtsov passed through the customs, the Guards demanded to examine his luggage. And he had quite a lot of luggage, about eight suitcases. Slovtsov invoked his diplomatic immunity. The customs officials and Guards answered that Slovtsov might be personally immune, but his personal luggage was not. The old refrain. At this point we naturally intervened as consular officials and started to argue diplomatic law. Slovtsov was extremely nervous. The guards categorically refused to let his luggage through without examination. We summoned an Iranian foreign ministry representative, who appeared at the airport with suspicious speed. He said that the guards believed that secret documents which could harm Iran were concealed in Slovtsov's luggage. That being so, they had the right to open his bags. But Mr Slovtsov also had the right to leave the customs if he did not wish his luggage to be examined. All this was done very politely, and it was obvious that it had all been set up in advance.

Finally we decided on a compromise. We suggested to Slovtsov that if he wanted to fly to Moscow that day, it would be better to allow them to examine the luggage. That way, we would bring the affair to an end without a row, and make fools of them as well. 'If you stay, then this performance is going to be repeated every time. Have you got anything really secret in your luggage?'

'Yes, I have,' Slovtsov replied. 'I'm carrying secret Trade Delegation documents which I can't send without the diplomatic bag.'

'All right,' we said. 'Then we'll have to go back. They won't let you out without an examination, and there's nothing else we can do.'

No sooner had he left the confines of the airport building than he was immediately surrounded by Revolutionary Guards brandishing submachine guns. Their commander, who had been extremely active in the customs, came up to Slovtsov.

'I am a representative of the procurator of the Islamic Republic,' he said. 'There in the customs hall, you were a diplomat to them. Out here you are nobody to me. So I'm not asking permission, but simply telling you that I'm going to examine your suitcases right now. If any of you tries to interfere, he will be arrested on the spot.'

We made a protest for form's sake, but it was clearly pointless. The Iranians were sure that at last they had found the evidence of Soviet espionage secrets that they had sought for so long. Slovtsov was white as a sheet.

The Guards began the examination right there on the pavement. Slovtsov, Polyakov, a GRU officer, several people from the Trade Delegation and I stood around. The first suitcase was opened and examined. No documents. The second – no documents. Then came the third, and the fourth. Finally the examination of the last suitcase, with the same result – no documents. The Guards were clearly dismayed. 'Why did he protest at the examination if he knew that his luggage was clean?' their baffled commander quite openly enquired. 'We've wasted all this time for nothing.'

We could not tell him the truth, so we read him an edifying lecture: Soviet people respected the law, observing it was dearer to them than anything, that was why we had protested. In fact, though, Slovtsov had had an altogether more solid reason for refusing to allow an examination of his luggage. Blinded by their obsessional quest for secret documents, the Revolutionary Guards had completely overlooked something else, and that was GOLD. Gold statuettes, gold portrait frames, gold ornaments. Gold and more gold in every suitcase. I do not know whom Slovtsov feared more at that moment, the Revolutionary Guards or us. Most likely us. This must have been only a small part of what he had managed to plunder during his eight-year stay in Iran. I was sorry that the guards had paid no attention to the gold.

'We can suggest to the guards that they've missed something,' the GRU officer whispered in my ear.

We looked at Slovtsov. He was silent, but his eyes were flicking back and forth. He was wilting but fidgety.

'Now that the examination has happened, do you want to go back to the embassy and make a protest to the Iranian authorities, or would you prefer to fly to Moscow right now?' I asked him indifferently.

'Can I?' asked Slovtsov, hardly believing that he could wriggle out so easily.

This time the customs officials did not insist on an examination, and let Slovtsov through without stopping him. He was a sorry sight at that moment, like a beaten dog with its tail between its legs.

'I shall report everything immediately,' Polyakov said on his way back to the embassy.

'Report away,' I said without enthusiasm. 'But it won't do any good. They won't do anything to him. What's more, the resident won't tell the Centre about it either.'

That is just what happened. Our report was listened to, and nothing was done about it. But I no longer cared about all that.

Vladimir Golovanov, the head of N line and my boss, was arrested while meeting an agent in mid-June 1980. The circumstances surrounding this case were not quite clear. Golovanov's agent, who had the pseudonym 'Sharov', was a Swiss by nationality. Golovanov had recently recruited him, and he observed all the rules of the art of espionage when he did so – acquaintanceship, study, cultivation and recruitment. 'Sharov' managed the Tehran branch of the Danzas transport company, so of course he was comfortably off financially, and that makes it hard to understand what made him collaborate with us. Was it perhaps a taste for risk and danger? He had stayed on in Iran although most foreigners had found the situation too dangerous to stay. Everything had been going smoothly, and Golovanov was planning to use 'Sharov' as a post-box, so that letters from illegals and KGB agents could be sent to his address. Beyond that, it was planned to train him for the role of a 'spetsagent', or special agent.

On the day of the incident, Golovanov's meeting with 'Sharov' was taking place as usual in the agent's home. In the course of the meeting, as the two of them were sitting quietly talking, armed men suddenly burst into the house. They said that they were members of the local revolutionary committee and that they were arresting Golovanov and 'Sharov' for espionage. It must be said that this Iranian action was absurd, since the meeting was taking place quite overtly between two foreigners. They had no secret documents on them, nor were they even drinking alcohol – something that could have put them in the wrong. In sum, there was nothing to compromise them.

All the same, the deed was done. Golovanov was put into a car, and without being spoken to or asked questions, he was driven to the Iranian foreign ministry. There the men with the guns handed him over to an official on duty and left the building. It was 9 o'clock in the evening. The perplexed official told Golovanov that he was free to go, and he walked back to the embassy, which was not far from the ministry. When he got there, he learnt that the Iranian official had rung the embassy and reported Golovanov's arrest, saying at the same time that he had already been released.

This whole episode was so strange that, after it had been discussed, it was concluded that it had all been a chance incident and the result of spy mania. Excessively vigilant committee people, trying to gain favour, had arrested 'two foreign spies', although they had absolutely no grounds for doing so. It was decided to treat the whole incident as a fortuitous occurrence.

Then something else happened soon after that strange arrest of Golovanov. It was summer, and all the diplomats were living at the embassy's summer residence in Zargande. One day, around noon, Golovanov's son left his mother at the swimming pool to get a drink of water at their bungalow. As he approached it, he saw two young Iranians emerge. They strolled up the hill to the outside brick wall, unhurriedly climbed over it and left the grounds of the summer residence. Golovanov's son went into the house, and froze in surprise. Inside was total devastation. Everything that could have been smashed was smashed. Everything that could have been broken was broken. The walls had been daubed with jam, and they dripped with broken eggs. The rest of what had been in the refrigerator had been trampled into the floor.

There was no question of burglary here, since nothing had been stolen. It was clear that the recent events had not been fortuitous after all, but were links in the same chain. SAVAK knew Golovanov from his first tour of duty in Iran. Immediately after his arrival back in the country to begin his second posting in 1977, SAVAK had begun to do all they could to make it impossible for him to work. Golovanov and his family were subjected to continual psychological pressure. They were kept under constant external surveillance, with the watchers totally and intentionally in evidence. In one version of foot surveillance, they even followed him and his wife so closely that they were almost breathing down their necks. Golovanov neither reacted nor panicked in the face of these provocations but continued to work away quietly. What annoyed SAVAK most of all was that, in spite of having their surveillance concentrated on him, they were unable to catch him red-handed carrying out an operation. Golovanov was a cool customer, with a complete mastery of surveillance detection methods.

For a time the revolution stopped the pressure on my boss. But now when the new forces of security had begun to operate, they decided to carry on with what had already been started. When they saw that Golovanov's arrest had failed to have the required effect, and that he had no intention of leaving the country, he was given a gentle hint in the form of the wrecking of his home. The insolence of this action against us exceeded anything they had done before, just as the open intrusion into embassy territory had never been done before. But anything could be expected from the new authorities.

The Residency and the Centre concluded that if Golovanov stayed in Iran, pure physical aggression would one day be used against him. The decision was taken to pull him out immediately, only in such a way that the Iranians would not suspect it, otherwise they would give him hell at the customs. We came to the decision that in order to fool Iranian security, Golovanov should be sent out of Iran alone and without his personal effects, leaving unexpectedly and travelling on a foreign airline, not by Aeroflot. The Iranian airline had a flight to Damascus the very next day, so it was decided to send him by this flight. The ticket was obtained by our agent in Aeroflot, and Golovanov's name was not put on the ticket when it was bought, but was written on it just before take-off. At Mehrabad airport, all the formalities involving the ticket were completed without him.

When we received the signal that everything was ready, we left for the airport in two cars. Golovanov was accompanied by four people: three consular officials and an operational driver, all KGB officers and all in good physical shape. He was nervous, but he never lost his dignity. We entered the airport building when boarding had already been announced, and went straight through all the controls, because Golovanov had no luggage. As diplomats we had the right to pass through the frontier controls at the airport. Just before boarding the bus to take us to the aircraft, we noticed some stir among a group of airport employees. One of them came over, asked which one of us was Golovanov, and asked him to produce his passport. Instead of his passport, he took out his diplomatic card. That was sufficient. The employee compared the photograph with the original and gave the card back.

We wanted to accompany Golovanov right up to the aircraft, but those in that airport group would not allow it. He was accompanied to the plane by an Aeroflot official. Shortly afterwards it took off safely. We left the airport with the feeling that we had won that round.

We realized the full extent of our victory only when we were sending Golovanov's family off to Moscow. That day the airport building was swarming with newspaper reporters. They were running about asking everyone where Golovanov was. It was evident that the Iranian authorities had been all set to stage a full-scale performance, with attendant publicity, around Golovanov's departure. Instead they got nothing out of it.

After Golovanov had gone, I was appointed the senior N line officer. Golovanov had formally handed over all the cases, which I knew very well anyway, before he left. Now another disagreeable duty was added to my work. I had to deal unassisted with all N line correspondence with the Centre. The second N line officer was working in the Soviet hospital. He had arrived not long before to replace Kharlashkin, but he had already proved to be a sensible and capable intelligence officer. There was no point in blowing him to the Iranians with frequent visits to the embassy.

The time soon came round for my own leave, and I departed for Moscow. There was nothing for me to fear from the Centre, as the work of the N line was going well.

'Ah, the celebrity!' said one of my friends in greeting.

I asked him what he meant.

'You're now a celebrity here. Your ears should burn at what

people say about you at all our meetings. "In the conditions of the complex situation in Iran, he gets results of high quality in his work," and stuff like that.'

This was news to me. We were never told about such things in the Residency, and I have to admit that, as I saw it, I had not achieved anything of importance. I had simply done my job conscientiously. Certainly I had managed to recruit an agent in a target that we had not been able to penetrate for about fifteen years, and there were other promising leads. The fact that I had also had no failures and that everything was going smoothly was also of great importance. I never worried about advancement. People who were always counting the days and months until they received their next military rank or career promotion always irritated me. Meanwhile my career was moving very rapidly ahead, and during this leave it advanced still further. After meeting KGB General Yuri Ivanovich Drozdov, the head of 'S' Directorate, I was officially appointed head of the N line in the Tehran Residency.

When I got back to Tehran, I felt that some Residency officers had changed in their attitude towards me. My promotion had clearly upset them, for some had started out with me. Wicked rumours and gossip went on behind my back.

'What evil and envious tongues some people do have,' the wife of one of our officers who worked as a Residency typist once said to me. 'Apart from the resident, you give me more work than all the others. I'm sometimes surprised at how you do it. But at the same time some of your "friends" are spreading gossip that you don't do anything, and that you're not capable of doing anything because you're stupid, and that your whole career is the result of sucking up to the bosses.'

Shebarshin once mentioned in conversation that there were complaints about my having become high-handed towards colleagues at work. I replied that that was pure gossip, and that I knew who was spreading it. I added that I was not the only one who had gossip spread about him. Shebarshin nodded agreement, but advised me to watch my step. I felt, and still feel, that the charge against me was completely absurd, since I am a person without ambition and I have never derived any satisfaction from ordering people about. This would have been against my nature.

They were levelling a charge of which I was not guilty. But nobody was accusing me of what I really was guilty of committing. Nobody was accusing me of disloyalty to the Soviet authority, although I did not conceal my views on this subject. I talked quite openly with my friends about the venality of the Party leaders, the corruption of institutional theft, and about the need to root out all these gangsters from our lives. When discussing ways in which our problems could be solved, I openly spoke in favour of abolishing the collective farms and transferring the land to the peasants for their own use. I argued for developing the private sector in light industry and the service industries, and most important of all, for removing from our lives the soul-destroying enervating burden which is the communist ideology.

I sometimes took pleasure from arguing with Sergei Polyakov's wife. She had passed through Moscow University before going to work there as a teacher of Marxism-Leninism, and she used to grow very annoyed when she was unable to find convincing arguments to defend the contrast between the odious Soviet reality and the magnificent theoretical promises. I expressed my open disgust at what was going on in the embassy and in the Soviet community as a whole, and nobody, including the heads in the Residency, ever reprimanded me for it. I doubt that they were unaware of it, but it was all the same to me whether they knew or not. I was ready to speak my mind to anybody. My frankness shocked no one, because most of our officers shared my views. Events in Poland gave me moral strength and encouraged the hope for possible changes. For me, Poland now even eclipsed Afghanistan.

In Afghanistan meanwhile the Soviet army was becoming more and more deeply bogged down. Hopes faded for a rapid destruction of the resistance and withdrawal of troops. The Soviet tank and armoured units, unaccustomed to carrying out military operations in the mountainous terrain of Afghanistan, could do nothing with the small partisan groups which were delivering lightning strikes from positions in the hills they had known since childhood. To make matters worse, Pakistan and Iran began to give help to the Afghan partisans. Their weaponry improved, and they began to deliver increasingly telling blows against Soviet military units. Raids were now being made with increasing frequency even into areas near Kabul. The Soviet forces replied with concentrated fire into the hills, but there was no one there any more. The military felt that they had been insulted and discredited before the whole world. The strongest army in the world unable to cope with a handful of insurgents. What a disgrace!

Officers in the GRU Residency in Tehran who had friends both on the ground in Afghanistan and among the planners on the General Staff disclosed when they came back from leave that the Soviet military command did in fact have a way to win in Afghanistan, a very rapid way which would involve using purely physical means to seal the Pakistani and Iranian frontiers and stop the flow of aid from these countries reaching the partisans. Airborne troops would then simultaneously annihilate the partisan formations shut up in Afghanistan. This plan would require increasing the strength of Soviet troops in Afghanistan to 300,000 men.

The plan was not to be realized, however, since the Politburo was afraid of sanctions from the West and did not want an escalation of the war. Instead it insisted that the military should do the job with the forces already at their disposal. 'What's the difference?' they asked. 'The damage is done already, so why stop halfway?' But the Politburo knew better. Instead of a rapid military solution to the problem, they preferred to operate in the communist manner, in secret. The KGB's 'S' Directorate was given the task of liquidating the partisan movement from within. This meant re-activating the Eighth Department, the direct action specialists, who formed a special detachment code-named 'Cascade'. It was manned by illegals who spoke Afghan languages. They had to locate Afghan partisans, join them, elicit as much information as possible and then either destroy them with their own forces or else lead them to Soviet troops. KGB residencies throughout the world were given the task of recruiting Afghans with pro-Soviet leanings and sending them to the Centre for special training.

In addition, in countries like Iran and Pakistan, the N line had to use its agents to penetrate Afghan immigration centres. We suggested using 'Vagif' for this purpose, but the Centre did not approve, judging it too dangerous. I knew one Afghan, a student at Tehran University, who had for long dreamt of going to the Soviet Union to study. After a short cultivation he agreed to collaborate, and I sent him off to Moscow for special training. I don't know what happened to him subsequently.

I did all this work with no great willingness. But as always happens in life, when you do not particularly want something, it will fall straight into your lap.

The Iran–Iraq war began on 22 September 1980. Its roots lay deep in the past, but the reason for it has always remained the same – the ownership of the Shatt al Arab. The Shatt al Arab is a waterway formed by the confluence of the rivers Tigris and Euphrates, which flows through both Iraqi and Iranian territory into an estuary on the Persian Gulf. The western bank of its lower course belongs to Iraq, the eastern bank to Iran. From time immemorial these two countries have never been able to resolve the problem of the ownership of these waters. An agreement was finally reached in 1975, during the reign of the last Shah, that the frontier between the two countries should pass down the middle of the river, and in this way both sides would have identical rights to use this stretch of water. It was a reasonable solution to the problem, but nothing is eternal.

The Islamic Republic of Iran, with its ideas of Islamic world revolution, began almost as soon as it was founded to interfere in the affairs of other countries in the region, especially in those where the Shiite current of the true Islamic creed predominated. The population in the eastern areas of Iraq is Shiite. In addition there were many emigrants from Iran living in Iraq. It was among these people that Iranian emissaries began to propagate their ideas, and the Iraqi authorities did not like it. Following the first disturbances by Shiites of Iranian origin, the Iraqis began to deport them from the country. At the same time, anti-Iranian propaganda started up in Iraq. This led first to tension and then to open armed conflicts in Iranian–Iraqi border areas. Iran hit Iraqi territory with artillery fire, and Iraq replied in kind.

On 17 September Iraq declared that it was unilaterally abrogating the 1975 agreement on the Shatt al Arab, and that it now considered these waters to be Iraqi territory. Fighting broke out on the Shatt al Arab between frontier troops, and then spread northwards along the frontier. Bani Sadr, who was president of Iran at the time, declared general mobilization on 20 September. On 22 September Iraqi troops invaded Iran on three fronts and launched air raids against airfields and military installations. Iran immediately declared its territorial waters in the Persian Gulf to be a military zone. A war of attrition had begun, which was to last until 1989. Throughout this period, the question has been asked, who was really responsible for starting the conflict and the hostilities that followed, Iran or Iraq?

Analytical information in the KGB Residency in Tehran indicated that the military conflict was advantageous mainly to the Khomeini regime, for the following reasons. First, the Iranian army, which the new regime did not quite trust and therefore feared, was busy at the front in wartime, and no longer offered a threat. Second, the ever-growing economic difficulties which had arisen as a result of the change in regime could be explained away by the war, and the people's attention diverted away from economic problems and on to political ones. Third, once the war had begun, the Iranian authorities could deal with the opposition under wartime laws. This meant only one thing – death.

The accuracy of the Residency's analysis was soon confirmed in practice. Beginning in April 1981, the Iranian authorities began a mass campaign for the physical extermination of the left-wing Mujahidin and Fedayin organizations. Open season was declared on them. Every day saw reports that dozens of their members had been shot dead in different towns, and hundreds arrested. In August 1981 alone, the Iranian security authorities and the Revolutionary Guards were each arresting roughly three hundred people a day. Soon hundreds were being executed daily. Terrible stories reached us about how, before they were shot, firing squad victims had blood taken from them for sending to the front. Let it not go to waste.

In order to wage war, an army must have weapons. The Iranian army which the regime of the Mosque inherited from the Shah had been fully equipped with weapons from Western countries. But because of the sharp deterioration of relations with the West, and especially with the United States, as a result of Khomeini's policies, the Iranians could no longer buy weapons in these countries. Now Iran had one natural choice, the Soviet Union, a country renowned for its massive deliveries of arms to revolutionary regimes throughout the world. The Iranians turned to the Soviet Union, but this time the circumstances were much more complicated.

At the beginning of the Iran–Iraq war, the Soviet Union was in a very delicate political position. A treaty between Iraq and the Soviet Union dated 1972 provided for cooperation and mutual assistance, including military assistance. At the same time, the Soviet government did not want to harm its relations with Iran and thereby push it back into the arms of the West. Having at last achieved its cherished aim (although not by its own hands) of removing the American presence from Iran, a country with which it shared a common frontier, the Soviet Union did not want a return to the past. On the other hand, support for Iran in a war against Iraq would mean a total loss of influence in the Arab world. In the end, the Soviet authorities found a solution. They declared themselves neutral in the conflict and observed this neutrality from the outset.

From the very beginning of the war, the Iranians kept on trying to send delegations to the Soviet Union to buy arms. Each time, they were turned down on various pretexts. I had to deal with the Iranians on all these occasions, since in their naivety they came straight to the consulate, bringing with them a bundle of passports belonging to members of the delegation, and saying that they needed visas in order to go to the Soviet Union to buy arms. These applications were always refused.

A curious thing happened once with one of these Iranian delegations. When they were making one of their usual applications for visas, I reported it to the consul, Dyatlov, and said that he should refer the matter to the ambassador. Dyatlov went off to the embassy, and then came back and instructed me to issue visas. I had some doubts about this, and usually on such occasions I would go to the ambassador and explain the situation, since it was quite out of the question to trust a fool like Dyatlov. But on that occasion I decided not to do it. I was fed up with always having to keep that idiot's nose clean. I asked Dyatlov once again whether he was sure that the ambassador's instruction was to issue the visas. Dyatlov said yes. I issued the visas.

Two days later, an almighty row broke out. The ambassador

demanded an explanation as to why I had issued visas to the Iranian delegation. I explained the facts to him. It was 9 o'clock in the morning, but when the ambassador sent for Dyatlov, he was nowhere to be found. He turned out to be at home, sleeping off his usual night's drinking.

It was 11 o'clock before Dyatlov could be roused. His eyes were glazed and bloodshot, and his ugly swollen face was even more bloated as a result of his hangover. Understanding, with difficulty, what was required of him, Dyatlov said that he had given me no instructions and that I had issued the visas on my own initiative – a lie so blatant that I burst out laughing. Nobody of course believed his ravings. I could not understand what had induced Dyatlov to give me that instruction. Most probably mere stupidity. The row kicked up by the indignant Iranian side was somehow defused. Did Dyatlov have to pay for this afterwards? Not at all. The consul was immune.

It was May 1982 before the first Iranian military delegation reached the Soviet Union. They were shown all the weapons they wanted to see and buy, but they returned to Iran empty-handed. The Soviet economy was planned, their hosts had explained, and this included the defence industry. All arms manufacture and arms deliveries had already been programmed, and the Iranian order could not be met until the end of 1983. This was a usual manoeuvre in the political balancing act between Iran and Iraq. Iranian efforts to buy Soviet-made weapons from the GDR and Czechoslovakia did not succeed either. A channel was finally found when North Korea decided to help Iran, and Kalashnikov submachine-guns began to appear in Khomeini's army.

This did not solve the problems confronting the Iranian army, for their main armament was of Western manufacture, and it required both ammunition and spare parts. This problem too was solved, and now the whole world knows how it was done. Through the mediation of private businessmen and Israel, Iran succeeded in fixing up deliveries of all the arms and spares it needed.

To buy the arms, Iran needed money, lots of it. Income from oil had dropped sharply as a result of the war, but the Residency learned that the Iranians were planning to sell a large quantity of their gold reserves on the open world market in order to obtain hard currency. This information alarmed Moscow. A move like this by the Iranian authorities could seriously affect price stability on the world currency markets and undermine the position of the Soviet Union as the largest gold producer. Moscow could not allow it, and the KGB Residency was given the task of setting up an operation to disrupt the Iranian plans.

Resident Shebarshin evolved a simple active measure. The editor of one of the main national newspapers in Tehran was then a Residency agent. He was given the job of starting a debate in the press about the inexpediency and danger of squandering the country's gold reserves. This theme was immediately seized upon by the other newspapers, and soon the argument spilled over into the Iranian parliament, which did not sanction the sale of the gold. The active measure had worked.

CHAPTER 19

When the campaign against the Mujahidin and Fedayin was at its height, the Iranian authorities made their first attempts to destroy the Tudeh Party. As they did not know how the Soviet Union would react, they began their campaign in a low-key way. At first Revolutionary Guards made attacks on some Tudeh Party local headquarters in towns in the provinces. Then there was a lull. Then Tudeh offices closer to Tehran were destroyed, and a number of rank-and-file members arrested. There followed the arrests of several Tudeh members in Tehran itself.

Kiyanuri, the Party secretary general, sounded the alarm. He demanded that Moscow should do something about 'the arbitrary rule of the reactionary Iranian authorities'. Moscow's response soon followed. A long article on the attacks on the Tudeh Party appeared in *Pravda*. In the initial phase the articles that followed were very sharp in tone. They said that the Soviet Union would not tolerate this despotic treatment of the Tudeh Party by the Iranian authorities. They would not leave their comrades in the lurch. In the middle phase, the tone began to soften. Iran was passing through a difficult stage. She was stabilizing herself politically, and at such times mistakes could happen. In the final phase the articles contained not one trace of the original menacing tone. They now said that, in spite of everything, the Iranian authorities must not forget the historic and traditional friendly relations which had prevailed between the two countries.

This article had something in it for everybody. The Tudeh Party was given the hope that it would be defended from complete destruction, while the Iranian authorities were given the hint that the

Soviet Union did not intend to intervene in their internal affairs and had certainly no intention of sacrificing a historic friendship just for the sake of the Tudeh Party.

The Iranian authorities responded fairly quickly. They banned the publication of *Mardom*, Tudeh's official newspaper, and there were more arrests. It was absolutely clear that the fate of the Tudeh Party had now been sealed. And this was not because it had been working against the Islamic regime. Quite the contrary, it had supported the regime throughout its own legal existence in Iran. It was because the Iranian clergy, just like the Bolsheviks after they came to power in Russia, had no intention of sharing power with anyone, regardless of their race or political complexion. The Residency had been predicting for some time that events would follow this course.

In this emergency, the Central Committee of the CPSU was desperate to save something from the wreckage, and the task of doing so fell to the 'S' Directorate of the KGB. Meanwhile the preparatory work went on. I was called back to the Centre for consultations, and there I learnt that our documentation section had instructions to provide forty Iranian internal passports, complete with photographs, which would enable the members of the Tudeh Party Central Committee to go underground in the event of their threatened arrest. The documents must allow these Tudeh people to enter the area of the Soviet–Iranian border and escape into the Soviet Union.

The Central Committee's instruction dismayed the documentation section of 'S' Directorate and offended my own sense of professional efficiency. Forty Iranian internal passports was more than we were holding in our entire operational archives. To squander them all on one-time operations was inadmissible extravagance. These documents had been collected over the years at a high cost in risk and expense by N line intelligence officers in Iran. They might have been used to put in place illegals who could live a long time in Iran without any risk of discovery. Now all this was having to be thrown to the dogs, and the question was, on whose behalf?

I could not contain my indignation, and spoke my mind candidly in the Directorate, insisting that I knew all about the leadership of the Tudeh Party, and that the venture was hopeless in any case, because the Iranian authorities knew every step these people took from their informants inside the Party. This enterprise was doomed to failure before it began, and its consequences would be to make the situation considerably more dangerous both for the Tudeh Party and for ourselves, since we should be giving the Iranian authorities irrefutable evidence of our involvement in Tudeh activities. And we knew in advance what the Tudeh people would all do, even under their very first interrogation. I recalled the liaison courier saying that, if he were arrested, he would tell everything; after twenty-six years in prison he no longer had the strength to stand up to torture. So why not break contact now, I asked, while it was still possible, and avoid trouble both for them and for ourselves? For nothing was going to change in their position in Iran. The Tudeh fate was sealed.

They agreed with me in the Directorate, but said that the directive from the Central Committee was an order and it was not in our power to change it in any way. This made me seethe with helpless anger. I even told a friend outside the service what was happening, cursing all the secrecy and conspiracy. He could not believe his ears, and he found it particularly hard to believe that the KGB had no rights under the Soviet Party authorities, but that was the reality. We drank up and dreamt of the time when all this nightmare would come to an end.

I returned to Tehran and got back to work without any enthusiasm. That latest clash with the Party had extinguished the zeal I usually brought to my job. Why make an effort, I thought, when one fine day the results of all my efforts would just be thrown away? It now seemed to me that those officers were quite right who chose to do nothing but simply serve out their time on their postings abroad.

The Tudeh Party liaison courier duly delivered forty photographs of the members of his Party Central Committee. I sent them to the Centre to be affixed to the documents. Shortly afterwards, Kiyanuri's passport arrived, complete with photograph. The remainder were to follow later. I had to put the finishing touches to Kiyanuri's passport by inserting entries about the elections which had taken place in Iran since the revolution. Great importance was then being attached to these entries in Iranians' passports, which testified to the holder's loyalty to the Islamic regime. The insertions were made and the passport given to Kiyanuri.

We later received the operational plan for taking Kiyanuri across the

Soviet–Iranian border. This revealed that it had been decided to save the captain of the sinking ship first. Three places had been selected where the frontier could be crossed. One was in the Afghan–Iranian border area, and the two others on the Soviet–Iranian frontier, in Turkmenistan and Azerbaijan. In the event of danger and of Kiyanuri having to go underground, he would send us a signal, and we would inform the Centre. At a given hour on a certain day of the week following reception of that signal, a KGB agent would wait for no more than ten minutes at an agreed place in a small Iranian frontier town. Kiyanuri would make his way to the frontier under his own steam, and go to the rendezvous. A password was provided for recognition purposes. The KGB agent would take him to the place where he was to cross the frontier, and Kiyanuri would then go over on to the other side. In case Iranian frontier troops showed up, a special group waiting on the other side on Soviet territory would take the necessary measures to ensure that Comrade Kiyanuri passed safely across. In other words, the special group would eliminate the Iranian troops. The same procedure was envisaged for the other members of the Tudeh Party Central Committee.

In order to develop a contingency plan for use in the event of the Tudeh leaders being arrested, the Residency was assigned to get in touch with one of the secret members of the Tudeh Party and devise a means of communicating with him. The secret member would then be able to inform us about the fate of his leaders. Shebarshin commissioned me to establish this link. An officer who in outward appearance looked no different from any Iranian was selected to make the contact with the secret member of the Tudeh Party. They met and discussed the communications arrangements. Every effort had been made to save the Tudeh Party.

It is no secret today that these efforts did not succeed. When the Iranian authorities finally struck, all the leaders of the Tudeh Party Central Committee were arrested. At the time, of course, all the blame for this was laid on me in the Western press, but I feel quite sure that whether I had been there or not, the fate of the Tudeh Party would have been exactly the same. Now that Khomeini is dead, and good relations between the Soviet Union and Iran have been restored, it is likely that the Tudeh Party members who are now in prison will eventually be released, if they have not been released already. This must have been one of the conditions imposed by the Soviet side at the negotiations.

But this was for the future. For the moment, late in 1981, relations between Iran and the Soviet Union had sharply deteriorated because of the Soviet attitude to the Iran–Iraq war. A bitter anti-Soviet campaign began. Now the slogan 'Death to the Soviet Union' was heard just as often as similar slogans against the United States, Israel and Saddam Hussein. Iran declared its own policy of joining 'Neither West nor East. The centre alone – the Islamic Republic!' The Iranians requested a price rise on the gas they sold to the Soviet Union. The Soviet Union refused to accept further gas supplies.

Many Soviet specialists were living in Iranian towns which were close to combat areas. In wartime of course attacks are made on both military and economic objectives. Iraq was unable to do this because of the thousands of Soviet specialists who were working at the steel plant at Isfahan and in the industrial establishments in Ahvaz. The Iraqi authorities approached the Soviet Union with a request that they withdraw their specialists from the target areas, stating that otherwise they would no longer be able to refrain from launching air strikes against these objectives.

There was no hesitation from Moscow. Relations with Iran had become so bad that there was really nothing left to lose, and the embassy was directed to reduce the numbers of specialists and to withdraw them. Here we came up against unforeseen difficulties. The Iranians refused to release the Soviet specialists from their posts. It was all done politely, without resort to any vulgar pressure, but the Iranians declined to cooperate in sending the Russians to Tehran, and having no transport of our own we could do nothing. The Iranians had two reasons for their attitude. First, they realized that the presence of Soviet citizens in their target areas would deter the Iraqis from destroying them completely. Second, the complete evacuation of the Soviet specialists would have quickly brought production to a standstill because of the shortage of skilled personnel in Iran. The Soviet specialists had in effect become hostages. There were further negotiations with the Iranians, and agreement was reached that we should leave behind the minimum number of specialists necessary to keep the various plants and factories going. The others were sent back to the Soviet Union to await better times.

In other respects Soviet–Iranian relations continued to languish. The Iranians openly declared their support for the Afghan resistance forces. Demonstrations by Afghans at the Soviet embassy in Tehran became more frequent. The Iranian authorities gave us protection of a sort, but in unofficial private conversations at different levels, they repeatedly warned us that they could not guarantee our complete safety. Nor did they wish to do so. I recall being told by one commander of a Revolutionary Guards detachment which was protecting us yet again from the encroaching mob, that he was only protecting us because he had been ordered to do so. If it was up to him, he would shoot us all down with his own hand. We knew that these sentiments were shared by Iran's highest ruling authority.

It was during this period that I was summoned by Resident Shebarshin.

'Our situation is becoming more complicated every day,' he began. 'We keep on getting reports that the Iranian authorities have not abandoned the idea of seizing the embassy. It might not be like the American seizure, with long-term detention of hostages, but there could at least be a quick seizure, aimed at capturing secret documents which they would then use for propaganda purposes. The highest levels are not unanimous about it, but there's no shortage of those who favour the idea of seizing the embassy using the Afghans for cover. If that's the case, don't you think that we ought to take additional security measures? Why don't we photograph all the most important documents and put them in a secret cache here in the Residency? In the event of everything in the Residency being destroyed in another assault, we should still have everything to hand when it's over. And we won't have to get our material back again from the Centre in dribs and drabs.'

'A good idea, Leonid Vladimirovich,' I said. 'But we must first ask the Centre.'

'Ach, you and your Centre!' Shebarshin said bad-temperedly. 'They'll start by taking their time, then they'll try to reconcile all views, and finally they'll end up saying no. But the idea is a good one, as you say.'

I had a slight gut feeling about this suggestion, but I brushed it aside and agreed.

Shebarshin had some quite substantial reasons for expressing his dissatisfaction with the Centre over illegal intelligence. Ever since the diplomatic bag between Tehran and Moscow was stopped, we had ourselves been processing all intelligence received from our illegals through dead letter-boxes. The reports from the illegals were written in secret writing. After receiving them, we developed them in the Residency and then sent summaries by telegram to the Centre. I remember the resident's enthusiasm as he waited to see the first intelligence sent by the two illegals 'Konrad' and 'Evi', which he expected to be much more interesting and richer in content than what otherwise came in. However, deep disappointment awaited all of us. First, the report, on seven typewritten pages, was in German. Although I did not speak that language, I had to copy the incomprehensible text into the telegram, but from what we could understand it was clear that it contained no intelligence at all. We received several such reports, and then insisted that 'Konrad' write his reports in Russian, since it made absolutely no difference from the security viewpoint. First, the operations with 'Konrad' were set up so that we collected the container with his information five minutes, or at most ten minutes, after he had dropped it. Second, his report was in secret writing, and even if it were to fall into the hands of the opposition it would be impossible to develop it without knowing the special chemical formula that was used only for 'Konrad'.

When Konrad's reports began to arrive in Russian it became very clear that they were quite useless in terms of intelligence information, and completely banal in character. The bulk of the messages consisted of 'Evi''s personal letters to her daughter, who was having trouble with her husband. As for the rest, 'Konrad' told about their daily lives – visits to receptions in Western embassies and to the private flats of their diplomatic and businessmen friends; a description of parties held in 'Konrad''s flat for his friends; complaints about 'Evi''s problems with the food shortages in Iran. It was clear to us from these messages that our illegals had first-rate intelligence potential. They were circulating among Western diplomats and businessmen.

They could obtain good information at will and without risk. But they were just not doing so.

Shebarshin was hopping mad, and I had to agree with him. All the effort and resources that the Residency had expended in their work on 'Konrad' and 'Evi' had been in vain. In terms of intelligence, there was no return at all from the two illegals. When he was in the Centre, Shebarshin visited 'S' Directorate and said what he thought about the case. It was natural that he should come up against the blind hostility of the heads of the Directorate. It had become a tradition that 'S' Directorate always adopted a very benevolent attitude towards illegals. The most important thing was to launch them safely abroad and set them up for a long and secure stay there. The question of obtaining intelligence was to all intents and purposes never raised. Illegals were cherished like children. Each one of them was surrounded by the care and efforts of dozens of 'S' Directorate officers both in the residencies and in the Centre.

Not all illegals were bone-idle, of course, and a definite opinion about each one of them existed in the Centre. Some of them were criticized. But the criticism was always made at the level of the officers who were working on the case. When personal meetings took place with the illegals themselves, usually no complaint was ever voiced to them, and if it were to be aired, it would be put in the form of a tentative wish – for example, 'Don't you think that it might be possible to pay just a little more attention to . . . ?' That was all the reprimand there was. Otherwise the illegals were told that they were irreplaceable and the best, and that the results they produced were highly valued by the senior heads of the KGB. This attitude is exemplified by what happened after the Residency had expressed its criticisms of 'Konrad' and 'Evi'. The pair were given decorations! I was in the Centre at the time, and I asked the head of section in the Seventh Department, who worked on these illegals, for what services they had been decorated. 'For a stay of long duration in a particularly complicated agent-operational environment,' Piskunov answered, without batting an eyelid. He added that I should not consult my resident for an explanation, as he didn't understand a damned thing about illegal intelligence.

From that time onwards, more and more caustic remarks began to appear in telegrams addressed to the Residency. Shebarshin replied in kind with sharp comments, altering telegrams which I had written. I was not in favour of escalating the conflict with the Centre, and often tried to persuade the resident that it was not worth while to wrangle, but there was no stopping Shebarshin. His attitude to N line had changed sharply, and now something akin to a state of conflict hung in the air.

I considered his attitude quite unfounded, since we in N line continued to go on as before producing results in our work. Besides 'Konrad' and 'Evi', we also had the illegal 'Vagif', who had begun to send in quite good political information of an analytical nature, in spite of his low social status and the short time he had spent in the country. We had active agents, one of whom was the Residency's most valuable source. In addition, both the second N line officer and I had several promising cultivations in hand. And bear in mind that all this was going on in a difficult environment of acute spy mania.

It was in these conditions that I consented to Shebarshin's suggestion that we should cache the most secret documents containing information on our illegals, their addresses and communications arrangements, and other information on N line agents. The location of the cache was suggested by Shebarshin himself. On the Residency premises on the fifth floor, our technical officer and I re-photographed the necessary documents and made a small container to hold the undeveloped film. Then in the corridor leading to the room occupied by the Impulse station, not far from the window, the plastic skirting board was prized off and a small hollow cut. The container was placed inside it, its opening lightly glued, and the skirting board replaced securely in its original position. No one, apart from the Residency technical officer, Shebarshin and myself, knew about the cache. An entry was made in our cipher clerks' log-book that I had copied the documents.

The technical officer went back to Moscow soon afterwards on the completion of his tour of duty. I checked the secret cache a couple of times after that. Everything was in order and I soon stopped thinking about it.

*

In order somehow to improve the quality of the intelligence reaching us from the illegals 'Konrad' and 'Evi', Shebarshin drew up a long list of political and economic questions on which he thought 'Konrad' might be able to shed some light without endangering his security. As an illegal, 'Konrad' had to have natural access to the intelligence being asked of him by virtue of the position he occupied in his daily life. The Centre transmitted these questions to 'Konrad' by radio, and proposed that they should always be reported upon in every future message he sent. The result was not long in coming. 'Konrad''s next report contained quite good and interesting information, and we began to hope that the situation had been put right. Shebarshin was satisfied. But no more information came in subsequent messages. The Residency asked why 'Konrad' was ignoring his brief, but no answer came.

Soon defects began to appear in work involving 'Konrad'. On one occasion the illegals did not go to the visual contact point, although they later maintained that they had acted completely in accordance with communications procedure. Then, during a dead letter-box operation, we were unable to find the container holding the information. 'Konrad' claimed later that he had in fact put it in place, but the second N line officer who was running the operation that evening had 'Konrad' continuously in his field of vision, and went up to the dead letter-box shortly after he did. It was empty, and there was no possibility that the container had been picked up by somebody else. But 'Konrad' stood his ground. Shortly after this we ceased receiving signals from him. It turned out that he had muddled the place where the signal was to have been put. Everything he said was now like this. What was more, 'Konrad' complained about the Residency officers and accused them of incompetence.

This state of affairs had begun to alarm me, and I suggested that the deteriorating situation should be discussed with 'Konrad' at a face-to-face meeting in the Centre, during his and my leave in June 1981. Before I went on leave, we received a signal from 'Konrad' indicating that he was leaving the country. Usually illegals travel first to Western Europe, visit several countries in order to establish their cover, and then, in Austria for example, they will switch to using their transit documents and then head for Moscow.

When I arrived at the Centre, fully prepared for a personal confrontation with 'Konrad', I learnt that neither he nor 'Evi' were in

Moscow. What was more, they had not given the signal to indicate that they had arrived in Europe. It was decided to wait until the end of the leave – perhaps they had been held up by something – but the time came for me to return to Iran, and there was still no news from the illegals.

Mild panic began in the Centre. They, and Piskunov in particular, advanced the theory that 'Konrad' and 'Evi' had been arrested in Iran. Back in Tehran, I began a search for the missing persons. We checked everything possible, and the results indicated that they had indeed left the country. But the Centre went on insisting that they were still in Iran, the tone of their telegrams growing increasingly accusatory. We defended ourselves as best we could.

Finally, in September 1981, a brief telegram arrived at the Residency. It read as follows:

> Konrad and Evi were arrested in Switzerland immediately on arrival from Tehran. During interrogations, they infringed KGB professional discipline and revealed their real names and that they belonged to the KGB intelligence service. The Residency must stop all action on the case of these illegals. N line officers must be particularly careful.

It now emerged that 'Konrad' and 'Evi' were Karl Kruminsch and Katarina Nummerk, who had been living under the names of Michel and Ursula Geschwinnt. The Centre later concluded that the reason for the débâcle was that 'Evi' had gone to the West German consulate to change her passport, as its validity had run out. It proved that on these occasions the Germans check everything. 'Evi''s documentation was easily traced back to the GDR. Now this whole line of thought was discarded, and all the blame was placed on me. It was easier that way, for no one in the Centre could then be blamed.

The prohibition of alcohol in Iran after the revolution had harmful consequences for the Soviet community, which was already suffering from a shortage of foodstuffs. Soviet specialists, made desperate by the drought of vodka, found other ways of quenching their thirst. The secret brewing of home-distilled vodka began, and several fatalities were caused by poisoning from methylated spirit. These cases must not be regarded as suicides. It is simply that Soviet methylated spirit is produced from natural ingredients, and is relatively safe to drink, as Soviet alcoholics have always done. Iranian methylated spirit however consisted completely of chemical ingredients and was lethal. But how could the Soviet work-horses know about such complications? The consequences were fearful. A man dies in torment from general dehydration, and his body shrivels up like a dried mushroom.

It was not only in the Soviet community that the brewing of distilled vodka was widespread. Practically all the Westerners did it, and they also brewed beer. Vodka was made on a grand scale in the Soviet embassy. Virtually everybody did it – the straight diplomats, the GRU and the KGB. But the past masters in moonshine were the embassy technical staff. They had experts among them who could make a drink which was not inferior to vodka, if not better. Drinking at that time became quite a popular dangerous sport. It was not that everybody was an alcoholic, it was simply that under the law it was forbidden fruit, which always tastes sweet. All relationships between people were now measured by the bottle. If you wanted someone to render you a service, put a bottle on his dinner table. This rule came to be observed even in operational relationships in the Residency. If you wanted help in an operation, you produced a bottle. If you did not do so, you would be looked at askance, as though to say 'He's not one of us.'

It seemed to me that many people drank in the embassy in the Shah's time, but next to what went on in 1981 and 1982 it was small beer. The Soviet hospital now became the main target to penetrate. There was pure medical spirit there, and it could be drunk. There were binges every day. Somebody would arrange one today, somebody else tomorrow, and so on until the circle was complete. But while most embassy officials drank only in the evenings and appeared at their desks next morning sober as judges, there were some who could not lay off it. One of these was Anatoli Efimovich Mylnikov, our Party leader and representative of the Central Committee of the CPSU.

Mylnikov came to the embassy in early 1981. He was aged about fifty. Medium build, rotund, with an ugly round little face, tiny piglet eyes, a small button of a snub nose and a permanent smile on his face. In short, a typical Party worker. Shebarshin, for what reasons I do not know, instructed Levakov, the security officer, to show Mylnikov the ropes, and to tell him who was who in the Soviet community. This was done to protect the Party leader from the outset against making undesirable friends. Levakov followed his instructions and gave Mylnikov a complete run-down on the Soviet community. Mylnikov listened, and embarked upon a lifestyle that began by his making friends with all those whom Levakov had particularly dispraised, and first and foremost with the director of the hospital.

That started it all. They drank and drank for days on end, both in the embassy and in other places. Mylnikov was repeatedly carried home from parties dead drunk. He knew the wives of two cipher clerks in the registry, women who were always trying to look younger than their age and had the reputation in the embassy of being gossips. They always went around arm in arm, with their mean eyes darting everywhere. After Mylnikov took up with them, I do not know what relationship they had, but he was often to be found first in the flat of one, then in the flat of the other, and they both visited him. All this went on while their husbands were at work. Then one day, all this carousing of Mylnikov's went over the edge. One evening when he had drunk everything he could lay his hands on, but still felt thirsty, he decided to visit one of his lady friends and get further tanked up. By then it was 11 o'clock at night, and the lady's husband was at home, but in the state Mylnikov was in when he arrived, that really did not matter to him. He knocked at the door, but no one answered. Then he knocked louder and still louder, and finally he began to hammer on the door with his fists and to kick it, shouting, 'Give me some vodka, you bitch, or I'll blow up the lot of you!' So the couple called the security officer, and he took Mylnikov home.

Next day the ambassador sent for Mylnikov and complained about his behaviour. As Mylnikov was going on leave next day, the ambassador said that he would not report him to the Central Committee, but he did obtain Mylnikov's solemn word that he himself would report what had happened when he got to Moscow. It came to light later that Mylnikov confessed to his 'moral lapse', with a flood of bitter tears and a promise that it would never happen again. 'The sword won't cut off the head that owns up,' especially if it's a Party head. Mylnikov returned to the embassy as though nothing had happened, and resumed where he had left off, and on the same scale as before.

Some time in the summer of 1981, the Residency potential for obtaining intelligence unexpectedly increased. Before joining the KGB, Azoyan, one of our officers, had served with an army radio interception unit. He suggested turning round the aerial dish in the room of the Mars station, and directing it towards the south-west, that is at the area where the fighting was taking place between Iraq and Iran. After a few days of painstaking searches, he suddenly came across an interesting frequency, which proved after investigation to be the radio telephone of the personal secretariat attached to the private office of Ayatollah Montazeri, the official religious heir of Ayatollah Khomeini. This office was connected to everybody who mattered both at the front and inside the country, and they spoke quite openly on a wide range of subjects. The success was considerable. Now the Residency was producing intelligence marked 'documentary'.

While I was in Moscow on leave in the summer of 1981, the heads of 'S' Directorate told me that a young officer had been selected to take my place, but they thought it desirable that he should spend another year in the Centre and gain more experience of operational work. In view of this, they suggested that I should stay in Iran for a fifth year. My first reaction was totally negative, along the lines of, I've had enough, I can't take any more, and apart from that, you promised me. I did not want to stay any longer in Iran. Intelligence work in extreme conditions had had its effect.

The chiefs were understanding, and said that I should first go off on leave for a rest, and then we could talk again. They knew what they were doing. Plunged once again into Soviet reality, I quickly changed my mind. The situation in Moscow was steadily changing for the worse, amid endless queues, empty foodshops, bitterness, greyness and depression. The people tried to drown their problems in vodka, and drunkenness was rising. So was crime. I learnt from my friends that burglary had reached epidemic proportions, and moreover that most of the burglaries were aimed at the flats of the ruling Party establishment and the people who served them. Corruption was now on such a scale that you could buy anything at all provided that you could pay. One of my school friends who grew up to be a big-time dealer on the black market bought himself a position in one of the leading institutions of the ruling establishment. The situation in the provinces was even worse.

All this had a very depressing effect on me. I had no desire to go out on to the street, and especially to go into the shops and see people who had been driven to despair. In these conditions, even Khomeini's Iran seemed like a paradise. When my leave ended, I agreed to stay on for another year.

Once they had finished with the Left, the Iranian authorities turned on the 'potential' enemies of the regime. The persecution of the Bahai began. The director of Russian language courses in Tehran was an Iranian of the Bahai faith. He was arrested for that. The fate of all those who were arrested at that time was almost always a foregone conclusion. In an effort to save his life, the director sought to heighten the authorities' interest in him and confessed that he had long been a KGB agent. It did not help. After rapidly interrogating him about his work with the KGB, the authorities imposed the death sentence and quickly carried it out. This example illustrates how right the KGB intelligence service is in instructing its agents without exception never to admit the connection.

The Russian language courses in Tehran were held under the aegis of the Soviet Cultural Centre. The KGB Residency expressly avoided using these courses, as it well understood that they were under SAVAK control. We knew from their director, who was also collaborating with SAVAK, that at any one time there were six or seven SAVAK people studying Russian on these courses. It would seem to have been a rewarding field for our counter-intelligence officers to work in, but there was no one among them so fool-hardy that he was prepared to play with fire. Thus these courses brought much more benefit to SAVAK than to us.

The last KGB Residency officer to maintain contact with the course director was Yuri Denisov, the head of the CI line. He was Denisov's only contact, and he ran him on embassy territory. When the course director named Denisov as his contact in the Residency, the reaction of the Iranians was swift. Denisov was expelled from the country. Although the situation was depressing, it also had its funny side. Yuri Denisov did not speak the local language. He did not even know the names of the streets around the embassy. He only conversed with Iranians through an interpreter, and did not even have contacts among English-speaking foreigners. All in all, he was for the Iranians the most harmless of opponents. Yet here he was, suddenly kicked out. In truth, God moves in a mysterious way.

The Iranian measures to rake up potential enemies of the regime dealt another blow to the KGB Residency. A former Iranian woman journalist was arrested for belonging to pro-Shah circles. In an effort to save her life, she too confessed to collaborating with the KGB. Her pseudonym was 'Lisa'. While she was being interrogated she recognized the man who had maintained contact with her from his photograph. He was Aleksei Panchenko, the head of the PI line in our Residency.

The Residency's first team was thus halved. Both these most recent expulsions of our officers, together with those that had gone before, had a debilitating effect on the calibre of the Residency staff. Those who were expelled were usually those who worked hard. Those who only went through the motions of working were left alone. The new officers who joined the Residency staff came mainly from the provinces, and were inadequately trained in both the language and the background of the country.

After the most recent expulsions of Denisov and Panchenko I became the longest-serving officer in Iran. Throughout my stay, not a day went by without my doing intelligence work. Logically, this now made me the prime target for Iranian counter-intelligence. Until that point, they had been unlucky. They had not been able to catch me out at anything. Every time they put me under surveillance, I had detected it and abandoned the operation. So whereas before they had tailed me about once a month, now they decided to keep me under constant surveillance. Every time I left the embassy, I was followed by car. They even came after me on foot when I went shopping. As before, I gave the appearance of not having noticed them.

All this was reminiscent of the tactics used against Golovanov, my old boss, and meant only one thing. I had been earmarked for expulsion. During one period towards the end of 1981, they had me under daily surveillance for almost two and a half months. That did not particularly disturb me. I used this intensified surveillance in order to sharpen up my methods of detecting surveillance. When I had to run an operation, I was smuggled out of the embassy. On one occasion I had to disappear for two days and sit in silence in the town flat of one of the Soviet specialists, so that I could finally emerge on the evening of the second day to go and meet an agent.

A military coup took place in Poland in December 1981, and a military government was set up under General Jaruzelski. The workers' democratic movement was suppressed. All my hopes that Poland would be the beginning of something much bigger came crashing to the ground. The Soviet rulers had invented a new method for controlling their satellites. This was to use a satellite's own army instead of sending Soviet troops into the recalcitrant country. There was no end to their totalitarian genius.

This defeat which the Polish people had suffered led me to the ultimate conclusion that it was essential to put up a fight against the Soviet regime. It was both stupid and quite pointless to sit and wait until they gave up power of their own volition. And they would have to be fought with their own methods, by using secrecy, cunning and perfidy. It was gratifying that I was not alone in thinking this. I had friends and others who thought as I did, who were prepared to do something positive against the Party mafia.

CHAPTER 20

By the beginning of 1982 the Soviet Union had decided on its policy towards the Iran–Iraq war. This policy favoured Iraq, which the Soviet Union began overtly to supply with arms, while showing itself increasingly contemptuous towards Iran. On several occasions the Soviet air force made raids on Iranian territory from Afghanistan, in order to strike at camps where Afghan partisans were undergoing training. No one fell over backwards to apologize.

It was obvious by now that as a result of the policies it had been pursuing, Iran had virtually isolated itself from the rest of the world. So long as Khomeini was alive, Iran would never return to the American fold. That was the prospect which had worried the Soviet rulers most of all. The Soviet Union was far better off with an Iran that was weak and stewing in its own juice. From the Soviet Union's standpoint, Iran was no longer an important country. This also found expression in the appointment of the new ambassador to Tehran. Vinogradov had been a member of the Party's Central Committee; Boldyrev, the new ambassador, had held the very modest position of head of the Middle East Department in the Soviet foreign ministry. Vinogradov left Iran in the spring of 1982, and he was given some high ceremonial post in the governing establishment.

Oddly enough, and much to our surprise, Iran reacted to the cooling Soviet attitude in an almost placatory way. The Iranian authorities grew less truculent. The press adopted a softer tone towards the Soviet Union. The slogan 'Death to the Soviet Union' was almost dropped. Furthermore, the Iranian–Soviet negotiations on economic cooperation were renewed on the Iranians' initiative. A new treaty on the further development of economic cooperation between Iran and the Soviet Union was signed in Moscow in February 1982. Soviet specialists began to return to Iran.

Against that background, the conditions around the Soviet embassy began to return to normal. Anti-Soviet Afghan demonstrators went on parading in Tehran, but this time we were very well protected. On the next anniversary of the Afghan revolution in April 1982, the demonstrators were not even allowed near the embassy, which was ringed by a remarkably large number of police and Revolutionary Guards. The Iranians were now afraid that something might happen to us, and were doing everything possible to carry out their promise, given earlier in Moscow, to guarantee the safety of Soviet citizens.

In these circumstances I decided that there was no longer any point in keeping the film of secret documents in the cache, and that it should now be taken out and destroyed. I went into the Impulse station premises during the lunch-break, when no one was there, and went to the cache. Then I squatted down and began to prise at the skirting board. To my surprise, it fell away from the wall at the first touch. That is a part of it fell off, near where the cache was. Under the skirting board gaped an empty hole. The container and the film had disappeared. I could not believe my eyes and checked everything again, but with the same result. The cache was empty. Only then did I realize that the skirting board had not been fixed tightly in place, as we had left it when we filled the cache, but had only been leaning against the wall. Whoever had removed the film in haste had not had time to stick the skirting board back.

I sat there in a state of shock still squatting, and stared long and hard at the empty opening in the wall. For me, this empty space was a tragedy. It was the end of the road. Under Soviet law, seven years in jail is the minimum sentence for losing top-secret documents. Whoever stole the film must have known this. In a mean, low-down way, in the Soviet way, someone had dealt me a fatal stab in the back. As to who it could have been, I could only guess. Officially, only Resident Shebarshin knew of the cache besides myself. Whom else he could have told about it, I did not know. But that no longer mattered. Whoever did it had created an irreversible situation. He could not put the film back in the cache, or, let us say, give it surreptitiously to the resident. That would be a clear indication that I had nothing to do with it. He could only destroy the film and sit and wait until its loss was officially discovered. In any event the responsibility for the loss of these top-secret documents lay on my shoulders.

My brilliant career was over. And that career had indeed been brilliant. I had been promoted three times in military rank, rising from lieutenant to major in the course of only one tour of duty in Iran. But more important than rank was promotion in the posts I held. In these too I was promoted three times during my tour of duty. From junior case officer I rose through the posts of case officer and senior case officer to that of assistant head of department. In addition, I had been given to understand unofficially in the Centre that my candidature was being seriously considered for the post of head of a geographical section after I had finally returned from Iran. In the KGB, such quick promotion in the course of only five years' service does not happen often. Now everything had come crashing down. And not only that. It was the ruin of all my secret plans for what I intended to do after I got back to the Soviet Union.

My first impulse was to go to the resident immediately and tell him everything, and then to find and punish the rat who had done it. But I realized that this would lead nowhere and would amount to virtual suicide. The resident would have to report it to the Centre, whose only possible response would be to recall me to Moscow for an inquiry. I decided to wait before reporting.

At that moment Arkadi Glazyrin, the Impulse station operator, returned from his lunch-break. When he saw me sitting there at the wall, he asked me what I was doing. I gave him the straight answer that I had opened my cache and had not found what should have been inside, but added that its contents were not too important. Arkadi inspected the empty cache, dug around inside it with his hand, and then, after muttering something, went off into his room. He cannot have attached any great importance to it. It was just as well that he did not.

I was in a strange state in the days that followed. I was one person who went to work, wrote telegrams to the Centre, and talked to my friends. At the same time I was another person who could think constantly of one thing only – WHAT CAN I DO? I could not eat. My body refused food. At night I was tortured by nightmares, or rather always by the same dream – a man dressed all in black, with an axe raised over his head, approaches my bed to finish me off. At that point I awoke in terror.

What could I do, I thought. Report it, or equally, sit and wait until it was discovered and then begin to prove my innocence? But that was no use. In my country, those who stumble and fall are trampled to death. To scorn danger and proudly take your punishment, while you fight on to prove your innocence, means adding your name to the list of the millions of victims of the Soviet system. And for the sake of what? For I already hated all that with all my heart. Nobody would appreciate my sacrifice, nobody needed it, and what did I have to prove to a system I despised?

'What would Comrade Lenin have done in your place?' I suddenly recalled the comical question often asked by the positive heroes of Soviet literature. All right, I thought, what would he have done? 'He would have emigrated,' were the words that sounded lucidly and clearly in my head. It seemed to me at that moment that it was not really my response, but that somebody else had said it. No, I thought. That's not for me. I had never been pro-Western. I always thought that the West had its own interests, and that it needed a strong Russia like a hole in the head, whether it was a communist Russia or a free Russia. I believed that we, the Russians, had to solve our own problems, and that changes in the Soviet structure were possible only from within, and absolutely not from outside. Interference from outside would as always unite the people and only strengthen the regime.

But the more I thought about this, the more I came to the conclusion that I had no other way out, no matter how I might try to avoid it. And in the West I should be able in some way or other to realize my plans. The thought again occurred that most of the Bolshevik leaders, who knew a thing or two about resistance, had spent a great part of their pre-revolutionary lives as emigrants abroad, and derived only advantage from it. What about Russia? I asked myself, for Russia does not like traitors. But the Russia that I was trying to serve, living on a diet of illusions, existed only in my head. The fact is that what has existed in Russia from the moment the Bolsheviks took power is hostile to her, and to fight it is the sacred duty of all Russians. So why waver now? That is what was going through my head at the time.

My nervous tension was so great that I began to take to the bottle to get rid of it. That helped. Then one evening I happened to run into Mylnikov, our Party leader. We met in the embassy grounds. He was drunk as usual, and when he saw me he invited me round to his flat to drink some more. I did not like the man, and it was never my habit to drink with his kind, but that evening something impelled me and I agreed. After a couple of drinks in Mylnikov's flat we had an argument, and at that point my dam burst. I told Mylnikov everything I thought about the Party, communism, the KGB, everything. For me at that moment, Mylnikov was the embodiment of everything I hated. That encounter would have ended fatally for Mylnikov had Levakov the security officer not arrived at the flat. The neighbours had complained about the racket from Mylnikov's flat. It turned out that Mylnikov had already had two rows with other people that day before he met me.

Levakov was surprised when he saw me, and said that he never expected that I might keep such company. 'I didn't expect it either,' I answered him. But it had happened, and a good many neighbours must have overheard our conversation. Sound carried far in the embassy block of flats. It was like talking face to face with everybody. I was certain that I would be reminded in due course of my candid revelations.

One day in a private conversation, one of our cipher clerks told me what he thought was a funny story. Friends in the Centre had told him that the commission that oversees the security systems for storing KGB documents had visited embassies in several Latin American countries and had found so many security breaches that it had now been decided to screen all Soviet embassies abroad. The cipher clerk said that it would be our turn soon, but there was nothing for him to worry about – he had all his records completely in order. If his story appeared funny to him, I for my part saw little in it to laugh about. The loss of my documents could be discovered even before the commission arrived, for our cipher clerks would begin their own check before the appearance of the commission. When I asked him when the commission was due, he replied that he didn't yet know exactly, but they were planning to come in the summer.

I had to act at once, since the preparations for my move could take a great deal of time. The first thing to decide was which route I should take to leave Iran. Of the existing passport check-points on the Iranian frontier, those on the Soviet, Afghan, Pakistani and Iraqi borders were out for a start. That left only Mehrabad airport in Tehran and the Bazargan check-point on the Turkish–Iranian frontier.

It would have been tempting of course to board an aircraft and fly off from Iran to the other end of the world. But there were serious objections to my using Mehrabad airport. First, practically everyone there had known me for several years, as I appeared there about once a week. Second, there were always many Soviet nationals knocking about in the airport. This meant that, if the airport were chosen, it would only be possible to fly out on my personal Soviet passport. Even buying the tickets on that passport would be very risky, as it would be noticed. It does not happen often in Iran that a Soviet official flies off to Europe on his own. But were it to happen, news about it could reach the Aeroflot representative. And it would have been quite stupid for me to use a foreign passport in Mehrabad airport, since everybody there knew me.

My work with illegals taught me to think out everything, down to the last detail, and to pre-empt all possible contingencies. Mistakes lead to failures. In my case, they would have led to catastrophe. There was only one way left – Bazargan, the check-point on the Turkish–Iranian frontier. The unfavourable factor here was that Bazargan was 900 kilometres from Tehran. In other respects, nothing could have been better. I had a solid reason to give to the Iranians for making a trip to the north-west. There were Soviet specialists in Tabriz, which is no more than 200 kilometres from Bazargan, and as a consular official I had the right to make a trip into that area. Also, I knew the procedures at the Bazargan check-point very well, as it was part of my duties to gather information of this nature. So that was to be the crossing point.

Now for the documents. Unfortunately I could not use a Soviet passport. Had it been an official journey, the Iranian foreign ministry would have given prior notification to the local authorities that a Soviet diplomat would appear at the Bazargan check-point. That meant that I should have to provide myself with a foreign passport.

Here I had to summon up all the knowledge I had accumulated as an officer of the documentation department of illegal intelligence. I obtained the passport.

In order to travel through Iran, a foreigner must hold a permit issued by the Iranian foreign ministry. I decided to travel on my Soviet diplomatic documents from Tehran as far as Tabriz, and I had no great difficulty in having a permit for the journey made out in the Iranian foreign ministry without anyone in our consulate knowing anything about it.

While I was in the process of preparing all the details of the plan, I was completely composed. I knew that the decision I had taken was the only right one. Not once did I have even the slightest niggle of a doubt. I simply kept constantly recalling some lines of a Vysotsky poem;

> Pure Truth will surely triumph
> If it does the same
> As blatant Falsehood.

This poem takes the form of an allegory relating how Truth was robbed by Falsehood (an allusion to the 1917 revolution). Falsehood did that in order to triumph. Now Truth must do the same.

It took me some time to make my preparations, but finally they were completed. Everything was ready. All that remained was to pick the day. In the end, it fixed itself. I knew that Levakov had been planning for months to make an inspection trip to the Soviet–Iranian border with Turkmenistan. There was a check-point there for travellers crossing from Iran to the Soviet Union and back, and there was nothing out of the ordinary in the embassy security officer planning to visit it. But now he was insisting that I should accompany him, and this put me on my guard. Perhaps there was nothing behind it. I do not know. But it would have been stupid to run the risk. What was more, Levakov was planning to cross over on to Soviet territory, just for familiarization purposes, and then come back. I did not like that at all.

In any case, even if I were mistaken in my thinking, it did not matter. The longer I stayed, the worse my chances grew. Of course I agreed to Levakov's proposal about the trip, and we fixed it for 18

June 1982. I also offered to draw up all the travel documents. My own departure would have to take place before then.

The day of my departure fell on Wednesday, 2 June 1982, in the evening. I spent that entire day as usual in the embassy, doing the usual things in the consular department in the morning before going on to the Residency. Once again I checked everything in my office, to be sure I had left no traces of what I had been doing with the documents. I had left my car outside the embassy grounds the previous day, but I told people that I had left it in a garage in town for servicing. The same day I visited the accounts desk in the Residency, in order to pay off what I owed. I did not want to be accused of peculation on top of everything else. After lunch I spent my allotted time in the Impulse station, following the Iranians' radio conversations. This enabled me to acquaint myself with the operational conditions in town that day. I then went back to my flat, checked everything again, and put it all in order.

At 6 o'clock in the evening I left the flat for the last time. I decided to leave the embassy by going through the quiet economic section, instead of through our guards' office, where all comings and goings were recorded. In the guards' office of the economic section, on the other hand, no one paid any attention to KGB officers who passed through it on their way out. And they knew me already. All I was carrying was a plastic bag, in which I had put my jacket and tie. It would have been unnatural to go out wearing them, as the weather was so hot.

On the way to the guards' office I bumped into a Residency officer who worked in the economic section, and he asked where I was going. To the dry cleaners, I replied. He was not really interested and hastened off on his own affairs. Once beyond embassy territory, I went to where I had parked the car. What if it wasn't there? The question crossed my mind. What if it had been stolen? But the car was there where I had left it.

I still had one more thing to do, and that was to carry out surveillance detection procedures. The Iranian security service could not be allowed to put their finger on my very last operation. On the detection route I could see no surveillance in my rear mirror. After checking thoroughly for two hours I was satisfied that I was not being tailed and decided to stop weaving through the town. As it was 8 o'clock in the evening, still too soon to leave Tehran, I decided to go to a quiet restaurant in the Abbasabad quarter and have a meal before setting out on my long journey, but I had no appetite. My nervous tension had begun to tell. Still, I made myself eat a shashlyk and drink some water. By then it was 9 o'clock, and darkness was beginning to fall on Tehran. The time had come. I nosed my car out of the narrow sidestreets and, no longer checking for surveillance, drove off towards the west.

The way out from town lay through Shahyad Square, one end of which was then guarded by soldiers and Revolutionary Guards. There a soldier armed with a rifle signalled me to stop and demanded to see my travel documents. I produced them. The soldier read through them unhurriedly.

'Odd,' he said. 'A Soviet diplomat driving westwards?'

'I'm going to Tabriz on embassy business,' I answered calmly. 'What's odd about that?'

The soldier was about to say something else, but just at that moment a large bus drove up from behind, and all the guards rushed to search it. They also called the soldier. He handed back my documents and waved me on. The danger had passed. I put my foot down on the accelerator, and my BMW disappeared into the darkness, leaving Tehran behind for ever.

It was a real pitch-black southern night, and I only saw what was picked up by my headlights. The excellent road ran in a north-westerly direction. Thanks to the French, who built it, I was making a fair speed, and about one hour later I passed through Qazvin, almost 140 kilometres from Tehran. I did not stop, for I had to pass through Tabriz as early in the morning as I could, in case some casual Soviet specialist should chance to see my car with its embassy number-plates.

After I had left Qazvin behind, I suddenly saw flashing lights in my mirror, approaching from the rear. It turned out to be a traffic police car. I slowed down. They caught up, and drove alongside for a time, inspecting me. I looked back at them. A moment later the police car accelerated and shot forward, its lights still flashing. What does that mean, I thought. Have they rumbled me, or was it just curiosity? But that was no longer important. I just had to press on ahead.

As I approached the town of Mianeh, I felt myself beginning to tire. My eyes were closing. I saw an illuminated parking area, and pulled into it. A small shop was open and I bought some water. I tried to take a nap for about fifteen minutes, but sleep did not come and I decided to continue my journey. It was 5 o'clock in the morning when I passed through Tabriz, which was still deserted. Just beyond the town, I found myself having to fight to stay awake, in fact at one point I realized that I had dozed off only when the car wheels hit the edge of the road. I could not take this risk any more, so I pulled over and fell asleep at once.

Instead of the fifteen minutes I had allowed myself, I slept for forty. This was a loss which I could not make up, but I floored the accelerator and drove on. I just had to arrive at the Bazargan check-point no later than 9 o'clock, by the time the frontier opened. After that hour, the main cross-border traffic began – huge lorries on their way through Turkey and beyond to Europe – and ordinary mortals could not pass. If I failed to cross the frontier on Thursday, I should have to wait until Saturday, for Friday was a holiday when the check-point was closed. I could not let this happen, since by then my absence from the embassy would have been discovered and the alarm raised.

Keyed up with speed and urgency, I reached Bazargan at 8.45 a.m. The road to the check-point, straight as an arrow, was full of lorries, which stretched in line for about a kilometre. I stopped the car, gathered up all my Soviet documents and hid them thoroughly inside it. Then with my foreign passport ready, I drove up to the gates that led into the frontier zone. The fairly sleepy civilian orderly on duty only glanced at my passport and let me through. Now I had to leave the car. I drove it into a parking area full of lorries, washed myself with what was left of the water, and put on my jacket and tie. The suitcase with my personal things was in the boot. I took it out, locked the car, and walked off towards the check-point.

The parking area where I had left the car lay in a hollow, and I had to stumble my way up a steep embankment. Reaching the top, I ran straight into a group of armed Revolutionary Guards, who were just walking past at that moment. They stopped right in front of me.

'Who are you?' one of them asked, speaking Farsi.

I answered in English that I did not understand. Then another of them, who looked fairly respectable for a Guard, asked the same question in English. I had begun to explain that I was going to Turkey, when it dawned on me that my listeners were becoming increasingly wide-eyed in astonishment. What was this? Suddenly I realized that, without having the foggiest idea I was doing so because of my nervousness, I had begun to explain myself in pure Farsi.

'Ah, so you do speak Farsi,' said the first Guard.

'Yes, but very little,' I answered in English again. That did not satisfy them.

'How did you get here?'

I explained that I had been brought by a friend, who had already gone back.

'Let's go and ask the duty orderly at the gates,' said the first Guard, unconvinced.

Everything inside me seized up. I preferred not to think what would happen now, as we walked back towards the gates. One Guard kept my passport, the other carried my suitcase. The sleepy duty orderly was getting ready to check the lorries. We went up to him.

'This is the end of my adventure,' I thought.

'Do you remember this gentleman?' the Guard asked the orderly, pointing at me.

The orderly nodded.

'How did he get here?'

It was obvious that the orderly was extremely frightened. He probably thought that the Guards wanted to pin something on him.

'By car,' the orderly answered.

'How many people were in the car?' the Guard continued, interrogating the orderly, with his eyes fixed penetratingly upon him.

At this point, without knowing how I did it, I whispered to myself under my breath in Farsi, 'Two, and the car has already gone back.'

'Two,' replied the orderly. 'And the car has already gone back.'

I could not believe my ears!

'Ah,' said the Guard turning to me, 'that means that you told the truth. May I offer our apologies for detaining you. Here are your passport and things. We'll give you a lift, as it's rather a long walk to the check-point.'

They called up a light vehicle, and the driver drove me straight to the check-point building. I did not say another word so as not to betray my nervousness.

Another surprise lay in wait at the check-point. Under the new rules, every foreigner who crossed the frontier had to be interviewed by a representative of the Iranian security service. Out of the frying pan into the fire. I was taken into a side room. At a desk sat, certainly not a former SAVAK official, but a bearded, scruffy-looking youth. I was in luck, for he spoke no English. An officer from passport control translated our conversation. I sat and looked the bearded one straight in the face, but his eyes were shifty. He asked what I had been doing in Iran.

'Business,' I answered curtly.

'And what do you think of Reagan and Margaret Thatcher?' he asked, looking somewhere to one side.

'Politics don't interest me, and I don't intend to discuss these matters with someone like you,' I answered impertinently.

The officer who was interpreting gave me a startled look and began to translate what I had said in considerably softer tones. But the bearded one had correctly understood my tone. He began to bustle about, and quickly handed my passport to the officer, who leafed through the pages and said that everything was in order. His colleague waved towards the door with his hand, allowing me to leave. There was a large black telephone on the bearded one's desk. Throughout the interview I kept thinking uneasily that it might ring, and that he would be told where I had just come from, and that they had discovered my car. The ring never came.

Out in the corridor, the officer smiled apologetically, heaved a long-suffering sigh and handed back my passport. He led me to the doors of the customs hall. They were still locked, and the man with the keys did not appear for some five minutes that seemed like an eternity. Finally he arrived, but then could not find the one he needed as he sorted through the enormous bunch of keys he was carrying. Everything seemed to be moving at a pace more leisurely than in a slow-motion film.

At last the door was opened, and I passed into the customs hall. In the middle was an enormous circular counter, one side belonging to Iran, the other to Turkey. Another Revolutionary Guard-cum-customs man examined my suitcase, and then, quite unhurriedly, I walked round the counter and found myself on Turkish territory. Probably on purpose to annoy the Iranians, the Turks had opened a duty-free shop on their side of the hall which sold liquor. Hardly anyone checked me on the Turkish side, except that they looked long and hard at the photograph in the passport.

When I came out of the Turkish customs building, I looked back and saw beyond the barrier the bustling guards of the Islamic revolution. Now all this was well and truly behind me. To the right rose the proud towering beauty of Mount Ararat, that ancient spiritual symbol of the Armenian people. It passed into Turkish ownership after the 1917 revolution as a consequence of the policies of the Bolsheviks. And the thought crossed my mind that, like Mount Ararat, I was with the Motherland in spirit, but in body I was now in a foreign land.

EPILOGUE

From the moment I found myself in the West, my life changed radically. I am not talking about material well-being. That has never been of great significance to me. The most important thing was that it was no longer necessary to pretend, to do things against my conscience, to think one thing and say another, and to live the double Soviet life. I experienced spiritual freedom for the first time. Now I could lead a full life, a life which was not a lie. I made many new good friends who helped me feel at home in this new life, and for that I am grateful to them.

Now it became possible to see from a distance all the Soviet problems in concentrated form, and what I saw was appalling. The entire Soviet economy had collapsed. The economic gulf between the West and the Soviet Union was so wide and deep that they could not even be compared. It was only after coming into contact in person with the political system of the West that it was possible to understand what true liberty was. Liberty is when nobody tells you what to do. There is no ideological conditioning of minds, to say nothing of ideological pressure. Conditioning of the minds of the populace exists only in the commercial world, where producers try through advertising to persuade customers to buy their goods instead of those of their competitors. There is only one word to describe this state of affairs – abundance. Of course, countries in the West have their problems, but compared to the problems of Soviet society they are banal and insignificant, so when emigrants from the Soviet Union, for example, see protest demonstrations in the West staged by left-wing organizations, all of them without exception are struck in effect by the same thought – 'All you left-wing people should be sent to any country where socialism has triumphed, and you would be quickly cured there of your left-wing illness, and understand what life in a communist society really means.' It is only with the passage of time that emigrants from the Soviet Union begin to understand what democracy and true liberty really are, and that individuals, just like organizations of all kinds, have the untrammelled right to express their opinions.

When you see the quiet measured life of a civilized democratic society, you experience a sense of bitter offence at the position of the entire Soviet people. Why have they had to bear this cross thrust on them by Soviet power for so many decades now? What have they done to anger the Almighty, that he visited such a punishment upon them?

After my disappearance from Tehran, the Soviet authorities adopted the story that I had been abducted by Afghan terrorists. For them this version was the most acceptable, since it obviated any need to look for someone to take responsibility or carry the blame, and as they say, none would be the wiser. However, when my presence in the West first became public knowledge, the Soviet side tried to have a meeting with me. I categorically refused to have one, and not entirely because I was afraid. It was simply because I did not have the slightest doubt about the rightness of what I had done, and therefore there was nothing to talk to them about.

Leonid Brezhnev, Secretary General of the CPSU, died at the end of 1982. A struggle for power began in the Kremlin and the resolution of such a minor matter as my own case receded into the background.

After Brezhnev died, Yuri Andropov, the former head of the KGB, came to power and the whole world declared in unison that power in the Soviet Union was now in the hands of the KGB. This was pure fantasy. Power has always been in the hands of the Party, and so it remained. Yuri Andropov had always been a professional Party official and had only been performing a Party task as leader of the KGB. He simply returned to Party work after that. George Bush, now President of the United States, previously held the post of Director of the CIA, yet it never enters anyone's head to say now that the CIA has come to power in the United States. But the West continues to propagate the myth of the all-powerful KGB. Thames

Television makes an authoritative series of programmes about Josef Stalin, and advertises it with the claim that 'getting the KGB to let us see the forced labour camps was anything but easy'. This could not be a KGB decision, but the image dies hard. The reason why paranoia is so dangerous is because there is no cure for it. And the cry about KGB power goes on, not only in the West, but in the Soviet Union itself.

Andropov fully realized that basic reforms had to be carried out in the Soviet Union. There were few people who had any idea that even in Brezhnev's time in the early Eighties, the KGB's reports on the conditions prevailing in the country constantly stressed that dissatisfaction among the population was on the increase, and that the economic position of the country was deteriorating. Throughout the land an explosive situation was developing which could only be defused by radical reforms both in the economy and in public life. If this were not done, the situation could get out of control. But at the time, nobody paid any attention.

Andropov's reforms began by striking a blow against the corruption that was rife among the Soviet nomenklatura, the ruling Party class, or rather among the entourage of Brezhnev, who was the greatest protector of rogues that Soviet history has ever seen. But because of his serious illness and subsequent death, Andropov did not succeed in achieving much.

A restoration of the Brezhnev–Stalin regime took place throughout the country. Chernenko, a close friend and drinking companion of Brezhnev's, became Secretary General of the CPSU. The decaying nomenklatura gave a sigh of relief. Even Brezhnev's relations reappeared in the political arena. But Chernenko was not to reign for long. A disease of the lungs carried him off to his grave only a few months after he had come to power.

The new Party leader elected in 1984 was the young, by Soviet standards, Mikhail Gorbachev, until that moment known to few people outside politics. I paid no attention at first to this new appointment. For me, Gorbachev was one of *them*, and I did not expect that any changes would result from his appointment. But it turned out that I was mistaken.

Once he had familiarized himself with his new post and gradually rid himself of the Brezhnev men in the Politburo, Gorbachev declared the need to carry out perestroika, or restructuring, and initiated a policy of openness or glasnost in all walks of Soviet life. The glasnost policy expressed itself in people speaking openly about the war in Afghanistan for the first time since it began, and admitting that the Soviet Army had sustained heavy losses in it. Glasnost was then directed at the period of Stalin's crimes. It was *permitted* to discuss these issues openly. In this way the Party decided to release the head of steam of dissatisfaction which had built up by using the safety-valve of hatred for the Stalin period. Censorship was abolished.

Then this small snowball of glasnost, rolling down the hill, rapidly began to grow into an enormous ball, which was by then difficult to stop. Now the truth began to be told officially about what had long been known by the people, namely the crimes of the regime in the name of an alien ideology. Serious investigations began into these matters, and uncovered their appalling details.

It was revealed that the terror against the people did not by any means begin in the Stalin period. It began in the first days of the revolution, and as a result of this red Bolshevik terror more than thirty million people were liquidated in Soviet concentration camps and prisons alone. In addition to this, twenty million Soviet people perished during the Second World War. The Soviet people now learnt that the Stalinist regime had done a deal with Nazi Germany and in fact bore the responsibility for the start of the Second World War. The deal between the Soviet Union and Germany led to Stalin occupying the Baltic countries, the western Ukraine and Bessarabia. These exposures led to an outbreak of disturbances in the Baltic republics and demands for their independence. Acute nationalist conflicts came to the surface in other republics in the Soviet Union.

Gradually, glasnost began to stretch out to the Brezhnev period as well. Now the press, growing increasingly bold, began to print facts showing that throughout Brezhnev's administration between 1964 and 1982, the whole Communist Party had been riddled with corruption and had to all intents and purposes merged with the black economy and organized crime. For this reason Gorbachev said that the Party also needed perestroika, a clean-out, and that the corrupt Party machine had to be curbed. And in fact, some cosmetic changes did take place in the Party apparatus. The most brazen embezzlers who had pushed their luck too far were expelled from the Party. But basically everything stayed the same. The abolition of Party privileges remained on paper.

The policy of glasnost however has done its work. Everyone has stood up to be counted. All the masks have been removed. Now it is clear to each and everyone in the Soviet Union that not just the organs of State security, but above all the Party apparatus itself, must bear the responsibility for all the terror that followed the revolution. The Party, which was proclaimed by its leaders to be 'the mind, the honour and the conscience of our epoch', has turned out in fact to be a mafia-style organization and rotten to the core. It holds on to its leading role in society only by force. Were it possible to hold free elections, not a trace would remain of the Soviet Communist Party, a fact that the Party apparatus realizes all too well, and which has already been demonstrated in a few of the Soviet republics, including Russia itself. They have been absolutely convinced of this by the example of what has happened in the Soviet Bloc countries, where the revolutions of 1988 and 1989 have virtually swept away the communist regimes.

But in spite of the threat to their staying in power, the Party apparatchiks have been compelled to put up with Gorbachev for the time being. There are several reasons for this.

First, there is the complete collapse of the Soviet economy, which cannot be halted without the support of the West. The West will give help only if the democratization process in the Soviet Union, begun by Gorbachev, is allowed to continue. Gorbachev is personally too popular in the West for him to be removed painlessly from power. The West sees in him a progressive man who has in effect halted the cold war between East and West, withdrawn Soviet troops from Afghanistan, and set in train a whole series of initiatives in the fields of disarmament and armed forces reduction. He has given freedom of choice and a free hand to the East European countries, improved the state of human rights inside the Soviet Union, and eased the emigration laws. The removal of Gorbachev from the political arena would lead again to the international isolation of the Soviet Union and all the unfavourable consequences that would flow from it.

As they are fully aware of all this, the Party apparatus has chosen to follow the tactic of covert resistance to and sabotage of the perestroika initiatives which are being taken in the fields of economic reforms. Everything perfectly according to Marx. Power in a country belongs to those who hold the means of production in their hands and who appropriate surplus production. In the Soviet Union, ownership of the means of production belongs to the State, in other words to the Party apparatus. That being so, the entire population is economically dependent on the State. If a market economy and private property are permitted to exist in the country, a large section of the population would gain economic independence from the State. It would develop its own political interests. It would create a political opposition which it would be able to finance, and this would put an end to the Party apparatus's authority. That is why even the rudiments of a market economy, like the creation of the cooperatives and the renting of land to peasants, are being sabotaged by the middle ranks of the Party apparatus. Such intolerable conditions of operating and taxation are being imposed on those running cooperatives and on those renting land, that many free traders are rapidly giving up, unable to break through the solid wall of bureaucracy.

The material condition of the people is continuing to deteriorate in these conditions. It has reached the point where the shortage of food throughout the country has caused ration cards for foodstuffs to be introduced. The last time there was rationing in the Soviet Union was during the Second World War. Rumours circulate throughout the country that Gorbachev's reforms are the cause of all the trouble. There is no doubt at all that these rumours are being spread by the Party apparatus. Such a policy is far from new. It was precisely discrediting tactics like these which were used against Khrushchev in 1964 in order to prepare public opinion for his overthrow.

This puts Gorbachev in a very difficult position. From one side, he is under pressure from the Party apparatus which does not want the reforms. But from the other, radical reforms are demanded by those who represent a variety of opposition organizations. Gorbachev has to manoeuvre constantly. He has manoeuvred himself into the presidency of the USSR, with almost unlimited powers, and no one can say what those powers will be used for. But while he is manoeuvring, the dissatisfaction in the country continues to grow. A large part of the Soviet population is disappointed in perestroika, or rather in the absence of any perestroika at all. Perestroika has been expressed in a multitude of economic initiatives from the top, but virtually none of them has actually become a reality. So far this dissatisfaction has been peaceful in character, but it is not difficult to imagine it spilling over into something else. For the patience of the people is not endless, especially after decades of waiting. This has been graphically demonstrated by the events in East European countries, where hated dictatorships have fallen one after the other. One dictator has been shot in Romania, while others are to be brought to trial in other countries. Those communists who still remain in power are hastening to renounce the ideology which their nations hate so much, and are changing themselves into something else in order to take the heat out of the popular anger.

In the Soviet Union, the country where all these transformations originated, there have so far been no changes. What is more, the most radical demands and energetic movements are being put down by armed force. That is what happened in Tbilisi, Azerbaijan and Armenia, and seems likely to happen elsewhere. Operations of this nature can demonstrate to the opposition that the Party has no intention whatever of releasing its hold on power.

There is a paradox. In the West there are more who believe in perestroika than in the USSR. In discussions between Soviet visitors and citizens of Western countries, often it is the Westerners who try to convince the Soviets that as a result of perestroika life in the USSR has changed fundamentally and that the standard of living has gone up. The Soviets cannot agree with this because they know the real state of affairs. The majority agree that perestroika is all show and that the changes are cosmetic. Westerners in turn do not agree with them, argue and in the end brand the Soviets they are talking with as extremists who want too much too soon. Then they repeat the idea which emanates from Moscow that the Communist Party is the only power in the country which is capable of keeping order. The alternative is anarchy.

Each new initiative of the Soviet leadership is perceived by the Western press as a *fait accompli*. When it was declared at the Central Committee plenum in Moscow in March 1990 that the Soviet Communist Party was relinquishing its monopoly on power, guaranteed by the Soviet constitution, hysteria broke out in the West about the latest historic victory of the leaders of perestroika. The development was presented as the Communist Party voluntarily and consciously intending to share power. Nothing of the sort! In the West it should have been realized long ago that perestroika has to be seen and judged in terms of its results and not its initiatives. Between the initiative and the achievement lies a zone of negativity that dominates the Soviet context. A prime example of this is the complete lack of results of all initiatives so far, initiatives which cannot pierce the blank wall of bureaucracy constructed by the 'apparatus' itself. All these initiatives are themselves used as a way of staying in power by whatever means, and of convincing the people that they have only to wait a little longer, and a little longer still . . . and maybe something will turn up.

As soon as a new threat of disturbances comes about in the country, so a new INITIATIVE is announced. Doubtless, somewhere in the Central Committee they have a whole stock of initiatives! Already they are planning to reorganize the structure of the Party. Then, when the pressure increases, they will change the Party's name. Later they will renounce the communist ideology and so try to carry on the process endlessly. There is only one thing that the Party will never voluntarily relinquish, and that is its power. The 'apparatus' understands this perfectly, and so every new initiative is accompanied by threats of a military coup and civil war. 'If you do not accept this initiative, there will be a disaster!' But this disaster can only come from the Party 'apparatus' itself, since the whole State machinery has remained unchanged. The sources of repression are firmly in the hands of the Party, and they are very strictly controlled.

Does the KGB have a future? It is doubtful, because in order to survive, the current regime is having to make more and more concessions to opposition elements. One of these concessions will surely be the disbanding of the KGB. But this will not happen at the moment, whilst the communists have sufficient power, but when popular dissatisfaction puts them under pressure and they have nowhere to turn. It will be then that they throw this bone to the people to calm them down.

If one supposes that truly democratic forces may come to power in the Soviet Union, then one of the first steps they take will doubtless be the disbanding of the KGB, which is so hated by all dissidents. If the Army came to power through a military coup, the KGB would be destroyed even if the new regime were an orthodox communist one. This would happen for one very good reason. Everyone in the Army without exception hates the KGB, because the KGB is responsible for security in the armed forces and consequently shadows the military organizations. The chances of the KGB itself taking power in the USSR through a civil coup are slight, since the Army would never accept it and would surely overthrow the KGB by force of arms.

The changes occurring in the country have also touched the KGB in certain ways. The first fact to consider is that since the death of Brezhnev the chairman of the KGB has changed three times. The latest reshuffle of the organization was instigated by Gorbachev, who sacked Chebrikov and appointed a former head of the intelligence division (PGU) of the KGB, Vladimir Kryuchkov. In the West this was interpreted as Gorbachev replacing a conservative with a progressive chief. I saw the move in a slightly different light. Just as all leaders in all ages have tried to surround themselves with people personally loyal to them, so Gorbachev appointed to the important post of KGB chairman Vladimir Kryuchkov, a person who was personally loyal to him and who until then had played no role in Soviet politics.

With Kryuchkov's move, certain changes occurred in the First Chief Directorate of the KGB, one of which was the appointment as its head of Leonid Shebarshin – the same Leonid Shebarshin who was my resident in Tehran. What a meteoric rise! Shebarshin has jumped a very long queue, and it would be instructive to know how he did it!

So the KGB has also been subjected to glasnost! Television cameras are admitted into the empty corridors of the Lubyanka itself. KGB generals appear in television discussions. In Moscow, a candle-lit human chain is formed around the KGB building to hon-our the memory of victims of Stalin's terror. People's Deputies call for the power of the KGB to be curbed, and for the names of all the people murdered by them to be carved on the walls of the Lubyanka. That is all very well, but once again one gets the impression that somebody is trying to deflect the anger of the people from himself and to direct it down the usual channel against the KGB. For it is clear to an increasing number of people that the KGB makes no decisions in USSR. Just as this organization was always under the full control of the Party and its leader, so it still is. Now the KGB appears to be more deprived of rights than it has ever been before. It does what it is ordered to do. Now it is ordered to take the blame for all the past sins of the regime, and it takes the blame. But the fact is that the proper place to carve the names of those tens of millions of murdered people is not the walls of the Lubyanka, but every inch of the building of the Central Committee of the Communist Party on Staraya Square.

These days we hear very little about the KGB. More and more is said about the Army, and the soldiers of the Ministry of Internal Affairs who have put down popular disturbances on the streets of USSR. Political life becomes more and more frenetic. With the blessing of the authorities – or sometimes even without it – many different sorts of organizations, movements and parties are being created. Dissidents who were once expelled from the USSR are either returning or can freely visit the country. An amnesty has been declared for soldiers who committed crimes in Afghanistan, even including deserters. But there is no amnesty for those in my position, the people whose grounds for 'defection' were provided by their sheer disgust with a corrupt Soviet system. For them, no changes are in sight – and what changes does it make sense to expect, when you consider that the operation described in the preface to this book, in which it was planned to eliminate me by using the services of the Communist Party of Great Britain, was still being run under the Gorbachev regime?

However, there is no point in supposing that the KGB is inactive. It still has plenty of work to do at home. On the orders of its masters it is now gathering material on the leaders and activists of the various fronts, movements and organizations, so that everything should be prepared for a possible suppression of the opposition. Those same masters have also ordered the KGB to put a human face on its activities, even to the point of opening certain of its archives to the public view. And there is no reason to doubt that, should the orders from the Party change tomorrow, our glorious Chekists will carry them out, and then carry out the next. Along with the Army and the MVD they will suppress the new democratic movement, after arresting its leaders and activists, whenever the Party sees fit. But is it likely to happen? Does the Party apparatus really consider that it will manage to hang on to power for ever? It does not seem very probable that it can.

I cannot help seeing Gorbachev as the driver of a runaway stagecoach in a cartoon film, desperately clinging by a precarious handhold as it careers downhill over ruts and boulders. Somewhere below is a splendid motorway where the cars and trucks roll smoothly by. To either side of the stagecoach track lie steep ravines and raging waters. Does the track even lead to that motorway? Gorbachev has no idea. He can only hang on.

The seeds of liberty have sprouted and grown shoots. The people of the Soviet Union, once politically passive, have awakened from the evil dream of unquestioning obedience to the Party, and are beginning to stand up to their full height, to shake off the chains of communism and to crush the hydra of the Party apparatus. This process can no longer be stopped – not by the Army, or by the KGB, or by any subterfuges, glasnost mirages, or receding perestroikas, that may be resorted to by those in power.

When Karl Marx was alive he wrote in the Communist Manifesto, 'A spectre is haunting Europe – the spectre of Communism!' There is no doubt that, as a result of the processes which are now unfolding throughout all the countries of socialism, a 'finis' will be written to the ideology which has brought so many calamities and so much suffering to generations of people, and that at the end of the day, all that remains of communism will be the spectre.

ABBREVIATIONS

GAI   *Gosudarstvennaya Avto-Inspektsiya.* The State Traffic Inspectorate (Traffic Police).

GKES   *Gosudarstvennyi Komitet SSR Po Vneshnim Ekonomicheskim Svyazam.* State Committee for Foreign Economic Relations.

GRU   *Glavnoe Razvedyvatel'noe Upravlenie.* Chief Intelligence Board (the Army intelligence service, and rival of the KGB).

KGB   *Komitet Gosudarstvennoi Bezopasnosti.* Committee of State Security.

MVD   *Ministerstvo Vnutrennikh Del.* Ministry of the Interior.

NKVD   *Narodnyi Kommissariat Vnutrennikh Del.* People's Commissariat for Internal Affairs.

OBKhSS   *Otdel Bor'by S Khishcheniem Sotsialisticheskoi Sobstvennosti.* Department for Combating the Theft of Socialist Property.

PGU   *Pervoe Glavnoe Upravlenie.* First Chief Directorate (of the KGB).

RT   *Razvedka Na Territorii Sovetskogo Soyuza.* Intelligence on the Territory of the Soviet Union. (It targets foreigners visiting the Soviet Union.)

SAVAK   *Sazman-i Amniyat va Ittila'at-i Kishvar.* The Organization for National Security and Intelligence. The Iranian secret police under the Shah.

SPETSNAZ   *Spetsial'noe Naznachenie.* 'Special Purpose' – referring to special forces troops.

USO   *Usovershenstvovanie.* A finishing or completion course, given to officers earmarked for leading posts.

VChK   *Vserossiiskaya Chrezvychainaya Kommissiya Po Borbe S Kontrrevolyutsiei Sabotazhem I Spekulyatsiei.* (Cheka for short.) All-Union Supreme Commission to Combat Counter-Revolution, Sabotage and Speculation. A precursor of the KGB.

INDEX